Homecoming

Homecoming

Our Return to Biblical Roots

Chuck and Karen Cohen

... I worship the God of my fathers,
believing all things which are written in the Law
and in the Prophets.
(Acts 24:14)

Sovereign World

Sovereign World Ltd
PO Box 784
Ellel
Lancaster LA1 9DA
England

Unless otherwise stated, all Scripture quotations are from the Authorized
King James Version of the Bible. Crown copyright.

Quotations marked NKJV are taken from the New King James Version,
copyright © 1983, 1992 by Thomas Nelson, Inc.

Some words and phrases within quoted scriptures have been set in italics for
emphasis. Bracketed words within quoted scriptures are the authors'.

Messianic terms used:
Messiah = Christ
Yeshua = Jesus
Tanach = Old Testament

ISBN: 978 1 85240 467 3

Poem on p. 6 by Karen Cohen
Cover design by David Lund Design
Typeset by CRB Associates, Reepham, Norfolk
Printed in Malta

בשבילו

Roots of faith from
Abraham's Seed
sown in the Promised Land's
blood-red soil.
The deepest roots drink
the Word of God
where earth marries heaven
in Yeshua.

Contents

Acknowledgments   9

Foreword   10

Introduction   11

Prologue   13

PART ONE: *Teachings*

Chapter 1   Is the Old Testament Still the Word of God
              Today?   17

Chapter 2   The Nature of God in the Old Testament   26

Chapter 3   Salvation in the *Tanach* – Passover   46

Chapter 4   Salvation in the *Tanach* – Grace and Faith   54

Chapter 5   Doctrines in the *Tanach* – Sin, Blood, Atonement   65

Chapter 6   Day of Atonement – *Yom Kippur*   73

Chapter 7   The New Birth   88

PART TWO: *Teachers*

Chapter 8   The Prophet Like Moses   99

Chapter 9   The Gospel According to the *Tanach*   118

Chapter 10   The Cross in the *Tanach* – Part 1   127

Chapter 11   The Cross in the *Tanach* – Part 2   138

Chapter 12   The Cross in the *Tanach* – Part 3   151

Chapter 13   The Resurrection   166

Chapter 14   The Deity of Messiah   175

Chapter 15   The Holy Spirit in the *Tanach* – Part 1   209

Chapter 16   The Holy Spirit in the *Tanach* – Part 2   218

Chapter 17   The Holy Spirit in the *Tanach* – Part 3   228

PART THREE: *Taught Ones*

Chapter 18   The Bride in the *Tanach*   243
Chapter 19   Israel and Our Salvation   254
Chapter 20   Your People Will Be My People – Part 1   264
Chapter 21   Your People Will Be My People – Part 2   272

Epilogue   287
About the Authors   289
Scripture Index   291
Topic Index   302

Acknowledgments

We praise God for the influence of His priceless grace and mercy in our lives, initially through the prayers of the Graziano family, when our eyes were opened to the call and claim of Yeshua. Their love for us and their open arms provoked us to jealousy.

Our former congregation in the USA, Temple Aron haKodesh, pastored for many years by Yosef and Marty Koelner, friends we don't see often enough, has been faithfully supportive in many ways. In the same category are Neil and Jamie Lash, and all the Jewish Jewels, who have personally stood with us and helped us with their time, energy, and resources – a real *mishpacha*! And we certainly thank King of Kings Assembly, Pastor Wayne Hilsden, his wife Ann and family, and the faithful staff for their love, encouragement, and prayers.

Many thanks to Christian Friends of Israel's Ray and Sharon Sanders for having the vision with us for *Homecoming*, for making our books possible, and for delicately balancing their desire to redeem the time with their patience. Thanks also to their faithful colaborers, especially Norma Megson, who "got it all together." We are grateful to Marita Brokenshaw for her availability to share her expertise and experience gained from the first time around. We have not forgotten Liz Baxter, who, with Marita, did so much work on our first book. Thanks also to Coral Mings for much proof-reading. There are others we appreciate for their contribution in other ways – like Walter C. Kaiser Jr whose teaching and books became an influential part of this book – in fact spurred us on to look more deeply at the importance of solid theology.

We love and appreciate our two sons, Michael and Jedidiah, who had to live with us while we worked on this book. Reparations aside, they deserve a huge thanks for continuing to love, pray for, and support us though the process.

Finally, thank You, Yeshua, precious Messiah and Lord, for bringing us to Your holy city and putting in our hearts and the hearts of all of these friends and family the desire to provoke our people to jealousy.

Foreword

Little Hebraic influence remains in the Church today because of replacement theology. Many gentile believers think of Christianity as a replacement for Judaism and that "Jewish roots" are unimportant. On the contrary, everything the Church possesses today has come through the Jewish people.

The Cohens' *Homecoming – Our Return to Biblical Roots* will help us recover the spiritual connection between the Church and Israel by restoring knowledge of Christianity's *biblical* roots. Theologically sound, *Homecoming – Our Return to Biblical Roots* will help believers who want to build a solid and more mature Messiah-centered life. We know that believers who read it will be challenged to deepen their relationship with the God of Israel.

In the Bible, Ruth is a portrait showing what our relationship with Israel should be. God forbid that the Church follows the way of Orpah, who parted from Naomi (Israel). Like Ruth we must cling to Naomi (Israel and our biblical roots) or forfeit many spiritual blessings in our lives and in the life of the Church worldwide.

As you read and study this book, know that around the world many others also will be rediscovering and reclaiming their biblical foundations. One of the greatest moves of the Holy Spirit in the Church now is a preparation for the restoration of all things – a preparation for restoring a biblical understanding of the foundations of our faith.

Ray and Sharon Sanders, Directors
Christian Friends of Israel – Jerusalem

Introduction

Chuck was on a plane heading for an Israel conference at Christ For the Nations Institute in Dallas, Texas. The Lord said something like this to him, "When you have finished teaching, someone will ask you where you studied, what seminary you went to, and what books you have read to be able to see the Scriptures in the way that you do. Here is what you are to say."

After Chuck's first teaching session, a young man did approach him, asking those very questions. Chuck replied, "You're the one God told me about. Here is what He said I should answer you: I simply read the Bible from the beginning!"

Many believers covertly think that their Bibles start with Matthew. They may give lip service to the fact that the Old Testament is part of the Word of God, but if they really believed in its validity for today, the major deception known as "replacement theology"[1] would not be rampant in the Church. In the second century the Church officially cut herself off from anything Jewish. Since then a dangerous mixture of truth and error has ruled over its theology.

We look at the Scriptures differently from many believers. Chuck is Jewish. After Yeshua revealed Himself to him, he needed assurance that what he now believed about the Messiah of Israel lined up with the Scriptures of Israel, the *Tanach*. Many believers have been taught to interpret the Old Testament through the filter of the New. But we interpret the New Testament through the filter of the Old. This is what Yeshua, His disciples, Paul and the first-century Body of Messiah did. They had no choice – all they had was the *Tanach* to prove that what they were saying was of God.

After making *aliyah* (immigrating to Israel) and living in a restored Jerusalem in the resurrected nation of Israel, we trust in the God of Israel's Word from Genesis onward. Our theological stance is holistic. We are not New Testament believers – we are Bible believers. Our Bible starts at Genesis and goes to the end of the book of Revelation.

Yet we do recognize the truth of progressive revelation. Often, what God reveals later in the Scriptures, especially in the New Testament, throws more light on the *Tanach*. But it does not conflict with it. God does not change or decide that "Plan A" won't work. The Lord is omniscient and knows everything in advance. His plan is prepared from beginning to end – He doesn't have to change. In fact He states this in the *Tanach*:

> For I am the LORD, I change not; therefore ye sons of Jacob are not consumed.   (Mal. 3:6)

The New Testament brings clarity to certain things which were declared beforehand. Chuck saw a wonderful analogy of this while sitting outside on a partly cloudy day. He was looking at a faint shadow cast by a tree. Then the sun broke through and the shadow of the tree became so sharp that he could distinguish even the outlines of individual leaves.

Parts of the Old Testament (especially the rituals and feasts of the Law) were shadows of the good things that were to come (Col. 2:17; Heb. 8:5; 10:1). But when Messiah Yeshua appeared and finished what His Father assigned to Him, the shadows didn't disappear – in fact, they became clearer, understandable, and edifying.

Our desire as you study this book is that you will become a "Bible" believer and have such deep Tanach roots in the Word of God that the various winds of doctrines blowing through the Church in the last days will not be able to uproot you.

> Blessed is the man that walketh not in the counsel of the ungodly, nor standeth in the way of sinners, nor sitteth in the seat of the scornful. But his delight is in the law of the LORD; and in his law doth he meditate day and night. And he shall be like a tree planted by the rivers of water, that bringeth forth his fruit in his season; his leaf also shall not wither; and whatsoever he doeth shall prosper.   (Ps. 1:1–3)

Notes

1. Replacement theology results from the pride about which Paul warned gentile believers in Romans 11. Its adherents believe that national Israel has been replaced by the Church which now inherits all blessings as the people of God, while Israel inherits the curses. Under this thought the only way that a Jew could have any relationship with the God of (spiritual) Israel, that is, with the God of the Church, would be if he or she becomes a Christian and forgoes every Jewish tradition.

Prologue

The ancient Israelites were not famed seafarers like their questing neighbors. Unlike the Phoenicians, Greeks, Egyptians, and Romans, who navigated, explored, and settled frontiers on three continents, the Israelites had already entered their Promised Land.

Thousands of years after Noah, the gentiles, busy conquering the earth and paganizing the world, would hear a call from that Promised Land. This call would lead them on a spiritual journey back to the source of eternal life in the One true God. In the last two thousand years many of them have heeded that call.

We have written this book to encourage and guide all travelers on their way back home. Their journey can be compared to a sea voyage, an appropriate illustration for those ancient mariners' countless offspring, those peoples whose strange-looking craft sail today between planets.

Here is the illustration – something like a parable – based on Psalm 107:23–31.

God did not create man and then leave him like a shipwrecked sailor, clinging to floating debris on an evil sea. He comes alongside and offers to all a berth and Provision in His "ark" of safety – the Messiah, who is both ship and Captain.

Although Noah's ark had no rudder or sails, Messiah's ship has both. To fill the sails He has sent His breath – the Holy Spirit. And to steer the ship He has placed in it a crew. But this is no pleasure cruise. No paying passengers wander the decks at their leisure. Everyone who has accepted Messiah's offer to come onboard becomes a member of the crew.

But where is this ship sailing and why? To answer these questions God has safely stowed onboard His maps and compass – the Scriptures. The "+" on the map marks the Tree of Life in the Promised Land. The Captain Himself marked the route in blood-red.

As His crew, we are on the most important and demanding quest of all time. The Golden Fleece, the Fountain of Youth, the Holy Grail, the Home Planet – all of them phantoms and shadows. We set course instead for reality, truth, and the eternal. God desires to share these with us.

Because He knows what's good for us, we should take Him seriously, studying the Scriptures to navigate well, obeying the Captain, and learning the ways of the ship. And one day, because of His faithfulness, we will step out into a glorious land and behold in its fullness the Tree of Life everlasting.

However, during our voyage, we only make progress toward that goal by correctly applying what we have learned from our studying the navigational charts and tackling without complaint our some-times tedious tasks onboard. One of our primary duties, easily crowded out by other things, is to guard the integrity of our ship, making sure it remains water-tight and seaworthy.

This duty is foundational and requires familiarity with the very unique properties of the wood from which our ship is made. We soon discover that the same type of tree which provided the material used to build our ship also provided the material used to make our navigational charts! Would it surprise us also to know that this wood came from the Tree of Life itself? It seems that our means and our goal are one and the same!

So let's begin "learning the ropes" by examining this tree on which our whole quest depends. It is an ancient olive tree, ever green . . .

PART ONE

Teachings

As members of the Body of Messiah we have a covenant obligation to become established in our faith. Every major teaching of the New Testament has roots deep in the *Tanach*. For a full understanding of these teachings we must dig into their Hebraic soil. Only well nourished by God's complete Word will we stand through the storm.

CHAPTER 1

Is the Old Testament
Still the Word of God Today?

In Romans 11[1] the apostle Paul compared believers in Yeshua to part of an olive tree. Since a tree needs deep roots to withstand strong winds, our community of faith also needs "deep roots." The Holy Scriptures contain warnings of many last days' deceptions and "winds" of false doctrines that would blow against the congregation of Yeshua.[2] We need God's complete revelation to strengthen the roots of our faith, in our daily walk as well as our theology, "that we henceforth be no more children, tossed to and fro, and carried about with every wind of doctrine, by the sleight [deception] of men, and cunning craftiness, whereby they lie in wait to deceive" (Eph. 4:14).

If we view ourselves as part of that Romans 11 Olive Tree, then the Spirit of God is the life-bearing sap which brings nourishment and water from our roots in the *Tanach* (Hebrew for the Old Testament) to the fruit-filled branches of believers. A partly uprooted tree is cut off from much of its strength. Sadly, roots without soil mirror the state of much of the organized Church during its history. Many old and resurgent heresies, such as gnosticism and replacement "theology," come from a misunderstanding or a misuse of the Word of God in the *Tanach*. Therefore, recognizing the validity of the Old Testament for our walk with God *today* is of the greatest importance to make us scripturally mature – our first line of defense against end-time deception.

Consider that when our Messiah walked the earth, there was no New Testament. When Peter preached to his fellow Jews on the Day of Pentecost (*Shavuot*), he preached from the *Tanach*. When Yeshua resisted Satan in the wilderness, He quoted from the "Law of Moses" (Deuteronomy) three times, and the Devil withdrew![3] Paul preaching to the gentiles used only the *Tanach*. In fact, to validate "New Testament" doctrines in the book of Romans alone, Paul uses or refers to Old Testament verses as his proof texts about sixty times. This indicates that the basis for Paul's doctrine, as well as the prophetic credentials for identifying the Messiah, were to be found in the *Tanach*.

Questions and Answers

Here are some vital questions for which believers must know the biblical answers:

- Do we trust in, and verify our faith by, the same Scriptures that Yeshua, the apostles, and the early believers did?
- If the *Tanach* was the Word of God then, is it still the Word of God today?
- Is it as much the Word of God for us today as is the New Testament?

To understand the total revelation of Himself that God has given us, the answers to these questions need to be settled in our minds and hearts. How often have you heard someone say, or maybe said yourself, "I'm a New Testament believer"? Personally, we prefer not to imply that we are cut off from our roots. We are Bible believers. We recognize that the written revelation of God begins at Genesis 1:1 and goes to the end of the book of Revelation. In fact, if Genesis 1:1 is not the foundation of our faith, that is, faith in God who is the Creator, then everything else we believe is built on sand.

Historically the New Testament uses the term "scripture" to refer only to the Old Testament. Keep that in mind as we look at the following verses:

> *the scripture* cannot be broken...[4] (John 10:35)

> Search *the scriptures*; for in them ye think ye have eternal life: and they are they which testify [bear witness] of me. (John 5:39)

The following passage is so important that we explore it in depth later on:

> *All scripture* is given by inspiration of God, and is profitable for doctrine, for reproof, for correction, for instruction in righteousness: That the man of God may be perfect, thoroughly furnished unto all good works. (2 Tim. 3:16–17)

The New Testament is saying this about the Old Testament.

If the *Tanach* is still God's Word for us today, we should be able to find convincing answers to the questions, "What is the New Testament view of the *Tanach*?" and "How did Yeshua view the *Tanach*?"

What Is the New Testament View of the *Tanach*?

According to Walter Kaiser Jr, in his excellent book *The Uses of the Old Testament in the New*,[5] the New Testament contains approximately 300 directly quoted verses, 200 unacknowledged quotes, and 1,100 re-worded or paraphrased verses from the *Tanach*. The New Testament uses these 1,600 Old Testament verses for proof that Yeshua is the promised Messiah, for doctrine and teaching, for encouraging and warning.

Kaiser points out other facts that demonstrate how the New Testament authors viewed their Bible, the *Tanach*. For instance, often the New Testament does not make a distinction between what God says and what the *Tanach* says. If the *Tanach* states something, the New Testament writers assume that it is God who states it, even if it is not directly credited to Him. Here are a couple of examples.

In Acts 4:24b–25 the apostles are praying,

> Lord, thou art *God*, which hast made heaven, and earth, and the sea, and all that in them is: *Who* by the mouth of thy servant David *hast said*, Why did the heathen rage [behave arrogantly], and the people imagine [devise, plot] vain things?

The apostles are quoting from Psalm 2 which was written by David, but they correctly assume that it was God who said it through David (see words in italics).

Paul, in Galatians 3:8 states,

> And the *scripture* [*Tanach*], foreseeing that God would justify [declare righteous] the heathen [gentiles] through faith, *preached* before the gospel unto Abraham, saying, In thee shall all nations[6] be blessed.

Paul claims that the scripture says this when, in the original account, God is speaking (see Gen. 12:1–3).[7]

We have already mentioned 2 Timothy 3:16–17, the pre-eminent New Testament statement on the relevance of the *Tanach* for believers. Do we grasp what God's Spirit is saying in this passage about the benefits of the Old Testament? Let's examine the passage in detail.

2 Timothy 3:16–17

> All scripture is given by inspiration of God, and is profitable for doctrine, for reproof, for correction, for instruction in righteousness: That the man of God may be perfect, thoroughly furnished unto all good works.

"*All scripture...*" today includes the Old and the New Testaments, but in its historical context Paul can only be referring to the *Tanach*.

"*All scripture is given by inspiration of God...*" By using the word "inspiration," Paul declares that the *Tanach* is God-breathed by the Holy Spirit and just as accurate as if God used the pen. Peter affirms such a high view of the *Tanach*. When speaking concerning *Tanach* prophecy he says, "Knowing this first, that no prophecy of the scripture is of [came into existence by] any private interpretation. For the prophecy came not in old time by the will [or desire; pleasure] of man: but holy men of God spake as they were moved [carried along] by the Holy Ghost" (2 Pet. 1:20–21).

"*All scripture ... is profitable for doctrine...*" "Profitable" means useful, advantageous; "doctrine" means teaching. Under the direct inspiration of God's Spirit, the apostle Paul is encouraging the Church to study the *Tanach* to get her doctrine and teaching material. He knew that we cannot have solid doctrine without the foundational part of God's Word. For example, how can we fully understand salvation and what occurred at the cross without understanding Leviticus 16 (*Yom Kippur*, the Day of Atonement), Isaiah 53 (the Suffering Servant), and the many other pictures in the *Tanach* that fully reveal what happened at Calvary?[8]

"*... profitable for ... reproof* [rebuke]...*" Reproof or rebuke is an act of mercy on God's part. For example,

> Turn [repent] you at my reproof: behold, I will pour out my spirit unto you, I will make known my words unto you.
>
>   (Prov. 1:23; see also 3:11–12)

Has God's Spirit ever rebuked you using the *Tanach*?

"*... profitable for ... correction...*" "Correction" literally means being restored to an upright position or right state, setting straight that which has become bent or twisted. The *Tanach* can often be used as a tool in the hand of God to restore us to Himself after we have sinned.

"*...profitable for...instruction in righteousness...*" This phrase pictures the submission of a disciple to the rules of instruction given by his teacher. It implies growth from childhood to maturity, from weakness to strength. Note also that such righteousness is by faith. The New Testament constantly uses Old Testament saints and/or verses to prove that "the just shall live by his faith," a verse originally found in Habakkuk 2:4b.[9] In fact, in Romans 10:6–8, Paul uses Deuteronomy 30:12–14 to describe "...the righteousness which is of faith...". We shall look at this in more detail in a later chapter.[10]

"*That the man of God may be perfect* [complete, mature], *thoroughly furnished unto all good works.*" To one who is born of the Holy Spirit, spiritual maturity requires understanding the *Tanach*. It is spiritual arrogance to think that we can know God and His will and yet not read, study, and believe more than 75 percent of the revelation of Himself that He has given us. It can lead to a misunderstanding of who God is, and that is a sure path to deception's door.

Previous to these verses, in 2 Timothy 3:14–15, Paul had encouraged Timothy to "continue thou in [do not depart from] the things which thou hast learned..." This specifically includes "the holy scriptures [the Holy Spirit's name for the Old Testament] which are able [have the power] to make thee wise unto salvation through faith which is in Messiah Yeshua."

People can, and do, get saved by reading or hearing God's Word in the *Tanach* and seeing that Yeshua is the promised Messiah. We should be able to preach the gospel out of the Old Testament just like Peter did on the Day of Pentecost. Can you, using only the *Tanach*, present the gospel message of Yeshua the Messiah? It is amazing how many Jewish people will listen to scriptures from "their" Bible.

> And when they had appointed him [Paul] a day, there came many to him ... to whom he expounded and testified the kingdom of God, *persuading them concerning Yeshua, both out of the law of Moses, and out of the prophets,* from morning till evening.   (Acts 28:23)

How Did Messiah Yeshua View the *Tanach*?

Yeshua saw the *Tanach* as the Word of God. In Matthew 5:17–18, He warns us against even thinking that He has come to do away with it, stating that it will stand as God's Word until all has been fulfilled, which means until there is a new heaven and earth (Isa. 65:17):

> Think not that I am come to destroy [or overthrow, render vain] the
> law, or the prophets: I am not come to destroy, but to fulfil [cause
> to abound, cause to be completed]. For verily I say unto you, Till
> heaven and earth pass, one jot or one tittle [smallest parts of letters of
> the Hebrew alphabet] shall in no wise pass from the law, till all be
> fulfilled.

In Mark 7:1–13 Yeshua pointed to a serious problem with the
Pharisees' attitude toward God's Word. In verses 7–13 He accused
them of worshiping God in vain because they taught man's tradition
as the basis of their doctrines and not "the commandment of God." In
effect, they had rejected God's Word, because the end result was
making "the word of God of none effect."[11] Before we look down on
the Pharisees too much, it would be worthwhile to consider in what
ways we in the Body may be guilty of the same thing.

Here is a sampling of other verses where Yeshua states that the
Tanach is still God's Word:

> And Yeshua answering said unto them, Do ye not therefore err [roam
> from the truth; become deceived], because ye know not the scriptures
> [the *Tanach*], neither the power of God?   (Mark 12:24)

> For David himself said by the Holy Ghost...   (Mark 12:36)

> Abraham saith unto him, They have Moses and the prophets; let them
> hear them ... If they hear not Moses and the prophets, neither will they
> be persuaded, though one rose from the dead.   (Luke 16:29, 31)

> ... and the scripture [the *Tanach*] cannot be broken...[12]
>   (John 10:35)

Yeshua also used the *Tanach* to settle arguments. In Matthew
12:1–7, when some Pharisees accused His disciples of breaking the
Sabbath law by plucking heads of grain to eat, Yeshua responded by
telling how David had used the Tabernacle showbread to feed his
hungry men and also pointed out that the priests in the temple worked
on the Sabbath.

Another time Yeshua quoted from Psalm 8:2 in the *Tanach* in
defense of children giving him praise:

> And Yeshua saith unto them [the priests], Yea; have ye never read
> [read and understood, or acknowledged that], Out of the mouth of
> babes and sucklings thou hast perfected [completed, repaired] praise?
>   (Matt. 21:16b)[13]

Yeshua had absolute faith in the power of God's Word as found in the *Tanach*. When tested in the wilderness, He resisted Satan by quoting three times from the book of Deuteronomy. Yes, Yeshua used "the Law of Moses" as a sword to defeat the Enemy (see Luke 4:1–13)!

His teaching used direct and indirect *Tanach* quotes frequently. For example, His teaching on His return (Matthew 24:29–31) is taken from many *Tanach* scriptures (referenced in brackets).

> Immediately after the tribulation of those days shall the sun be darkened, and the moon shall not give her light, and the stars shall fall from heaven, and the powers of the heavens shall be shaken [from Isa. 13:10; 34:4]: And then shall appear the sign of the Son of man in heaven: and then shall all the tribes of the earth mourn [from Zech. 12:10–12], and they shall see the Son of man coming in the clouds of heaven with power and great glory [from Dan. 7:13–14]. And he shall send his angels with a great sound of a trumpet [from Isa. 27:12–13], and they shall gather together his elect from the four winds, from one end of heaven to the other [from Deut. 30:4; Zech. 2:6].

Even His ethical teachings are rooted in the same soil. Here are two classic examples:

> Therefore all things whatsoever ye would that men should do to you, do ye even so to them: for this is *the law and the prophets*.
>
> (Matt. 7:12)

> And, behold, one came and said unto him, Good Master, what good thing shall I do, that I may have eternal life? And he said unto him, Why callest thou me good? there is none good but one, that is, God: but if thou wilt enter into life, keep *the commandments*. He saith unto him, Which? Yeshua said, Thou shalt do no murder, Thou shalt not commit adultery, Thou shalt not steal, Thou shalt not bear false witness, Honour thy father and thy mother: and, Thou shalt love thy neighbour as thyself.
>
> (Matt. 19:16–19)

Finally, consider that the whole basis of His own role as the Messiah depended entirely on His conviction that He must fulfill the *Tanach*. There are many verses in the Gospels to support this but we will cite only three and list a few others in the endnotes.

To answer John the Baptizer's question of whether He, Yeshua, was the one prophesied to come, Yeshua says "yes" by telling John's disciples to report what works they see Him do – works listed in several prophecies from Isaiah: 29:18–19 and 35:4–6,

> The blind receive their sight, and the lame walk, the lepers are cleansed, and the deaf hear, the dead are raised up, and the poor have the gospel preached to them.   (Matt. 11:5)

In a synagogue in Nazareth, when Yeshua first proclaimed who He was, He quoted Isaiah 61:1–2a,

> The Spirit of the Lord is upon me, because he hath anointed me to preach the gospel to the poor; he hath sent me to heal the broken-hearted, to preach deliverance [release from bondage] to the captives, and recovering of sight to the blind, to set at liberty them that are bruised [broken, shattered], To preach [proclaim publicly] the accept-able year of the Lord.   (Luke 4:18–19)

Then He said, "This day is *this scripture* fulfilled in your ears" (Luke 4:21b).

And in John 5:39 Yeshua declares that we need to "Search *the scriptures* [the Old Testament]; for in them ye think ye have eternal life: and they are they which testify of me." The Old Testament is where He directs us for proof of His Messiahship.[14]

Conclusion

There is no doubt that the New Testament authors viewed the *Tanach*, the Old Testament, not only as the Word of God, but as still valid for them in their walk with the Lord. There is not one sermon or teaching in the New Testament lacking a solid doctrinal foundation in the *Tanach*.

In the following chapters we will explore the roots of the gospel and of much of the New Testament's doctrinal teachings. We will see how all of it is grounded in God's Word as found in the *Tanach*. That is where the seeds were planted, the tree watered and weeded, pruned back and watched, until the fullness of time. Then the fruit was ripe, and our Messiah appeared,

A light to lighten the Gentiles, and the glory of thy people Israel.
(Luke 2:32)

Notes

1. Rom. 11:16–24.
2. Matt. 24:4–5, 11, 24; Rom. 16:17–18; 2 Thess. 2:2–4.
3. All three were from the same book – Deuteronomy: Matt. 4:4 from Deut. 8:3b; Matt. 4:7 from Deut. 6:16; and Matt. 4:10 from Deut. 6:13a and/or 10:20a.
4. This could be translated, "there is no power or authority which can annul, subvert, dissolve, destroy, overthrow, deprive of its authority or declare unlawful the Old Testament…"!
5. Walter Kaiser Jr, *The Uses of the Old Testament in the New* (Moody Press, Chicago, 1985), pp. 2–3.
6. This is the same Greek word that was translated "heathen" previously in this verse.
7. Here are some other examples: Matt. 19:4–5 with Gen. 1:27; 2:23–24; Rom. 9:17 with Exod. 9:16.
8. See Chapters 10, 11, and 12, "The Cross in the *Tanach*," for a study on this theme.
9. See Rom. 1:16–17; Gal. 3:11; Heb. 10:38; also Rom. 4:3 and 10:5–6.
10. See "Salvation by Faith in the *Tanach*" in Chapter 4, and "Saved by Faith" in Chapter 9.
11. Mark 7:7–13: "Howbeit *in vain* [unsuccessfully] *do they worship me, teaching for doctrines the commandments of men. For laying aside* [used of a man divorcing his wife; also disregarding, omitting, neglecting] the commandment of God, ye hold [seize; retain] the tradition of men, as the washing of pots and cups: and many other such like things ye do … Full well [With great skill] ye reject [nullify or violate] *the commandment of God, that ye may keep* [guard carefully] *your own tradition.* For Moses said, Honour thy father and thy mother; and, Whoso curseth father or mother, let him die the death: But ye say, If a man shall say to his father or mother, It is Corban, that is to say, a [sacred] gift, by whatsoever thou mightest be profited by me; he shall be free. And ye suffer [allow] him no more to do ought [anything] for his father or his mother; *Making the word of God of none effect* [depriving it of force and authority] *through your tradition*, which ye have delivered: and many such like things do ye."
12. See note 4 above.
13. Some other examples, see Matt. 22:29–46 and John 5:39, 45–47.
14. Here are a few of many other examples: Matt. 22:41ff.; 23:37–39; 26:24; 27:46; Luke 12:49–53; 18:31–34; 22:22, 37; 24:25–27, 44–49.

CHAPTER 2

The Nature of God in the Old Testament

Many doctrines which believers in Yeshua consider essential to the gospel have their roots in the *Tanach*. The truth of "progressive revelation," the idea that God gave more revelation to His people in the course of completing the Holy Scriptures, does not change the fact that certain concepts were revealed early in history.[1] Malachi 3:6a states, "For I am the LORD, I change not..." If this is true then the revelation of His nature and person through His Son, Yeshua,[2] and through the New Testament must have deep roots in the *Tanach*.

Already in the second century certain "Christian" sects, Marcionism and gnosticism, were identified as heresies. Among other errors, they alleged that the God of the *Tanach* was inferior to the God of the New Testament. Unfortunately people today, especially those unfamiliar with the *Tanach*, can be vulnerable to the same false teaching. As we will soon discover, God is the same in both Testaments.

God is Love

He that loveth not knoweth not God; *for God is love.*   (1 John 4:8)

And we have known and believed [been persuaded of; placed confidence in] the love that God hath to us. *God is love*; and he that dwelleth [remains; abides] in love dwelleth in God, and God in him.
(1 John 4:16)

Perhaps the most common phrase that believers use to express the essence of the Good News to an unbeliever is "God loves you!" This is a tremendous truth brought out in all its fullness in the New Testament. But it is sad, even shameful, that some believers talk of the God of love in the New Testament as though in contrast to a God of judgment in the *Tanach*. Don't they believe that He is the same God, the same loving, righteous Father from Genesis to Revelation?

It is important to avoid compartmentalizing God into the various characteristics of His nature. As A.W. Tozer expressed in his highly recommended book *The Knowledge of the Holy*, "The words 'God is love' mean that love is an essential attribute of God. Love is something true of God but it is not God. It expresses the way God is in His unitary being, as do the words holiness, justice, faithfulness and truth. Because God is immutable He always acts like Himself, and because He is a unity He never suspends one of His attributes in order to exercise another."[3]

For this reason we should learn to see His mercy and love in action even in the midst of His judgments. One of the best examples of this doctrine is found in the story of Israel's exodus from Egypt. Instead of delivering Israel out of bondage without giving the Egyptians warning, the Lord sent ten plagues over a span of time not only to increase the faith of His people, but to give the Egyptians a chance to know that He, the LORD, is the Almighty God:

> *And the Egyptians shall know that I am the* LORD, when I stretch forth mine hand upon Egypt and bring out the children of Israel from among them. (Exod. 7:5)[4]

Not only does God judge in mercy, but He judges because He loves. We are redeemed because God is a God of judgment. Our sins separated us from Him (Isa. 59:1–2). If God had not judged our sins on the cross, then we would never have been able to approach or know Him. And Psalm 9:16a states exactly that, "The LORD is known by the judgment which he executeth . . . "

If our God is ". . . the same yesterday, and today and forever" (Heb. 13:8), then He is a God of love in the *Tanach* as well as in the New Testament, and also a God of judgment in the New Testament as well as in the *Tanach*. Before we search the *Tanach* Scriptures concerning His love, consider these New Testament verses concerning His judgment. He is the same God in all of Scripture.

The God of Judgment in the New Testament

> And fear not them which kill the body, but are not able to kill the soul [lit: breath; fig. life essence]: but rather *fear* [Gk *phobeo*, to be afraid of, be terrified of] *him* which is able to destroy both soul and body in hell. (Matt. 10:28)

Contrary to some explanations of this verse, Yeshua is telling His followers to fear God, in agreement with the many commandments in the *Tanach* that encourage the fear of the LORD.[5]

Acts 5:1–11 records God's judgment on Ananias and Sapphira because they lied to the Holy Spirit. The result was that "*great fear* [dread, terror] came upon all the church [believers] and upon as many as heard these things" (v. 11).

> For we must all appear [lit: we must all be seen] before the judgment seat of Messiah; that every one may receive the things done in his body ... whether it be good or bad. Knowing therefore *the terror* of the Lord, we persuade men... (2 Cor. 5:10–11a)

The Greek word translated "terror" is *phobos* from which we get "phobia." It literally means, fear, dread, or terror.[6]

The New Testament letter to the Hebrews contains two strong statements concerning God:

> For we know him that hath said, Vengeance [revenge] belongeth unto me, I will recompense [pay back], saith the Lord. And again, The Lord shall judge his people. It is *a fearful thing* to fall into [be trapped by] the hands of the living God. (Heb. 10:30–31)

A few chapters later, the writer declares, "For our God is a consuming [destroying] fire" (Heb. 12:29) in the context of encouraging godly fear.

In the final book of the New Testament, the gentle Lamb of God, our Messiah and Lord, Yeshua, gives two strong warnings – to believers!

> And *I will kill her children with death*; and all the churches shall know that I am he which searcheth [examines] the reins [inmost thoughts, feelings, and purposes] and hearts [mind, emotions and will]: and I will give unto every one of you according to your works [deeds]. (Rev. 2:23)

> So then because thou art lukewarm [fig. apathetic] ... I will [intend to] spue [lit: vomit] thee out of my mouth. (Rev. 3:16)

These New Testament verses reveal that God's justice and judgment are still valid even after the cross. But is His love as clearly shown in the *Tanach* as is His justice in the New Testament?

The God of Love in the *Tanach*

Ahavah and *chesed* are two Hebrew words used in the *Tanach* to describe two different aspects of God's love. Both contribute to a solid understanding of Israel's and the Church's election and security in God's faithfulness.

The Election-Love of God – Ahavah

Ahavah is the modern Hebrew term for "love." According to Norman Snaith in *The Distinctive Ideas of the Old Testament*,[7] *ahavah* in the *Tanach* stands for the "election-love" of God. He observes, "...when the [Hebraic root for *ahavah*, or *ahabah*] is used of loving persons, it is used of the attitude of a superior to an inferior" (p. 132). We will see later the same parameter for the biblical concept of grace, showing a superior favoring an inferior.

Snaith points out, "*ahabah* is the Election-love as against *chesed* [explained in the next section], which is the Covenant-love ... the origin of the Covenant is due to Jehovah's *ahabah* (election love) ... She [Israel] is His elected people" (pp. 133–134).

"The one thing of which all Old Testament writers are certain is that God's love for Israel was not because of anything that Israel had done or was" (p. 136). Already we see how close this idea conforms to New Testament "grace." Snaith says, "Either we must accept this idea of choice on the part of God with its necessary accompaniment of exclusiveness, or we have to hold to a doctrine of the Love of God other than that which is Biblical" (p. 139).

Finally, concerning God's command that His people love Him with all their heart, soul, mind and strength, Snaith states that the love of God which chose Israel is also the power which God gives them to obey Him (p. 142).

Several different words are translated as "love" in the Bible. The word *ahavah* and its derivatives are translated "love" in many verses. Let us look at how these different words (in bold) are used.

In Deuteronomy 7:7–8a the Lord speaks to Israel through Moses as they are poised to enter the Promised Land:

> The LORD did not set his *love* [*chashaq* – longing or delight] upon you, nor choose you, because ye were more in number than any people; for ye were the fewest of all people: But because the LORD *loved* [*ahavah*] you ...

Moses goes on to say that if Israel will listen to and do all that the Lord commands, then "the LORD thy God shall keep unto thee the covenant and the mercy which he sware unto thy fathers: And he will *love* [*ahavah*] thee, and bless thee, and multiply thee . . . " (vv. 12b–13a). Remember, this promise is not New Testament: this is in the Law of Moses.

The following verse shows the difference between *chashaq*, a longing for and delight in someone, and *ahavah*. It also declares God's election of Israel.

> Only the LORD had a delight [*chashaq*] in thy fathers to *love* [*ahavah*] them, and he chose their seed after them, even you above all people, as it is this day.   (Deut. 10:15)

In Deuteronomy 23:5 Moses refers to the Balaam incident found in Numbers 23–25 and states,

> Nevertheless the LORD thy God would not hearken unto Balaam; but the LORD thy God turned the curse into a blessing unto thee, because the LORD thy God *loved* [*ahavah*] thee.

In the same way, didn't the LORD through the cross overturn the curse due to us? Didn't Yeshua take on Himself the judgment for breaking the Law and put in its place the blessing of our God who so abundantly loves us? Because of God's love,

> Messiah hath redeemed us from the curse of the law, being made a curse for us: for it is written, Cursed is every one that hangeth on a tree: That the blessing of Abraham might come on the Gentiles through Yeshua the Messiah.   (Gal. 3:13–14a)

Isaiah 63:7–64:12 calls on God to remember His lovingkindness to Israel (63:7) and to again turn to her because of His covenant relationship with her – a model for interceding for Israel. In this passage is found,

> In all their affliction he was afflicted, and the angel of his presence saved them: in his *love* [*ahavah*] and in his pity he redeemed them; and he bare [lifted] them, and carried them all the days of old.
>   (Isa. 63:9)

Jeremiah 30:23–31:1 is a prophecy of Israel's final restoration. What is God's reason for restoring His people to His land and to Himself at the present time? Why does God say that He wants to draw Israel closer to Himself? Because of His love! Verse 31:3 states,

The LORD hath appeared of old [from afar] unto me, saying, Yea [Yes], I have *loved* [*ahavah*] thee with an everlasting *love* [*ahavah*]: therefore with lovingkindness [*chesed* – see below] have I drawn thee.

Ezekiel 16 is one of the classic Bible chapters on God's relationship with Israel. In the first part, verses 1–14, God recalls His love for Israel when He first chose her. Then He states Israel's harlotries against Him in verses 15–34. The reason God called Israel adulterous and a harlot is because He saw her as His wife! This is evident from verse 8, where God remembers His initial love for Israel:

Now when I passed by thee, and looked upon thee, behold, thy time was the time of *love* [Heb. *doe-deem'*, lit. loves, fig. marriage]; and I spread my skirt over thee,[8] and covered thy nakedness: yea, I sware unto thee, and entered into a covenant with thee, saith the Lord GOD, and thou becamest mine.

And although, in verses 35–59, God announces her judgments, in verses 60–63 He prophesies that in the end He will establish an everlasting covenant with the house of Israel.

Hosea 14:4 is from the scripture portion read in synagogues on *Shabbat Shuvah*, the Sabbath of Repentance, which is the Sabbath falling between *Rosh haShanah*, the New Year, and *Yom Kippur*, the Day of Atonement. In Judaism the ten days between these two holy days are called "The Days of Awe," a time of heart-searching and of seeking reconciliation with God and man. This scripture from Hosea, so appropriate for such a sacred time, concerns the undying love of God for Israel. He only waits for her to acknowledge her sin and return to her Lord, her Husband.

Hosea urges in verses 1–2a,

O Israel, return unto the LORD thy God; for thou hast fallen by thine iniquity. Take with you words, and turn [return; repent] to the LORD: say unto him, Take away all iniquity, and receive us graciously . . .

The Lord responds with a promise that has kept the flame of hope alive in the Jewish people through many centuries of exile and darkness,

I will heal their backsliding [apostasy], I will *love* [*ahavah*] them freely: for mine anger is turned away from him.   (Hos. 14:4)

We do not have room to explore the many other verses in the *Tanach* which speak of God's *ahava*.[9] However, in ending this section we look into the Song of Songs which the famous second-century Rabbi Akiva declared the "Holy of Holies" of the Holy Scriptures. Many see it as an allegory of the love between God and Israel and also between Yeshua and His Bride, whose character in the song says, "He brought me to the banqueting house, and his banner [flag, standard] over me was *love [ahavah]*" (Song 2:4). God's nature is unchanging and He has been a God of love from the beginning, from eternity.

> The LORD thy God in the midst of thee is mighty; he will save, he will rejoice over thee with joy; he will rest in his *love [ahavah]*, he will joy over thee with singing. (Zeph. 3:17)

The Covenant-Love of God – Chesed

The Hebrew word *chesed* is central to explaining God's relationship with Israel, but it is a difficult concept to translate into English. The best explanation we have found is in Snaith's book.[10] He emphasizes, "*ahabah* [see previous section] is God's Election-Love, whilst *chesed* is His Covenant-Love" (p. 95). In the following sentence we have italicized Snaith's definition of *chesed*. "When the word came to be used predominantly of the covenant between Jehovah and Israel, it was realized by the prophets that such a covenant could be maintained only by that *persistent, determined, steadfast love of God, which transcends every other love by its nature and depth*" (p. 99).

Although at times *chesed* is translated as "lovingkindness" or "mercy," Snaith points out that "these renderings are often far too weak to convey the strength, the firmness, and the persistence of God's sure love ... The most important of all the distinctive ideas of the Old Testament is God's steady and extraordinary persistence in continuing to love wayward Israel in spite of Israel's insistent waywardness" (p. 102). The same can be said for God's "extraordinary persistence in continuing to love" the Church, those of us who are now grafted into Israel's Olive Tree (see Rom. 11:17).

Snaith declares that *chesed* underlies God's faithfulness to His Covenant with Israel. " ... [Hosea] came to know that the *chesed* of God meant God's steadfast determination to be true to His share of the Covenant obligation whatever Israel did" (p. 111). Snaith again, "But through all the troubles which beat against and broke the marriage covenant between Jehovah and Israel, there was one factor which never changed ... God's sure love for Israel. Because of this sure, unswerving love, the Covenant can never be finally and completely broken" (p. 113).

Snaith concludes, "Arising, then, out of this sure, unswerving love of God, we get the doctrine of the Remnant, and with it the belief that God will accomplish in Israel that repentance and turning to Him without which there can never be any hope of better days, or indeed any Remnant" (p. 122). Romans 9–11 says the same.

Although sometimes confused, *chesed* is not the same as grace. Snaith points out that grace, *chen*, "tends to carry with it ... the idea of unmerited favor ... " He clarifies how both work together, " ... the whole secret of God's mercy towards Israel was that they were the people of His choice [by love and grace] ... [But] her hope of salvation was in God's persistent covenant-love (*chesed*)" (pp. 128–129).

In biblical times, as we have seen, a name was often an indication of character. In Exodus 33:18, when Moses asked the Lord, "I beseech thee, shew me thy glory," God proclaimed His Name. In that passage, the King James Version translates *chesed* with two different English words:

> And the LORD passed by before him, and proclaimed, The LORD, The LORD God, merciful and gracious, longsuffering, and abundant in *goodness* [*chesed*] and truth, Keeping *mercy* [*chesed*] for thousands, forgiving iniquity and transgression and sin, and that will by no means clear the guilty ... "   (Exod. 34:6–7a)

We can see from this *Tanach* revelation of God's name that, although He does say that He must deal with sin, His character is one of covenant-love, mercy and grace.

After God redeems us by His grace, He leads us by His *chesed*, his faithful love, into what He has promised.[11]

> Thou in thy mercy [*chesed*] hast led forth the people which thou hast redeemed: thou hast guided them in thy strength unto thy holy habitation.   (Exod. 15:13)

Although this verse applies to the children of Israel in its original setting, according to the apostle Paul, the principles of the Lord's dealings with Israel also apply to His Church:

> Now all these things happened unto them [Israel in the wilderness] for examples [patterns]: and they are written for our admonition [attention, warning], upon whom the ends [also "goals" or "purposes"] of the world [ages, eternity] are come [have arrived].
>   (1 Cor. 10:11)

Moses intercedes for Israel based on God's *chesed*, an essential aspect of who God is!

> Pardon [forgive], I beseech thee, the iniquity of this people according unto the greatness of thy *mercy* [*chesed*], and as thou hast forgiven this people, from Egypt even until now.   (Num. 14:19)

In Psalm 51:1, King David pleads for the Lord to forgive his murder and adultery. He bases his plea on a number of characteristics of God's nature, including *chesed*:

> Have mercy [lit: grace; pity] upon me, O God, according to thy *lovingkindness* [*chesed*]: according unto the multitude of thy tender mercies blot out my transgressions [rebellion].

We see it in the context of repentance again in Psalm 86:5,

> For thou, Lord, art good, and ready to forgive; and plenteous in *mercy* [*chesed*] unto all them that call upon thee.

David says that *chesed* enables God to deal with His people according to who He is and not according to what we deserve:

> He hath not dealt with us after our sins; nor rewarded us according to our iniquities. For as the heaven is high above the earth, so great [strong; mighty] is his *mercy* [*chesed*] toward them that fear him.
>   (Ps. 103:10–11)

Why does anyone, Jew or Gentile, ever have a chance to draw near to this holy God? Because of God's covenant love.

Psalm 136, the Great Hallel, has twenty-six verses, at the end of every one of which is, "for his *mercy* [*chesed*] endureth for ever." David understood the concept of covenant love, trusting that God's relationship with Israel was based on His *chesed*.

Jeremiah pleads with apostate Israel to repent because God is a covenant-keeper and will have mercy on them:

> Return, thou backsliding Israel, saith the LORD; and I will not cause mine anger to fall upon you: for I am *merciful* [from *chesed*], saith the LORD, and I will not keep anger for ever.   (Jer. 3:12b)

God's great *chesed* also endures forever for those who believe in Messiah Yeshua, then fall into unbelief, but finally repent.

Micah states that the reason God wants to forgive and be gracious is because He takes pleasure in acting on the basis of His *chesed*:

> Who is a God like unto thee, that pardoneth iniquity, and passeth by
> the transgression of the remnant of his heritage? he retaineth not his
> anger for ever, because he delighteth in *mercy* [*chesed*].   (Mic. 7:18)

Of all the *Tanach* verses that talk about God's *chesed*, one of the
most moving is found in Lamentations. Jeremiah the prophet, author
of this dirge, is watching the destruction of Jerusalem, the beloved
city. He is witnessing horrible sights and sounds (see Lam. 2:20; 4:10).
He cries out his anguish to his God. Yet, in the midst of his heart-
rending lament, Jeremiah utters one of the greatest expressions of
faith in Scripture,

> It is of the LORD's *mercies* [*chesed*] that we are not consumed, because
> his compassions fail not. They are new every morning: great is thy
> faithfulness.   (Lam. 3:22–23)

The God of Mercy

Although *chesed*, or covenant love, is often translated "mercy" or
"mercies," there is another Hebrew word – *rachamim* – which is
closer to the current English usage of the word "mercy." The word
rachamim is always found in the *Tanach* in the plural, as in
"mercies," and points to specific instances of God's compassion and
patient love for His people. The root of this word is related to the
Hebrew word for a mother's womb, *recham*. We do not serve an
unfeeling God.

Yeshua said that if we have seen Him, we have seen the Father
(John 14:6–11), and the Gospels record many incidents when Yeshua
evidenced His feelings: feeding and healing the multitudes in compassion (Matt. 9:36; 14:14); crying over Lazarus' tomb (John 11:35) and
over Jerusalem (Luke 19:41); angry and grieved against the hard
hearts of some of the people (Mark 3:5); angry at merchandise sellers
in His Father's house (Matt. 21:12–13); joyful over the disciples'
works done in His name (Luke 10:17–22); disappointed with His
disciples' unbelief (Matt. 8:25–26; 14:29–31), etc.

Many of the Psalms read like excerpts from Yeshua's autobi-
ography. In passages that express profound and powerful feelings,[12]
we can rejoice in God's deep love for us – and share with Him a
loathing for our sin.[13] He even commands us to join Him in hating
evil. "Ye that love the LORD, hate evil... " (Ps. 97:10a).[14]

In studying the word *rachamim*, we will look again at some of the
same verses examined in the section on *chesed*, covenant-love.

Remember, we cannot separate God's attributes or psychoanalyze Him. In fact, it is especially true of God that He is more than the sum of His characteristics.

A.W. Tozer writes, "Mercy is an attribute of God ... which disposes God to be actively compassionate. Both the Old and New Testaments proclaim the mercy of God, but the Old has more than four times as much to say about it as the New."[15] As Tozer points out, probably the best definition for *rachamim* would be "actively compassionate." Just as love is a lifestyle, a choice, and not a feeling, so mercy, or mercies, are actions and not just feelings. Pity is a feeling, but mercy is an action "on" a recipient. *Rachamim* and its derivatives are highlighted in the following texts.

As with *chesed*, covenant love, God declares that mercy, *rachamim*, is also His essential character,

> And the LORD passed by before him, and proclaimed, The LORD, The LORD God, *merciful* and gracious, longsuffering, and abundant in goodness [*chesed*] and truth...   (Exod. 34:6)

Mercy is the first attribute He lists after His Name.

In Deuteronomy 4 Moses prophesies that Israel will provoke the Lord to anger (v. 25), resulting in a God-driven global scattering (vv. 26–27). But He says that in the last days (v. 30), when Israel truly seeks God, they will find Him. Knowing all that Israel would do, how does Moses explain this conclusion?

> (For the LORD thy God is a *merciful* God;) he will not forsake thee, neither destroy thee, nor forget [ignore] the covenant of thy fathers which he sware unto them.   (Deut. 4:31)

Nehemiah and Daniel, confessing Israel's constant rebellion against God, proclaim that Israel survives because of God's continual mercies to His people,

> Nevertheless for thy great *mercies'* sake thou didst not utterly consume them, nor forsake them; for thou art a gracious and *merciful* God.
>   (Neh. 9:31)

and,

> To the Lord our God belong mercies and forgivenesses, though we have rebelled against him...   (Dan. 9:9)

King David puts this idea on an individual level:

> Have mercy [lit: grace; pity – not *rachamim*] upon me, O God, according to thy lovingkindness [*chesed*]: according unto the multitude of thy *tender mercies* blot out my transgressions. (Ps. 51:1)

Proverbs 28:13, concerning the result of confessing sin, says,

> He that covereth his sins [lit: transgressions; rebellions] shall not prosper: but whoso confesseth and forsaketh them shall have *mercy*.

That is one of the root verses for John's declaration in 1 John 1:9,

> If we confess our sins, he is faithful and just to forgive us our sins, and to cleanse us from all unrighteousness.

The prophets described God's merciful compassion as one of the "rewards" of repentance:

> Let the wicked forsake his way, and the unrighteous man his thoughts: and let him return [repent] unto the LORD, and he will have *mercy* upon him; and to our God, for he will abundantly pardon. (Isa. 55:7)

and also,

> rend your heart, and not your garments, and turn [repent] unto the LORD your God: for he is gracious and *merciful*... (Joel 2:13a)

Look once more at that verse in Lamentations which contains both *chesed* and *rachamim*:

> It is of the LORD's mercies [*chesed*, covenant-love] that we are not consumed, because *his compassions* [*rachamim*, mercies] fail not. They are new every morning: great is thy faithfulness.
> (Lam. 3:22–23)

You probably know many of those verses and even quote some of them by heart. Such great revelations of God's character are found frequently in the Old Testament. The *Tanach* saints needed God's mercy as much as we do.

> Gracious is the LORD, and righteous; yea, our God is *merciful*.
> (Ps. 116:5)

The God of Grace

God never saved by means of the Law in the *Tanach*. Salvation by works does not exist anywhere in Scripture. God's way of salvation has always depended on grace through faith in His Word. "Grace"

(Hebrew root word *chen*, sometimes translated "favor") can be defined as the pleasure, goodwill, and favor from a superior to an inferior; the stronger coming to the help of the weaker. God's grace means He delights in bestowing benefits on His undeserving children. The simplest theological definition of grace is God's unmerited favor on sinners.

His grace blooms everywhere in the *Tanach*. (The Hebrew word *chen* and its derivatives are highlighted in the following verses.) Starting in Genesis, how were Noah and his family saved from the Flood? By God's grace. "But Noah found *grace* in the eyes of the LORD" (Gen. 6:8), and Scripture only then talks about Noah being just and "perfect in his generations" (Gen. 6:9).

Moses knew God's grace. In the previously discussed "show me your glory" episode and its introduction (Exod. 33:12–19; 34:5–9), the word *chen* ("grace," "gracious") is found nine times!

> And Moses said unto the LORD, See [consider], thou sayest unto me, Bring up this people: and thou hast not let me know whom thou wilt send with me. Yet thou hast said, I know thee by name [I know all about you], and thou hast also found *grace* in my sight. Now therefore, I pray [ask, plead with] thee, if I have found grace in thy sight, shew me now [lit: please let me know] thy way, that I may know thee, that I may find *grace* in thy sight: and consider that this nation is thy people.
>
> And he [God] said, My presence shall go with thee, and I will give thee rest.
>
> And he [Moses] said unto him, If thy presence go not with me, carry us not up hence. For wherein shall it be known here that I and thy people have found grace in thy sight? is it not in that thou goest with us? so shall we be separated [distinguished], I and thy people, from all the people that are upon the face of the earth.
>
> And the LORD said unto Moses, I will do this thing also that thou hast spoken: for thou hast found *grace* in my sight, and I know thee by name.
>
> And he [Moses] said, I beseech thee, shew me thy glory.
>
> And he [God] said, I will make all my goodness pass before thee, and I will proclaim the name of the LORD [which includes His characteristics] before thee; and will be *gracious* to whom I will be *gracious*, and will shew mercy [*rachamim*] on whom I will shew mercy...
>
> And the LORD descended in the cloud, and stood with him there,[16] and proclaimed the name of the LORD. And the LORD passed by before him, and proclaimed, The LORD, The LORD God, merciful [*rachamim*]

and *gracious*, longsuffering, and abundant in goodness [*chesed*] and truth, Keeping mercy [*chesed*] for thousands, forgiving [bearing, carrying] iniquity and transgression and sin, and that will by no means clear the guilty; visiting the iniquity of the fathers upon the children, and upon the children's children, unto the third and to the fourth generation.

And Moses made haste, and bowed his head toward the earth, and worshipped. And he said, If now I have found *grace* in thy sight, O LORD, let my LORD, I pray [ask, plead with] thee, go among us; for it is a stiffnecked [stubborn; obstinate] people; and pardon our iniquity and our sin, and take us for thine inheritance.

In pleading with God that He, and not just an angel,[17] would continue to accompany the children of Israel, Moses based his request on God's grace. Note the context; this dialogue occurs right after the sin of idolatry when Israel made and worshiped the golden calf (Exod. 32–33). But here God reaffirms[18] grace, unmerited favor, as the basis of His relationship with Moses and the children of Israel.

God commanded Israel's priests to bless the children of Israel by placing His name on them, using the "Aaronic benediction." Part of this wonderful blessing asks God to deal with His children by grace:

> The LORD bless thee, and keep [guard; protect] thee: The LORD make his face shine upon thee, and be *gracious* unto thee: The LORD lift up his countenance upon thee, and give thee peace.   (Num. 6:24–26)

This peace, *shalom* in Hebrew, results from God's grace. It means much more than the cessation of strife. *Shalom* includes completeness, welfare, health, safety, contentment and prosperity.

Although oppressed by the king of Syria, Israel was not destroyed.

> And the LORD was *gracious* unto them, and had compassion [*rachamim*] on them, and had respect unto them, because of his covenant with Abraham, Isaac, and Jacob, and would not destroy them, neither cast he them from his presence as yet.   (2 Kgs. 13:23)

There did come a time when Israel was "cast ... from his presence," but even then God's promise not to destroy them still stood – as it does to this day (Jer. 31:35–37; 51:5).

The plea for God's grace occurs at least twenty times in the Psalms, but it is often translated "mercy."

> Have *mercy* upon [grace toward] me, O LORD; for I am weak: O LORD, heal me; for my bones are vexed.   (Ps. 6:2)

> I said, LORD, *be merciful* [gracious] unto me: heal my soul; for I have
> sinned against thee.   (Ps. 41:4)

(See also 4:1; 6:2; 9:13; 25:16; 51:1; 119:58, etc.)

Psalm 84:11 is a wonderful promise to those of us who are
righteous in God's sight because of abiding in Messiah (2 Cor. 5:21;
Phil. 3:9) and who are working out our salvation with fear and
trembling (Phil. 2:12b–13). Among the things God promises to us is
more grace!

> For the LORD God is a sun and shield: the LORD will give *grace* and
> glory: no good thing will he withhold from them that walk uprightly.

Psalm 102:13 is one of the verses that gives us hope:

> Thou shalt arise, and have mercy [*rachamim*, active compassion] upon
> Zion: for the time to *favour* [from *chen*, grace] her, yea, the set time,[19]
> is come.

Note that God deals with Israel because of His great compassion
and grace – not because Israel is perfect or always obedient (cf. Jer.
31:1–3). He deals with believers in the same way – for which we will
be eternally thankful!

Proverbs 3:34 is a root verse that is used by James (Jas. 4:6) and
Peter (1 Pet. 5:5),

> Surely he scorneth the scorners: but he giveth *grace* unto the lowly
> [humble, meek, poor, broken hearted].

We close this section on grace with two end-time prophecies
concerning Israel. In Isaiah 30:18–19, the prophet says that God is
waiting for Israel's cry to Him,

> And therefore will the LORD wait, that he may be *gracious* unto you,
> and therefore will he be exalted, that he may have mercy [*rachamim*]
> upon you: for the LORD is a God of judgment [justice]: blessed are all
> they that wait for him. For the people shall dwell in Zion at Jerusalem
> thou shalt weep no more: he will be very *gracious* unto thee at the voice
> of thy cry; when he shall hear it, he will answer thee.

This situation resembles one described in Ezekiel 36:37a – after the
Lord promises to do many wonderful things for Israel, He waits for
Israel to ask for them:

> Thus saith the Lord GOD; I will yet for this be inquired of by the house
> of Israel, to do it for them ...

But when will Israel cry out to their God? Zechariah 12 gives a picture of all the nations coming against Jerusalem (vv. 2–11), and God still dealing with His people by grace!

> And I will pour upon the house of David, and upon the inhabitants of Jerusalem, the spirit of *grace* and of *supplications* [from the same root word as grace]: and they shall look upon [pay attention to; consider] me whom they have pierced, and they shall mourn for him, as one mourneth for his only son, and shall be in bitterness for him, as one that is in bitterness for his firstborn. (Zech. 12:10)

God had already stated this spiritual principle of crying out for His grace earlier in Zechariah when He said to Zerubbabel, whom some rabbis consider a foreshadow of the Messiah,

> This is the word of the LORD unto Zerubbabel, saying, Not by might, nor by power, but by my spirit, saith the LORD of hosts. Who art thou, O great mountain? before Zerubbabel thou shalt become a plain: and he shall bring forth the headstone thereof with shoutings, crying, Grace, grace unto it. (Zech. 4:6b–7)

God our Father

For believers, being able to call God "Abba, Father,"[20] is one of the priceless benefits we obtain by our faith in Messiah. However, some have the impression that God's fatherhood was a new doctrine revealed by Yeshua. Like all New Testament doctrines, this one also has its roots in the *Tanach*. Here are some of the root verses in the *Tanach*.

God commanded Moses to approach Eygpt's king this way,

> And thou shalt say unto Pharaoh, Thus saith the LORD, *Israel is my son*, even my firstborn . . . (Exod. 4:22)

The Egyptians considered Pharaoh a god, and in a symbolic sense as a father. So God challenges Pharaoh,

> And I say unto thee, Let my son go, that he may serve me: and if thou refuse to let him go, behold, I will slay thy son, even thy firstborn. (Exod. 4:23)

Moses testified to God's father relationship with the children of Israel. In his final message to them, Moses declared, "Ye are *the children of the* LORD *your God...*" (Deut. 14:1a). Later on in the same book, he asked Israel this pointed question,

> Do ye thus requite the LORD, O foolish people and unwise? is not he thy *father* that hath bought thee? hath he not made thee, and established thee?   (Deut. 32:6)

King David also had the revelation of God as a father to Israel:

> Wherefore David blessed the LORD before all the congregation: and David said, Blessed be thou, LORD God of Israel our *father*, for ever and ever.   (1 Chr. 29:10)

Here are two interesting verses from the prophet Isaiah. In Isaiah 63:16, it appears that a believing remnant in Israel[21] is confessing that although they have not walked completely in the faith of their forefathers, Abraham and Israel, still,

> Doubtless thou art our father, though Abraham be ignorant of us, and Israel acknowledge us not: thou, O LORD, art our father, our redeemer; thy name [reputation; character] is from everlasting.

This remnant, having confessed their sins, pleads in Isaiah 64:8 for God to have mercy on Israel because of His father relationship to them:

> But now, O LORD, thou art our father; we are the clay, and thou our potter; and we all are the work of thy hand.

The Lord justifies giving the people of Israel possession of the land of Israel, saying that when He saves her as a nation she will recognize Him as her Father and will serve and worship Him:

> But I said, How shall I put thee among the children, and give thee a pleasant [precious] land, a goodly [prominent] heritage of the hosts of nations? and I said, Thou shalt call me, *My father*; and shalt not turn away from me.   (Jer. 3:19)

and,

> They shall come with weeping, and with supplications will I lead [carry] them: I will cause them to walk by the rivers of waters in a straight [upright, righteous] way, wherein they shall not stumble: for I am a *father* to Israel, and Ephraim is my firstborn.   (Jer. 31:9)

This last verse is a definite end-time prophecy being fulfilled in a remnant of Israel today.

In the *Tanach* there are even instances of God being called a father of individuals. In declaring the Davidic covenant, God says about Solomon, "I will be his *father*, and he shall be my son..." (2 Sam. 7:14a). There exists also a group of underprivileged individuals for whom God is declared to be a father:

> A *father* of the fatherless, and a judge of [dispenser of justice for] the widows, is God in his holy habitation.　　　　　(Ps. 68:5)

We can see that before Yeshua came in the flesh, many *Tanach* verses had revealed God as our Father. Yeshua emphasized God's fatherhood more than anyone had before, but He could do so in total biblical correctness because of the deep *Tanach* roots that we have just reviewed.

The fatherhood of God also has a prominent role in rabbinic Judaism. A. Cohen observes that, "God is constantly addressed, or referred to, as 'Father Who is in heaven' ... It was considered a mark of exceptional grace on His part that this intimate relationship exists and was revealed to man." He continues in his book *Everyman's Talmud*, "Especially when in the act of prayer, the individual was exhorted to think of himself as addressing his petitions to One Who stood to him in the relationship of Father."[22] In the traditional Hebrew prayer book, the Siddur, in the beautiful liturgical confession of sins read in every synagogue on *Yom Kippur*, the Day of Atonement, each line starts with "Our Father, our King."

> He shall cry unto me, Thou art my *father*, my God,
> and the rock of my salvation.
> (Ps. 89:26)

Notes

1. Walter Kaiser makes this observation: "Once in a while historical progress ... allowed a full maturation of an aspect of the record, and at those points the text amazes us with the way in which meaning and teaching outstrip experience and the times" (Walter J. Kaiser Jr, *Toward An Old Testament Theology*, Grand Rapids, MI: Academie Books, Zondervan Pub. House, 1978, pp. 8–9).

2. "And the Word [Yeshua] was made flesh, and dwelt among us, (and we beheld his glory, the glory as of the only begotten of the Father,) full of grace and truth" (John 1:14); "[Yeshua] ... is the image of the invisible God ... For it pleased the Father that in him should all fulness dwell" (Col. 1:15a, 19); "[God] Hath in these last days spoken unto us by his Son ... Who being the

brightness of his glory, and the express image of his person, and upholding all things by the word of his power, when he had by himself purged our sins, sat down on the right hand of the Majesty on high" (Heb. 1:2a, 3).

3. A.W. Tozer, *The Knowledge of the Holy* (New York, NY: Harper & Row Pub. Inc., 1961, p. 105).

4. See also Exod. 7:16–17; 8:10, 19, 22; 9:14–16, 20, 29; 10:1–2; 11:7; 14:4, 18, 31.

5. Here are a few *Tanach* examples: "O that there were such an heart [mind, will, soul, inner man] in them, that they would fear [both revere and be afraid of] me, and keep all my commandments always, that it might be well with them, and with their children for ever!" (Deut. 5:29); "Serve the LORD with fear, and rejoice with trembling" (Ps. 2:11); "Surely his salvation is nigh them that fear him; that glory may dwell in our land" (Ps. 85:9); "The fear of the LORD is the beginning of knowledge . . . " (Prov. 1:7a); "But unto you that fear my name shall the Sun of righteousness arise with healing in his wings . . . " (Mal. 4:2a). Other references on the fear of the Lord include: Josh. 24:14; 1 Sam. 12:14; Ps. 19:9; Prov. 1:7; Eccl. 12:13; Isa. 8:13.

6. *Strong's Concordance* #5401.

7. Norman H. Snaith, *The Distinctive Ideas of the Old Testament* (NY: Schocken Books, 1964), Chapter VI, "The Election-Love of God," pp. 131–142.

8. KJV "skirt," and the Hebrew "wing" both indicate betrothal. (Compare this to Ruth 3:9b, "I am Ruth thine handmaid: spread therefore thy skirt over thine handmaid; for thou art a near kinsman [my kinsman-redeemer].")

9. Here are a few more: 1 Kgs. 10:9; 2 Chr. 2:11; Hos. 3:1; 11:4.

10. Norman H. Snaith, op. cit., pp. 94–130.

11. The New Testament describes God's faithfulness in many places. For example: Rom. 16:25; 2 Cor. 1:21; Phil. 1:6; 2:13; Col. 1:22; 1 Thess. 5:24; 2 Thess. 3:3–4; 2 Tim. 4:18 and this incredible statement in Jude 24–25: "Now unto him that is able [has the power and authority] to keep you from falling, and to present you faultless [as an unblemished sacrifice] before the presence of his glory with exceeding joy, To the only wise God our Saviour, be glory and majesty, dominion and power, both now and ever. Amen."

12. For example, Ps. 22:1–22 [see Chapter 11, section "Psalm 22"]; 41:5–13; 69:4, 7–9, 19–26.

13. Prov. 6:16; Isa. 61:8; Jer. 44:4; Amos 5:21; Zech. 8:17. Yeshua hates things that pervert His Church (Rev. 2:6, 15).

14. See also Pss. 101:2–3; 119:104, 113, 128, 163; 139:21–22; Prov. 8:13; Amos 5:14–15.

15. A.W. Tozer, op. cit., pp. 96–97.

16. Who was this LORD who stood with Moses on the mount and revealed to him the essential nature of the God of Israel? According to John, it was the pre-incarnate Son of God: "No man hath seen God at any time; the only begotten Son, which is in the bosom of the Father, he hath declared him" (John 1:18).

17. See Exod. 32:34–33:3.

18. We say reaffirmed because God chose Abraham, Isaac, and Jacob, and redeemed Israel from Egyptian bondage on the basis of His grace and love.

Moses knows God's grace personally, and God reaffirms it here by saying yes to Moses' request.

19. The Hebrew word for "set time" is *moed*. It refers to a God-set appointment to meet with His people. Translated "feast" in Leviticus 23, which describes the "Feasts" of the LORD, it means more than just a holiday dinner.

20. Rom. 8:15; Gal. 4:6. *Abba* (Daddy) is heard in the streets and homes of Israel today.

21. As Paul indicates in Romans 9:27 and 11:5, there has always been a "remnant according to the election of grace."

22. A. Cohen, *Everyman's Talmud* (New York: Schocken Books, 1975 (reprint of 1949 edn by E.P. Dutton), pp. 20–21.

CHAPTER 3

Salvation in the *Tanach* – Passover

Passover Redemption

Participating in the feast of the Lord known as *Pesach*, or Passover, is a wonderful way to obtain a panoramic view of God's plan for salvation. By means of an unforgettable experience this "feast of [the] LORD" (see Lev. 23)[1] portrays salvation by grace through faith in the blood of a lamb.

The story of Israel's redemption from slavery[2] and their subsequent freedom to receive God's Law at Mount Sinai illustrates our redemption from the control of sin and Satan and of our freedom to live under God's rule. This is legitimate exegesis because, as we note in our comments on the covenant-love of God, Paul often used *Tanach* scriptures for examples of our walk with the Lord, explaining that "all these things happened unto them [Israel] for examples [warnings or prophetic types]: and they are written for our admonition [consideration], upon whom the ends [prophetic purpose or goal] of the world [lit: ages] are come" (1 Cor. 10:11).

Besides teaching us spiritual truths, *Tanach* stories recount the penetration of world history by the God of the universe, the God of Israel. These episodes happened to a real flesh and blood people. Israel is never just a symbol.

Background

The book of Exodus opens with Israel in severe bondage to cruel taskmasters under a tyrant who is using them to build an empire and glorify himself. God hears their cries (Exod. 2:23–25) and chooses an ambassador (apostle or "sent one"), an instrument to set His people free. God sends Moses as a prophet, in many ways a type of Yeshua,[3] to tell Pharaoh, whom the Egyptians claimed as a god, "Thus saith the LORD God of Israel, Let my people go..." (Exod. 5:1b).[4]

Before Pharaoh ever hears this word, God tells Moses that Pharaoh will not listen:

> And I am sure [I know] that the king of Egypt will not let you go, no, not by a mighty hand. (Exod. 3:19)

Pharaoh hardens his heart, then God hardens it further, allowing ample opportunity for God to display His power and draw many to Him. This process, stated in Exodus 9:16 by God and in Romans 9:17, shows God's sovereignty in the affairs of men:

> And in very deed for this cause have I raised thee [Pharaoh] up, for to shew in thee my power; and that my name [character] may be declared throughout all the earth. (Exod. 9:16)[5]

The display of God's sovereignty also attacks the concept of dualism, the idea of equally powerful good and evil forces fighting for the souls of men. Dualism undergirds many false religions but it cannot stand in light of the Scriptures which declare our God as Lord of heaven and earth. The following verses emphasize this:

> And I will sever [set apart, sanctify] in that day the land of Goshen, in which my people dwell, that no swarms of flies shall be there; to the end [in order that] thou mayest know that *I am the* LORD *in the midst of the earth*. (Exod. 8:22)

> And Moses said unto him, As soon as I am gone out of the city, I will spread abroad my hands unto the LORD; and the thunder shall cease, neither shall there be any more hail; that thou mayest know how that *the earth is the* LORD'*s*. (Exod. 9:29)

> At that time Yeshua answered and said, I thank [lit: acknowledge; confess] thee, O Father, LORD *of heaven and earth* ... (Matt. 11:25a)[6]

We are all familiar with the story of the ten plagues the Lord sent upon Egypt. The complete description is found in Exodus 7:14–12:30. These plagues pointedly attacked the many gods of Egypt. The last plague destroyed all the first-born animals and the first-born children (heirs) from every level of dynastic Egyptian society, including Pharaoh's son, the future god-king.

> For I will pass through the land of Egypt this night, and will smite all the firstborn in the land of Egypt, both man and beast; and against all the gods of Egypt I will execute judgment: I am the LORD.
> (Exod. 12:12)

God specified these judgments for the purpose of redemption, and not just Israel's, but also that of the Egyptians. The Lord states nine times that He sends these plagues so that "the Egyptians shall know that I am the LORD ... "[7] This is an excellent example of the thought in Psalm 9:16a, "The LORD is known by the judgment which he executeth ... "

Our God still executes judgment and will continue to do so until the whole world knows that He is the God of Abraham, Isaac and Jacob, the God of Israel. This has been and will continue to be accomplished through God's dealings with Israel.

> He hath remembered his mercy [*chesed*][8] and his truth [lit: faithfulness] toward the house of Israel: all the ends of the earth have seen the salvation [also deliverance, *yeshuah* – feminine form of Jesus' Hebrew name] of our God.   (Ps. 98:3)

On the cross, the Father executed His judgment on our sin and laid it on Messiah Yeshua (see Isa. 53:4–6) for the purpose of our redemption. God's righteous judgment removed the barrier separating us from Himself. Now we can enjoy a mutual love relationship with Him because of his judgment:

> Behold, the LORD's hand is not shortened, that it cannot save; neither his ear heavy [insensitive], that it cannot hear: But your iniquities [perversity; depravity] have separated between [divided] you and your God, and your sins have hid [concealed] his face [presence] from you, that he will not hear.   (Isa. 59:1–2)

As we saw above, God demonstrated His Lordship by protecting His people in Egypt from His wrath. After the first three plagues the "Israeli" neighborhood of Goshen was set apart " ... to the end thou mayest know that I am the LORD in the midst of the earth." And at the last plague,

> But against any of the children of Israel shall not a dog move his tongue, against man or beast: that ye may know how that the LORD doth put a difference [distinguishes] between the Egyptians and Israel.
> (Exod. 11:7)[9]

Believers in Yeshua are also protected from God's wrath. We face the wrath of man (John 16:33) and the discipline of our Father (Heb. 12:5–11), but in Yeshua we will escape the wrath God will pour out on unbelievers:

For God hath not appointed us to wrath [His punishment or judgment], but to obtain salvation [deliverance, rescue] by our Lord Yeshua the Messiah.   (1 Thess. 5:9)

Exodus 12 – The First Passover

The final book of the Bible proclaims Yeshua as "the Lamb slain from the foundation of the world" (Rev. 13:8b). Why? Why is He called a lamb? Because the lamb is the Passover.

Exodus 12, the story of the Passover in Egypt, relates to our salvation through Yeshua and brings out facets of God's glorious redemption that the New Testament alone does not. The New Testament does not expand on many of these "root" issues because all of its writers assumed that believers would study and know Yeshua's Bible, the *Tanach*, as their scriptural foundation.[10] Here is a brief commentary on the Exodus account of the first Passover as it parallels our salvation. We encourage you to follow in your Bible.

Exodus 12:1–2
By telling Moses and Aaron, "This month shall be unto you the beginning of months: it shall be the first month of the year to you" (v. 2), God indicates that redemption from bondage in Egypt will mark the start of a new life. We also start a new life when we trust in the sacrifice of Yeshua, our Passover Lamb (1 Cor. 5:7), and become new creatures in the Messiah (2 Cor. 5:17).

Exodus 12:5
The "lamb ... without blemish" is a type of the Messiah as a man without sin:

> For we have not an high priest which cannot be touched with the feeling of our infirmities [weaknesses]; but was in all points tempted [tested; proved] like as we are, yet without sin.   (Heb. 4:15)

The Hebrew word translated "without blemish," *tamiyim*, lines up perfectly with Yeshua's character, meaning complete, whole, entire, sound, innocent, having integrity and truth.[11] In the life of sheep, a "male of the first year" indicates a male in the prime of its life, as was Yeshua at thirty-three when He gave His life.

Exodus 12:6
The lamb was examined for four days to see if there was any defect in

it and only then was it killed. Yeshua walked and taught openly throughout the land of Israel for over three years so all could examine Him. He once asked, "Which of you convicteth me of sin?" (John 8:46). As Peter states, He is the spotless Lamb of God,

> Forasmuch as ye know that ye were not redeemed with corruptible [perishable] things, as silver and gold, from your vain [profitless; empty] conversation [behavior, lifestyle] received by tradition from your fathers; But with the precious blood of Messiah, *as of a lamb without blemish and without spot* ...   (1 Pet. 1:18–19)

Exodus 12:8–11

God commanded Israel to eat the flesh of the lamb, which is described in verse 11 as "the LORD's passover." Comparing this with verses 21 and 27, we realize that in this chapter God is often speaking of the lamb when He uses the term "the Passover." By the Holy Spirit, Paul said, "Messiah our passover is sacrificed for us" (1 Cor. 5:7b). Therefore, calling Yeshua "our Passover" is parallel to calling Him "the Lamb of God," the title used of Yeshua more often than any other in the New Testament except for "the Messiah," "the Christ."[12] "Messiah our Passover is sacrificed for us" makes perfect sense against the background of Exodus 12.

What the Church calls "Communion" has roots in the annual Passover *Seder*, a meal God ordained to commemorate the Exodus from Egypt. Yeshua broke the bread, which is called "the bread of affliction" in the modern *Seder*, and told His disciples to eat it, saying, "This is my body ... " (Luke 22:19). This bread was unleavened according to the commandment in Exodus 12:8. Leaven represents the spreading nature of sin (1 Cor. 5:6–8). Yeshua, the sinless Lamb, used the *Seder*'s unleavened bread to represent His body.[13]

Jewish *Seder* tradition names the cup of wine after supper "the cup of Messianic redemption." Yeshua said that this cup represented His blood which would seal the New Covenant promised in Jeremiah 31:31–34:

> Likewise also the cup after supper, saying, This cup is the new testament [covenant] in my blood, which is shed for you.
>
> (Luke 22:20)

Exodus 12:12

This verse identifies the one who destroys evil; the one who brings judgment on Egypt and its gods. The Lord God of Israel declares,

For *I will* pass through the land of Egypt this night, and *[I] will* smite all
the firstborn in the land of Egypt, both man and beast; and against
all the gods of Egypt *I will* execute judgment: I am the LORD.

If we compare this with verses 13, 23, 27 and 29, we see that only in
verse 23 is there a reference to "the destroyer." This is not Satan! Satan
would not destroy his own kingdom, rooted so firmly in Egypt. God
states four times that He Himself is the destroyer of Egypt's gods. We
see this destroyer as none other than the pre-incarnate Son of God
Who later destroyed the authority of the Devil over our lives at His first
coming and will totally destroy Satan's kingdom at the end of time!

> For this purpose the Son of God was manifested, that he might destroy
> the works of the devil.   (1 John 3:8b)

Exodus 12:13
In verse 7, the children of Israel were commanded to smear the blood
of the Passover lamb on the lintel and doorposts of their houses. They
were then to go inside and eat the Passover meal. Once inside, they
would no longer see the blood – it was a sign for God.

Yeshua presented His blood to His Father and the Father accepted
it.[14] We trust in this blood sacrifice initially, and afterwards for
forgiveness of each sin. God the Father is looking for the "sign" of the
blood of His Son applied in our lives. When God sees the blood, His
wrath will pass over us, while it falls on the world.

> And to wait for his Son from heaven, whom he raised from the dead,
> even *Yeshua, which delivered* [rescued] *us from the wrath* [punish-
> ment] *to come* ... For God hath not appointed us to wrath, but
> to obtain salvation [safety; deliverance] by our Lord Yeshua the
> Messiah...   (1 Thess. 1:10; 5:9)

Another similarity to our salvation is that, unlike the later
sacrificial system, the Passover was a "once for-all" deliverance from
within enemy territory!

> Yea, though I walk through the valley of the shadow of death, I will
> fear no evil: for thou art with me; thy rod and thy staff they comfort
> me. Thou preparest a table before me *in the presence of mine enemies*:
> thou anointest my head with oil; my cup runneth over.   (Ps. 23:4–5)

God commanded the children of Israel to eat this meal to
remember forever His redemption. Jews and the gentiles who joined
themselves to the house of Israel were to keep this feast (Exod. 12:19,

47–49) as a way to teach the next generation about God's goodness and power:

> And it shall come to pass, when your children shall say unto you, What mean ye by this service? That ye shall say, It is the sacrifice of the Lord's passover, who passed over the houses of the children of Israel in Egypt, when he smote the Egyptians, and delivered our houses. And the people bowed the head and worshipped...   (Exod. 12:26–27)

We declare redemption when we keep the Passover as well as when we celebrate Communion:

> For as often as ye eat this bread, and drink this cup, ye do shew [publicly proclaim] the Lord's death [the Atonement] till he come.
> (1 Cor. 11:26)

We encourage you to participate in a believers' Passover *Seder*. You will find it edifying and exciting, and will end up with a new appreciation of the continuity of God's great plan of salvation.

Conclusion

"Behold the Lamb of God which taketh away[15] the sin of the world" (John 1:29b). The Passover, while celebrating a historic event, also illustrates the dynamics of salvation by grace through faith in the blood of the Lamb. Grace applies because it was God who delivered the children of Israel when, through faith, they obeyed His instructions to apply the blood. They rested and ate under the protection of the blood until the Lord delivered them. We too apply the blood of God's Passover Lamb, rest in Him, partake of Him, and remain under His protection. We "stand still, and see the salvation of the Lord..." (Exod. 14:13b).

> Oh, taste and see [consider] that the Lord is good;
> *blessed is the man that trusteth in him.*
> (Ps. 34:8)[16]

Notes

1. The seven-yearly feasts in Leviticus 23 are divided into two seasons. The spring feasts: Passover (*Pesach* – v. 5); Unleavened Bread (*Matzot* – vv. 6–8); First Fruits [of the barley harvest] (*Bikkurim* – vv. 9–14); Pentecost or Weeks (*Shavuot* – vv. 15–21). Then the fall feasts: Day of the Blowing of the Shofar

(*Yom Teruah*, known today as *Rosh haShanah*, i.e., the Jewish New Year – vv. 24–25); The Day of Atonement (*Yom Kippur* – vv. 26–32); finally Tabernacles or Booths (*Succot* – vv. 33–43).

2. The children of Israel should have made a "clean break" from Egypt. They were no longer slaves and the gods of Egypt had been humiliated. Instead, in one of the great tragedies in the *Tanach*, many of the Israelites took Egyptian idols with them (see Ezek. 20:7, 8, 16, 18, 24). Those who did, remained spiritual slaves. This is a picture of many believers in Messiah Yeshua who, although saved and set free from past sins, still hold on to their "idols" as well. The Israelites who professed love for the Lord, yet could not part with their idols, died in the wilderness.

3. Deut. 18:15, 18–19: "The LORD thy God will raise up unto thee a Prophet from the midst of thee, of thy brethren, like unto me; unto him ye shall hearken ... [the LORD said] I will raise them up a Prophet from among their brethren, like unto thee, and will put my words in his mouth; and he shall speak unto them all that I shall command him."

4. This is the first time in Scripture that God uses the name "LORD God of Israel."

5. See Dan. 4:17, 25, 32, 34–35; 5:21.

6. See also Pss. 2:1–9; 24:1; Isa. 40:17–26; Hag. 2:8; Acts 10:36.

7. See Exod. 7:5, 17; 8:10, 19, 22; 9:14, 29; 14:4, 18.

8. See Chapter 2.

9. See also Exod. 9:4, 26 and 10:23.

10. See 2 Tim. 3:16–17 and Chapter 1.

11. Brown-Driver-Briggs Hebrew lexicon, PC Study Bible; Biblesoft Inc.

12. John 1:29, 36; 1 Pet. 1:19 plus 26 times in the book of Revelation!

13. Unleavened bread is called *matzah*. It is baked today as it was in Yeshua's day except then the shape was probably round. This special bread, representing Messiah's body, is pierced and has the appearance of being striped and bruised. It is broken before being eaten. *Matzah* is the most symbolic bread to use when taking Communion.

14. Acts 20:28; Eph. 1:7; Heb. 9:12, 22.

15. "Takes away" is literally to lift up, carry away or bear on oneself. It is a Hebraism for atoning for, or redeeming from sin. Cf. Isa. 53:4 – "he hath borne ... carried"; 53:5 – "upon him"; 53:6 – "laid on him."

16. Alternative paraphrase: How happy is the valiant warrior that seeks refuge, flees for protection to, confides and hopes in Him.

CHAPTER 4

Salvation in the *Tanach* –
Grace and Faith

Salvation by Grace in the *Tanach*

We have seen that our God is a God of grace, that grace is just as much His nature as love or justice. The Passover story clarifies that God's salvation is and always was by grace through faith, and not through the "Law," as some have it. Unfortunately, for centuries many have been led to believe that in the Old Testament salvation was accomplished only through works. That is a serious misconception of what the *Tanach* and the New Testament clearly teach.

Look at grace and the Law, or faith and works, in the *Tanach*. Think about the "Law of Moses," also called the "Law of the Lord" even in the New Testament.[1] When was the "Law" (a better translation would be "Instruction" or "Teaching") first revealed to the children of Israel? It was given after they were freed from Egypt. By faith in God's Word to Moses they had already applied the blood of the Passover Lamb to their doorposts, and they had already been "baptized,"[2] in faith passing through the Red Sea at God's Word (Heb. 11:29).

The children of Israel were redeemed and dedicated for His special purposes before they ever received His Law. At Sinai He said to His blood-bought,[3] water-baptized people that He wanted His people to live by this Law, so as to be a kingdom of priests proclaiming His name to the nations.[4] The Law was given as a set of divine rules and instructions so the people of God would be holy (literally, "set-apart") and protected in the midst of the world and its traps.

Over time, and because of man's tendency to trust in works of the flesh, the Law became distortedly seen as the way of salvation (see Rom. 9:31–32) – the thinking that one can do something to earn God's favor. But it has always been and ever will be that " ... the just

54

shall live by his faith" (Hab. 2:4; Heb. 10:38). The Law's nature never changed. According to Paul, the Law of God is still "holy, and the commandment holy, and just, and good" (Rom. 7:12b).

Confusion has arisen due to translations saying that believers are no longer "under the Law." Bible expositors unfamiliar with Hebrew theology did not understand that "under the Law" is just a shortened way of saying "under the system for atonement found in the Mosaic Law." After all, what kind of believer would think it is now "legal" to break the Ten Commandments?

The Law of Moses no longer provides for an effective means of atonement for "Law-breakers" (sinners) because of the fulfillment in Messiah's blood atonement. However, the Law still contains God's standard of righteousness. Breaking the Law still requires blood atonement. The Jewish people no longer believe in blood atonement (animal blood is no longer accepted by God), and for that reason they are not saved outside of their Messiah Yeshua.[5] As for gentiles, so for Jews, for it has always been and ever will be that " . . . the just shall live by his faith" (Hab. 2:4; Heb. 10:38).

The doctrine of salvation by grace lies at the root of our proclamation of the Good News. Paul states,

> For by grace are ye saved through faith; and that not of yourselves: it is the gift [or sacrificial offering] of God: Not of works, lest any man should boast.   (Eph. 2:8–9)

And where do we find the root doctrine of grace? As we have seen, it appears in the Hebraic soil of the Old Testament as an attribute of God. But more than that, God actually saves us through His grace.

Here is another definition of grace which emphasizes its role in salvation. The Hebrew word most often translated "grace" or "favor" is *chen*. According to Colin Brown's *New International Dictionary of New Testament Theology*, this word "clarifies the meaning of 'grace' in history and actions. It denotes the stronger coming to the help of the weaker who stands in need of help by reason of his circumstances or natural weakness. [The stronger] acts by a voluntary decision, though he is moved by the dependence or the request of the weaker party."[6]

This is often expressed as "to find favor in someone's eyes," an idiom still in use in modern Hebrew. Brown makes the observation that "*chen* denotes relatively seldom the activity of God. It is used mostly in the sense of His undeserved gift in election."[7] Or as Paul puts it,

In whom also we have obtained an inheritance, being predestinated according to the purpose of him who worketh all things after the counsel of his own will...
(Eph. 1:11b)

Tanach Verses

Here are some *Tanach* verses picturing God's grace, *chen* (in italics), variously translated as "grace" or "favor":

But Noah found *grace* in the eyes of the LORD.
(Gen. 6:8)

Although verse 9b says, "Noah was a just [righteous][8] man and perfect [had integrity] in his generations, and Noah walked with God," yet the reason he acted righteously was because he had been chosen by God's grace. In that grace Noah responded as we all must, but ultimately he and his household were saved by the grace of God.

After worshiping the golden calf in Exodus 32, Israel deserved death. Moses knew that it was not by any merit on the part of the children of Israel that he could approach the Lord and intercede for them. So he came on the basis of grace. God answered him on the same basis (33:17) and even stated that it is His divine nature to be "gracious" (34:6).[9] As we saw in this brief exchange between God and Moses, the word *chen*, or a word based on the same root, is used nine times.

Psalm 51 is David's prayer of confession, asking the Lord for forgiveness because of his sins of murder and adultery (2 Sam. 11). "Have mercy upon me, O God, according to thy lovingkindness [*chesed*]" (Ps. 51:1a). The word "mercy" in this verse comes from the Hebrew root meaning "grace." David realized that he was lost if God did not deal with him in accordance with His grace and mercy, based on God's *chesed*, His covenant love.[10] So David, the greatest king of Israel, like the great prophet Moses before him, came to his Lord on the basis of who God is and not with any merit of his own. Although David's life afterwards proved the spiritual principle that we reap what we sow (Gal. 6:7–8), yet we must note that God did deal with His servant based on His grace – because according to His law, murder and adultery are worthy of the death penalty (Lev. 24:17; 20:10).

Proverbs 3:34 states,

Surely he scorneth the scorners: but he giveth *grace* unto the lowly [humble, meek, afflicted].

James and Peter quote the last part of this *Tanach* verse. James says,

> But he giveth more *grace*. Wherefore he saith, God resisteth the proud, but giveth grace unto the humble.   (Jas. 4:6)

and Peter says,

> ...Yea, all of you be subject one to another, and be clothed with humility: for God resisteth the proud, and giveth *grace* to the humble.
> (1 Pet. 5:5b)

James 4:6 uses this principle of obtaining grace through humility to encourage believers to "Submit yourselves therefore to God. Resist the devil..." (Jas. 4:7a). Peter brings out the same principle using slightly different terms as a proof text to encourage us to submit to God:

> Humble yourselves therefore under the mighty hand of God, that he may exalt you [give grace/favor] in due time...   (1 Pet. 5:6)

In Jeremiah's prophesied restoration of the nation of Israel (chapters 30–33), God declares in 31:2,

> Thus saith the LORD, The people which were left [lit: "survivors," or "remnant"] of the sword found *grace* in the wilderness; even Israel, when I went to cause him to rest.

God's rest is an example of His grace. The New Testament ties in God's rest with salvation:

> For he that is entered into his rest, he also hath ceased from his own works, as God did from his.   (Heb. 4:10)

Obviously, ceasing from trusting in our own works depends on trusting in God's grace through salvation.[11]

Zechariah 12:10 is a promise of Israel's national salvation (see Rom. 11:26), the result of God's grace pouring out on them:

> And I will pour upon the house of David, and upon the inhabitants[12] of Jerusalem, the spirit of *grace* and of supplications: and they shall look upon [intently regard] me whom they have pierced, and they shall mourn for him, as one mourneth for his only son, and shall be in bitterness for him, as one that is in bitterness for his firstborn.

The Hebrew for "supplications" also comes from the same Hebrew root as "grace."

In just these six *Tanach* passages among the many showing God's grace, we have seen grace in connection with election, salvation, God's nature, the forgiveness of sin, and the national salvation of the house of Israel. These are the roots of that same grace proclaimed in the New Testament. And since our salvation is "by grace through faith," let us look next at what the *Tanach* says about faith.

Salvation by Faith in the *Tanach*

As we have mentioned before, and contrary to what many believers think, salvation in the *Tanach* was never obtained just by obeying the Mosaic Law. God, who never changes (Mal. 3:6), has always offered salvation to those who believe and trust in His Word. And His Word consistently points to salvation through faith in God's provision for atonement. This theme runs through the Old Testament as well as the New. As the following New Testament verses state, our God wants faith with works, not faith in works:

> Therefore whosoever heareth these sayings of mine, *and doeth them*, I will liken him unto a wise man, which built his house upon a rock ... And every one that heareth these sayings of mine, *and doeth them not*, shall be likened unto a foolish man, which built his house upon the sand... (Matt. 7:24, 26)

> If ye love me, *keep my commandments*... (John 14:15)[13]

> This is a faithful saying, and these things I will that thou affirm constantly, that they which have believed in God might *be careful to maintain* good works... (Titus 3:8a)

Here is that often misunderstood section of James:

> What doth it profit, my brethren, though a man say he hath faith, and have not works? can faith save him? ... Yea, a man may say, Thou hast faith, and I have works: shew me thy faith without thy works, and I will shew thee my faith by my works ... But wilt thou know, O vain man, that faith without works is dead? ... For as the body without the spirit is dead, so *faith without works is dead* also.
> (James 2:14, 18, 20, 26)

Works are the manifestation of the fruits of the Spirit. This fruit consists of the forming in us of godly characteristics (listed in Galatians 5:22–23) and includes faith and goodness. If we would keep in mind that our works are good only if they are validated by faith, our trusting and obeying God's Word to us, and empowered by His Spirit and not our own questionable motives, then all of the above verses make perfect sense.

The words "faith" and "belief" are commonly used in two different but valid ways. They are sometimes used to designate a creed or set of religious beliefs, for example: Christian belief, the Jewish faith, etc. However, in this section we use "faith" and "belief" in the usual biblical sense of trusting in, relying on, remaining steadfast in, and believing the Lord. Genesis 15:6 says about Father Abraham, "And he believed in the LORD; and he counted it to him for righteousness" or as the Amplified Version states, "And [Abram] believed, (trusted in, relied on, remained steadfast to the Lord); and He counted it to him as righteousness [right standing with God]."

In Hebrew, three important words come from a single root. "Faith" (or "faithfulness"), "truth," and "amen" are linked linguistically and theologically. Their root word means "to build up or support; to foster as a parent; figuratively, to render [or be] firm or faithful, to trust or believe, to be permanent or quiet . . . to be true or certain" (*Strong's Concordance*, #539).

The Hebrew word for "faithful" denotes a trusting certainty, as well as faithfulness in the sense of dependability. This word is used of men:

> My servant Moses is not so, who is *faithful* in all mine house . . .
> (Num. 12:7)

> And I will raise me up a *faithful* priest [Samuel], that shall do according to that which is in mine heart . . .   (1 Sam. 2:35a)

> Thou art the LORD the God, who didst choose Abram, and broughtest him forth out of Ur of the Chaldees, and gavest him the name of Abraham; And foundest his heart faithful before thee, and madest a covenant with him to give the land of the Canaanites . . .
> (Neh. 9:7–8a)

This word is also used of God, the One to whom all true faith looks:

> Know therefore that the LORD thy God, he is God, the *faithful* God, which keepeth covenant and mercy [*chesed*] with them that love him and keep his commandments to a thousand generations . . .
> (Deut. 7:9)

> Kings shall see and arise, princes also shall worship, because of the

LORD that is *faithful*, and the Holy One of Israel, and he shall choose
thee . . .   (Isa. 49:7b)

It is of the LORD's mercies [*chesed*] that we are not consumed, because
his compassions fail not. They are new every morning: great is thy
faithfulness.   (Lam. 3:22–23)

This word is also used of God's covenant, highlighting its reliability
because God stands behind it:

My mercy [*chesed*] will I keep for him for evermore, and my covenant
shall stand fast with him.   (Ps. 89:28)

Although the root word under discussion is not found in the
following passage, this quote thoroughly embodies the concept of
God's faithfulness to His covenant:

Thus saith the LORD; If ye can break my covenant of the day, and my
covenant of the night, and that there should not be day and night in
their season; Then may also my covenant be broken [frustrated;
violated] with David my servant, that he should not have a son to
reign upon his throne; and with the Levites the priests, my ministers . . .
Thus saith the LORD; If my covenant be not with day and night, and if
I have not appointed the ordinances of heaven and earth; Then will I
cast away [or despise] the seed of Jacob, and David my servant, so that
I will not take any of his seed to be rulers over the seed of Abraham,
Isaac, and Jacob: for I will cause their captivity to return, and have
mercy on them.   (Jer. 33:20–21, 25–26)

The *Tanach* on Faith

And he [Abraham] *believed* in the LORD; and he counted it to him for
righteousness.   (Gen. 15:6)

More than once the New Testament uses this incident in the *Tanach*
as a specific example of faith as trust. For example in James 2:23,

And the scripture was fulfilled which saith, Abraham *believed* [trusted]
God, and it was imputed [accounted] unto him for righteousness: and
he was called the Friend of God.[14]

Paul also uses this verse to support his argument for salvation by faith
in Romans 4, and also in Galatians 3:6 to encourage believers not to
try to gain God's favor by works of the Law (Gal. 5:4), but by
continuing in faith (Gal. 3:3).

Even the rabbis declare, "Our father Abraham, came into the possession of this world and the world hereafter [eternal life] only by the merit of his faith" (Mechilta 33a). In an interesting comment found in the ArtScroll Tanach Series, Hirsch explains in connection with this verse, "the concept of believing someone, in the sense that his promise is accepted, would be expressed as ["he believed him"]. The phrase in this verse, ["he believed in Him"], however, represents a much deeper concept than mere belief. It suggests total submission in the sense that one places his total confidence and seeks all his guidance and attitudes in God."[15]

The Tabernacle in the wilderness (Exod. 25:1–40:38) symbolizes the pattern of our salvation, of how to relate to God His way. It ties together God's provision for the forgiveness of sins and our response of obedient service to Him in faith. Without the ordained priesthood and offerings, the Tabernacle was just a pretty tent. Without God's order, timing and Law functioning in the Tabernacle, all that man can offer is "profane fire" (Lev. 10:1–5), "filthy rags" (Isa. 64:6), and works and service through the flesh. Israel was saved through the Tabernacle not by bringing sacrifices, but only by acting in belief in what God said about blood, and atonement, and bringing sacrifices. There's a huge difference.

Leviticus 1:1–7:38 describes the sacrificial offerings. The sinner brought his sacrifice to the priest and confessed his sin over the head of the animal (Lev. 4:29, 33), then slew the offering. The priest applied the blood to the altar, making atonement for the sin. The sinner was then forgiven (Lev. 4:31, 35). What is the pattern? To gain acceptance by God, all the sinner needed to do was trust the Word of the Lord which told him that the blood of his sacrificial offering would atone for, literally "cover," his sin. The sinner did no work other than to trust and obey the Word! This atoning power of the shed blood models the forgiveness of sins. It is a foreshadow of our salvation accomplished on the cross through our sacrificial offering, Yeshua. All we "do" for salvation is believe God's Word and trust Him to fulfill it; and the fruit of that faith comes when we obey God's commands.

We read in 2 Chronicles 20:20b,

> Hear me, O Judah, and ye inhabitants of Jerusalem; *Believe* in the Lord your God, so shall ye be established; *believe* his prophets, so shall ye prosper.

The Hebrew in that verse has the same wording as in Genesis 15:6, to believe in the Lord. This charge, given by King Jehoshaphat to the nation of Judah when they were about to be attacked by a greatly superior army, demonstrates the Hebrew concept behind the word "faith," translated here as "believe." We are "established," "built up," when we trust in God's Word (see Matt. 7:24–27). In fact the Hebrew for "so shall ye be established" has the same Hebrew root as "believe"!

The negative side of the above verse is found in Isaiah 7:9b, "If ye will not believe, surely ye shall not be established." Again, the word translated "believe" means to trust, to be certain, and has the same root as the word translated "ye shall ... be established."

Habakkuk 2:4 is one of the most important of the "faith" verses found in the *Tanach*,

> Behold, his soul which is lifted up is not upright in him: but the just shall live by his *faith* [or faithfulness].

That second part is quoted several times in the New Testament as a proof text for our life of faith:

> For I am not ashamed of the gospel of Messiah: for it is the power of God unto salvation to every one that *believeth*; to the Jew first, and also to the Greek. For therein is the righteousness of God revealed [disclosed] from *faith* to *faith*: as it is written, The just shall live by *faith*. (Rom. 1:16–17)

> But that no man is justified [rendered righteous] by the law in the sight of God, it is evident [obvious]: for, The just shall live by *faith*. (Gal. 3:11)

> For yet a little while, and he that shall come will come, and will not tarry. Now the just shall live by *faith*. (Heb. 10:37–38a)

When the New Testament authors wanted to give solid examples of men and women of God who lived by faith, they pointed to the heroes of the *Tanach*. The most quoted chapter in this regard is Hebrews 11 which presents a "great cloud of witnesses" (Heb. 12:1) who overcame, stood in their faith, trusting in God through all kinds of trials, including death.

Scripture emphatically states that these saints of God pleased Him (Heb. 11:6), not through their works per se, although we see their faith by their works, but through trusting the One who did the works through them. Here is the key – not faith in our faith or in our ability to believe, but faith/trust in the living God of the Scriptures, who is faithful.

> Looking unto Yeshua the author [leading example] and finisher [perfector] of our *faith*; who for the joy that was set before him endured the cross, despising the shame [disgrace], and is set down at the right hand of the throne of God. (Heb. 12:2)

Paul mentions God's faithfulness as the pillar of Abraham's faith,

> He staggered [withdrew] not at the promise of God through unbelief; but was strong in *faith*, giving glory to God; And being fully persuaded that, *what he had promised, he was able also to perform.* And therefore it was imputed [accounted] to him for righteousness.
> (Rom. 4:20–22)

Paul further tells us in 2 Timothy 2:13 that we can trust in God because of who He is. It is God's character to be faithful:

> If we believe not, yet he abideth [remains] *faithful*: he cannot [is not able to] deny himself.

Finally, in Revelation 3:14 Yeshua calls Himself "the *Amen,* the *faithful* and *true* witness…," combining all three of the major concepts rooted in the Hebrew word for "faith." Yeshua, and He alone, must be the focal point of our faith.

> Thus saith the LORD, the Redeemer of Israel, and his Holy One,
> to him whom man despiseth, to him whom the nation abhorreth, to a
> servant of rulers, Kings shall see and arise, princes also shall worship,
> because of the LORD that is *faithful*, and the Holy One of Israel,
> and he shall choose thee.
> (Isa. 49:7)

Notes

1. "And when the days of her purification according *to the law of Moses* were accomplished, they brought him to Jerusalem, to present him to the Lord; (As it is written in *the law of the Lord*, Every male that openeth the womb shall be called holy to the Lord;) And to offer a sacrifice according to that which is said *in the law of the Lord*, A pair of turtledoves, or two young pigeons" (Luke 2:22–24).
2. "Moreover, brethren, I would not that ye should be ignorant, how that all our fathers were under the cloud, and all passed through the sea; And were all *baptized* unto Moses in the cloud and in the sea" (1 Cor. 10:1–2).

3. See Exod. 15:16; cf. with Acts 20:28.

4. Here is that paraphrase as it appears in the KJV: "And Moses went up unto God, and the LORD called unto him out of the mountain, saying, Thus shalt thou say to the house of Jacob, and tell the children of Israel; Ye have seen what I did unto the Egyptians, and how I bare you on eagles' wings, and brought you unto myself. Now therefore, if ye will obey my voice indeed, and keep my covenant, then ye shall be a peculiar treasure unto me above all people: for all the earth is mine: And ye shall be unto me a kingdom of priests, and an holy nation. These are the words which thou shalt speak unto the children of Israel" (Exod. 19:3–6).

5. For this reason, any attempts to help the Jewish people rebuild their Temple and reinstitute animal sacrifices are misguided and hindering their salvation.

6. *The New International Dictionary of the New Testament*, ed. Colin Brown, Vol. 2, p. 116.

7. Ibid., p. 116.

8. As Isaiah 64:6a states: "But we are all as an unclean thing, and all our righteousnesses are as filthy rags."

9. See Chapter 2, section "God of Grace" for a more complete look at this section of Scripture.

10. See Chapter 2, section "The Covenant-Love of God – *Chesed*".

11. "Even so then at this present time also there is a remnant according to the election of grace. And if by grace, then is it no more of works: otherwise grace is no more grace. But if it be of works, then is it no more grace: otherwise work is no more work" (Rom. 11:5–6; also Eph. 2:8–9).

12. This word in modern Hebrew is translated "settlers." Considering the current uproar over the "Israeli settlers," it is good to know that these people will also be recipients of God's grace.

13. See also John 14:21–24; 1 John 2:3–5; 5:2–3.

14. See also Rom. 4:3–6, 9, 20–25 and Gal. 3:6–14. Also see Hebrews 11:8 for another New Testament use of Abraham as someone whose faith should provoke us to jealousy.

15. Bereshis (Genesis), ArtScroll Tanach Series (Brooklyn: Mesorah Publications), Vol. 1, p. 512.

CHAPTER 5

Doctrines in the *Tanach* – Sin, Blood, Atonement

Having studied some basic concepts of salvation illustrated in the feast of Passover, we turn our attention to *Yom Kippur*, the Day of Atonement, another *Tanach* holy day in which several teachings of our faith take root. We will look at teachings in four areas: sin, blood atonement, forgiveness, and the mediation of the High Priest.

Sin

As mentioned before, Rabbi Shaul (apostle Paul), who had been carefully educated in "the holy scriptures" (called the *Tanach* or "Old Testament" – 2 Tim. 3:15), referred to or quoted the *Tanach* about sixty times in his one letter to the Romans. Only by doing so could he have proven that the major New Testament doctrines are of God. Paul knew that for a doctrine to be true it must confirm what God had previously said in the *Tanach*. The Lord stated this through His prophet Isaiah,

> To the law and to the testimony: if they speak not according to this word, it is because there is no light in them.   (Isa. 8:20)

So do we find in the *Tanach* any sweeping statements about sin like Paul's declaration in Romans 3:23, "For all have sinned and come short of the glory of God"?

As early as Genesis 6:5, before the Flood, the Bible observes,

> And GOD saw that the wickedness of man was great in the earth, and that every imagination [purpose, idea] of the thoughts of his heart was only evil continually ("continually" in the Hebrew is *kol yom*, literally, all or every day).

After the Flood God declares that He will "not again curse the ground any more for man's sake; for the imagination [purpose] of man's heart is evil from his youth..." (Gen. 8:21b). In these verses God focuses on the state of the "heart," which in both Hebrew and Greek stands for the inner man, the mind, emotions and will. In both verses, the condition of man's heart is described as "evil" all through his life. Or as God declares through the prophet Jeremiah,

> The heart is deceitful [sly; insidious; lit: slippery] above all things, and desperately wicked [incurably sick]: who can know it?   (Jer. 17:9)

In the *Yom Kippur* instructions found in Leviticus 16, which we will study in a later section, the High Priest made atonement for everyone in the camp of Israel, including himself. No one was free from the need of atonement for his sins.[1]

King Solomon, whom the Scriptures declare was the wisest man who ever lived (1 Kgs. 3:12; 4:29–34), knew about our tendency to sin. When dedicating the Temple in Jerusalem, he prayed to God, "If they sin against thee, (for there is no man that sinneth not,)..." (1 Kgs. 8:46a). In Proverbs 20:9, Solomon has this insight,

> Who can say, I have made my heart clean, I am pure from my sin?

Later in life, he came to a further realization,

> For there is not a just man upon earth, that doeth good, and sinneth not.   (Eccl. 7:20)

Even the righteous person who wants to please God does not avoid all sin.

The prophet Isaiah says in 64:6a, "But we are as an unclean [impure; defiled] thing, and all our righteousnesses are like filthy rags..." These last two verses reprove those who try to earn their salvation. Not only is there "no man," not even a "just man" who never sins, but the literal Hebrew declares that even our righteous acts are, in His sight, like clothing that has been soiled and stained.

The Psalmist exclaims in 130:3,

> If thou, LORD, shouldest mark iniquities, O Lord, who shall stand?

In Psalm 143:2, King David pleads with the Lord,

> And enter not into judgment with thy servant: for in thy sight shall no man living be justified.

If God judged us according to His legal right as our Creator, insisting that we walk before Him without fault, as He says in both the *Tanach* and the New Testament,[2] no one would be found blameless. Isaiah confirms this in 53:6a, "All we like sheep have gone astray; we have turned every one to his own way..."

In the New Testament Paul says that we have inherited our "old man," our propensity to sin, from our father Adam, the natural head of the human race.[3] Can we find the roots of that truth in the *Tanach*?

Psalm 51:5 ("Behold, I was shapen in iniquity; and in sin did my mother conceive me") and Psalm 58:3 ("The wicked are estranged from the womb: they go astray as soon as they be born, speaking lies") indicate that babies are born with the first Adam's nature. If you have ever seen a precious little baby suddenly change into a screamer because it could not have its way, you have seen a perfect demonstration of a rebellious spirit whose vocabulary is largely limited to "I," "Me" and "Mine."

In Genesis 5:1–3 we have an insightful commentary by Moses on the result of Adam's sin:

> This is the book of the generations of Adam. In the day that *God created man, in the likeness of God* made he him; Male and female created he them; and blessed them, and called their name Adam, in the day when they were created. And Adam lived an hundred and thirty years, and *begat a son in his own likeness, after his image*; and called his name Seth...

Since "God is a Spirit..." (John 4:24), it was Adam's spirit that was created in God's likeness. That likeness died when Adam and Eve sinned (Eph. 2:1, 5) and all their offspring were then born with their spiritual likeness – the tendency to sin, which we all have inherited. Only by being "born from above" are our spirits reborn or resurrected in God's likeness (John 3:6–7). Our lives then begin to be conformed into the likeness of the life of the Son of God, Yeshua (Rom. 8:29).

The *Tanach* scriptures given above undergird the New Testament doctrine that all people are sinners. Here are specific terms that the *Tanach* uses to describe manifest sin: unbelief, lack of trust, hardness of heart, disobedience, stiff-neck, rebellion.

Atonement and Blood

The Hebrew root word *kopher* means literally "to cover," but figuratively "to pay" or "to ransom." We have a good example of it in Exodus 21:30, "If there be laid on him a sum of money, then he shall *give for the ransom* of his life whatsoever is laid upon him," or as it states in the New King James Version, "he shall *pay* [*kopher*] to redeem his life..." The Hebrew noun for atonement, *kaphar*, is derived from this root word.

Kaphar, atonement, literally means a protective covering, but figuratively it takes on the meaning of forgiveness, including the "covering" and "payment" for sins. *The Theological Wordbook of the Old Testament* states the following about *kaphar*: "From the meaning of *kopher*, 'to ransom', the meaning of *kaphar* can be understood ... 'to atone by offering a substitute'."[4]

Hebrews 9:22 contains the clearest position statement on blood atonement in the New Testament,

> And almost all things are by the law purged [cleansed] with blood; and without shedding of blood is no remission [forgiveness; pardon].
>
> (based on Lev. 17:11 – see following)

That verse occurs in the context of the writer's argument that Yeshua's blood sacrifice was necessary to establish a new covenant between God and man. The phrase "make a covenant" literally says in Hebrew "cut a covenant," referring to a blood sacrifice to seal the covenant.[5]

When we realize that sealing a covenant requires blood to be shed we obtain a better understanding of Yeshua's words spoken over the cup of wine during His last supper (the Passover meal),

> And he took the cup, and gave thanks, and gave it to them, saying, Drink ye all of it; For this is my blood of the new testament [covenant], which is shed for many for the remission [forgiveness; pardon] of sins.
>
> (Matt. 26:27–28)[6]

Throughout the Scriptures God makes it clear that blood is not some arbitrary magical substance that provides atonement. Blood is required because it contains the life of the creature. The Lord states, "The soul that sinneth, it shall die" (Ezek. 18:20a). "Soul" (Hebrew *nephesh*) "denotes the 'life' of an individual."[7] Look at Leviticus 17:11–12:

> For the life [*nephesh*] of the flesh is in the blood: and I have given it to you upon the altar to make an atonement [covering] for [or over] your souls [*nephesh*]: for it is the blood that maketh an atonement for the soul [*nephesh*]. Therefore I said unto the children of Israel, No soul [*nephesh*] of you shall eat blood, neither shall any stranger that sojourneth among you eat blood.

Forty years later, as Israel prepared to enter the Promised Land, Moses reminded them of that commandment (Deut. 12:23). This divine instruction was not new; it had been given to all mankind from the time that God made a covenant with Noah after the Flood. Included in His instructions to Noah and his sons is,

> But flesh with the life [*nephesh*] thereof, which is the blood thereof, shall ye not eat.　　　　　　　　　　　　　　　　(Gen. 9:4)[8]

God uses the physical red liquid as a symbol for the life of the flesh. The New King James Version translates the Hebrew word "blood" as "life." Leviticus 19:16b in the New King James Version reads "against the *life* of your neighbor"; but in the King James Version and the original Hebrew it is "against the *blood* of your neighbor." A sacrifice whose blood was sprinkled on the altar of God became a substitute for the sinner's soul, that is, the sinner's life, which would have been forfeit through sin. It fulfilled the divine Law of a life [*nephesh*] for a life [*nephesh*] (Exod. 21:23; Deut. 19:21).

Our salvation depends on that fact. Yeshua gave His life for us by offering His blood as our substitute/sacrifice; His life for our lives. Matthew 20:28 says,

> Even as the Son of man came not to be ministered unto [to be served], but to minister [to serve], and to give his life a ransom for many.[9]

As mankind's substitute, Yeshua had to die in a certain way. He could not be suffocated or poisoned. His blood had to be shed like that of a sacrificed animal.[10] This legally satisfied God's justice while releasing His mercy in forgiveness.

> For all have sinned, and come short of the glory of God; Being justified [rendered righteous] freely [undeservedly] by his grace through the redemption that is in Messiah Yeshua: Whom God hath set forth to be a propitiation [satisfaction of divine justice] *through faith in his blood*...　　　　　　　　　　　　　　　　(Rom. 3:23–25a)

The following was prophesied in Isaiah 53:10,

> Yet it pleased the LORD [the LORD willed] to bruise [crush] Him; he hath put him to grief: when thou shalt make his soul [*nephesh*] an offering for sin...

It was Yeshua's soul, His life, His blood, that was offered for our sin. As Judas finally realized, "I have sinned in that I have betrayed the innocent blood" (Matt. 27:4a). God is proclaiming that the sinless life

of Yeshua was exchanged for our sinful lives by His blood poured out
on the cross.

Isaiah 53 analyzes the exchange our Lord accomplished by dying in
our place. It states that Yeshua took our griefs and carried our
sorrows (53:4); He was wounded for our transgressions, bruised for
our iniquities and the chastisement for our peace was upon Him
(53:5); He had the iniquity of us all laid on Him (53:6); Yeshua was
stricken for the transgression of the people (53:8); His soul was an
offering for sin (53:10); and He bore the sin of many (53:12).

All of that was made possible because as Yeshua said,

> Think not that I am come to destroy the law, or the prophets: I am not
> come to destroy, but to fulfill.   (Matt. 5:17)

In this case, with reference to His death on the cross, he fulfilled,
brought to its ultimate goal, the doctrine of substitutionary blood
sacrifice as spelled out in the *Tanach*.

How did the people who offered sacrifices to God obtain forgiveness before Yeshua's atonement? "But without faith it is impossible to
please Him..." (Heb. 11:6a). Remember that in the *Tanach* "faith"
is often found embodied in the word "trust." The author of Hebrews
goes on to give examples of this biblical faith by looking to that "great
... cloud [vast multitude] of witnesses" (Heb. 12:1), heroes and
heroines of the *Tanach*.[11]

So it was, that before Yeshua's death, as a witness of the truth of
God's Word, any member of Israel instructed in God's Word,
realizing that he needed atonement for his sin, brought a substitutionary sacrifice to the priests. He believed/trusted what God said was
true, that blood must be shed in order for sins to be forgiven. The
sinner acted on that Word and was reconciled to God. Even Yeshua
commanded this before His death, telling the leper to offer what
Moses commanded as a testimony/witness to the priests of his healing
(Matt. 8:2). However, if the rite was performed not in belief but only
as dead tradition, God, who has always looked on the condition of the
heart, would not forgive.[12]

Works do not, and never did, lead to salvation. However, coupled
with faith, they evidence and witness to a relationship with the living
God, as Paul emphasizes to Titus,

> Looking for that blessed hope, and the glorious appearing of the great
> God and our Saviour Yeshua the Messiah; Who gave himself for us,
> that he might redeem us from all iniquity [lawlessness], and purify unto

himself a peculiar people, *zealous of good works* ... This is a faithful saying, and these things I will that thou affirm constantly [confidently; strongly], that *they which have believed* in God might be careful to *maintain* [give attention to; practice] *good works*. These things are good and profitable unto men ... And let ours also learn to maintain good works for necessary uses, that they be not unfruitful.

(Titus 2:13–14; 3:8, 14)

Works without faith are just as dead as faith without works (Jas. 2:20), but together faith and works make an unbeatable combination.

And they overcame him by the blood of the Lamb
and by the word of their testimony [witness],
and they loved not their lives unto the death.
(Rev. 12:11)

Notes

1. See Lev. 16:6, 11, 17, 24, 33–34.
2. Lev. 11:44–45; 1 Pet. 1:16.
3. Rom. 5:14–21; 1 Cor. 15:21–22.
4. Harris, Archer, Waltke, *Theological Wordbook of the Old Testament* (Chicago: Moody Press), Vol. I, p. 453.
5. Ibid., p. 128.
6. Obviously the wine was not literal blood. Yeshua was speaking symbolically. His Jewish listeners would have understood this. Drinking blood is absolutely forbidden under both Old and New Covenants. See Lev. 17:10 and Acts 15:29.
7. Harris, Archer, Waltke, op. cit., Vol. 2, p. 589.
8. Even in the New Testament, the Jerusalem Council included this injunction as one of the four things gentile believers needed to do so that Jew and gentile in the Body of Messiah could have fellowship together. See Acts 15:29 where three of the four "necessary things" had to do with food laws! How do we deal with these New Testament commandments?
9. See also John 6:47–54; 1 John 3:16.
10. Incredible as this sounds to some ears, the Bible specifically claims that when Yeshua died on the tree, it was *God's blood* that was shed: "Take heed therefore unto yourselves, and to all the flock, over the which the Holy Ghost hath made you overseers, to feed the church of God, which *he hath purchased with* [through] *his own blood*" (Acts 20:28).

    A similar thought is brought out in Israel's victory song on the other side of the Red Sea: "Thou in thy mercy [*chesed* – covenant love] hast led forth *the people which thou hast redeemed*: thou hast guided them in thy strength unto thy holy habitation. The people shall hear, and be afraid: sorrow shall take hold on the inhabitants of Palestina ... Fear and dread shall fall upon them;

by the greatness of thine arm they shall be as still as a stone; till thy people pass over, O LORD, *till the people pass over, which thou hast purchased"* (Exod. 15:13–14, 16).

11. Our word "martyr" comes from the Greek word meaning "witness." But, though all these died in the faith, not all witnesses are killed because of their faith.

12. See, for example, Gen. 4:4, cf. Heb. 11:4; 1 Sam. 15:22; Ps. 34:22; 51:16–19; Prov. 21:27; Isa. 1:10–20; Jer. 7:21–23; Hos. 6:6; Amos 5:21–24; Mic. 6:6–8; Mal. 3:3; Mark 12:33–34.

CHAPTER 6

Day of Atonement –
Yom Kippur

Atonement in *Yom Kippur*

Yom Kippur, the sixth of the seven annual convocations instituted by God (Lev. 23:26–32), occurs on the tenth day of the seventh month of the Hebrew calendar (*Tishrei*), and has been observed as a complete fast in Judaism at least since the time of the Second Temple.[1] On that day, according to Scripture, atonement was made for all of Israel's iniquities, transgressions, and sins (see comments on Lev. 16:21 below). God says that He has provided a way to make atonement.

> For the life of the flesh is in the blood: and I have given it to you upon the altar to make an atonement for your souls: for it is the blood that maketh an atonement for the soul. (Lev. 17:11)

This has always been the most solemn day of the year for the Jewish people. On this day religious Jews spend the day in synagogues fasting, praying prayers of repentance, and believing that God will hear and answer their prayers. The whole nation of Israel shuts down to observe this biblical holy day. The city of Jerusalem is closed and, except for an occasional ambulance, there is no traffic.[2]

Concerning this day we agree with Matthew Henry's statement in his *Commentary*, "The Day of Atonement ... has as much gospel in it as perhaps any of the ... ceremonial law."[3]

Leviticus 16

Leviticus 16 gives a detailed description of the duties of the high priest on *Yom Kippur*. Without an understanding of that chapter it is impossible to fully comprehend the New Testament book of Hebrews which declares Yeshua as the High Priest of all believers:

> Wherefore, holy brethren, partakers of the heavenly calling, consider the Apostle and High Priest of our profession [confession], Messiah Yeshua . . .   (Heb. 3:1)

> Now of the things which we have spoken this is the sum [summary]: We have such an high priest, who is set on the right hand [metaphorically, the place of honor and/or authority] of the throne of the Majesty [God] in the heavens; A minister [public servant; priest] of the sanctuary, and of the true tabernacle, which the Lord pitched, and not man.   (Heb. 8:1–2)[4]

After each of the verses quoted below, we give a brief description of the God-ordained rituals for this most holy of days and their fulfillment by Yeshua, our High Priest.

Leviticus 16:2

> And the LORD said unto Moses, Speak unto Aaron thy brother, that he come not at all times into the holy place within the veil *before the mercy seat*, which is upon the ark; that he die not: for I will appear in the cloud upon the mercy seat.

These instructions applied originally to the Tabernacle in the wilderness and later to the Temple in Jerusalem. The Lord warned that Aaron, the first high priest, should not come through the veil into the Holy of Holies except yearly on that one day. Aaron needed to approach God in God's way, bringing something to cover his sin, making an atonement. The word translated "mercy seat" in this verse comes from a Hebrew word, *kaporah*, literally meaning a protective cover,[5] and is derived from the same word from which Hebrew also derives the word for "atonement."

Leviticus 16:3

> Thus shall Aaron come into the holy place: with a young bullock for a sin offering, and a ram for a burnt offering.

Aaron needed protection, a covering. The penalty for his own sin first needed to be purged by the blood of a sin offering and a burnt offering before he could enter into the presence of Israel's holy God. In the next chapter of Leviticus God says He has provided a way to make atonement,

> For the life of the flesh is in the blood: and I have given it to you upon the altar to make an atonement for your souls: for it is the blood that maketh an atonement for the soul. (Lev. 17:11)

Yeshua presented Himself as the offering for sin by His own blood (Heb. 9:12–14, 22). He was also the perfect burnt offering, offering His whole life completely to His Father's will (Heb. 10:5–10).

> But Messiah being come an high priest of good things to come, by a greater and more perfect [complete] tabernacle, not made with hands, that is to say, not of this building [creation]; Neither by the blood of goats and calves, *but by his own blood he entered in once into the holy place*, having obtained eternal redemption for us.
> (Heb. 9:11–12)

He is there in the true Tabernacle (Heb. 8:2; 9:24), interceding for us now (Rom. 8:27, 34).

Believers have continual access to God's presence, but not because we are priests. Regular priests were never allowed to enter that special place. We have access because of the blood of our Messiah and because we are part of the body of the High Priest (Eph. 5:30–32). Therefore, we belong within the veil.

> Having therefore, brethren, boldness [assurance] to enter into the holiest by the blood of Yeshua, By a new and living way, which he hath consecrated [initiated] for us, through the veil, that is to say, his flesh... (Heb. 10:19–21)

Leviticus 16:4

> He shall put on the holy linen coat, and he shall have the linen breeches upon his flesh, and shall be girded with a linen girdle, and with the linen mitre shall he be attired: these are holy garments; therefore shall he wash his flesh in water, and so put them on.

The high priest needed to wear ordained holy garments made out of unadorned linen when entering God's presence. "Holy" means separated from the world and consecrated to God. Linen is symbolic of righteous deeds.

> And to her [the wife of the Lamb] was granted that she should be arrayed in fine linen, clean [pure] and white [shining]: for the fine linen is the righteousness [righteous deeds of faith] of saints.
> (Rev. 19:8; see also Eph. 2:10)

The high priest wore these symbolic yet simple garments in the Holy of Holies when he represented the people before a holy God. When he appeared as God's representative to the people (v. 23), he changed into his elegantly adorned high priest's garments symbolizing God's glory and majesty (see Exod. 39:1–31).

Leviticus 16:5

And he shall take of the congregation of the children of Israel two kids of the goats for a sin offering, and one ram for a burnt offering.

These offerings made atonement for the sins of the people of Israel (see v. 15). Other than here and in Leviticus 14:2–7, there is no other instance of two animals presented together as one offering. We will see what this represents in verse 22.

Leviticus 16:6

And Aaron shall offer [lit: come near with] his bullock of the sin offering, which is for himself, and make an atonement for himself, and for his house.

Aaron, or any human high priest, needed to deal with his own sin before he could stand in the gap for the sins of the people. Yeshua did not need to do that since He was without sin.

For such an high priest became [was suitable for] us, who is holy, harmless [free from guilt], undefiled, separate from sinners, and made higher [more exalted] than the heavens; Who needeth not daily, as those high priests, to offer up sacrifice, first for his own sins, and then for the people's: for this he did once, when he offered up himself.

(Heb. 7:26–27)

Because He had no sin, nothing separated Him from His Father (see Isa. 59:2).

Leviticus 16:7–8

And he shall take the two goats, and present them before the LORD at the door of the tabernacle of the congregation. And Aaron shall cast lots upon the two goats; one lot for the LORD, and the other lot for the scapegoat.

After presenting the bull's blood for his own sins, Aaron was able to mediate for Israel. He took both goats to the door of the Tabernacle before the Lord and cast lots. One goat became the Lord's and was killed as a sin offering. The other goat, called *azazel* in Hebrew or "scapegoat" in some English versions, was released in the wilderness. (See vv. 20–21 below for a detailed discussion on the scapegoat.)

Leviticus 16:9

> And Aaron shall bring the goat upon which the LORD's lot fell, and offer him for a sin offering.

The Lord's goat was slain to be a propitiation, a satisfaction of divine justice. "The soul that sinneth, it shall die" (Ezek. 18:4b, 20a). "For the wages of sin is death..." (Rom. 6:23a). Justification is what Yeshua's death on the cross accomplished for all who believe.

> Being justified freely by his grace through the redemption that is in Messiah Yeshua: Whom God hath set forth to be a propitiation through faith in his blood...   (Rom. 3:24–25a)

Leviticus 16:10

> But the goat, on which the lot fell to be the scapegoat, shall be presented alive before the LORD, to make an atonement with him, and to let him go for a scapegoat into the wilderness.

This is an amazing ritual. The live goat released in the wilderness was also part of the atonement. But atonement for sin can only be accomplished through the shedding of blood (Lev. 17:11). We will reconcile that contradiction in a later section (vv. 20–22).

Leviticus 16:11

> And Aaron shall bring the bullock of the sin offering, which is for himself, and shall make an atonement for himself, and for his house, and shall kill the bullock of the sin offering which is for himself...

This repeats verse 6 with the added detail that Aaron is the one who killed the sin offering. Yeshua laid down His life. "No man taketh it from me, but I lay it down of myself" (John 10:18a, see also 1 John 3:16).

Leviticus 16:12–13

> And he shall take a censer full of burning coals of fire from off the altar before the LORD, and his hands full of sweet incense beaten small, and

> bring it within the vail: And he shall put the incense upon the fire
> before the LORD, that the cloud of the incense may cover [clothe or
> conceal] the mercy seat that is upon the testimony, that he die not...

Aaron brought incense into the Holy of Holies to cover the mercy seat
so that he would not die (v. 2). Incense is a type of the prayers of the
saints (Rev. 5:8; 8:3–4), a sweet-smelling offering to God. We may
not see our prayers as always pleasing God but, in Proverbs 15:8,
Solomon writes,

> The sacrifice of the wicked is an abomination to the LORD: *but the
> prayer of the upright is his delight...*

Since He sees us as righteous by our position in Messiah Yeshua,[6] our
prayers are His delight!

Leviticus 16:14

> And he shall take of the blood of the bullock, and sprinkle it with his
> finger upon the mercy seat eastward; and before the mercy seat shall he
> sprinkle of the blood with his finger seven times.

In the Holy of Holies, the high priest sprinkled the blood once on the
mercy seat and seven times on the ground. "This act constituted the
rite of expiation [atonement] ... "[7] The blood-sprinkled mercy seat is
a foreshadow of Messiah Yeshua's atonement. In fact, in the Greek
New Testament, the same word used for "mercy seat" in Hebrews 9:5
is also used for "propitiation" in Romans 3:25. Commenting on this,
C.I. Scofield states that the "mercy seat was sprinkled with the
atoning blood on the Day of Atonement (Lev. 16:14),[8] representing
that the righteous sentence of the Law had been executed, changing
the judgment seat into a mercy seat (Heb. 9:11–15; cf. "throne of
grace," Heb. 4:14–16; place of communion, Exod. 25:21–22)."[9] On
the basis of Yeshua's finished work, we can boldly enter the Holy of
Holies to meet with our God.

Leviticus 16:15

> Then shall he kill the goat of the sin offering, that is for the people, and
> bring his blood within the vail, and do with that blood as he did with
> the blood of the bullock, and sprinkle it upon the mercy seat, and
> before the mercy seat...

That verse foreshadows the point at which Yeshua as the High Priest begins His ministry for us. All the sacrifices to that point in Leviticus 16 were for the sins of the high priest. Yeshua, being sinless, had no need to offer these sacrifices for Himself (see Heb. 7:26–27, under Lev. 16:6 above). An incredible thing about God's Messiah is that He is our High Priest and our sacrifice.

> For even the Son of man came not to be ministered unto, but to minister [serve], and to give his life a ransom [redemption price, atonement] for many ... (Mark 10:45)

> Behold the Lamb of God, which taketh away [carries upon oneself] the sin of the world ... (John 1:29b)

By crying out, "It is finished" (John 19:30b), Yeshua indicated that the payment for our salvation was accomplished by His voluntary death, His blood freely offered for us.

Another important point that Leviticus 16:15 brings to mind is the biblical concept of a mediator. How cleverly the Enemy has deceived multitudes into thinking they can be on good terms with God without needing a mediator. Israel needed one.

> And [Aaron] stood between the dead and the living; and the plague was stayed [stopped].
> (Num. 16:48; see 41–48 for the context of that incident)

Even righteous Job (Job 1:1, 8) recognized his need for a mediator:

> For he is not a man, as I am, that I should answer him, and we should come together in judgment. Neither is there any daysman [mediator] betwixt us, that might lay his hand upon us both. (Job 9:32–33)

You cannot find any verse in the Scriptures saying that God did away with the necessity of a mediator to stand between us and Him.

God had given the priesthood to Israel. He desired them to become a nation of mediators between Him and the rest of the world, but they had to keep His covenant and obey His voice:

> Now therefore, if ye will obey my voice indeed, and keep my covenant, then ye shall be a peculiar [specially chosen] treasure unto me above all people: for all the earth is mine: And ye shall be unto me a *kingdom of priests*, and an holy [separated] nation ... (Exod. 19:5–6a)

But only Messiah Yeshua, as the representative of the children of Israel,[10] was able to live in perfect obedience to God's Word. He was the long-awaited mediator.

> For there is one God, and one mediator [intercessor; reconciler] between God and men, the man Messiah Yeshua... (1 Tim. 2:5)

> And if any man sin, we have an advocate [intercessor; helper] with the Father, Messiah Yeshua the righteous... (1 John 2:1b)

Leviticus 16:16

> And he shall make an atonement for the holy place, because of the uncleanness [impurity] of the children of Israel, and because of their transgressions [rebellions] in all their sins: and so shall he do for the tabernacle of the congregation, that remaineth among them in the midst of their uncleanness.

This verse explains what God desired when He gave the plans for the Tabernacle and what He desires from us as His Temple.[11] He wants to dwell among us (Exod. 25:8), but our sin prevents it. Both the Tabernacle in the wilderness and then the Temple in Jerusalem provided a way for sins to be covered, or "atoned for," by the blood of a sacrifice. And ever since the cross, the blood of God's own Son covers our sins, allowing God to dwell in our midst, even inside of us – by His Spirit.

> Yeshua answered and said unto him, If a man love me, he will keep my words: and my Father will love him, and we will come unto him, and make our abode [home] with him. (John 14:23)

Leviticus 16:17

> And there shall be no man in the tabernacle of the congregation when he goeth in to make an atonement in the holy place, until he come out, and have made an atonement for himself, and for his household, and for all the congregation of Israel.

No one could help the high priest; he had to face God alone. So too, Yeshua was the only one who could accomplish His Father's will and become a ransom for us.

> Neither is there salvation in any other: for there is none other name under heaven given among men, whereby we must be saved.
> (Acts 4:12)

Yeshua knew He must do it alone to fulfill Zechariah 13:7:

> Awake, O sword, against my shepherd, and against the man [valiant warrior] that is my fellow [associate; comrade], saith the LORD of

hosts: smite [even "slay"] the shepherd, and the sheep shall be scattered: and I will turn mine hand upon the little ones.[12]

Leviticus 16:18–19

And he shall go out unto the altar that is before the LORD, and make an atonement for it; and shall take of the blood of the bullock, and of the blood of the goat, and put it upon the horns of the altar round about. And he shall sprinkle of the blood upon it with his finger seven times, and cleanse it, and hallow it [sanctify; set apart] from the uncleanness [spiritual impurity] of the children of Israel.

The blood was ordained by God to make atonement; to cleanse and sanctify men and things.

Leviticus 16:20–21

And when he hath made an end of [accomplished; finished] reconciling [lit: making atonement for] the holy place, and the tabernacle of the congregation, and the altar, he shall bring the live goat: And Aaron shall lay both his hands upon the head of the live goat, and confess over him all the iniquities of the children of Israel, and all their transgressions in all their sins, putting them upon the head of the goat, and shall send him away by the hand of a fit man into the wilderness...

Here the high priest's concentration turned to the live goat, the other part of the composite sin offering. He laid hands on the head of the "scapegoat" and confessed, or literally "cast" or "threw," the sins of Israel onto it, transferring them onto the goat. This is more than symbolism. The Israelite received forgiveness (see v. 30) and sanctification by faith because the ritual was done in obedience to God's direct word as found in this chapter of Leviticus.

Therefore for sin, God's forgiveness came through faithful, obedient animal sacrifice. However, under this sacrificial system no indwelling Spirit routinely brought to the moral consciousness the purifying fire, the agony of conviction of sin. That had to wait for the better sacrifice of the blood of God's Son. Hebrews 9:13–14 puts these two truths together like this,

For if the blood of bulls and of goats, and the ashes of an heifer sprinkling the unclean, sanctifieth to the purifying of the flesh: How much more shall the blood of Messiah, who through the eternal Spirit offered himself without spot to God, purge [cleanse] your conscience from dead works to serve [obey and worship] the living God?

What does the Hebrew word for the scapegoat signify? " 'Azazel' [is] a rare Hebrew noun meaning, 'dismissal' or, 'entire removal' ... It is the ancient technical term for the entire removal of sin and guilt of the community..."[13] What sins did God forgive on *Yom Kippur*? Here are the Hebrew meanings for "iniquities," "transgressions" and "sins." See how truly forgiving God was through the Law:

- *iniquities* – crookedness; disobedience; denotes a willful departure from the Law of God
- *transgressions* – the Hebrew is strong, literally meaning rebellion
- *sins* – missing the mark; unintentional deviation from the right path.

Although in the *Tanach* God provided forgiveness for sins through a believing obedience, Yeshua dealt with the root of sins – our "old man." By taking our death penalty on Himself, He made it possible for us to consider our "old man" dead and buried (Rom. 6:4), making new creations of us who trustingly depend on Him. When we abide in Him, walking in His Spirit and repenting as needed, we appropriate His newness of life.[14]

Leviticus 16:22

And the goat shall bear upon him all their iniquities unto a land not inhabited: and he shall let go the goat in the wilderness.

The live goat was released in the wilderness to carry away all the sins of Israel. The ideas of "to bear or carry" and "to forgive" are often covered by the same Hebrew verb (in italic), as we read in Isaiah 53:

Surely he hath *borne* our griefs, and carried our sorrows ... he hath poured out his soul unto death: and he was numbered with the transgressors; and he *bare* the sin of many, and made intercession for the transgressors.   (Isa. 53:4a, 12b)

The same verb is emphasized in Psalm 32,

Blessed is he whose transgression is *forgiven*, whose sin is covered ... I said, I will confess my transgressions unto the LORD; and thou *forgavest* the iniquity of my sin. Selah.   (Psalm 32:1, 5b)

The scapegoat part of the offering carried away each sin, never to be seen again. Micah, in a declaration full of prophetic hope, states the conclusion of the matter when he says,

> He will turn again, he will have compassion upon us; he will subdue [conquer] our iniquities; and thou wilt cast all their sins into the depths of the sea. (Mic. 7:19)

Why did God use two animals to represent one sin offering? All that Yeshua accomplished in purchasing our salvation could not be demonstrated by either one alone. The Lord's goat represents Yeshua's death on the cross, and the scapegoat, His resurrection. His death atoned for our sins (Rom. 3:25) and His resurrection declared us justified (Rom. 4:25). His resurrection was God's formal announcement that our sins had been carried away to be remembered no more. Two goats; one offering. The first one dead; the other alive. Our Redeemer is portrayed in these two, dead and then alive. We too, if living sacrifices to our God, are to be dead to self but alive to Him (Rom. 6:2–8, 11–12).

Leviticus 16:23–24

> And Aaron shall come into the tabernacle of the congregation, and shall put off the linen garments, which he put on when he went into the holy place, and shall leave them there: And he shall wash his flesh with water in the holy place, and put on his garments, and come forth, and offer his burnt offering, and the burnt offering of the people, and make an atonement for himself, and for the people.

By our count, that is the twenty-seventh of thirty-two statements in Leviticus saying that a priest makes atonement for the people. We may be assured that sinners need a mediator to atone for their sins (see v. 15). We are not able to do it by ourselves.

The type we see is this. The high priest made atonement by presenting the sacrificial blood on the mercy seat in the Most Holy place. That he remained alive and came back out to the people indicated that God accepted the sacrifice. Those who by faith believed what God said about this ritual, were then forgiven their sins.

The anti-type is this: Yeshua's death on the cross made atonement for us. Three days later He rose from the dead, demonstrating His Father's approval of His sacrifice as acceptable payment for sin. Those who believe this Good News are forgiven.

Leviticus 16:27

> And the bullock for the sin offering, and the goat for the sin offering, whose blood was brought in to make atonement in the holy place, shall one carry forth without the camp; and they shall burn in the fire their skins, and their flesh, and their dung.

The remains of the sin offering, whose blood was brought within the veil, were burned outside the camp. The writer to the Hebrews sees that verse as a foreshadow of Messiah Yeshua's sacrifice and encourages us to join Him outside the camp of this world's religions and values. Our eyes should be fixed on the city whose builder and maintainer is God (Heb. 11:10). Here is what he says in Hebrews 13:11–14,

> For the bodies of those beasts, whose blood is brought into the sanctuary by the high priest for sin, are burned without [outside] the camp. Wherefore Yeshua also, that he might sanctify the people with his own blood, suffered without the gate. Let us go forth therefore unto him without the camp, bearing his reproach. For here have we no continuing [permanent] city, but we seek one to come.

Leviticus 16:29

> And this shall be a statute for ever unto you: that in the seventh month, on the tenth day of the month, ye shall afflict [humble] your souls, and do no work at all, whether it be one of your own country, or a stranger that sojourneth among you...

Afflicting or humbling ourselves before God has been interpreted by Jewish and Christian commentators as fasting. This interpretation can be derived from several verses in the Bible:

> Then I proclaimed a *fast* there, at the river of Ahava, that we might afflict [humble] ourselves before our God.　　　　　　(Ezra 8:21a)

> *I humbled my soul with fasting*...　　　　　　　　　　　(Ps. 35:13b)

> When I wept, and *chastened my soul with fasting*, that was to my reproach...　　　　　　　　　　　　　　　　　　　(Ps. 69:10)

> Therefore also now, saith the LORD, turn ye even to me with all your heart, and with *fasting*, and with weeping, and with mourning...
> 　　　　　　　　　　　　　　　　　　　　　　　　　(Joel 2:12)

This day has been a complete fast throughout the history of the Jewish people.

Notice to whom the Lord directs this command. The Lord states that this day's observance be "a statute for ever..." for the children of Israel and for the "stranger that sojourneth among you..." The "strangers," referring to non-Jews who had chosen to live with the children of Israel and follow the God of Israel, are a foreshadow of the non-Jewish part of the Body of Messiah.[15]

Leviticus 16:30

> For on that day shall the priest make an atonement for you, to cleanse [purify] you, that ye may be clean from all your sins before the LORD.

Here is the reason why this day is called the holiest day of the year in Judaism. Not only did the atonement accomplished on *Yom Kippur* enable the sinner to be forgiven all his/her sins, but, since the words "the priest" are not in the Hebrew, some rabbis say that the day itself provides atonement to the person who humbles himself and confesses his sins before God. As believers, we know that Messiah and not fasting, repentance, or a special day provides atonement, but we still see the importance of the day as a divinely appointed time to commune with God and to pray for Israel and the Church.

Verse 30 also offers further proof that forgiveness of sins was available to those who lived in obedience to the Law of God concerning atonement (see 16:21–22 above). Of course, Yeshua's atoning death has made continuing these blood sacrifices unnecessary and ineffectual for the cleansing of sins:

> For Messiah is not entered into the holy places made with hands, which are the figures of the true; but into heaven itself, now to appear in the presence of God for us: Nor yet that he should offer himself often, as the high priest entereth into the holy place every year with blood of others; For then must he often have suffered since the foundation of the world: *but now once in the end of the world* [completion of the ages] *hath he appeared to put away* [abolish; annul] *sin by the sacrifice of himself.* (Heb. 9:24–26)

Leviticus 16:31

> It shall be a sabbath of rest unto you, and ye shall afflict [humble] your souls, by a statute for ever.

This was to be a day of complete rest which is called in Hebrew *shabbat shabbaton*. The high priest did all the work required to remove the sins; the sinner rested in that work and was required only to recognize his need of forgiveness. The Day of Atonement perfectly illustrates God's grace at work.

Leviticus 16:32

> And the priest, whom he shall anoint, and whom he shall consecrate to minister in the priest's office in his father's stead, shall make the atonement, and shall put on the linen clothes, even the holy garments...

The priest who made the atonement for Israel was anointed (the same Hebrew root from which we get the word "Mashiach," Messiah, Anointed One – translated "Christ" in English from the Greek)[16] and consecrated to minister in his father's stead. This foreshadows Yeshua, who is consecrated to the High Priest's office as a representative of His Father and of us, His brethren:

> For there is one God, and one mediator between God and men, the man Messiah Yeshua... (1 Tim. 2:5)

> Wherefore, holy brethren, partakers [sharers] of the heavenly calling, consider the Apostle and High Priest of our profession [declaration or confession], Messiah Yeshua... (Heb. 3:1)

Summary

As we have seen from the *Tanach*, God declares that without His grace we are all hopelessly lost in our sins. But Leviticus 16 has shown us the Day of Atonement when the high priest entered into the Holy of Holies, going behind the veil, making atonement for sins with the blood of the God-ordained sin offering. We heard him confess the people's sins as he laid them on the head of the scapegoat. We watched that goat driven into the wilderness never to be seen again. Israel's iniquities, transgressions and sins were forgiven and removed. God provided for His people this way of purification so that He could dwell among them. This divine illustration of forgiveness in the *Tanach* points unmistakably to the death and resurrection of Messiah Yeshua.

> Having therefore, brethren, boldness [confidence] to enter into
> the holiest by the blood of Yeshua, By a new and living way,
> which he hath consecrated [renewed or inaugurated] for us,

through the veil, that is to say, his flesh;
And having an high priest over the house of God;
Let us draw near with a true heart in full assurance of faith,
having our hearts sprinkled [purified] from an evil [bad] conscience,
and our bodies washed with pure water.
(Heb. 10:19–22)

Notes

1. Zech. 7:5; Acts 27:9.
2. What other nation shuts down for a full day just because God's Word says so? Despite this nation's large measure of unbelief at this time, she is still a witness to the eternal truth of God's Word.
3. Matthew Henry, *Matthew Henry's Commentary*, Vol. 1, p. 504.
4. See also Heb. 2:17; 4:14–15; 5:10; 6:20; 7:26–28; 9:11; 10:21. Scripturally it was used in describing pitch's ability to protect from water. It also described the protection afforded by a village.
5. Idiomatically it was used to denote protection money – used for both good (a ransom) or bad (a bribe).
6. See 1 Cor. 1:30 and 2 Cor. 5:21 and compare with these *Tanach* verses: Ps. 119:40; Isa. 45:24–25; 46:12–13; 54:17; Jer. 23:5–6.
7. Dr J.H. Hertz (ed.), *The Pentateuch and Haftorahs* (Soncino Press, 1980), p. 482.
8. Concerning sprinkling, see comments on Isaiah 52:15a, in Chapter 10, section "Isaiah 52:13–53:12."
9. *The New Scofield Reference Bible* (Oxford University Press), p. 1214; note #4, Rom. 3:25.
10. In Isaiah 49:3, the servant of the Lord is called "Israel" and in the context of that chapter specifically means the Messiah.
11. See 1 Cor. 3:16–17; 6:19–20; 2 Cor. 6:16; Eph. 2:19–22; 1 Pet. 2:5.
12. See Matt. 26:31, 56; John 16:32.
13. Hertz (ed.), op. cit., p. 481.
14. For example, see Romans chapters 5–6 and 2 Cor. 5:17.
15. In Part Three we see how this statement proves accurate.
16. In Matthew 24:23–25 and Mark 13:21–23, Yeshua warns about "false christs" arising in the last days. Literally, this term translates into false "anointed-ones."

CHAPTER 7

The New Birth

Since some believers endorse the mistaken idea that God required only outward works of ritual and sacrifice in the *Tanach*, they may also think that after the inauguration of the New Covenant, He is concerned only with "inward works," the spiritual condition of our hearts. However, neither of these views agrees with the Word of God. In both the *Tanach* and the New Testament, God's emphasis is the faith of the heart manifested through works of obedience.

A New Heart

The concept of being born again, or born from above, is so central to our belief, that Yeshua said if a person is not born again he cannot enter the kingdom of God (John 3:3). Yeshua stated, "Marvel not that I said unto thee, Ye must be born again" (John 3:7). He was talking to Nicodemus, a ruler of the Jews, who many scholars believe was the leading teacher in Israel at that time. Nicodemus was surprised at His statement, but Yeshua indicated that it should not have taken him by surprise, asking, "Art thou a master of Israel, and knowest [understand] not these things?" (John 3:10b). He was implying that this crucial belief is found in the *Tanach*, Nicodemus' Bible.

"Born again" – what does it mean? "Regeneration, or new birth, is an inner re-creating of fallen human nature [spirit] by the gracious sovereign act of the Holy Spirit..."[1]

In the *Tanach* and the New Testament "heart" refers to the soul, and at times the spirit, that must be renewed or regenerated. Look at what "heart" means in the original Hebrew and Greek.

Hebrew – *lev*.: "the heart, the center, or the middle of something ... it is common to interpret the term [in the *Tanach*] as the totality of man's inner or immaterial nature ... In the Bible, the whole spectrum of human emotions is attributed to the heart ... Wisdom and understanding reside in the heart (1 Kgs. 3:12; Prov. 16:23). It is almost a synonym for "mind" (2 Chr. 9:23) or perceptive nature (1 Kgs. 3:12). However, it can be deceived (Isa. 44:20). The heart is the seat of the will [self] (Num. 16:28 [in Hebrew, the "mind" of the KJV, and the "will" in the NKJV is *lev.*, heart.]; Judg. 9:3; 2 Chr. 12:14). To refuse to make the right choice is to harden the heart (Exod. 10:1; Josh. 11:20). The heart is the seat of moral evil (Jer. 17:9)."[2]

Greek – *kardia*: "The Scriptures attributed to the heart thoughts, reasonings, understanding, will, judgment, designs, affections, love, hatred, fear, joy, sorrow, and anger ... Therefore, the heart is used for the mind in general (Matt. 12:34; John 13:2; Rom. 2:15; 10:9–10); the understanding (Luke 3:15; Acts 28:26–27; Rom. 1:21; 2 Cor. 4:6); the will (Acts 11:23; 13:22); the memory (Luke 1:66; 2:51); the intention, affection or desire (Matt. 6:21; 18:35; Mark 7:6; Luke 1:17; Acts 8:21); the conscience (1 John 3:20–21)."[3]

According to the above definitions and biblical usage the term "heart" refers to the inner man, the mind, emotions and will together, or any of those parts separately or in combination.

The Heart of the Issue in the New Testament

God wants our hearts to be humble and upright before Him. One of the chief benefits of the "born again" experience is that God begins to purify our hearts by faith.

> And God, which knoweth the *hearts*, bare them [the gentiles] witness, giving them the Holy Ghost, even as he did unto us; And put no difference between us and them, purifying [cleansing] their *hearts* by faith. (Acts 15:8–9)

> To the end he may stablish your *hearts* unblameable in holiness before God, even our Father, at the coming of our Lord Yeshua the Messiah with all his saints. (1 Thess. 3:13)

Here are some other New Testament scriptures that label as "heart" the sphere God changes through regeneration, the theological term for being "born again" (born from above, given a new spirit, saved, redeemed, etc.). Speaking to His disciples, Yeshua declares,

> Blessed are the pure in *heart*: for they shall see God. (Matt. 5:8)

But speaking to some of the religious leaders of His day, He says,

> Ye hypocrites, well did [Isaiah] prophesy of you, saying, This people

> draweth nigh [near] unto me with their mouth, and honoureth me with
> their lips; but their heart is far from me.   (Matt. 15:7–8)

The writer of Hebrews gives us this warning,

> Take heed, brethren, lest there be in any of you an evil *heart* of
> unbelief, in departing from the living God.   (Heb. 3:12)

In Paul's Spirit-led prayer for believers, he uses a parallelism to
identify our inner man with our heart, asking that the Spirit of
Messiah would abide there – in His spiritual temple:

> That he would grant you, according to the riches of his glory, to be
> strengthened with might by his Spirit in the *inner man*; That Messiah
> may dwell in your *hearts by faith* . . .   (Eph. 3:16–17a)

In Romans 10, Paul shows the difference between the righteousness
of works versus the righteousness of faith. He demonstrates that both
are mentioned in the Law but that, even there, God points to faith as
essential to approach and be reconciled to Him.[4]

> But what saith it?[5] The word is nigh thee, even in thy mouth, and in thy
> *heart*: that is, the word of *faith*, which we preach; That if thou shalt
> confess [declare; acknowledge] with thy mouth the Lord Yeshua, and
> shalt believe in thine *heart* that God hath raised him from the dead,
> thou shalt be saved. For with the heart man believeth [trusts] unto
> righteousness; and with the mouth confession is made unto salvation.
>   (Rom. 10:8–10, see Acts 8:37)

From just these few New Testament examples, we see God dealing
with the heart in and after the new birth. But the term "heart" as used
throughout the Bible has other associations as well.

Tanach Roots of Regeneration

Using the biblical definition of "heart," we now discover the roots of
being "born again" in the *Tanach*. The most graphic metaphor used
is "heart circumcision." "In [*Tanach*] prophecies, regeneration is
depicted as the work of God renovating, circumcising, and softening
Israelite hearts, writing His laws upon them, and thereby causing their
owners to know, love, and obey Him as never before (Deut. 30:6; Jer.
31:31–34; 32:39–40; Ezek. 11:19–20; 36:25–27). It is a sovereign
work of purification from sin's defilement (Ezek. 36:25; cf. Ps.
51:10)."[6]

Many *Tanach* passages concerning the heart are referenced in the above quote taken from a theological dictionary. We will look at several of these. Here are two which promise Israel's final salvation after she is restored to God's land. We see these promises coming to pass today.

> And I will give them *one heart*, and one way, that they may fear[7] me for ever, for the good of them, and of their children after them: And I will make [lit: cut] an everlasting covenant with them, that I will not turn away from them, to do them good; but I will put my fear *in their hearts*, that they shall not depart [turn away] from me.
>
> (Jer. 32:39–40)

The second passage, from Ezekiel, is arguably the best description of what it means to be "born again" in all of Scripture:

> Then will I sprinkle clean water upon you, and ye shall be clean [pure; undefiled]: from all your filthiness, and from all your idols, will I cleanse [purify] you. *A new heart* also will I give you, and *a new spirit* will I put within you: and I will take away the *stony heart* out of your flesh, and I will give you *an heart of flesh*. And I will put my spirit within you, *and cause you to walk in my statutes*, and ye shall keep my judgments, and do them. (Ezek. 36:25–27)

In other "heart" verses, the *Tanach* states the precise demands that God makes on those who desire to approach Him. One example would be Psalm 24:3–4,

> Who shall ascend into the hill of the LORD? or who shall stand in his holy place? He that hath clean [innocent] hands, and *a pure* [purified] *heart*; who hath not lifted up his soul unto vanity [falsehood], nor sworn deceitfully.

The same criterion is found in Matthew 5:8,

> Blessed are the pure in heart: for they shall see God.

David in Psalm 51:10 implores his King to "Create in me a clean [purified, cleansed] *heart*, O God; and renew *a right spirit* within me." The Hebrew word "create" in that verse is the same word used in Genesis 1:1 for God's creation of the universe out of nothing. David, like Paul, understood that in his flesh dwelt no good thing (Rom. 7:18). For David to be able to conquer his sin, it was necessary for God to make of him a new creature (2 Cor. 5:17).

As we saw in the last chapter, the *Tanach* declares that all have sinned; all people have chronic and terminal "heart disease." God pinpoints this problem through the prophet Jeremiah:

> The sin of Judah is written with a pen of iron, and with the point of a diamond: it is graven upon the table of their *heart* ... *The heart* is deceitful above all things, and desperately wicked [incurably sick]: who can know it? (Jer. 17:1a, 9)

To make us aware that we need heart "surgery" ("heart circumcision" in the *Tanach*), God challenges us to do it ourselves. Through Moses, the Lord says,

> *Circumcise* therefore the foreskin of *your heart*, and be no more stiffnecked [stubborn, rebellious]. (Deut. 10:16)

The results of any attempts to follow this most important command show us we cannot do it without Him.

Moses continues to list all that God requires from us if we choose to live by our own righteousness. Yet as Moses frequently reminds us in Deuteronomy, which is a divine summary of God's Law, the heart is the core issue.[8] Finally in chapter 30 verse 6, Moses prophesies about the new birth,

> And the LORD thy God will *circumcise thine heart*, and the heart of thy seed, to love the LORD thy God with all thine heart, and with all thy soul, [so] that thou mayest live.

God performs the heart surgery. As Paul states, we are saved by grace (Eph. 2:8).

Results of the New Birth

In these times, with a what-can-God-do-for-me attitude permeating the Church, it is important we understand why God saves us. He saves us so we can love and obey Him with our whole lives. Yeshua says that loving Him (not Him loving us) entails obeying His commands, His words, in other words, the Word of God:

> If ye love me, keep my commandments ... He that hath my commandments, and keepeth them, he it is that loveth me ... If a man love me, he will keep my words ... He that loveth me not keepeth not my sayings ... (John 14:15, 21a, 23b, 24a)

(John restates this in 1 John 2:3–6.)

In the *Tanach* God promised to the houses of Israel and Judah that the new birth into the new covenant would make possible that obedience! Through Jeremiah God prophesies about the New Covenant,

> Behold, the days come, saith the LORD, that I will make [lit: cut] *a new covenant* with the house of *Israel*, and with the house of *Judah*: Not according to the covenant that I made with their fathers in the day that I took them by the hand to bring them out of the land of Egypt; which my covenant they brake [violated], although I was an husband unto them, saith the LORD: But this shall be the covenant that I will make with the house of Israel; After those days, saith the LORD, *I will put my law in their inward parts, and write it in their hearts*; and will be their God, and they shall be my people. And they shall teach no more every man his neighbour, and every man his brother, saying, Know the LORD: for they shall all know me, from the least of them unto the greatest of them, saith the LORD: for [because] I will forgive their iniquity, and I will remember their sin no more.   (Jer. 31:31–34)

That entire passage becomes the longest *Tanach* quote in the New Testament. It is quoted or referred to twice in the book of Hebrews (8:8–12; 10:16–17). The writer uses these verses to prove that Yeshua's High Priestly ministry and sacrifice instituted that "new covenant" of which Jeremiah spoke.

The writer of Hebrews goes on to say in 8:13 that the "old" was now obsolete. The question is, "old what?" That "old" referred to the system of the Levitical priesthood and animal sacrifices for sin. It did not, indeed, could not, refer to "the Law" because God's Law or, literally, Teaching, is holy, just and good (Rom.). The word "Law" (in the Hebrew *Torah*) means God's instruction, His teachings, His way, His guidance, and not just a list of commands and restrictions.

The Lord never said either in Jeremiah or Hebrews that the New Covenant would replace His Law, but that by the New Covenant He would sovereignly place His Law in our minds and write it on our hearts. Paul says,

> That the righteousness of the law might be fulfilled in us, who walk not after the flesh, but after the Spirit.   (Rom. 8:4)

Paul implies that only those who are born from above and led by the Spirit can fulfill God's Law, His *Torah*. The new birth provides new wineskins for the new wine, the indwelling Holy Spirit.

Ezekiel also talks about the new birth. In 11:19, the prophet proclaims that God will give Israel one heart and put a new spirit in them. Why?

> That they *may walk in my statutes, and keep mine ordinances*, and do them: and they shall be my people, and I will be their God.
>
> (Ezek. 11:20)

Do we remember that our Lord Yeshua and the writers of the New Testament said that as well? Yes, we are saved by grace through faith. It is a gift of God that does not depend on anything we do so that we have no reason to boast (Eph. 2:8–9). But how do we live after salvation? Can we claim to be believers and do what we want, or are we commanded in the New Testament to do the good works God has ordained for us?

In the beginning of the Sermon on the Mount, Yeshua says to His disciples,

> Let your light so shine before men, that they may see *your good works*, and glorify your Father which is in heaven.   (Matt. 5:16)

And He sums up that teaching by stating,

> Therefore whosoever heareth these sayings of mine, *and doeth them*, I will liken him unto a wise man, which built his house upon a rock ...
>
> (Matt. 7:24)

A few people may protest that these sayings of Yeshua were spoken before He died and do not apply to believers after the cross. Or they may say that all these statements were made to Jewish believers and do not apply to gentiles in Messiah. However, consider the following verses written to the universal community of believers after Yeshua's resurrection:

> Looking for that blessed hope, and [even] the glorious appearing of the great God and our Saviour Yeshua the Messiah; Who gave himself for us, that he might redeem us from all iniquity [lawlessness], and purify unto himself a peculiar people, *zealous of good works*.
>
> (Titus 2:13–14)

> This is a faithful saying, and these things I will that thou affirm constantly, that they which have believed [placed their confidence] in God might be careful to *maintain good works*. These things are good and profitable unto men ... And let ours also learn to *maintain good works* for necessary uses, that they be not unfruitful.
>
> (Titus 3:8, 14)

What doth it profit, my brethren, though a man say he hath faith, and have not works? can faith save him? ... Even so faith, if it hath not works, is dead, being alone. Yea, a man may say, Thou hast faith, and I have works: shew me [give proof of] thy faith without [apart from] thy works, and *I will shew thee my faith by my works*.

(Jas. 2:14, 17–18)

Here is the patience [steadfastness] of the saints: here are they *that keep the commandments of God, and the faith of Yeshua*.   (Rev. 14:12)

From Genesis through Revelation God's constant appeal is to the heart of man, which He alone can read (Jer. 17:9–10). When we see our need of Him, beginning with trusting His atonement for our sins, then our Father gives us new hearts and new spirits. In time we will do what God created us for – worship (serve) Him in faith through obedient works that bring Him glory.

Let your light so shine before men, that they may see your good works, and glorify your Father which is in heaven.   (Matt. 5:16)

Hear, O Israel: The Lord our God is one Lord:
And thou shalt love the Lord thy God with all thine heart,
and with all thy soul, and with all thy might.
And these words, which I command thee this day,
shall be in thine heart...
(Deut. 6:4–6)

Notes

1. Walter A. Elwell (ed.), *Evangelical Dictionary of Theology*, p. 924.
2. Spiros Zodhiates Th.D. (ed.), *Lexical Aids to the Old Testament, The Hebrew – Greek Key Study Bible*, p. 1603.
3. Ibid., p. 1701.
4. See Chapter 9, section "Saved by Faith," for a more detailed explanation of these verses from Romans 10.
5. This "it" refers back to "the righteousness which is of faith" in verse 6, which is taken from the *Tanach* in Deut. 30:14.
6. Elwell, op. cit., p. 925.
7. This Hebrew word occurring over 300 times in Scripture is here correctly translated "to fear" and includes to be afraid, fearful or to make afraid.
8. See Deut. 4:9, 29; 5:29; 8:2, 5; 9:4–5; 10:12; 17:17; 28:47; 30:14.

PART TWO

Teachers

Old Testament Scripture roots filled the hearts and minds of Yeshua and the New Testament writers. Only by nourishing those roots in them could the Spirit of God use these men to "fulfill" metaphorically, to explain and exemplify the true meaning of the Law of God.

CHAPTER 8

The Prophet Like Moses

Deuteronomy 18:15–19

Deuteronomy contains many prophecies of the coming Messiah. But the prophetic promise found in chapter 18:15–19 stands out like a beam of sunlight on a shaded landscape:

> The LORD thy God will raise up unto thee a Prophet from the midst of thee, *of thy brethren, like unto me*; unto him ye shall hearken [hear with the intent to obey]; According to all that thou desiredst of the LORD thy God in Horeb in the day of the assembly, saying, Let me not hear again the voice of the LORD my God, neither let me see this great fire any more, that I die not. And the LORD said unto me, They have well spoken that which they have spoken. *I will raise them up a Prophet from among their brethren, like unto thee, and will put my words in his mouth; and he shall speak unto them all that I shall command him. And it shall come to pass, that whosoever will not hearken unto my words which he shall speak in my name, I will require it of him.*

The Prophet in the New Testament

The New Testament actually refers to these verses on several occasions, but if we are not aware of the perspective of the speakers, we lose the full implication of what they are saying. For example, why do people in the following New Testament verses all refer to the "prophet"? Because the Jewish people of Yeshua's time were looking for the one promised in Deuteronomy 18.

> And they asked him [John the Baptist], What then? Art thou Elias [Elijah]? And he saith, I am not. *Art thou that prophet?* And he answered, No ... And they asked him, and said unto him, Why

> baptizest thou then, if thou be not that Messiah, nor Elias [Elijah],
> neither *that prophet?*   (John 1:21, 25)

> Then those men, when they had seen the miracle that Jesus did, said,
> This is of a truth *that prophet* that should come into the world.
>   (John 6:14)

> Many of the people therefore, when they heard this saying, said, Of a
> truth this is the Prophet. Others said, This is the Messiah...
>   (John 7:40–41a)

After Yeshua's resurrection, the disciples used the Deuteronomy
passage as an apologetic to declare that Yeshua is that Prophet, and
then stated that He is the Messiah, the Anointed One. Note how Peter
tied these together:

> But those things, which God before had shewed [promised] by the
> mouth of all his prophets, that Messiah should suffer, he hath so
> fulfilled ... For Moses truly said unto the fathers, A *prophet* shall the
> Lord your God raise up[1] unto you of your brethren, like unto me; him
> shall ye hear in all things whatsoever he shall say unto you. And it shall
> come to pass, that every soul, which will not hear that *prophet*, shall be
> destroyed from among the people. Yea, and all the prophets from
> Samuel and those that follow after, as many as have spoken, have
> likewise foretold of these days.   (Acts 3:18, 22–24)

Stephen's message to the Sanhedrin also uses this prophecy to
demonstrate that Israel had a history of not believing Moses:

> This is that Moses, which said unto the children of Israel, A *prophet*
> shall the Lord your God raise up[2] unto you of your brethren, like unto
> me; him shall ye hear.   (Acts 7:37)

In fact, Yeshua pointed out this issue as a stumbling block to Israel
believing in Him:

> For had ye believed Moses, ye would have believed me: for he wrote of
> me [He could be referring to Deuteronomy 18]. But if ye believe not his
> writings, how shall ye believe my words?   (John 5:46–47)

Isn't not believing Moses one of the major problems in the Church?
The word "believe" in this passage means to have faith, confidence, or
trust in. How many really believe that what Moses wrote is still
foundational for us today?

The Prophet To Be Like Moses

The Deuteronomy prophecy promises the coming of a prophet like Moses. Even the rabbis point out that the coming Messiah would be like Moses: "The Rabbinic literature often presents parallels between similar types of fact . . . *One of the most frequently used parallels is the likening of the Messiah to the 'first savior', Moses*" (emphasis in the original).[3] So we should expect that the lives of Moses and Yeshua should contain some parallels, and they do – extensive ones. Let's look at some of these.

Lineage

Moses and Yeshua are both children of Israel, what we would today call Jews, descendants of Abraham through Isaac and Jacob (Israel).

> The book of the generation of Yeshua the Messiah, the son of David, the *son of Abraham.*   (Matt. 1:1)

> Who are *Israelites*; to whom pertaineth the adoption, and the glory, and the covenants, and the giving of the law, and the service of God, and the promises; Whose are the fathers, and *of whom as concerning the flesh Messiah came*, who is over all, God blessed for ever. Amen.
>   (Rom. 9:4–5)

Childhood

The parallels here are so astounding that we can truly call them supernatural! Both Moses and Yeshua were born when the people of Israel were under gentile rule, Moses in Egypt (Exod. 1:8–10) and Yeshua in Roman-occupied Israel (Luke 2:1, 3–5).

Both were, out of necessity, placed by their mothers in unusual beds, Moses in a waterproof basket (Exod. 2:3), and Yeshua in a feeding trough (Luke 2:7). Each was saved from a death decree placed on many of the Hebrew boys by the ruling gentile king; Moses was saved from the decree of Pharaoh (Exod. 1:22), and Yeshua from the decree of Herod (Matt. 2:13b, 16).

They were not only rescued in their infancy, but also preserved miraculously in the same foreign country. Moses was rescued and raised by Pharaoh's daughter (Exod. 2:5–6), although God even arranged to have Moses' own mother nurse him (Exod. 2:9). Yeshua, like Moses, was preserved in Egypt because Joseph believed the Word of the Lord brought by an angel:

> When he arose, he took the young child and his mother by night, and departed into Egypt: And was there until the death of Herod: that it might be fulfilled which was spoken of the Lord by the prophet, saying, Out of Egypt have I called my son.   (Matt. 2:14–15)

The women who raised them were both daughters of a kingly line, Pharaoh's daughter (Exod. 2:5–10), and Miriam, who was a direct descendant of King David (Luke 1:26–33; 3:23–32).[4]

Finally, they were raised in the home of men who were not their real fathers. Moses was raised in Pharaoh's house, as the *Tanach* and New Testament point out (Exod. 2:9–10; Acts 7:21–22). In Yeshua's case, Matthew states that Joseph obeyed the Lord and took Miriam to be his wife when an angel told him about Yeshua's miraculous conception (Matt. 1:18–25).

Other Life Similarities

Here are some other interesting parallels that we find between the lives of Israel's Lawgiver and Israel's Messiah: they had to flee the land of their birth because of a king's wrath, Moses from Pharaoh (Exod. 2:15), and Yeshua from Herod (Matt. 2:13). Each returned to that land and was used by the God of Israel to perform many miracles there (Exod. 4:21; Matt. 2:19–21).

They shared the experience of being criticized and challenged by family members and fellow Israelis.

> And when Pharaoh drew nigh, the children of Israel lifted up their eyes ... and they were sore afraid: and the children of Israel cried out unto the LORD. And they said unto Moses, Because there were no graves in Egypt, hast thou taken us away to die in the wilderness? wherefore hast thou dealt thus with us, to carry us forth out of Egypt?
> (Exod. 14:10–11)

And again Moses is criticized:

> And Miriam and Aaron [Moses' sister and brother] spake against Moses because of the Ethiopian woman whom he had married: for he had married an Ethiopian woman.   (Num. 12:1)

In Yeshua's case,

> His brethren therefore said unto him, Depart hence, and go into Judaea, that thy disciples also may see the works that thou doest ... If

thou do these things, shew thyself to the world. For neither did his
brethren believe in him. (John 7:3–5)

And again,

But though he had done so many miracles before them, yet they
believed not on him: That the saying of [Isaiah] the prophet might be
fulfilled ... Lord, who hath believed our report? and to whom hath the
arm of the Lord been revealed? (John 12:37–38)

They endured murmuring from God's people.

And the people murmured against Moses, saying, What shall we
drink? (Exod. 15:24, see 16:2)

The Jews then murmured at him [Yeshua], because he said, I am the
bread which came down from heaven. (John 6:41)

Moses and Yeshua had seventy chosen helpers at some point in
their ministries.

And the LORD said unto Moses, Gather unto me seventy men of the
elders of Israel, whom thou knowest to be the elders of the people, and
officers over them; and bring them unto the tabernacle of the
congregation, that they may stand there with thee. (Num. 11:16)

After these things the Lord [Yeshua] appointed other seventy also, and
sent them two and two before his face into every city and place,
whither he himself would come. (Luke 10:1)

They each sent out twelve men on special missions.

And the LORD spake unto Moses, saying, Send thou men, that they
may search the land of Canaan, which I give unto the children of Israel:
of every tribe [12] of their fathers shall ye send a man, every one a ruler
among them. (Num. 13:1–2)

And when he [Yeshua] had called unto him his *twelve* disciples, he
gave them power against unclean spirits, to cast them out, and to heal
all manner of sickness and all manner of disease ... These twelve
Yeshua sent forth ... (Matt. 10:1, 5a)

They experienced forty-day fasts.

And he [Moses] was there with the LORD *forty* days and forty nights;
he did neither eat bread, nor drink water. And he wrote upon the tables
the words of the covenant, the ten commandments. (Exod. 34:28)

> Then was Yeshua led up of the Spirit into the wilderness to be tempted of the devil. And when he had fasted forty days and forty nights, he was afterward an hungred. (Matt. 4:1–2)

Moses and Yeshua are spoken of as men of deep humility despite their greatness and position.

> (Now the man Moses was *very meek*, above all the men which were upon the face of the earth). (Num. 12:3)

> Come unto me, all ye that labour and are heavy laden, and I will give you rest. Take my yoke upon you, and learn of me; for I [Yeshua] am *meek and lowly* in heart: and ye shall find rest unto your souls. For my yoke is easy, and my burden is light. (Matt. 11:28–30)

They fed multitudes through miraculous means.

> And when the children of Israel saw it, they said one to another, It is manna: for they wist not what it was. And Moses said unto them, This is the bread which the LORD hath given you to eat ... And the children of Israel *did eat manna* forty years ... (Exod. 16:15, 35a)

> And he [Yeshua] commanded the multitude to sit down on the grass, and took the five loaves, and the two fishes, and looking up to heaven, he blessed, and brake, and gave the loaves to his disciples, and the disciples to the multitude. *And they did all eat*, and were filled ... And they that had eaten were about five thousand men, beside women and children. (Matt. 14:19–21)

Both of these servants of God had a supernatural experience of having their faces shine with God's glory.

> ... when Moses came down from mount Sinai with the two tables of testimony in Moses' hand ... Moses wist not that the skin of *his face shone* while he talked with him. And when Aaron and all the children of Israel saw Moses, behold, the skin of his face shone; and they were afraid to come nigh him. (Exod. 34:29–30)

> And after six days Yeshua taketh Peter, James, and John his brother, and bringeth them up into an high mountain apart, And was transfigured before them: and *his face did shine* as the sun, and his raiment was white as the light. (Matt. 17:1–2)

We are not half finished but already we see a likeness of Yeshua to Moses that goes far beyond coincidence. As a friend of ours has said, it is a "God-incidence"!

Their Relationship with God

In Numbers 12 God describes His relationship with Moses as one that no lesser prophet would ever have, an extraordinary relationship which is best described as "face to face":

> ... Hear now my words: If there be a prophet among you, I the LORD will make myself known unto him in a vision, and will speak unto him in a dream. My servant Moses is not so, who is faithful in all mine house. With him will I speak *mouth to mouth*, even apparently, and not in dark speeches; and the similitude of the LORD shall he behold: wherefore then were ye not afraid to speak against my servant Moses?
> (Num. 12:68)

Deuteronomy confirms this special relationship,

> And there arose not a prophet since in Israel like unto Moses, whom the LORD knew *face to face*.   (Deut. 34:10)

Messiah Yeshua also had a singular relationship with His Father that could also be described as talking "face to face" (see examples below). This idiomatic term can be interpreted as having direct access to God and His revelation. In fact, we see examples of God speaking audibly to both of them:

> And the LORD said unto Moses, Lo, I come unto thee in a thick cloud, that the people may hear when I speak with thee, and believe thee for ever. And Moses told the words of the people unto the LORD ... And when the voice of the trumpet sounded long, and waxed louder and louder, Moses spake, and *God answered him by a voice*.
> (Exod. 19:9, 19; see also 34:5–6)

> And Yeshua answered them, saying, The hour is come, that the Son of man should be glorified ... Now is my soul troubled; and what shall I say? Father, save me from this hour: but for this cause came I unto this hour. Father, glorify thy name. Then came there *a voice* from heaven, saying, I have both glorified it, and will glorify it again.
> (John 12:23, 27–28)

Because of their direct access to the Father, both spoke as oracles of God.

> And Moses came and told the people all the words of the LORD, and all the judgments: and all the people answered with one voice, and said, All the words which the LORD hath said will we do.
> (Exod. 24:3, cf. 20:18–19)

I [Yeshua] have many things to say and to judge of you: but he that sent
me is true; and I speak to the world those things which I have heard
of him.　　　　　　　　　　　　　　　　　　　　　　　(John 8:26)

For I [Yeshua] have not spoken of myself; but the Father which sent
me, he gave me a commandment, what I should say, and what I should
speak. And I know that his commandment is life everlasting: whatsoever I speak therefore, even as the Father said unto me, so I speak.
　　　　　　　　　　　　　　　　　　　　　　　(John 12:49–50)

Their special relationship with God was based on God's sovereign
choice in sending them to the children of Israel and was maintained by
faithfulness to Him.

My servant Moses is not so, who is *faithful* in all mine house.
　　　　　　　　　　　　　　　　　　　　　　　　(Num. 12:7)

Wherefore ... consider the Apostle and High Priest of our profession,
Messiah Yeshua; Who was *faithful* to him that appointed him, as also
Moses was *faithful* in all his house.　　　　　　　　(Heb. 3:1–6)

Of course, their being sent by God is another divine parallel.

I will *send* thee unto Pharaoh, that thou mayest bring forth my people
the children of Israel out of Egypt ... And Moses said unto God,
Behold, when I come unto the children of Israel, and shall say unto
them, The God of your fathers hath *sent* me unto you; and they shall
say to me, What is his name? what shall I say unto them? And God said
unto Moses, I AM THAT I AM ... Thus shalt thou say unto the children
of Israel, I AM hath *sent* me unto you ... The LORD God of your fathers,
the God of Abraham, the God of Isaac, and the God of Jacob, hath *sent*
me unto you: this is my name for ever, and this is my memorial unto all
generations.　　　　　　　　　　　　(selections from Exod. 3:10–15)

John the Baptist testified of Yeshua,

For he whom God hath *sent* speaketh the words of God: for God giveth
not the Spirit by measure unto him.　　　　　　　　　(John 3:34)

And Yeshua described Himself as "sent":

Say ye of him, whom the Father hath sanctified, and *sent* into the
world, Thou blasphemest; because I said, I am the Son of God?
　　　　　　　　　　　　　　　　　　　　　　　(John 10:36)

Mediator

Moses was called on to be a mediator between God and Israel; he passed on God's words and commands to them.

> (I [Moses] stood between the LORD and you at that time, to shew you the word of the LORD: for ye were afraid by reason of the fire, and went not up into the mount;). (Deut. 5:5)

> But as for thee, stand thou here by me [God], and I will speak unto thee all the commandments, and the statutes, and the judgments, which thou shalt teach them, that they may do them in the land which I give them to possess it. (Deut. 5:31)

Messiah Yeshua also acted as such a mediator – as a vessel to bring God's words, thoughts, and actions to man, to express the Father's name or nature.

> Then answered Yeshua and said unto them, Verily, verily, I say unto you, The Son can do nothing of himself, but what he seeth the Father do: for what things soever he doeth, these also doeth the Son likewise. For the Father loveth the Son, and sheweth him all things that himself doeth: and he will shew him greater works than these, that ye may marvel. (John 5:19–20)

> I have many things to say and to judge of you: but he that sent me is true; and I speak to the world those things which I have heard of him. (John 8:26)

They were used by God as mediators of a covenant which was sealed with blood.

> And he [Moses] took the book of the covenant, and read in the audience of the people: and they said, All that the LORD hath said will we do, and be obedient. And Moses took the *blood*, and sprinkled it on the people, and said, Behold the *blood of the covenant*, which the LORD hath made with you concerning all these words. (Exod. 24:7–8)

> And as they were eating, Jesus took bread, and blessed [God], and brake it, and gave it to the disciples, and said, Take, eat; this is my body. And he took the cup, and gave thanks, and gave it to them, saying, Drink ye all of it; For this is my *blood of the new testament*, which is shed for many for the remission of sins. (Matt. 26:26–28)

Intercessor

Moses interceded by standing in the gap between God's righteous anger and sinful man, in this case Israel, to turn that anger aside.

> Therefore he said that he would destroy them, had not Moses his chosen stood before him in the breach, to turn away his wrath, lest he should destroy them.   (Ps. 106:23, see Exod. 32:11–14)

> And Moses returned unto the LORD, and said, Oh, this people have sinned a great sin, and have made them gods of gold. Yet now, if thou wilt forgive their sin–; and if not, blot me, I pray thee, out of thy book which thou hast written.
>   (Exod. 32:31–32, see also Deut. 9:13–20; 10:10)

Yeshua is the Anointed One (Messiah) whose sacrifice turns aside God's wrath from sinful, but repentant, man.

> For even the Son of man came not to be ministered unto, but to minister, and to give his life a ransom for many.   (Mark 10:45)

> For there is one God, and one mediator between God and men, the man Messiah Yeshua; Who gave himself a ransom for all, to be testified in due time.   (1 Tim. 2:5–6)

> Therefore will I divide him a portion with the great, and he shall divide the spoil with the strong; because he hath poured out his soul unto death: and he was numbered with the transgressors; and he bare the sin of many, and made intercession for the transgressors.   (Isa. 53:12)

Moses interceded in prayer for Israel. Here are some examples:

> And when the people complained, it displeased the LORD: and the LORD heard it; and his anger was kindled; and the fire of the LORD burnt among them, and consumed them that were in the uttermost parts of the camp. And the people cried unto Moses; and when Moses *prayed* unto the LORD, the fire was quenched.   (Num. 11:1–2)

> And the LORD spake unto Moses and unto Aaron, saying, Separate yourselves from among this congregation, that I may consume them in a moment. And *they fell upon their faces, and said*, O God, the God of the spirits of all flesh, shall one man sin, and wilt thou be wroth with all the congregation?   (Num. 16:20–22)

Yeshua also used prayer to intercede for God's people.

I pray for them: *I pray* not for the world, but for them which thou hast given me; for they are thine. (John 17:9)

And when they were come to the place, which is called Calvary, there they crucified him, and the malefactors, one on the right hand, and the other on the left. Then said *Yeshua, Father, forgive* them; for they know not what they do. (Luke 23:33–34a)

Of course, He is still interceding for us today.

Who is he that condemneth? It is Messiah that died, yea rather, that is risen again, who is even at the right hand of God, who also maketh intercession for us. (Rom. 8:34)

Wherefore he is able also to save them to the uttermost that come unto God by him, seeing he ever liveth to make intercession for them. (Heb. 7:25)

Deliverer

God chose Moses to deliver Israel from slavery in Egypt.

Now therefore, behold, the cry of the children of Israel is come unto me: and I have also seen the oppression wherewith the Egyptians oppress them. Come now therefore, and I will send thee unto Pharaoh, that thou mayest *bring forth my people* the children of Israel out of Egypt. (Exod. 3:9–10)

For he supposed his brethren would have understood how that God by his hand would *deliver* them: but they understood not.

(Acts 7:25)

So, too, God chose Yeshua to deliver us from slavery to sin and from other afflictions. At the start of His public ministry, Yeshua claimed that what God had prophesied in Isaiah was fulfilled in Himself,

The Spirit of the Lord is upon me, because he hath anointed me to preach the gospel to the poor; he hath sent me to heal [make whole] the brokenhearted, to preach *deliverance* [freedom, pardon] to the captives, and recovering of sight to the blind, to *set at liberty* [same as "deliver"] them that are bruised [lit: crushed, shattered], To preach the acceptable year of the Lord. (Luke 4:18–19)

Paul explains deliverance from slavery to sin in a comprehensive way in Romans 6. This verse seems to sum up his thoughts:

> But God be thanked, that ye were the *servants of sin*, but ye have obeyed from the heart that form of doctrine which was delivered you. Being then *made free from sin*, ye became the servants of righteousness.
>
> (Rom. 6:17–18; see in context 6:16–23)

To accomplish this salvation, both contended with evil. Moses resisted the magicians of Pharaoh (Exod. 7:11, 22), and when finally free from Egypt, he became the spiritual focal point of Israel's fight with Amalek (Exod. 17:8–13). Then in Exodus 32:26–28 he called those on the Lord's side to himself. The Levites responded and obeyed, killing three thousand idolaters in the camp of Israel.

Yeshua was confronted by Satan but resisted his temptations in the wilderness (Matt. 4:1–11). He also freed people from demons on many occasions (e.g. Matt. 8:28–32; 17:14–18).

Another important parallel is that deliverance by Moses from Egypt and by Yeshua from sin were accomplished through the shedding of blood – which in both instances provided protection against God's righteous judgment. The Passover Lamb is the type of Yeshua, the Lamb of God.[5]

The Lord told Moses,

> And they shall take of the *blood* [of the lamb], and strike it on the two side posts and on the upper door post of the houses, wherein they shall eat it ... [The lamb] is the LORD's passover. For I will pass through the land of Egypt this night, and will smite all the firstborn in the land of Egypt, both man and beast; and against all the gods of Egypt I will execute judgment: I am the LORD. And the *blood* shall be to you for a token upon the houses where ye are: and when I see the *blood*, I will pass over you, and the plague shall not be upon you to destroy you, when I smite the land of Egypt.   (Exod. 12:7, 11b-13)

The writer to the Hebrews teaches about Yeshua's blood atonement,

> But Messiah being come an high priest of good things to come ... by his own *blood* he entered in once into the holy place, having obtained eternal redemption for us. For if the blood of bulls and of goats, and the ashes of an heifer sprinkling the unclean, sanctifieth to the purifying of the flesh:[6] How much more shall the *blood* of Messiah, who through the eternal Spirit offered himself without spot to God, purge your conscience from dead works to serve the living God? And for this cause he is the mediator of the new testament [covenant], that by means of death, for the redemption of the transgressions that were

under the first testament, they which are called might receive the promise of eternal inheritance. (Heb. 9:11–15)

Moses and Yeshua each established covenant meals to help us remember and give thanks to God for His great deliverance/salvation. God commanded Israel to keep a meal on Passover as a memorial for them and their children (Exod. 12:3–11, 25–27, 42–49; Lev. 23:5). Of course, when Yeshua instituted Communion, it was during the Passover meal (Luke 22:14–20; 1 Cor. 11:26). And the New Testament goes on to identify Yeshua as the Passover Lamb, "For even Messiah our passover is sacrificed for us . . ." (1 Cor. 5:7b).[7]

Authority
Both Yeshua and Moses were empowered to declare God's word with authority. Deuteronomy 18:18 states that the promised prophet would speak in God's name with God's authority!

I will raise them up a Prophet from among their brethren, like unto thee, and will put my words in his mouth; and he shall speak unto them all that I shall command him.

Moses displayed this power in his ministry, it being promised him by God when He first called him to go to Egypt:

Now therefore go, and I will be with thy mouth, and teach thee what thou shalt say. (Exod. 4:12)

At Mt Sinai, the children of Israel recognized that Moses spoke the words of the Lord to them. They had pleaded to hear them from him rather than directly from God,

And they said unto Moses, Speak thou with us, and we will hear: but let not God speak with us, lest we die. (Exod. 20:19)

Yeshua also revealed the authority of God when He spoke and/or performed miracles.

And they went into Capernaum; and straightway on the sabbath day he entered into the synagogue, and taught. And they were astonished at his doctrine: for he taught them as one that had *authority*, and not as the scribes ... And they were all amazed, insomuch that they questioned among themselves, saying, What thing is this? what new doctrine is this? for with authority commandeth he even the unclean spirits, and they do obey him.

(Mark 1:21–22, 27; see also Matt. 7:28–29; Luke 4:20–21)

Verily, verily, I say unto you, He that heareth my word, and believeth on him that sent me, hath everlasting life, and shall not come into condemnation; but is passed from death unto life ... The hour is coming, and now is, when the dead shall hear the voice of the Son of God: and they that hear shall live. For as the Father hath life in himself; so hath he given to the Son to have life in himself; And hath given him *authority* to execute judgment also, because he is the Son of man.

(John 5:24–27)

Judge

Moses became the supreme judge in Israel. At His return, Yeshua will be the Judge of the whole world. Although Jethro gave Moses the idea to have faithful men help him, Moses was still the final authority when it came to difficult cases, as Jethro said,

Moreover thou shalt provide out of all the people able men, such as fear God, men of truth, hating covetousness; and place such over them, to be rulers of thousands, and rulers of hundreds, rulers of fifties, and rulers of tens: And let them judge the people at all seasons: and it shall be, that *every great matter they shall bring unto thee*, but every small matter they shall judge: so shall it be easier for thyself, and they shall bear the burden with thee.

(Exod. 18:21–22, see context: vv. 13–23)

Yeshua stated that He did not come the first time as a judge:

Ye judge after the flesh; *I judge no man*. And yet if I judge, my judgment is true: for I am not alone, but I and the Father that sent me.

(John 8:15–16)

And if any man hear my words, and believe not, *I judge him not*: for I came not to judge the world, but to save the world.   (John 12:47)

Of course He will be the judge when He returns, and not just of Israel, but of all the earth.

Let the field be joyful, and all that is therein: then shall all the trees of the wood rejoice; Before the LORD: for he cometh, for he cometh to *judge* the earth: he shall *judge* the world with righteousness, and the people with his truth.   (Ps. 96:12–13)

For we must all appear before the *judgment seat of Christ*; that every one may receive the things done in his body, according to that he hath done, whether it be good or bad.   (2 Cor. 5:10)

I charge thee therefore before God, and the Lord Jesus Christ, who shall *judge* the quick and the dead at his appearing and his kingdom...
(2 Tim. 4:1)

(See also Matt. 25:31–46; Acts 10:40–42; Rev. 19:11.)

Shepherd
Moses and Yeshua are called shepherds of God's people.

Thou leddest thy people like a flock by the hand of Moses and Aaron.
(Ps. 77:20)

Then he remembered the days of old, Moses, and his people, saying, Where is he that brought them up out of the sea with the *shepherd* of his flock?
(Isa. 63:11a)

I [Yeshua] am the good *shepherd*: the good *shepherd* giveth his life for the sheep ... I am the good *shepherd*, and know my sheep, and am known of mine. As the Father knoweth me, even so know I the Father: and I lay down my life for the sheep. And other sheep I have, which are not of this fold: them also I must bring, and they shall hear my voice; and there shall be one fold, and one shepherd.   (John 10:11, 14–16)

(See also Heb. 13:20; 1 Pet. 2:5; 5:4)

Miracles
Both men demonstrated the Kingdom of God in word and power as they performed many mighty public miracles. Yet each was constrained to do only what they were told by God the Father.

In Moses' life all ten plagues on Egypt were commanded by God:

And I will stretch out my hand, and smite Egypt with all my wonders which I will do in the midst thereof: and after that he will let you go.
(Exod. 3:20, see also 4:28)

Thus saith the LORD, In this thou shalt know that I am the LORD: behold, I will smite with the rod that is in mine hand upon the waters which are in the river, and they shall be turned to blood.
(Exod. 7:17, see also 8:2, 16, 21, etc.)

Also in the wilderness, God specifically showed Moses what miracles He would do through him:

And the people murmured against Moses, saying, What shall we drink? And he cried unto the LORD; and the LORD shewed him a tree, which when he had cast into the waters, the waters were made sweet: there he made for them a statute and an ordinance, and there he proved them. (Exod. 15:24–25)

And the LORD said unto Moses, Go on before the people, and take with thee of the elders of Israel; and thy rod, wherewith thou smotest the river, take in thine hand, and go. Behold, I will stand before thee there upon the rock in Horeb; and thou shalt smite the rock, and there shall come water out of it, that the people may drink. And Moses did so in the sight of the elders of Israel. (Exod. 17:5–6)

Yeshua said He did only what He saw His Father doing, so He also obeyed, performing only miracles God ordained Him to perform.

Then answered Jesus and said unto them, Verily, verily, I say unto you, The Son can do nothing of himself, but what he seeth the Father do: for what things soever he doeth, these also doeth the Son likewise. For the Father loveth the Son, and sheweth him all things that himself doeth: and he will shew him greater works than these, that ye may marvel. (John 5:19–20)

Their Deaths
The deaths of both were previously revealed in Scripture by God.

So Moses the servant of the LORD died there in the land of Moab, according to the word of the LORD. (Deut. 34:5, cf. 32:48–52)

For I delivered unto you first of all that which I also received, how that Messiah died for our sins according to the scriptures; And that he was buried, and that he rose again the third day according to the scriptures... (1 Cor. 15:3–4)

Amazingly, each reappeared after death. Moses actually did "enter" the Promised Land when he appeared with Elijah talking to Yeshua on the mountain of transfiguration:

And, behold, there appeared unto them Moses and Eliahu [Elijah] talking with him. (Matt. 17:3)

Of course, Yeshua's resurrection from the dead climaxes the gospel story (Luke 24:13ff.; Acts 1:3, etc.).

Relationship with Israel
Since God sent both Moses and Yeshua to Israel we would expect

them to have a special relationship with the Jewish people. Again the parallels are quite extraordinary.

Each was initially rejected by Israel.

> And it came to pass . . . when Moses was grown, that he went out unto his brethren, and looked on their burdens: and he spied an Egyptian smiting an Hebrew, one of his brethren. And he looked this way and that way, and when he saw that there was no man, he slew the Egyptian, and hid him in the sand.
>
> And when he went out the second day, behold, two men of the Hebrews strove together: and he said to him that did the wrong, Wherefore smitest thou thy fellow? And he said, *Who made thee a prince and a judge over us?* intendest thou to kill me, as thou killedst the Egyptian? And Moses feared, and said, Surely this thing is known.
> (Exod. 2:11–14)

In Acts 7:23–28, Stephen reviews this part of Moses' story adding in verse 35,

> This Moses whom they refused, saying, Who made thee a ruler and a judge? the same did God send to be a *ruler and a deliverer* by the hand of the angel which appeared to him in the bush.

The majority of Israel also rejected Yeshua at His first appearing although perhaps one-third believed Him to be the promised Messiah.

After Israel rejects them, they each obtain a gentile bride. Moses married Zipporah, daughter of Jethro, the priest of Midian (Exod. 2:16–21), and also an Ethiopian woman (Num. 12:1). And Paul writes to the gentiles in Corinth,

> For I am jealous over you with godly jealousy: for I have espoused you to one husband, that I may present you as a chaste virgin to the Messiah. (2 Cor. 11:2)

And in the letter to the Ephesians, which most biblical scholars view as a general letter to the Church, he says,

> For we are members of his body, of his flesh, and of his bones. For this cause shall a man leave his father and mother, and shall be joined unto his wife, and they two shall be one flesh. This is a great mystery: but I speak concerning Messiah and the church. (Eph. 5:30–32)

Although it is true that the initial Church was made up exclusively of Messianic Jews and that there has always been a Jewish remnant in the Church throughout history,[8] it is also true that the overwhelming majority of the Church in membership and culture for the past two millennia has been non-Jewish.

When Moses returned to Israel, he was accepted.

> And Moses and Aaron went and gathered together all the elders of the children of Israel: And Aaron spake all the words which the LORD had spoken unto Moses, and did the signs in the sight of the people. *And the people believed*: and when they heard that the LORD had visited the children of Israel, and that he had looked upon their affliction, then *they bowed their heads and worshipped.*   (Exod. 4:29–31)

Yeshua also will be accepted when He returns to Israel. Paul says so,

> For I would not, brethren, that ye should be ignorant of this mystery, lest ye should be wise in your own conceits; that blindness in part is happened to Israel, until the fulness of the Gentiles be come in. And so all Israel shall be saved: as it is written, There shall come out of Sion the Deliverer, and shall turn away ungodliness from Jacob . . .
> (Rom. 11:25–26)[9]

Conclusion

This extensive look at the parallels between the lives of Moses and Yeshua, the prophet promised to be like Moses, proves that when the Lord God states something in His Word, He means it.

> So shall my word be that goeth forth out of my mouth: it shall not return unto me void, but it shall accomplish that which I please, and it shall prosper in the thing whereto I sent it.   (Isa. 55:11)

God's faithfulness should be a source of great comfort and encouragement for us as we look at all the wonderful promises He has made to Israel, and to the Church. He will fulfill His Word. No wonder Messiah Yeshua said to Israel,

> Search the scriptures; for in them ye think ye have eternal life: and they are they which testify of me.   (John 5:39)

Finally, rabbis knew that the greatness of the Messiah would overshadow the greatness of Moses!

> In fact the Messiah is such a prophet as it is stated in the Midrash[10] on the verse, "Behold my servant shall prosper" . . . Moses by the miracles which he wrought drew but a single nation to the worship of god, but the Messiah will draw all nations to the worship of God.[11]

Philip found Nathanael and said to him,
We have found Him of whom Moses in the law,
and also the prophets, wrote – Yeshua of Nazareth,
the son of Joseph.
(John 1:45).

Notes

1. This Greek word is also used for being raised from the dead. For example: Mark 8:31; 9:9–10; 12:23–25; Luke 9:8, 19; 16:31; 24:46; John 6:54; 11:23–24; 20:9; Acts 2:24, 32; 13:33–34; Eph. 5:14; 1 Thess. 4:14, 16.
2. See note 1.
3. Risto Santala, *The Messiah in the Old Testament in the Light of Rabbinical Writings* (Jerusalem: Keren Ahvah Meshihit, 1992).
4. Most commentators say that the genealogical record in Luke traces Miriam's family line, while the one in Matthew traces Joseph's side of the family.
5. The New Testament uses the title "Lamb" to describe Yeshua more often than any other title except "Messiah" and the most frequent use is in the book of Revelation.
6. The New Testament says that the *Tanach* blood sacrifices sanctified the offerers from sins of the flesh. Those sacrifices could not deal with our inherited sin nature, but Messiah's sacrifice made each of us "a new creature" in the Messiah (2 Cor. 5:17).
7. See Chapter 3 on Passover.
8. Note in Rom. 11:17, "among them," and in 11:25 "blindness in part."
9. Standing before the Sanhedrin, Stephen emphasizes the Second Coming when he compares Yeshua's life with the patriarch Joseph's and says, "*And at the second time* Joseph was made known to his brethren . . . " (Acts 7:13a).
10. A *midrash* is a Jewish commentary on the Scriptures.
11. F. Kenton Beshore, *The Messiah of the Targums, Talmuds and Rabbinical Writers* (World Bible Society, Box 1, LA, CA 90053, 1971), Chart 17 quoting R. Levi ben Gershom.

CHAPTER 9

The Gospel
According to the *Tanach*

Where Are the Roots of the Gospel Found?

The gospel, literally "good news,"[1] was not totally unexpected when
the angel announced to the Jewish virgin Miriam that she would give
birth to the promised Messiah. Many in Israel were waiting for His
appearing, for example Simeon and Anna (see Luke 2:25–38). In fact
we see that the inspired writers of the New Testament are constantly
pointing back to the *Tanach* as their proof text for what they proclaim
about Messiah Yeshua, His life and ministry, His miracles, and most
importantly His death on the cross, His burial, and His resurrection.

We want to look at a number of New Testament texts that will
demonstrate that the gospel, the "good news" we have believed, was
based on the Word of God found in the *Tanach*.

The New Testament Looks Backward for Proof

From the opening line of the New Testament, our attention is focused
on what went before,

> The book of the generation of Yeshua the Messiah, the son of *David*,
> the son of *Abraham*.   (Matt. 1:1)

Why was it so important that Yeshua was the son, or descendant, of
both Abraham and David? Because God covenanted with them that
one of their offspring would be the promised Messiah.

To Abraham, God said,

> Get thee out of thy country, and from thy kindred, and from thy
> father's house, unto a land that I will shew thee: And I will make of
> thee a great nation, and I will bless thee, and make thy name
> [reputation, fame] great; and thou shalt be a blessing: And I will bless

them that bless thee, and curse him that curseth[2] thee: and *in thee shall all families of the earth be blessed.*   (Gen. 12:1b–3)

We have already seen in Chapter 1 that, according to Paul, that phrase prophesied the gospel to the gentiles,

And the scripture, foreseeing that God would justify [make righteous] the heathen [*ethnos*][3] through faith, preached before the gospel unto Abraham, saying, In thee shall all nations [*ethnos*] be blessed.

(Gal. 3:8)

Even from Matthew 1:1, the New Testament looks backward to God's promises to Abraham and forward to the message going out to the whole world.

God also promised that David's greater Son would be the Messiah who would reign on David's throne forever:

And when thy days be fulfilled, and thou shalt sleep with thy fathers, I will set up thy seed after thee, which shall proceed out of thy bowels, and I will establish his kingdom. He shall build an house for my name [honor, glory], *and I will stablish the throne of his kingdom for ever.* I will be his father, and he shall be my son ... And thine house and thy kingdom shall be established [confirmed] for ever before thee: thy throne shall be established for ever.   (2 Sam. 7:12–14a, 16)

Solomon, although a type, was not the final fulfillment of these promises because a natural son could not possibly fulfill them. Yeshua, called the "Son of David" in many New Testament verses, is the Promised One.[4]

Incidentally, both Abraham and David were also promised the inheritance of the Land of Israel, making Matthew 1:1 one of several New Testament texts which affirm that the coming of Israel's Messiah did not do away with God's promises to the Jewish people concerning that inheritance. See Genesis 12:1 above for the promise to Abraham. To David, God states in 2 Samuel 7:10a,

Moreover I will appoint a place for my people Israel, and will plant [establish] them, that they may dwell [abide, settle] in a place of their own, and move [move with fear, be agitated] no more ...

Matthew continually points back to the *Tanach* by using the following or similar phrases repeatedly,

Now all this was done [brought into being], *that it might be fulfilled which was spoken of the Lord by the prophet...*   (Matt. 1:22)[5]

John,[6] like Matthew, is also careful to link his Gospel account with the fulfillment of *Tanach* prophecies. He often uses that same phrase. For example:

> But though he had done so many miracles before them, yet they believed not on [did not put confidence in] him: *That the saying of [Isaiah] the prophet might be fulfilled*, which he spake, Lord, who hath believed our report? and to whom hath the arm of the Lord been revealed? Therefore they could not [were not able to, did not have the power to] believe, because that *[Isaiah] said again*, He hath blinded their eyes, and hardened their heart [understanding]; that they should not see with their eyes, nor understand [comprehend] with their heart, and be converted [turned around 180 degrees], and I should heal them.
> (John 12:37–40)[7]

This does not refer to all the Jewish people. If it did, the gospel would never have spread to the gentiles. It did not even refer to all the Levitical priests, many of whom believed![8] In the original context of the quote from Isaiah (Isa. 6), the previous chapter (Isa. 5) speaks about self-indulgent and corrupt nominal believers in Israel and Judah who were already under God's judgment.

Yeshua Points to the *Tanach*

Imagine for a moment you are walking on the road to Emmaus with the resurrected Messiah, but your eyes have been blinded to His identity. Writing the script for this fantasy, wouldn't you have Him say something like, "Hey – wake up! It's me. I am risen from the dead. Look at Me, touch Me – and believe!" But what did Yeshua really say to His disciples on that road?

> ...O fools, and slow of heart [mind, inner man] to *believe* [be persuaded, place confidence in] *all that the prophets have spoken*: Ought not Messiah to have suffered these things, and to enter into his glory?

What did He do next?

> *And beginning at Moses and all the prophets, he expounded unto them in all the scriptures* the things concerning himself.   (Luke 24:25b–27)

Yeshua's proof of his Messiahship is based on what the Word of God, the *Tanach*, states and not just physical evidence – no matter how miraculous.[9] God's people in Yeshua's day, just like many of His people today, were seeking signs and a miraculous deliverance. Yeshua strongly warned against signs becoming their main focus.[10] Instead, He turned His disciples' attention back to the Word.

Many Jews were crucified in the first century AD and several Jews were even resurrected in the Gospel accounts – Lazarus, a widow's son, and a synagogue ruler's little girl. So Yeshua's crucifixion or resurrection alone do not prove He is Messiah. His birth, crucifixion, burial, and resurrection prove He is Israel's promised Anointed One, and the world's Savior, only because they exactly fulfill what the *Tanach* prophesied concerning the Jewish Messiah!

How did Yeshua challenge those who doubted He was the Messiah?

> Search the *scriptures* [the *Tanach*]; for in them ye think ye have eternal life: and they are they which testify [bear witness] of me ... Do not think that I will accuse you to the Father: there is one that accuseth you, even *Moses*, in whom ye trust. For had ye *believed Moses*, ye would have believed me: for *he wrote of me*. But *if ye believe not his writings*, how shall ye believe my words?   (John 5:39, 45–47)

That particular saying of the Messiah is a stumbling block to many in the Church when it should be a foundation. If we do not have confidence that what Moses wrote is still the Word of our God, then how can we really trust in Yeshua as Messiah, Savior, and Lord? Yeshua always used the *Tanach* as proof of His Messiahship.

God wants us to believe in what Moses wrote – forever!

> And the LORD said unto Moses, Lo, I come unto thee in a thick cloud, [in order] that the people may hear when I speak with thee, *and believe thee for ever*. And Moses told the words of the people unto the LORD.
> (Exod. 19:9)

A Rabbi Satisfied with Yeshua's Messiahship

Why was Rabbi Saul, the apostle Paul, so convinced that Yeshua was the true Messiah? Because he found that the gospel was the fulfillment of what the *Tanach* says. He declared before both Roman and Jewish authorities,

> But this I confess unto thee, that after the way which *they* call heresy, so worship [and serve] I the God of my fathers, *believing* [trusting in] *all things which are written in the law and in the prophets*...
> (Acts 24:14)

In Romans 1:1–2 Paul not only calls the *Tanach* "the holy scriptures," but he states that the gospel was promised in the *Tanach*,

> Paul, a servant [slave] of Yeshua the Messiah, called to be an apostle, separated unto the gospel of God, *(Which he had promised afore by his prophets in the holy scriptures)*...[11]

Saved by Faith

In Romans 10:5–8, the apostle quotes Moses, arguing in favor of God's righteousness imparted through trusting God, as opposed to the idea that man can achieve righteousness by keeping all of God's Law. Although what follows may sound like Moses was contradicting himself, he was not. Moses only points out that if a person wants to be righteous in God's sight by his own works, he must perfectly keep all of God's Law. But Moses knows this is impossible. He then says that there is another way of being righteous with God, a way that achieves its goal, and that is by faith.

Paul uses these points from Moses in his argument,

> For Moses describeth the righteousness which is of the law, That the man which doeth those things shall live by them.   (Lev. 18:5)

He then contrasts that impossible approach to righteousness *by again quoting from Moses,*

> But the righteousness which is of faith speaketh on this wise, Say not in thine heart, Who shall ascend into heaven [Deut. 30:12]? (that is, to bring Messiah down from above:) Or, Who shall descend into the deep? (that is, to bring up Messiah again from the dead.) But *what saith it? The word* is nigh thee, even in thy mouth, and in thy heart [Deut. 30:14]:[12] that is, the *word of faith*, which we preach.

So to establish what God means by "the righteousness which is of faith," Paul has quoted Moses – he quotes the Law! In the Law (lit: Teaching), both types of righteousness are proclaimed. Righteousness by faith never negates the righteousness of the Law, but rather upholds it as a standard (Rom. 3:31).

Paul continues presenting his gospel evidence from the *Tanach* (here in italics) throughout Romans 10:9–21,

> That if thou shalt confess with thy mouth the Lord Yeshua, and shalt believe [trust] in thine heart that God hath raised him from the dead, thou shalt be saved. For with the heart man believeth unto

righteousness; and with the mouth confession is made unto salvation. For the scripture [the *Tanach*] saith, *Whosoever believeth on* [trusts in] *him shall not be ashamed* [Isa. 28:16; 49:23]. For there is no difference between the Jew and the Greek: for the same Lord over all is rich unto all that call upon him. *For whosoever shall call upon the name of the Lord shall be saved* [Joel 2:32]. How then shall they call on him in whom they have not believed? and how shall they believe [trust] in him of whom they have not heard? and how shall they hear without a preacher? And how shall they preach, except they be sent? as it is written, *How beautiful are the feet of them that preach the gospel of peace, and bring glad tidings of good things* [Isa. 52:7; Nah. 1:15]. But they have not all obeyed the gospel. For [Isaiah] saith, *Lord, who hath believed our report?* [Isa. 53:1] So then faith cometh by hearing, and hearing by the word of God.[13] But I say, Have they not heard? Yes verily, *their sound went into all the earth, and their words unto the ends of the world* [Ps. 19:4]. But I say, Did not Israel know? First Moses saith, *I will provoke you to jealousy by them that are no people* [ethnos], *and by a foolish nation* [ethnos] *I will anger you* [Deut. 32:21]. But [Isaiah] is very bold, and saith, I was found of them that sought me not; I was made manifest unto them that asked not after me [Isa. 65:1]. But to Israel he saith, *All day long I have stretched forth my hands unto a disobedient* [rebellious] *and gainsaying* [unwilling, contrary] *people* [Isa. 65:2].

At this point in Paul's argument in Romans, you might think that God is finished with Israel. After all, the *Tanach* verses that Paul quotes are critical of God's chosen people. But the Spirit of God knew that many people might reach this conclusion and so continued in the very next verse[14] with this statement, "I say then, Hath God cast away [rejected] his people? *God forbid*" (Rom. 11:1a). And to prove this, Paul quotes from or alludes to the *Tanach* in many other verses.[15]

In Paul's classic chapter on the resurrection of the dead, again and again he uses the *Tanach* as God's sanctified foundation for his belief.

For I delivered [committed, transmitted] to you first of all what I also received, how that Messiah died for our sins *according to the scriptures* [the *Tanach*]; that he was buried, and he rose again the third day *according to the scriptures* [the *Tanach*]. (1 Cor. 15:3–4)

It should be quite obvious by now that if Paul cannot find the "roots" of some doctrine in the *Tanach*, he will not ask you to believe it in the New Covenant. Even with an issue like speaking in tongues, Paul finds a *Tanach* proof text,

> *In the law it is written,* With men of other tongues and other lips will I speak unto this people; and yet for all that will they not hear me, saith the Lord. Wherefore tongues are for a sign, not to them that believe, but to them that believe not: but prophesying serveth not for them that believe not, but for them which believe.   (1 Cor. 14:21–22)

Other New Testament Proofs

The letter to the Hebrews states also that the gospel was preached to the children of Israel in the wilderness after the Law was given:

> Let us therefore fear, lest, a promise being left us of entering into his rest, any of you should seem to come short of it. *For unto us was the gospel preached, as well as* [lit: exactly as] *unto them*: but the word preached did not profit them, *not being mixed with faith* in them that heard it. For we which have believed [trusted, have confidence] do enter into rest, as he said, *As I have sworn in my wrath, if they shall enter into my rest* [Ps. 95:11]: although the works were finished from the foundation of the world.   (Heb. 4:1–3)

This is similar to another *Tanach* verse in which God said to Israel through the prophet Jeremiah,

> Thus saith the LORD, Stand ye in the ways, and see, and ask for the old [lit: everlasting, eternal] paths, where is *the good way,* and walk therein, and ye shall find [attain] *rest for your souls.* But they said, We will not walk therein.   (Jer. 6:16)

Finally, Peter declares that the Word of the Lord as found in the *Tanach* was the same Word that the apostles used to preach the gospel, the good news of Yeshua the Messiah. And why not? It was the only Word of God they had.

> Being born again, not of corruptible seed, but of incorruptible, by [through] *the word of God, which liveth and abideth for ever.* For all flesh is as grass, and all the glory [beauty, influence, dignity] of man as the flower of grass. The grass withereth, and the flower thereof falleth away: *But the word of the Lord endureth for ever* [Isa. 40:6, 8]. *And this is the word which by the gospel is preached unto you.*
>
>   (1 Pet. 1:23–25)

In Conclusion

Try this most informative, eye-opening, and profitable word study. Trace all the places where the New Testament uses the word "scripture" and in your mind substitute "*Tanach*." You are not doing a disservice to the text – in fact just the opposite. You will be reading the text with the mindset of the writers whom God used to write it.

Here is the question. Do you think your own personal theological view of the Old Testament is as "high and holy" as that of the New Testament authors and Messiah Yeshua? If not, why not?

We cannot afford to believe in just the New Testament.

> Yeshua answered and said unto them, Ye do err [go astray, are deceived and in error], not knowing [understanding] *the scriptures* [the *Tanach*], nor the power of God. (Matt. 22:29)

We cannot afford such error. Why call ourselves "New Testament believers"? We should more accurately call ourselves "Bible believers." We must realize that the *Tanach* is vital to our faith.

> For I am not ashamed of the gospel of Messiah:
> for it is the power of God unto salvation to every one that believeth;
> to the Jew first, and also to the Greek. For therein is the
> righteousness of God revealed from faith to faith:
> *as it is written* [in Hab. 2:4], The just shall live by faith.
> (Rom. 1:16–17)

Notes

1. Prov. 25:25.
2. The two words translated "curse" in this verse are not the same in Hebrew. Paraphrased, it reads: "I will bitterly curse, or put under a curse, them that treat you with contempt, make you despicable and dishonor you."
3. The Greek *ethnos* and the Hebrew *goyim* can be translated as heathens, or nations, according to the context.
4. See Chapter 14, section "God's Son."
5. See also Matt. 2:15, 23; 8:17; 12:17; 13:35; 21:4.
6. Many scholars list John's as the least Jewish of the gospels, but according to *Tanach* rabbinic thinking, it would be one of the more "kosher" accounts, as seen by John's frequent *Tanach* references.
7. See also John 15:25; 17:12; 18:9; 19:24, 28, 36–37.
8. Acts 6:7.
9. See also Luke 24:44.
10. Matt. 24:24; Mark 13:22; John 4:48; 2 Thess. 2:9.

11. Whenever the New Testament mentions "scriptures," in the historical context it is referring only to the *Tanach*. How many believers in Messiah Yeshua today understand that their Holy Scriptures must include the Old Testament?

12. Through Paul, the Spirit of God gives this inspired commentary, or *midrash*, on what the *Tanach* says.

13. In some manuscripts, "the word of Christ."

14. In the original Greek and Hebrew Scriptures there were no chapter or verse divisions. The current numbering system, although very helpful, can at times cut through the thought flow. Often it is helpful, before tackling the beginning of a new chapter, to read the last couple of verses in the previous chapter to check for a vital connection.

15. Rom. 11:2–4, 7–12, 15–16, 20–21, 24–29, 33–36.

CHAPTER 10

The Cross in the *Tanach* – Part 1

Believers can run into many problems if they don't fully understand what Scripture says about the cross. However, to comprehend what happened on the cross, we need to know more than just what the New Testament reveals. We can safely assume that the New Testament authors depended on their readers studying and knowing the *Tanach*. Although the cross as a means of execution was first used only a couple of centuries before Yeshua, yet there are prophecies in the *Tanach* from much earlier which give deep insight about what was to occur on that "tree."

The New Testament says that the prophets had many things revealed to them about the Messiah except the exact time of His coming:

> Of which salvation the prophets have inquired and searched diligently [in the *Tanach*], who prophesied of the *grace* that should come unto you: Searching what, or what manner of *time* the Spirit of Messiah which was in them did signify [make clear; give understanding], when it testified beforehand the *sufferings of Messiah*, and the *glory that should follow*. (1 Pet. 1:10–11)

One of the most complete revelations of "Yeshua the Messiah and Him crucified" (1 Cor. 2:2) is found in Isaiah 52:13–53:12. The following verse-by-verse discussion of this and other passages will demonstrate the necessity of looking into the *Tanach* in order to fully understand the New Testament.

Isaiah 52:13–53:12 [1]

Isaiah 52:13

> Behold, *My Servant* shall deal prudently [prosper, deal wisely, succeed in that for which He is sent], He *shall be exalted* [raised up on high, lit. and/or fig.] and extolled, and be very high.

In Yeshua's time there were Aramaic translations of the *Tanach* with commentaries, called the *targums*. They give insight into the thinking of the Jewish people of that day. *Targum Jonathan* translates the verse: "Behold, My Servant Messiah ... shall be exalted ... "[2] Yeshua must have had this verse in mind when He said,

And I, if I be lifted up from the earth, will draw all men unto me.
(John 12:32)

Here is an interesting quote: "Our Rabbis expound this [verse] ... of the King Messiah, saying, 'He shall be higher than Abraham, exalted above Moses, and loftier than the ministering angels.'"[3] It is difficult to see how this interpretation could apply to any mere human. It sounds similar to what the New Testament writer to the Hebrews says about Messiah Yeshua in the first three chapters of his letter.

In both the Hebrew and Greek, the word "servant" can also be translated "worshiper." Servants obey, and Yeshua was obedient – even to his death on the cross. Obedience is the essence of worship. Simply put, to serve and worship God we must obey Him.

Isaiah 52:14

Just as many were astonished [appalled, horrified] at you, so *His visage* [appearance] *was marred* more than any man, and His form *more than the sons of men* ...

Yeshua received a beating and scourging before His crucifixion. By the time Messiah was crucified He was a bleeding, shocking sight. If we remember that Messiah was standing in our place, taking the punishment for sin that we rightly deserve from a holy God, we can understand why our sin repulses God. Just as it marred Yeshua's body, it destroys what is holy, the likeness of God in man.

Isaiah 52:15a

So shall He *sprinkle* many nations [*goyim* – gentiles].

The Hebrew word translated "sprinkle" is used for ceremonial cleansing through the sprinkling of blood. Peter refers to this section of Isaiah several times in his first letter. For example:

Elect according to the foreknowledge of God the Father, through sanctification of the Spirit, unto obedience and *sprinkling of the blood* of Jesus Christ: Grace unto you, and peace, be multiplied.   (1 Pet. 1:2)

Isaiah 52:15b

> *Kings* shall shut their mouths at Him; for what had not been told them they *shall see*, and what they had not heard they shall consider [discern, understand].

Compare this with Isaiah 49:7:

> Thus saith the LORD, the Redeemer of Israel, and his Holy One, to him *whom man* [*nephesh* – lit. a soul] *despiseth,* to him *whom the nation* [in context – Israel] *abhorreth,* to a servant of rulers, *Kings shall see* and arise, *princes also shall worship, because of the* LORD *that is faithful,* and the Holy One of Israel, and he shall choose thee.

These two verses prophesy that the Servant of the LORD, the Messiah, will be revealed to, and worshiped by, gentiles and their leaders. In fact, Isaiah 49:7 (above) states that the reason Israel will despise, but the gentiles accept, this Sent One, is because God is faithful to His promises to Israel! This perhaps startling thought is confirmed by Paul in Romans 11.[4]

Isaiah 53:1a

> Who has believed our report?

John 12:37–38 gives the reason more Jewish people did not believe in Yeshua despite His miracles:

> But though he had done so many miracles before them, yet *they believed not* on him: That *the saying of* [Isaiah] *the prophet might be fulfilled,* which he spake, Lord, who hath believed our report? and to whom hath the arm of the Lord been revealed?

God was confirming His Word by executing it. He blinded Israel's eyes as John says in the verses following:

> Therefore they *could* not believe, because that [Isaiah] said again, He hath blinded their eyes [metaphorically, the mind, the faculty of knowing], and hardened their heart [soul, mind, will, understanding]; that they should not see [know, perceive] with their eyes, nor understand with their heart, and be converted [lit. turn back; fig. change one's mind], and I should heal [to free from errors and sins; save] them.
> (John 12:39–40)

Remember, in context this referred to the unbelievers among the Jews and many of the religious authorities, not to all Israel.

In Romans 10 Paul shows that although the gospel was preached as was prophesied, not all believed, also as was prophesied. By combining Isaiah 52:7 with 53:1 in the following verse, he demonstrates the scriptural principle of God watching over His Word to perform it (see Jer. 1:12):

> And how shall they preach, except they be sent? as it is written, How beautiful are the feet of them that preach the gospel of peace, and bring glad tidings of good things! But they have not all obeyed the gospel. For [Isaiah] saith, Lord, who hath believed our report?
>
> (Rom. 10:15–16)

Paul confirms the divine blinding of most of Israel for the sake of the salvation of gentiles:

> For I would not, brethren, that ye should be ignorant of this mystery,[5] lest ye should be wise in your own conceits; that blindness [hardness] *in part* is happened to Israel, until the fulness of the Gentiles be come in.
>
> (Rom. 11:25)

Isaiah 53:1b

And to whom has *the arm of the* LORD been revealed?

Isaiah 52:10 proclaims that,

> *The* LORD *has made bare His holy arm* in the eyes of all the nations; and all the ends of the earth shall see *the salvation*[6] *of our God.*

In context (Isa. 52:7–10), this occurs when Israel receives her salvation. That scripture is part of the *Tanach* foundation for Paul's theology that the salvation of Israel as a nation will bring even greater blessings to the world:

> Now if the fall of them be the riches of the world, and the diminishing of them the riches of the Gentiles; how much more their fulness? ... For if the casting away of them be the reconciling of the world, what shall the receiving of them be, but life from the dead?
>
> (Rom. 11:12, 15)

Faith for salvation comes only by revelation; it is a gift from God (Eph. 2:8). Yeshua gave His Father all the glory for "opening Peter's eyes," making sure that "flesh and blood" did not get any credit for Peter's ability to "see" that He was "the Messiah, the Son of the living God" (Matt. 16:16–17).

Isaiah 53:2

For He shall grow up before Him [in God's presence] as a tender plant, and as *a root out of dry ground.* He has *no form or comeliness* [appearance or excellence]; and when we see Him, there is *no beauty* that we should desire [take pleasure, delight in] Him.

This verse describes Yeshua's humanity and Israel's spiritual condition at the time of the first coming of Messiah. Yes, there was a righteous remnant, but most of the community could be described as "dry ground."

Isaiah 11:10 declares that one of the names of the Messiah is "Root of Jesse":

And in that day there shall be a root of Jesse, which shall stand for an ensign [*nes* – banner, sign, standard lifted up, a rallying point; can be translated as "miracle"] of the people; to it shall the Gentiles seek: and his rest shall be glorious.

Isaiah 53:3

He is despised and rejected by men, a man of sorrows [or pain] and acquainted with [knows intimately] grief [also sickness, both physical and mental]. And we hid, as it were, our faces from Him; *He was despised,* and we did not esteem Him.

Some rabbis and *Targum Jonathan* saw this verse as referring to the Messiah whom Israel would despise.[7] Read Matthew 27:30–31 with this verse in mind.

Isaiah 53:4a

Surely [or but] *He has borne our griefs and carried our sorrows* [borne = lifted; carried = carried away] . . .

This was and still is fulfilled in Yeshua's healing ministry.

When the even was come, they brought unto him many that were possessed with devils: and he cast out the spirits with his word, and healed all that were sick: That it might be fulfilled [accomplished] which was spoken by [Isaiah] the prophet, saying, *Himself took our infirmities, and bare our sicknesses.*   (Matt. 8:16–17)

Isaiah 53:4b

> ...yet we esteemed [thought, judged] him stricken, *smitten by God*, and afflicted.

Psalm 69:26 also predicts this attitude:

> For they persecute him whom *thou hast smitten*; and they talk to the grief of those whom thou hast wounded.

This last phrase literally translates as "they recount near the anguish of the fatally-pierced." In other words this means: in the presence of the agony of the Crucified, they recite His faults.

Isaiah 53:5

> But *He* was wounded [profaned, defiled, pierced] for *our* transgressions [rebellion], *He* was bruised [crushed, broken] for *our* iniquities [faults, perversity, depravity]; the chastisement for *our* peace [completeness, well-being, prosperity] was upon *Him*, and by *His* stripes [lashings] *we* are healed.

Four times "He" and "we" are contrasted, emphasizing that His suffering was for us, a substitutionary atonement. The first two times explain the reason He suffered – for our sins; the last two times present us with the results of His suffering – our peace and healing. Rabbi Simeon ben Yochai states: "since the Messiah bears our iniquities, which produce the effect of His being bruised, it follows that whosoever will not admit that the Messiah thus suffers for our iniquities, must endure and suffer for them himself."[8]

Another rabbinic comment: "And when Israel is sinful, the Messiah seeks for mercy upon them, as it is written, 'By His stripes we were healed, and He carried the sins of many; and made intercession for the transgressors'."[9]

Isaiah 53:6

> All we like sheep have gone astray [erred, wandered, been seduced, been deceived, staggered as if drunk]; we have turned, every one, to his own way; and the Lord has laid on [made fall upon; same root word is used for "intercession"] Him the iniquity of us all.

"[W]e have turned, every one, to his own way..." is a short but encompassing definition of sin.

Isaiah 53:7

> He was oppressed, and He was afflicted, yet *He opened not His mouth*; He was led as a lamb to the slaughter, and as a *sheep* before its shearers is *silent*, so *He opened not His mouth.*

This verse predicts the Servant's lamb-like quiet submission, which we see clearly in Mark 15:3–5:

> And the chief priests accused him of many things: but he *answered nothing*. And Pilate asked him again, saying, Answerest thou nothing? behold how many things they witness against thee. But Yeshua yet *answered nothing*; so that Pilate marvelled.

Messiah Yeshua's death as the slain lamb is extolled in heaven and crowns the Lamb's glory:

> And I beheld, and, lo, in the midst of the throne and of the four beasts, and in the midst of the elders, stood a *Lamb as it had been slain*, having seven horns and seven eyes, which are the seven Spirits of God sent forth into all the earth. And he came and took the book out of the right hand of him that sat upon the throne.
>
> And when he had taken the book, the four beasts and four and twenty elders fell down before *the Lamb*, having every one of them harps, and golden vials full of odours, which are the prayers of saints. And they sung a new song, saying, *Thou art worthy* to take the book, and to open the seals thereof: for thou wast slain, and hast redeemed us to God by thy blood out of every kindred, and tongue, and people, and nation; And hast made us unto our God kings and priests: and we shall reign on the earth.
>
> And I beheld, and I heard the voice of many angels round about the throne and the beasts and the elders: and the number of them was ten thousand times ten thousand, and thousands of thousands; Saying with a loud voice, *Worthy is the Lamb* that was slain to receive power, and riches, and wisdom, and strength, and honour, and glory, and blessing. And every creature which is in heaven, and on the earth, and under the earth, and such as are in the sea, and all that are in them, heard I saying, *Blessing, and honour, and glory, and power, be unto him that sitteth upon the throne, and unto the Lamb for ever and ever.*
>
> (Rev. 5:6–13)

Isaiah 53:8a

> He was taken from prison and from *judgment* [or justice], and *who will declare His generation?*

The Spirit led Philip to the Ethiopian eunuch as he was reading this and the previous verse in Isaiah:

> ... He was led as a sheep to the slaughter; and like a lamb dumb before his shearer, so opened he not his mouth: In his humiliation his *judgment* [or justice] was taken away: and *who shall declare his generation?* for his life is taken from the earth.
>
> And the eunuch answered Philip, and said, I pray thee, of whom speaketh the prophet this? of himself, or of some other man? Then Philip opened his mouth, and began at the same scripture, and preached unto him Yeshua. (Acts 8:32b–35)

Isaiah 53:8b

> For He was *cut off* [destroyed] from the land of the living; *for the transgressions* [rebellions] *of My people* He was stricken.

Again we see the substitutionary atonement. The modern rabbinic argument for why this cannot refer to Yeshua says that Isaiah 53 refers to Israel as a nation. But this verse is proof that Isaiah 53 cannot be referring to the nation of Israel as a whole because they were Isaiah's/God's people for whom "He," someone else, "was stricken." Isaiah prophesies that someone will be "cut off," or die, for Israel. Daniel 9:26a is a confirmation of this verse:

> And after threescore and two weeks shall *Messiah be cut off, but not for himself* ...

Isaiah 53:9

> And they made [assigned] His grave [metaphor for death] *with the wicked* [criminals] – but [yet] *with the rich* [a rich man] at His death, because *He had done no violence* [or wrong], *nor was any deceit in His mouth.*

Matthew 27:44, 57–60 describes in detail the fulfillment of this verse when Yeshua was crucified between two thieves yet buried in a rich man's tomb, while 1 Peter 2:22 declares that Yeshua was sinless: "Who did no sin, neither was guile found in his mouth ... "

Isaiah 53:10a

Yet it pleased [it was the desire of, the will of] the LORD to bruise [crush] Him; He [God] *has put Him to grief* [lit: worn Him out].

God the Father is the One who bears ultimate responsibility for the crucifixion of His Son, Yeshua (and our salvation). As David says in Psalm 118:22–23:

The stone which the builders refused [cast off, reject, refuse, despise] is become the head stone of the corner. *This is the* LORD's *doing*; it is marvellous [lit.: wonderful; metaphorically: accomplished or fulfilled] in our eyes.

See again Psalm 69:26.

Yeshua understood that His death was His Father's will:

Then said Yeshua unto Peter, Put up thy sword into the sheath: the cup which *my Father hath given me*, shall I not drink it?   (John 18:11)

This occurred after Messiah's struggle in Gethsemane to do His Father's will, to drink that cup of suffering. Because of this, and although the agents of evil were men, the death of Yeshua was in God's will, and this was eventually recognized and accepted by the apostles:

For of a truth against thy holy child Yeshua, whom thou hast anointed, both Herod, and Pontius Pilate, with the Gentiles, and the people of Israel, were gathered together, *For to do whatsoever thy hand and thy counsel determined before to be done.*   (Acts 4:27–28)

Isaiah 53:10b

When You make [appoint] His soul [life] an *offering for sin* [lit. a sin, guilt or trespass offering], He shall see His seed [children], He shall prolong His days, and the pleasure [will] of the LORD shall prosper [advance, succeed] in His hand.

This verse points to Yeshua's death as an offering for sin, fulfilling the entire sacrificial system as the book of Hebrews declares in the section from chapter 8 verse 1 to chapter 10 verse 18. It also hints at His resurrection, because immediately after Messiah is sacrificed, it states that "he shall prolong his days," and God's pleasure, His will, shall go forward through this One.

Isaiah 53:11

He shall see the travail [labor, trouble] of His soul, and be satisfied. By His knowledge My righteous [just, law abiding, obedient] Servant shall justify many[10] [will cause many to be accounted righteous – many, not all!], for *He shall bear* [carry away] *their iniquities* [perversity, depravity].

With this prophecy we again see Messiah as our substitutionary sacrifice. In Acts 13:38, Paul notes this, proclaiming the fulfillment of what Isaiah prophesied:

Be it known unto you therefore, men and brethren, that through this man is preached unto you the forgiveness of sins...

Isaiah 53:12

Therefore will I divide [issue, assign] Him a portion with the great, and He shall divide the spoil with the strong, because *He poured out His soul unto death*, and He was *numbered with the transgressors*, and *He bore* [lifted up, carried] *the sin of many, and made intercession for the transgressors.*[11]

Hebrews 9:28a is the New Testament verse confirming that Isaiah was speaking about Yeshua: "So Messiah was once offered to bear the sins of many..."

Paul may have been thinking about this verse, especially about Messiah's soul being poured out in death when he wrote to the Philippians:

Let this mind be in you, which was also in Messiah Yeshua: Who, being in the form of God, thought it not robbery to be equal with God: But made himself of no reputation, and took upon him the form of a servant, and was made in the likeness of men: And being found in fashion as a man, he humbled himself, and *became obedient unto death*, even the *death* of the cross.   (Phil. 2:5–8)

Mark also pointed out a fulfillment of Isaiah 53:12 when he wrote:

And with him they crucify two thieves; the one on his right hand, and the other on his left. And the scripture was fulfilled, which saith, And he was *numbered with the transgressors*.   (Mark 15:27–28)

Targum Jonathan also applies this verse to the Messiah, speaking about His dying and interceding for the transgressors.[12]

Conclusion

In Luke 22:37, Yeshua recognizes Isaiah 53 as a picture of His death:

> For I say unto you, that *this that is written must yet be accomplished in me, And he was reckoned among the transgressors* [lawless, wicked]: for the things concerning me have an end [goal, purpose].

For even hereunto were ye called:
because Messiah also suffered for us, leaving us an example,
that ye should follow his steps: Who did no sin,
neither was guile found in his mouth:
Who, when he was reviled, reviled not again; when he suffered,
he threatened not; but committed himself
to him that judgeth righteously:
Who his own self bare our sins in his own body on the tree,
that we, being dead to sins, should live unto righteousness:
by whose stripes ye were healed.
(1 Pet. 2:21–24).

Notes

1. Verses quoted from Isaiah 53 are taken from the New King James Version.
2. F. Kenton Beshore, *The Messiah of the Targums, Talmuds & Rabbinical Writers* (World Bible Society, Box 1, LA, CA 90053, 1971), Chart 15.
3. Ibid.
4. See Rom. 11:11–15, 25–32.
5. See Chapter 18, section "The Mystery of Messiah."
6. *Yeshuat* is the feminine form of Yeshua with the possessive ending, the salvation that belongs to our God.
7. Kenton Beshore, op. cit., Chart 21.
8. Robert R. Gorelik, *Messiah, Another Jewish View* (Irvine, CA: Eshav Books), p. 27.
9. Kenton Beshore, op. cit., Chart 26.
10. Cf. Prov. 11:9: "An hypocrite with his mouth destroyeth his neighbour: but through knowledge shall the just be delivered."
11. This is His present priestly role: Rom. 8:34; Heb. 7:25.
12. Burt Yellin, *Messiah, A Rabbinic and Scriptural Viewpoint* (Denver: Congregation Roeh Israel), p. 43, note 37.

CHAPTER 11

The Cross in the *Tanach* – Part 2

Psalm 22

Psalm 22 is another *Tanach* chapter that helps us understand the cross and its results. Although the Gospel accounts give the disciples' view of the cross and the events associated with it, in this psalm we hear Yeshua expressing His feelings and reaction to the cross – while hanging on it. Dying, Yeshua declared for all who had ears to hear that His death was fulfilling prophecy, especially this psalm.

One of the rabbinic teaching techniques of Yeshua's day was called *remez*, or hinting. Because the *Tanach* was not easily portable, large portions were committed to memory. The rabbis only needed to quote a verse or a phrase and the context would come to the minds of their disciples. David Stern points out, "In Judaism, when a Bible verse is cited its entire context is implied, if appropriate. Thus Yeshua refers all of Psalm 22 to himself..."[1] The proof for this? Yeshua quoted both the first and last lines of this psalm during His execution. Using *remez*, Yeshua implied that "this is that which was spoken by the prophet...," that is, he was referring to His crucifixion and beyond. So we will examine this psalm verse by verse as prophetic of Yeshua on the cross.

On the Cross

Psalm 22:1

> My God, my God, why hast thou forsaken me? why art thou so far from helping [lit. saving[2] me, and from the words of my roaring [groaning]?

A Jewish commentator, Rev. Dr A. Cohen, says about this verse, "He feels that he has been abandoned by God, and his faith is sorely tried."[3] A.M. Hodgkin, a Christian commentator, points out that, "The Hebrew shows not one completed sentence in the opening verses, but a series of brief ejaculations, like the gasps of a dying man whose breath and strength are failing, and who can only utter a word or two at a time."[4]

Many believers struggle with questions concerning Yeshua's crucifixion. For instance His cry, "My God, my God, why hast thou forsaken Me?" (Matt. 27:46b). Didn't Yeshua know His Father was going to turn His back to Him?

Yeshua knew what would happen on the cross. The separation between Him and His Father probably was the major issue He struggled with at Gethsemane. He resolved that issue, but He wanted His disciples to resolve it also. Using *remez* from the cross, He "hints" at Psalm 22, giving a biblical perspective and foundation concerning His death.

God placed on Him the sins of the world. Yeshua understood that sin separates us from God.

> Behold, the LORD's hand is not shortened, that it cannot save; neither his ear heavy, that it cannot hear: But your iniquities have separated between you and your God, and your sins have hid his face from you, that he will not hear [Isa. 59:1–2].

He always quoted from the Scriptures, the *Tanach*, for evidence that He was the One who was to come, the promised Messiah. And by quoting from Psalm 22, Yeshua was declaring to His disciples, and all who would ever hear or read about His death, that it was so prophesied.

Also after His resurrection He pointed, not to His resurrection in itself, but to the *Tanach* prophecies for proof of who He was.[5] To sum up, He did not say, "I am risen...," He said, "It is written..."

Psalm 22:6

> But I am a worm, and no man; a reproach of men [Heb.: *adam* = mankind], and despised of the people [Heb.: *am* = the national group].

Rev. Cohen writes, "The language of this section is reminiscent of Isaiah's description of the suffering 'Servant of the Lord'." Cohen continues concerning the phrase "and no man," "I am so disfigured by cruelty that I have not the appearance of a man, as in Isa. [52]:14..." and concerning "despised of the people" he points to Isaiah 53:3 (see also Isa. 49:7). Amazingly even rabbis tie together these two crucial chapters describing the death and resurrection of the Messiah.

Psalm 22:6 finds its fulfillment in Luke 23:35–37,

> And the people stood beholding. And the rulers also with them derided
> him, saying, He saved others; let him save himself, if he be Messiah, the
> chosen of God. And the soldiers also mocked him, coming to him, and
> offering him vinegar, And saying, If thou be the king of the Jews, save
> thyself.

Psalm 22:7–8

> All they that see me laugh me to scorn: they shoot out the lip, they
> shake the head, saying, He trusted on the LORD that he would deliver
> [rescue] him: let him deliver him, seeing he delighted in him.

It is easy to forget that this is a quote from the *Tanach* and not from
the New Testament. The chief priests, scribes, and elders spoke these
same things against Yeshua while He was hanging on the cross:

> And they that passed by reviled [blasphemed] him, wagging their
> heads, And saying, Thou that destroyest the temple, and buildest it in
> three days, save thyself. If thou be the Son of God, come down from the
> cross. Likewise also the chief priests mocking him, with the scribes and
> elders, said, He saved others; himself he cannot save. If he be the King
> of Israel, let him now come down from the cross, and we will believe
> [trust in] him. He trusted in God; let him deliver him now, if he will
> have him: for he said, I am the Son of God. The thieves also, which
> were crucified with him, cast the same in his teeth.
>
> (Matt. 27:39–44; see also Mark 15:29)

When biblical prophecy comes to pass, we should expect to see a
literal fulfillment. Although predicting how God will perform His
Word is impossible, after the fact we can say with Peter "this is that
which was spoken by the prophet..." (Acts 2:16). The consistent
literal fulfillment of God's Word allows no excuse to those who reject
it! For example, what will believers say who reject the modern-day
nation of Israel as a fulfillment of prophecy?

Psalm 22:9–10

> But thou art he that took me out of the womb: thou didst make me
> hope [trust, be bold, secure, confident (in You)] when I was upon
> my mother's breasts. I was cast upon thee from the womb: thou art my
> God from my mother's belly [womb].

The psalmist mentions his mother three times, but not his earthly father. The prophetic scriptures never contradict the virgin birth.

Psalm 22:12

> Many bulls have compassed [surrounded] me: strong bulls of Bashan have beset me round.

In another Jewish commentary,[6] Rabbi A.C. Feuer states that the literal interpretation of "beset me" is "they crown me!" The Roman soldiers who crowned Yeshua's head with thorns (Matt. 27:29) were "strong as bulls," whether in themselves or as representatives of a conquering empire.

Psalm 22:14

> I am poured out like water, and all my bones are out of joint: my heart is like wax; it is melted in the midst of my bowels.

This is a poetic, yet accurate, description of what a crucified person would go through. Christian doctors have written articles on the similarities of this description to actual physical events and processes which would occur in a body during crucifixion.[7]

Psalm 22:15

> My strength is dried up like a potsherd; and my tongue cleaveth [clings] to my jaws; and thou hast brought me into the dust of death.

Rev. Cohen comments on "thou hast brought me into the dust of death," "If his persecutors succeed in destroying his life, it must be God's will; 'for the Jew could never think of anything as happening without God'."[8] Yeshua had already expressed this thought to Peter and Pilate:

> Then said Yeshua unto Peter, Put up thy sword into the sheath: the cup which my Father hath given me, shall I not drink it?   (John 18:11)

and to Pilate,

> Yeshua answered, Thou couldest have no power at all against me, except it were given thee from above...   (John 19:11a)

Besides this thirst described in Psalm 22, Psalm 69:21 also speaks of thirst,

They gave me also gall for my meat; and in my thirst they gave me vinegar to drink.

Here is the perfect New Testament fulfillment of both these verses:

After this, Yeshua knowing that all things were now accomplished, that the scripture [the *Tanach*] might be fulfilled, saith, I thirst. Now there was set a vessel full of vinegar: and they filled a sponge with vinegar, and put it upon hyssop, and put it to his mouth.

(John 19:28–29)

(See Endnote 9 for further possible *remez*)[9]

Psalm 22:16

For dogs have compassed [surrounded] me: the assembly of the wicked have inclosed me: they pierced my hands and my feet.

Following some modern translations, Rev. Cohen has "like a lion, they are at my hands and my feet" as the wording for the last part of this verse. But he admits that the "Hebrew is difficult . . . A.V. and R.V. render they pierce, adopting the reading of the LXX, to accord with the Christological interpretation of the Psalm."[10] This is an amazing statement! The Septuagint, often designated by "LXX," is the Greek version of the *Tanach* translated by seventy Jewish scholars/rabbis around 200 BC. So, more than two centuries before Yeshua was crucified, Jewish scholars understood this verse to read "pierce"!

This is not the only place in the *Tanach* which points to Messiah being pierced:

And I will pour upon the house of David, and upon the inhabitants of Jerusalem, the spirit of grace and of supplications: and they shall look upon [regard with favor, consider] me whom they have pierced, and they shall mourn for him, as one mourneth for his only son, and shall be in bitterness for him, as one that is in bitterness for his firstborn.

(Zech. 12:10)

Psalm 22:17

I may tell [count] all my bones: they look and stare upon me.

Again, the first part is an accurate description of a crucified man.

Psalm 22:18

> They part [divide] my garments among them, and cast lots upon my vesture [clothing].

So many *Tanach* prophecies like this one were fulfilled on the day Yeshua was crucified that we can know for a fact God was in control. There was no human way Yeshua could have set up everything that happened to Him just to fulfill those scriptures.

> Then the soldiers, when they had crucified Yeshua, took his garments, and made four parts, to every soldier a part; and also his coat: now the coat was without seam, woven from the top throughout. They said therefore among themselves, Let us not rend it, but cast lots for it, whose it shall be: that the scripture might be fulfilled, which saith, They parted my raiment among them, and for my vesture they did cast lots. These things therefore the soldiers did.
>
> (John 19:23–24; see also Matt. 27:35)

The literal fulfillment of Psalm 22 is another witness to the divine inspiration of the Scriptures (Isa. 55:11). How else could Roman soldiers at the foot of the cross, unknowingly accomplish what had been written a thousand years before?

Ibn Ezra, a famous twelfth-century Jewish commentator, makes an interesting observation about this verse, " 'they are royal vestments; if he were not a king these words would make no sense'."[11]

Psalm 22:20

> Deliver my soul [fig. my life] from the sword; my darling [precious life] from the power of the dog.

Rev. Cohen correctly points out that "the sword" symbolizes death by violence.

After the Resurrection

Psalm 22:21b–22

> ... for thou hast heard me from the horns of the unicorns [NKJV: "You have answered Me."]. I will declare thy name [reputation, fame] unto my brethren: in the midst of the congregation will I praise thee.

The declaration of triumph from this verse onward is one reason Yeshua quoted from this psalm while dying on the cross. By doing so,

He was giving His disciples "hints" that, because of His Father's faithfulness to perform His Word (Jer. 1:12), He would pass through this ordeal in victory.

Quoting verse 22:22, Yeshua says that after His death He will declare His Father's "name," that is, His essential nature, to His disciples. This occurs in John 17:26a, in the last sentence of His last speech to His disciples before He goes to the cross, when Yeshua says, "And I have declared to them your name, and *will* declare it . . . " He also praises the Father from within and through "the congregation" of His "called-out-ones," thus fulfilling the last half of verse 22.

Concerning Yeshua's suffering, Hebrews 2:10–12 points to this verse to say that Messiah is one with those whom He has saved:

> For it became [was fitting for] him, for whom are all things, and by whom are all things, in bringing [leading, guiding] many sons unto glory, to make the captain [leader] of their salvation perfect [complete] through sufferings. For both he that sanctifieth [makes holy, sets apart] and they who are sanctified [made holy, set apart] are all of one: for which cause he is not ashamed to call them brethren, Saying, *I will declare thy name unto my brethren, in the midst of the church* [congregation] *will I sing praise unto thee.*

Note how this psalm predicts the current work of the Holy Spirit, which is to lead us to be conformed to Yeshua's likeness, to establish the "Kingdom" – literally, the Rulership of God – in the human heart.[12]

Psalm 22:23

> Ye that fear [lit. be afraid of; revere with trembling] the LORD, praise him; all ye the seed [descendants] of Jacob, glorify him; and fear[13] [or abide in] him, all ye the seed of Israel.

This verse may reflect the situation that all Israel is saved as a nation after the elect God-fearers among the gentiles enter God's Kingdom. When the *Tanach* talks about God-fearers, or "Ye that fear the LORD," in context with other groups which are definitely Jews it is referring to proselytes – gentiles who have converted and become part of the community of Israel (see also Pss. 115:9–13; 118:2–4). Psalm 22:23 first lists the God-fearers, then the "seed of Jacob/Israel" as those who will praise and glorify Him.

Although the early Church was almost exclusively Jewish, by the time of the Jerusalem Council in Acts 15 multitudes of non-Jews were being saved. So many were finding salvation through the Jewish Messiah that James refers to their first visitation by God,

> Simeon [Peter] hath declared how God at the first did visit [inspect, attend to] the Gentiles, to take out of them a people for his name. And to this agree the words of the prophets; as it is written, After this I will return, and will build again the tabernacle of David, which is fallen down; and I will build again the ruins thereof, and I will set it up: That the residue of men might seek after [worship; seek to obey] the Lord, and all the Gentiles, upon whom my name is called, saith the Lord, who doeth all these things.
>
> (Acts 15:14–17; James is quoting from the *Tanach* – Amos 9:11–12)

God has saved a remnant mostly from among the gentiles (nations, pagans, heathens). Next He will save all Israel ("After this I will return and will build again the tabernacle of David," Amos 9:11). In Luke 2:30–32, as the reward of his patient waiting on God, Simeon prophesies with what could be seen as the same order of events. While holding baby Yeshua he declared by the Spirit,

> For mine eyes have seen thy salvation, Which thou hast prepared before the face of all people; A light to lighten [give understanding to] the Gentiles, and the glory of thy people Israel.

After Yeshua's resurrection, the early believers (the first Messianic Jews) and proselytes, God-fearers from among the nations, are the first to praise the Lord (see Acts 13:16). Even so, for almost two millennia, the good news of Yeshua has gone out mostly to the gentiles of the earth. Now, however, many Jews are having their blindness removed and receiving Yeshua as Messiah and Lord, and a time will come when "all ye the seed of Israel" (Ps. 22:23) will be saved. This in turn will lead many more gentiles from every nation to know that the LORD God of Israel is the only true God (see Ezek. 36:23; Rom. 11:15). All of Jacob/Israel will join in with the elect from every nation and tongue to worship the Lord in Jerusalem!

Psalm 22:25

> My praise shall be of thee in the great congregation: I will pay my vows before them that fear him.

Concerning this congregation Rabbi Feuer says, "This refers to all of the gentile nations who will ultimately come to fear God when they witness His salvation."[14] Amen!

Psalm 22:26

> The meek [poor, humble] shall eat and be satisfied: they shall praise the LORD that seek him: your heart shall live for ever.

Rev. Cohen states, "A votive [thanksgiving] sacrifice was eaten by the offerer ... and he invites the humble [poor] to share in it. By participating in this common meal, they become knit into a brother-hood."[15] Communion is symbolized by such a common meal. The humble eat of this grace feast – and by eating are forever satisfied. Who but "the poor in spirit," knowing they are spiritual beggars before a holy God and Savior, will inherit the kingdom of heaven (Matt. 5:3)?

Even some rabbis link this verse with the promised Messiah. "The most renowned commentator in Judaism, Rashi, says that this verse refers to *"the time of deliverance, to the days of the Messiah"* (italics in the original).[16]

Psalm 22:27

> All the ends of the world shall remember and turn [return or repent] unto the LORD: and all the kindreds [families] of the nations shall worship before thee.

Rabbi Feuer continues in his commentary to say about this verse, "When the nations ... see the good which will come to us [Israel] in the future they will remember our previous poverty and degradation ... This will arouse them to repent and return to God."[17] Paul has already declared this in Romans 11:15:

> For if the casting away of them [Israel] be the reconciling [restoration] of the world [lit: cosmos], what shall the receiving of them be, but life from the dead?

Those who believe that what God proclaims in the *Tanach* is still applicable today, understand the enormity of what the salvation of Israel means for the world.

Psalm 22:28

> For the kingdom is the LORD's: and he is the governor [He rules] among the nations.

Belief (trust) in Messiah's death and resurrection establishes God's rulership, His "Kingdom" among the nations/gentiles.

Psalm 22:29b

… all they that go down to the dust shall bow before him …

The psalmist says that even the dead will bow before Him. Paul agrees, stating in Philippians 2:9–11,

Wherefore God also hath highly exalted him, and given him a name which is above every name: That at the name of Yeshua every knee should bow, of things in heaven, and things in earth, and things under the earth; And that every tongue should confess [acknowledge, agree fully] that Yeshua the Messiah is Lord, to the glory of God the Father.

What total faith in God's Word Yeshua evidenced while on the cross by referring to that *Tanach* promise!

Isaiah 45:22–23 has the same sequence as those last two verses, with all the nations coming under God's rule and all the peoples bowing before Him:

Look [turn] unto me, and be ye saved, all the ends of the earth: for I am God, and there is none else. I have sworn by myself, the word is gone out of my mouth in righteousness, and shall not return, That unto me every knee shall bow, every tongue shall swear.

James E. Smith points out that, "No Old Testament person [such as Psalm 22's author, King David] could have imagined that his personal deliverance from death could be the occasion for the world's conversion. Such a hope must be restricted to the future Redeemer. Under inspiration of the Holy Spirit, David … saw his descendant resembling, but far surpassing, himself in suffering. Furthermore, the deliverance of this descendant would have meaning for all mankind."[18]

Psalm 22:30

A seed shall serve him; it shall be accounted to the Lord for a generation.

"Serve" in both Hebrew and Greek can be translated "worship." To worship God we must serve Him. And this verse says Messiah will have descendants, people related to Him as in the same family, who shall worship, serving Him.[19]

Psalm 22:31

> They shall come, and shall declare his righteousness unto a people that shall be born, that he hath done this.

These descendants of Messiah will declare "His righteousness." This is fulfilled in many New Testament epistles where the righteousness of God and His Messiah are constantly declared. For example:

> For I am not ashamed of the gospel of Messiah: for it is the power of God unto salvation to every one that believeth [trusts]; to the Jew first, and also to the Greek. For therein is the righteousness of God revealed from faith to faith: as it is written, The just shall live by faith.
>
> (Rom. 1:16–17)

> Being justified freely by his grace through the redemption that is in Messiah Jesus: Whom God hath set forth to be a propitiation[20] through faith [trust] in his blood, to declare [demonstrate] his righteousness for the remission of sins that are past, through the forbearance of God...
>
> (Rom. 3:24–25)

> But of him are ye in Messiah Yeshua, who of God is made [become] unto us wisdom, and righteousness, and sanctification, and redemption...
>
> (1 Cor. 1:30)

> Now then we are ambassadors for the Messiah, as though God did beseech you by us: we pray you in Messiah's stead, be ye reconciled to God. For he hath made him to be sin for us, who knew no sin; that we might be made [become] the righteousness of God in him.
>
> (2 Cor. 5:20–21)

Finally, in our verse (Ps. 22:31) the Hebrew word for "he hath done this," can also be translated, "It is finished!" In saying this, Yeshua was quoting the last line of Psalm 22 as well as having quoted the first. He thereby applied all of this psalm to Himself. Even in His agony on the Cross, Yeshua encouraged His disciples using *remez* from prophetic songs of praise to God by His ancestor, Israel's great King David.

And he said unto them, These are the words which I spake unto you,
while I was yet with you, that all things must be fulfilled,
which were written in the law of Moses, and in the prophets,
and in the psalms, concerning me. Then opened he their understanding,
that they might understand the scriptures [the *Tanach*],

And said unto them, Thus it is written,
and thus it behoved Messiah to suffer, and to rise from the dead
the third day: And that repentance and remission
[forgiveness, pardon] of sins should be preached in his name
among all nations, beginning at Jerusalem.
And ye are witnesses of these things.
(Luke 24:44–48)

Notes

1. David H. Stern, *Jewish New Testament Commentary* (Clarksville, Maryland: Jewish New Testament Publications, 1992), p. 84.
2. From the same Hebrew root as the name "Yeshua."
3. Rev. Dr A. Cohen, *Soncino Books of the Bible, The Psalms*(New York: The Soncino Press Ltd, 1985), commentary on Psalm 22.
4. A.M. Hodgkin, *Christ in All the Scriptures* (Pickering Classic), p. 117.
5. Luke 24:25–27, 44–46: "Then he said unto them, O fools, and slow of heart to believe all that the prophets have spoken: Ought not Messiah to have suffered these things, and to enter into his glory? And beginning at Moses and all the prophets, he expounded unto them in all the scriptures the things concerning himself … And he said unto them, These are the words which I spake unto you, while I was yet with you, that all things must be fulfilled, which were written in the law of Moses, and in the prophets, and in the psalms, concerning me. Then opened he their understanding, that they might understand the scriptures, And said unto them, Thus it is written, and thus it behoved Messiah to suffer, and to rise from the dead the third day."
6. Rabbi A.C. Feuer, *Psalms*, The Artscroll Tanach Series (Brooklyn: Tehillim, Mesorah Pub. Ltd, 1969), commentary on v. 13, p. 276.
7. For several articles, see www.ldolphin.org/sixhours.html
8. Cohen, op. cit.
9. Consider that John 19:28 explicitly links Yeshua's knowledge that He had fulfilled the Scriptures with His simple statement, "I thirst." Could this short phrase be another case of *remez*, or "hinting"? If so, Yeshua may have been referring to other psalms which speak of thirst – psalms which seem to emphasize His heart-breaking separation from, and His ultimate trust in, His Father. Read these psalms: 42, 63, and 143. Could Yeshua's "I thirst" point to the witness of these three psalms in what may be, in spite of His having hardly the strength to speak two words, His dying prayer from the cross?
10. Cohen, op. cit.
11. Risto Santala, *The Messiah in the Old Testament* (Jerusalem: Keren Ahvah Meshihit, 1992), p. 130.
12. The Greek *basilea* is usually translated "kingdom" in most Bible versions. However, PC Study Bible (Biblesoft 1993–1998) defines this word first of all: "1) royal power, kingship, dominion, rule a) not to be confused with an actual kingdom, but rather the right or authority to rule over a kingdom." If we use a less confusing term – "rulership" for example – in many of the NT verses

where "kingdom" is mentioned, the shift in meaning can be quite enlightening and makes a provocative word study.

13. The two words translated "fear" in this verse are different words in Hebrew.
14. Feuer, op. cit., p. 282.
15. Cohen, op. cit., commentary on v. 27, p. 65.
16. Risto Santala, *The Messiah in the New Testament* (Jerusalem: Keren Ahvah Meshihit, 1992), p. 211.
17. Feuer, op. cit., commentary on v. 28, pp. 283–284.
18. James E. Smith, *What the Bible Teaches About the Promised Messiah* (Thomas Nelson Pub.), p. 146.
19. See comments on vv. 21b–22.
20. Propitiation is the satisfaction of divine justice. This is the same Greek word used in the Septuagint for the "mercy seat" on top of the Ark of the Covenant in the Holy of Holies. It became a "mercy seat" when the High Priest sprinkled on it the blood of the *Yom Kippur* sacrifice.

CHAPTER 12

The Cross in the *Tanach* – Part 3

We want to examine two other sections of the *Tanach* which also foreshadow the cross of Messiah Yeshua.

The Binding of Isaac

Known as the *Akedah* in Judaism, the binding of Isaac is found in Genesis 22. In that scenario Abraham's willingness to sacrifice his son Isaac becomes a type, or foreshadow, of God the Father's willingness to sacrifice His only Son, Yeshua. As with all types, we should not expect every detail to fit the anti-type, but the similarities are amazing.

Genesis 22:1–2

> And it came to pass after these things, that God did tempt [test, prove] Abraham, and said unto him, Abraham: and he said, Behold, here I am. And he said, Take now thy son, thine only son Isaac, whom thou lovest, and get thee into the land of Moriah [Heb.: "seen of God" or "chosen by God"]; and offer him there for a burnt offering upon one of the mountains which I will tell thee of.

Sometimes believers make idols out of God's gifts and promises and end up worshiping the gift more than the Giver. God tested Abraham's willingness to let go of the divine promise, and to just trust in God, so proving by his works that his faith was genuine.

> Was not Abraham our father justified by works, when he had offered Isaac his son upon the altar? Seest [discern, understand] thou how faith wrought [cooperated, worked together] with his works, and by works was faith made perfect [brought to completion]? And the scripture was fulfilled which saith, Abraham believed [trusted in] God, and it was imputed unto him for righteousness: and he was called the Friend of God. (Jas. 2:21–23)

Interestingly, in the Hebrew "*Take now*" is not a command from God to Abraham, but is literally, "Please take." God is making His will clear, although it is couched as a request.

Isaac is the son of the promise described in Genesis 17:15–19:

> And God said unto Abraham, As for Sarai thy wife, thou shalt not call her name Sarai, but Sarah shall her name be. And I will bless her, and give thee a son also of her: yea, I will bless her, and she shall be a mother of nations; kings of people shall be of her.
>
> Then Abraham fell upon his face, and laughed, and said in his heart, Shall a child be born unto him that is an hundred years old? and shall Sarah, that is ninety years old, bear? And Abraham said unto God, O that Ishmael might live before thee!
>
> And God said, Sarah thy wife shall bear thee a son indeed; and *thou shalt call his name Isaac: and I will establish my covenant with him for an everlasting covenant, and with his seed after him.*

As the promised son, Isaac is a type of Yeshua, who also is a fulfillment of a promised Son, He who was promised to King David in 2 Samuel 7:12–14. The New Testament identifies Yeshua as that One,

> He shall be great, and shall be called the Son of the Highest: and the Lord God shall give unto him the throne of his father David...
>
> (Luke 1:32)

In fact, the New Testament opens up by looking backwards and declaring that the promised sons of David and Abraham find their complete fulfillment in the Messiah Yeshua:

> The book of the generation [or nature] of Yeshua the Messiah, the son of David, the son of Abraham.   (Matt. 1:1)

In Genesis 22:2, God is careful to note that Isaac is Abraham's "only" son (cf. John 3:16). Abraham fathered Ishmael through Hagar, Sarah's servant, but that was not God's perfect will, whereas Isaac was the promised one through whom, as we have already seen in Genesis 17:19, God swore to establish His covenant.

This verse contains Scripture's first usage of the word "love": "thine only son Isaac, whom thou lovest." Amazingly, the initial occurrence of "love" becomes a type for its greatest fulfillment on the cross. Just as Yeshua is God's "beloved Son,"[1] so Isaac was to Abraham. But how much greater was God's sacrifice in that He gave Himself in human form for us and no one could or did stop Him!

Greater love hath no man than this, that a man lay down his life for his
friends...   (John 15:13)

Hereby perceive [know, understand] we the love of God, because he
laid down his life for us...   (1 John 3:16a)

Both Judaism and ancient literature portray Isaac as fully grown,
somewhere between twenty-three and thirty-seven years old, causing
"the realization that the sacrifice derived its full value from the fact
that Isaac accepted God's will as well as his father."[2] The same can be
said about Yeshua who was thirty-three when, accepting His Father's
will, He was crucified.

God directed Abraham to the "land of Moriah" where Jerusalem is
now located, and where the future temple of Solomon would be built.

> Then Solomon began to build the house of the LORD at Jerusalem
> in mount Moriah, where the LORD appeared unto David his father, in
> the place that David had prepared in the threshing floor of Ornan the
> Jebusite.   (2 Chr. 3:1)

In that same geographic area, on one of Jerusalem's hills, Messiah
Yeshua would lay down His life.

Isaac was to be offered as "a burnt offering." Yeshua's sacrifice
was also a type of burnt offering. The instructions for that sacrifice, a
voluntary, free-will offering, are found in Leviticus 1:3–9.[3] Noting
how God really asked Abraham, "Please take..." we can see that
there was a voluntary aspect to it. Yeshua also stated that He was the
One who decided to submit to His Father and lay down His life:

> I am the good shepherd, and know my sheep, and am known of mine.
> As the Father knoweth me, even so know I the Father: and *I lay down
> my life for the sheep* ... Therefore doth my Father love me, because *I
> lay down my life*, that I might take it again. No man taketh it from me,
> but *I lay it down of myself. I have power* [of choice, liberty] *to lay it
> down*, and I have power to take it again. This commandment have I
> received of [accepted from] my Father.   (John 10:14–15, 17–18)

Other instructions for the burnt offering included that it should not
be killed by the priests, but by the offerer. Abraham was ready to offer
Isaac, and we will see that ultimately God the Father offered His Son.
Also, the sacrifice was to be totally consumed on God's altar. Isaac
was willing to die, and Yeshua did die at His Father's hand (Heb.
10:5–10).[4]

Finally, a burnt sacrifice made in obedient faith was a "sweet savor" pleasurable to God. What God asked both Abraham and Yeshua to do, in fact the whole system of animal sacrifices, was not the thing that God really desired, but the eventual outcome of all faithful sacrifices greatly pleased Him. As Yeshua prophetically declared,

> Sacrifice and offering thou didst not desire; mine ears hast thou opened: burnt offering and sin offering hast thou not required. Then said I, Lo, I come: in the volume of the book it is written of me, I delight to do thy will, O my God: yea, thy law is within my heart.
> (Ps. 40:6–8; see Heb. 10:5–12)[5]

The Hebrew of Genesis 22:2 gives another hint that points to Yeshua. The original for "offer him" literally means "lift him up," and can also mean "exalt him."[6] Yeshua was both. He was lifted up on the cross and exalted to the right hand of the Father.

Genesis 22:3–4

> And Abraham rose up early in the morning, and saddled his ass, and took two of his young men with him, and Isaac his son, and clave the wood for the burnt offering, and rose up, and went unto the place of which God had told him. Then on the third day Abraham lifted up his eyes, and saw the place afar off.

Abraham took three days to get to where God was leading him. Undoubtedly thoughts of Isaac and death were never far away. One might say that for three days Isaac was dead in his father's mind. Of course, Yeshua really was dead three days.

> Then opened he their understanding, that they might understand the scriptures [the *Tanach*], And said unto them, Thus it is written, and thus it behoved Messiah to suffer, and *to rise from the dead the third day*..."   (Luke 24:45–46)

> For I delivered unto you first of all that which I also received, how that Messiah died for our sins according to the scriptures [the *Tanach*]; And that he was buried, and that *he rose again the third day* according to the scriptures [the *Tanach*]...   (1 Cor. 15:3–4)

Genesis 22:5–6

> And Abraham said unto his young men, Abide ye here with the ass; and I and the lad will go yonder and worship [sacrificial obedience],

and come again to you. And Abraham took the wood of the burnt offering, and laid it upon Isaac his son; and he took the fire in his hand, and a knife; and they went both of them together.

Abraham burdened Isaac with the wood for the offering. Yeshua also bore on His back the wood of the cross used, in a sense, to "consume" His offering (see John 19:17).

Now to answer that crucial question: Who was responsible for Yeshua's crucifixion? As can be seen from the following verses, it was God the Father:

> The stone which the builders refused [rejected, despised] is become the head stone of the corner. *This is the* LORD*'s doing*; it is marvellous [extraordinary, beyond understanding] in our eyes.[7]
>
> (Psalm 118:22–23)

> All we like sheep have gone astray [erred, been deceived]; we have turned every one to his own way; and *the* LORD *hath laid*[8] *on him the iniquity*[9] *of us all ... Yet it pleased* [was willed by] *the* LORD *to bruise* [crush, break] *him; he hath put him to grief*: when thou shalt make his soul an offering for sin, he shall see his seed, he shall prolong his days, and the pleasure [will] of the LORD shall prosper [advance, succeed] in his hand.   (Isaiah 53:6, 10)

> Then said Yeshua unto Peter, Put up thy sword into the sheath: *the cup which my Father hath given me, shall I not drink it?*
>
> (John 18:11)

> Him, *being delivered by the determinate* [appointed, decreed] *counsel* [purpose, intention] *and foreknowledge of God*, ye have taken, and by wicked [lawless] hands have crucified and slain ...   (Acts 2:23)

> For of a truth against thy holy child Jesus, whom thou hast anointed, both Herod, and Pontius Pilate, with the Gentiles, and the people of Israel, were gathered together, For *to do whatsoever thy hand* [power] *and thy counsel* [purpose, intention] *determined before to be done.*
>
> (Acts 4:27–28)

Continuing in Genesis 22, we see that Abraham is the active player in the drama, while Isaac is passive. So too were God the Father and His Son as we see at Gethsemane:

> And he went a little further, and fell on his face, and prayed, saying, O my Father, if it be possible, let this cup pass from me: nevertheless *not as I will, but as thou wilt* ... He went away again the second time, and

> prayed, saying, O my Father, if this cup may not pass away from me,
> except I drink it, *thy will be done* ... [He] prayed the third time, saying
> the same words.   (Matt. 26:39, 42, 44b)

Genesis 22:7–8

> And Isaac spake unto Abraham his father, and said, My father: and he
> said, Here am I, my son. And he said, Behold the fire and the wood: but
> where is the lamb for a burnt offering? And Abraham said, My son,
> God will provide himself a lamb for a burnt offering: so they went both
> of them together.

"[B]ut where is the lamb ... ?" Isaac asked. Abraham's answer is
prophetic for what was about to happen that day and for what God
was going to do many centuries later. "God will provide [lit. see or
consider] himself a lamb ... " That statement could just as accurately
be written with "himself" capitalized, "God will provide Himself ... "! Prophetically, this was fulfilled when John the Baptizer
proclaimed about Yeshua, "Behold the Lamb of God, which taketh
away the sin of the world" (John 1:29b).

Genesis 22:9–10

> And they came to the place which God had told him of; and Abraham
> built an altar there, and laid the wood in order, and bound Isaac his
> son, and laid him on the altar upon the wood. And Abraham stretched
> forth his hand, and took the knife to slay his son.

Abraham and Isaac climbed to the top of Mount Moriah. There Abraham built the altar, placed the wood on it, bound Isaac, and took the
knife to kill him. Again and again in this foreshadow of the cross, we
see God the Father, symbolized by Father Abraham, as the One in
control. Isaac could have resisted. Instead he becomes a type of
the Greater Son who was willing to be "brought as a lamb to the
slaughter ... " (Isa. 53:7b).

Genesis 22:11–12

> And the angel of the LORD called unto him out of heaven, and said,
> Abraham, Abraham: and he said, Here am I. And he said, Lay not thine
> hand upon the lad, neither do thou any thing unto him: for now I know
> that thou fearest God, seeing thou hast not withheld thy son, thine only
> son from me.

Only at the last possible moment does God break in and prevent the sacrifice. The pre-incarnate Son of God speaks as "the Angel of the LORD,"[10] confirmed in verse 12, where the Angel identifies Himself as God when He says, "thou hast not withheld thy son, thine only son from me."

Dr J.H. Hertz, the late Chief Rabbi of Britain, makes an incisive comment about the issue of human sacrifice: "In that age, it was astounding that Abraham's God should have interposed to prevent the sacrifice, not that He should have asked for it."[11]

> If any man come to me, and hate not his father, and mother, and wife, and children, and brethren, and sisters, yea, and his own life also, he cannot be my disciple. And whosoever doth not bear his cross, and come after me, cannot be my disciple. (Luke 14:26–27)

Literal hate is not meant here, but a love that is less than that for Yeshua. Loving others more than loving God is idolatry.

Genesis 22:13

> And Abraham lifted up his eyes, and looked, and behold behind him a ram caught in a thicket by his horns: and Abraham went and took the ram, and offered him up for a burnt offering in the stead of his son.

God miraculously provides a ram that has his horns tangled in the bushes. This becomes an example of substitutionary sacrifice. The ram died in the place of Isaac just as Yeshua died in our place.

> For when we were yet without strength, in due time Messiah died for the ungodly. For scarcely for a righteous man will one die: yet peradventure for a good man some would even dare to die. But God commendeth [proved] his love toward us, in that, while we were yet sinners, Messiah died for us. (Rom. 5:6–8)

All of the animal sacrifices in the *Tanach* portrayed, in various ways, certain aspects of Yeshua dying for us sinners.

The Hebrew word for "ram" is not the same as the Hebrew word for "lamb." So although the ram is the God-given substitute for Isaac, it is not the fulfillment of that prophesied lamb that Abraham mentioned in verse 8 when he said that God would "provide himself a lamb."

Genesis 22:14

> And Abraham called the name of that place Jehovahjireh: as it is said to this day, In the mount of the LORD it shall be seen.

Or in the New King James Version,

> And Abraham called the name of the place, The-LORD-Will-Provide; as it is said ... In the Mount of The LORD it shall be provided.

That name looked forward to the day when the Lord Himself would provide the Lamb. And it was in that mountain, the mount of the Lord, that He did provide His Son. Dr Hertz translates the end of that verse as "where the LORD is seen" and then comments, "i.e., where He reveals himself..."[12] God ultimately revealed Himself in the Mount of the Lord through His Son Yeshua.

> Yeshua saith unto him, I am the way, the truth, and the life: no man cometh unto the Father, but by me. If ye had known me, ye should have known my Father also: and from henceforth ye know him, and have seen [perceived, known, become acquainted with] him.
>
> Philip saith unto him, Lord, shew us the Father, and it sufficeth [is enough for] us.
>
> Yeshua saith unto him, Have I been so long time with you, and yet hast thou not known me, Philip? he that hath seen me hath seen the Father; and how sayest thou then, Shew us the Father?
>
> (John 14:6–9)

Genesis 22:15–18

> And the angel of the LORD called unto Abraham out of heaven the second time, And said, By myself have I sworn, saith the LORD, for because thou hast done this thing, and hast not withheld thy son, thine only son: That in blessing I will bless thee, and in multiplying I will multiply thy seed as the stars of the heaven, and as the sand which is upon the sea shore; and thy seed shall possess [inherit, occupy] the gate of his enemies; And in thy seed shall all the nations of the earth be blessed; because thou hast obeyed my voice.

Finally, we have from the Angel a repeat of the promise God made to Abraham in Genesis 12:3 that through his seed the blessing of the Good News would come to the gentiles, to "all the nations of the earth." We see this fulfilled through Yeshua, descendant of Abraham, who came through the inheritors of the promise, the Jewish people.

Paul emphasizes to the Romans that when the Son of God manifested Himself in the flesh, it was as a member of the nation of Israel:

> Concerning his Son Yeshua the Messiah our Lord, which was made of the seed of David *according to the flesh* . . .   (Rom. 1:3)

> Who are Israelites; to whom pertaineth the adoption, and the glory, and the covenants, and the giving of the law, and the service of God, and the promises; Whose are the fathers, and of whom as *concerning the flesh* Messiah came, who is over all, God blessed for ever. Amen.   (Rom. 9:4–5)

And to the Galatians, he declares that the gospel to the gentiles was already proclaimed to Father Abraham,

> And the scripture [*Tanach*], foreseeing that God would justify the heathen through faith, preached before the gospel unto Abraham, saying [in Gen. 12:3], In thee shall all nations be blessed.   (Gal. 3:8)

A quote from Herbert Lockyer's excellent book *All the Messianic Prophecies of the Bible*[13] is a good way to summarize this section on the likeness of Yeshua revealed in Isaac: "Thus, in Isaac, we have a conspicuous type of Him who was freely 'delivered up for us all' and who was received from the dead by His Father (Rom. 8:32; 1 Tim. 3:16)."

The Bronze Serpent

Yeshua, talking to Nicodemus about being born again, points to the bronze serpent in the *Tanach* as a type of His death on the cross. What analogy was He making with this illustration? Look at the verses.

Yeshua said,

> And as Moses lifted up [or exalted] the serpent in the wilderness, even so [in this way] must the Son of man be lifted up: That whosoever believeth [have faith; put confidence] in him should not perish, but have eternal life.   (John 3:14–15)

Here is the story He was referring to:

> And the people spake against God, and against Moses, Wherefore have ye brought us up out of Egypt to die in the wilderness? for there is no bread, neither is there any water; and our soul loatheth [hates] this light [contemptible, worthless] bread.

> And the LORD sent fiery serpents among the people, and they bit the people; and much people of Israel died. Therefore the people came to Moses, and said, We have sinned, for we have spoken against the LORD, and against thee; pray [intercede] unto the LORD, that he take away the serpents from us. And Moses prayed [interceded] for the people.
>
> And the LORD said unto Moses, Make thee a fiery serpent, and set it upon a pole: and it shall come to pass, that every one that is bitten, when he looketh upon it, shall live. And Moses made a serpent of brass, and put it upon a pole, and it came to pass, that if a serpent had bitten any man, when he beheld the serpent of brass, he lived.
>
> (Num. 21:5–9)

From the Wisdom of Solomon Hertz quotes something that may shed light on why Yeshua related His approaching death to that incident in Israel's history. The Wisdom of Solomon, one of the apocryphal books written before 200 BC, says, "The brazen serpent was 'a token of salvation to put them in remembrance of the commandments of Thy Law, for he that turned toward it was not saved because of that which was beheld but because of Thee, the Savior of all'."[14]

Targum Pseudo-Jonathan, a well-known Aramaic translation/ commentary of Yeshua's day, states concerning Numbers 21:8–9, "He who lifted up his heart to the name of the Memra (i.e. the Word) of Jehovah, lived."[15] Why does this commentary seem to link the serpent on the pole to the Word of God? The answer may lie in the symbolism of the serpent as a curse.

The first occurrence of the word "curse" in Scripture occurs in the passage after the Fall of Man. God declares to the serpent, "thou art cursed . . . " (Gen. 3:14). The serpent has ever since been a symbol for the curse of sin. In the case of the serpent on the pole, we are reminded of the scriptures which state,

> And if a man have committed a sin worthy of death, and he be to be put to death, and thou hang him on a tree: His body shall not remain all night upon the tree, but thou shalt in any wise bury him that day; *for he that is hanged is accursed of God*;) that thy land be not defiled, which the LORD thy God giveth thee for an inheritance.   (Deut. 21:22–23)

And in Galatians 3:13, Paul says,

> Messiah hath redeemed us from the curse of [curse for breaking] the law, being made a curse for us: for it is written, *Cursed is every one that hangeth on a tree* . . .

We have read in Numbers 21 that God sent deadly serpents to bite the people because they loathed, they despised, His provision, calling the manna light or worthless bread (v. 5). That bread was a type of Yeshua, the bread from Heaven, as we read in John 6:31–35:

> Our fathers did eat manna in the desert; as it is written, He gave them bread from heaven to eat.
>
> Then Yeshua said unto them, Verily, verily, I say unto you, Moses gave you not that bread from heaven; but my Father giveth you the true bread from heaven. For the bread of God is he which cometh down [descends] from heaven, and giveth life unto the world.
>
> Then said they unto him, Lord, evermore give us this bread.
>
> And Yeshua said unto them, I am the bread of life: he that cometh to me shall never hunger; and he that believeth on me shall never thirst.

To despise Him, which is the sin of unbelief, leads to death by God's own hand of judgment, the greatest curse, as seen in Numbers 21:6. The New Testament adds this warning,

> Neither let us tempt Messiah, as some of them also tempted, and were destroyed of serpents.   (1 Cor. 10:9)

The word translated "tempt" means to entice, provoke, try to manipulate, from a root meaning "to pierce." When we entice, provoke, or try to manipulate God it is as though we are piercing Him. That is why Paul gave this serious warning.

God's swift response to His people's blasphemous remarks, withdrawing His protection, resulted in Israel's quick repentance: "We have sinned, for we have spoken against the LORD, and against thee [Moses]..." (21:7). Moses, always the compassionate leader, interceded for the people. God's answer seems strange, even to us who can now look at the anti-type of Yeshua's death:

> Make thee a fiery serpent, and set it upon a pole: and it shall come to pass, that every one that is bitten, when he looketh upon it, shall live.
>   (Num. 21:8)

The serpent was made of bronze, which throughout the Scriptures is symbolic of judgment. For example, the bronze altar in both the Tabernacle and the Temple was where the sacrifices for sin were offered, where judgment on sin was carried out.

The serpent was lifted up "upon a pole." *Nes*, the Hebrew word used here for "pole," can also mean standard, ensign, signal, banner, something lifted up and used as a rallying point. In many *Tanach* prophecies, that is the Hebrew word that stands for the future cross of Messiah! Here are a few examples:

> Thou hast given a banner [*nes*] to them that fear thee, that it may be displayed because of [in the face or presence of] the truth. Selah.
>   (Ps. 60:4)

> And in that day there shall be a root of Jesse, which shall stand for an *ensign* [*nes*] of the people; to it shall the Gentiles seek: and his rest shall be glorious. And it shall come to pass in that day, that the Lord shall set his hand again the second time to recover [possess] the remnant of his people, which shall be left ... And he shall set up [lift up, exalt] an *ensign* [*nes*] for the nations, and shall assemble [gather, receive] the outcasts of Israel, and gather together the dispersed [scattered] of Judah from the four corners of the earth.   (Isa. 11:10, 11a, 12)

> Thus saith the Lord GOD, Behold, I will *lift up* [exalt] mine hand[16] to the Gentiles, and set up my *standard* [*nes*] to the people: and they shall bring thy sons in their arms, and thy daughters shall be *carried* upon their shoulders.   (Isa. 49:22)

In the Hebrew, there is a poetic repetition of the word for "lift up" because it is also used for "carried."[17]

Returning to the comparison of Yeshua's death with the bronze serpent, the Greek for "lifted up" in John 3:14 can, as we have indicated, also be translated as "exalted." In that verse Yeshua compares His crucifixion to the lifting up of the bronze serpent. He was certainly hinting[18] that His crucifixion would result in His exaltation.

In the wilderness the Israelites who were already bitten were dying. God did not just heal them from a sickness, He delivered them from certain death by requiring their obedient looking at the uplifted serpent. The Hebrew for "looketh" (Num. 21:8), and "beheld" (21:9), although not the same word, have similar meanings. Both mean not just a physical glance, but beholding, considering, regarding. As you read these verses, all using one of these Hebrew words, you will obtain a better understanding of what the Lord desires:

> I sought the LORD, and he heard me, and delivered me from all my fears. They *looked* unto him, and were lightened: and their faces were not ashamed.   (Ps. 34:4–5)

> Open [uncover] thou mine eyes, that I may *behold* wondrous things out of thy law.[19]   (Ps. 119:18)

Hear,[20] ye deaf; and *look*, ye blind, that ye may see.   (Isaiah 42:18)

Hearken to me, ye that follow after [run after, pursue] righteousness, ye that seek [search out, strive after, desire] the LORD: *look* unto the rock whence ye are hewn, and to the hole of the pit whence ye are digged. *Look* unto Abraham your father, and unto Sarah that bare you: for I called him alone, and blessed him, and increased him.

(Isaiah 51:1–2)

Behold ye among the heathen, and *regard*, and wonder marvellously [be amazed, astonished]: for I will work a work in your days, which ye will not believe, though it be told you.   (Habakkuk 1:5)

And I will pour upon the house of David, and upon the inhabitants of Jerusalem, the spirit of grace and of supplications: and they shall *look* upon [better: "look to"] me whom they have pierced, and they shall mourn for him, as one mourneth for his only son, and shall be in bitterness for him, as one that is in bitterness for his firstborn.

(Zechariah 12:10)

Of all the *Tanach* symbolism of His death and resurrection, the serpent on the pole is the only one Yeshua used to illustrate His being lifted up on a cross. We believe that another reason He used it is found in 2 Corinthians 5:21 where Paul declares,

For he [God] hath made him [Messiah Yeshua] to be sin for us, [Messiah] who knew no sin; that we might be made the righteousness of God in him.

Since the Garden, the serpent has represented the Tempter, the temptation, and the curse of sin; he has become the personification of sin just as Yeshua is the personification of righteousness. We benefit from a brutal exchange on the cross – we gain Yeshua's righteousness by His taking upon Himself the death curse for our sin.

Finally, from a nineteenth-century commentary, "Among the Jews, the brazen serpent was considered a type of the resurrection – through it the dying lived . . . "[21]

Look [Turn] unto Me, and be ye saved, all the ends of the earth:
for I am God, and there is none else. I have sworn by Myself,
the word is gone out of My mouth in righteousness,
and shall not return, That unto Me every knee shall bow,
every tongue shall swear. Surely, shall one say,
in the LORD have I righteousness and strength: even to Him shall men come;

> and all that are incensed against Him shall be ashamed.
> In the LORD shall all the seed of Israel be justified,
> and shall glory [celebrate, boast].
> (Isa. 45:22–25)

Notes

1. Matt. 3:17; 2 Pet. 1:17.
2. H.L. Ellison, *Fathers of the Covenant* (R.N. Haynes Publishers, Inc., 1981), p. 53.
3. "If his offering be a burnt sacrifice of the herd, let him offer a male without blemish [complete, whole]: he shall offer it of his own voluntary will at the door of the tabernacle of the congregation before the LORD. And he shall put his hand upon the head of the burnt offering; and it shall be accepted for him to make atonement for him. And he shall kill the bullock before the LORD: and the priests, Aaron's sons, shall bring the blood, and sprinkle the blood round about upon the altar that is by the door of the tabernacle of the congregation. And he shall flay the burnt offering, and cut it into his pieces. And the sons of Aaron the priest shall put fire upon the altar, and lay the wood in order upon the fire: And the priests, Aaron's sons, shall lay the parts, the head, and the fat, in order upon the wood that is on the fire which is upon the altar: But his inwards and his legs shall he wash in water: and the priest shall burn all on the altar, to be a burnt sacrifice, an offering made by fire, of a sweet savour unto the LORD" (Lev. 1:3–9).
4. "Wherefore when he cometh into the world, he saith, Sacrifice and offering thou wouldest not, but a body hast thou prepared me: In burnt offerings and sacrifices for sin thou hast had no pleasure. Then said I, Lo, I come (in the volume of the book it is written of me,) to do thy will, O God.
   "Above when he said, Sacrifice and offering and burnt offerings and offering for sin thou wouldest not, neither hadst pleasure therein; which are offered by the law; Then said he, Lo, I come to do thy will, O God. He taketh away the first, that he may establish the second. By the which will we are sanctified through the offering of the body of Yeshua the Messiah once for all" (Heb. 10:5–10).
5. See also 1 Sam. 15:22; Jer. 7:21–23.
6. See the section on "The Bronze Serpent" following.
7. See Matt. 21:42; Mark 12:10–11; Luke 20:17; and Acts 4:11 for the New Testament confirmation that this verse is pointing to Messiah Yeshua's death.
8. This same Hebrew root can mean "to intercede."
9. In Hebrew, it means not just the iniquity itself, but also the consequence and/ or punishment of our iniquity.
10. See Chapter 14, section "The Angel of the LORD."
11. Dr J.H. Hertz, *The Pentateuch and Haftorahs* (Soncino Press, 1980), p. 201.
12. Ibid., p. 75.
13. Herbert Lockyer, *All the Messianic Prophecies of the Bible* (Zondervan Pub. House, 1973), p. 221.
14. Hertz, op. cit., p. 660.

15. Alfred Edersheim, *The Life and Times of Jesus the Messiah* (MacDonald Pub. Co.), p. 388.

16. The hand, or right hand, of God is often used in the *Tanach* as a metaphor of the coming Messiah.

17. It is easy to see Psalm 60:4 and Isaiah 11:10 as foreshadows of the cross, but what about the other verses from Isaiah about carrying Israel's sons and daughters? God is telling the Church that He wants them involved in regathering the Jewish people to the land of Israel. See Chapter 18, section "Mystery of Messiah" for a more detailed explanation.

18. See *remez*, Chapter 11, section "Psalm 22."

19. Here is our paraphrase from the Hebrew: "By revelation, show me things in Your Word that cannot be understood by human knowledge alone." Paul often talked about this – that God's revelation enabled him to understand Messiah and His Body. See Rom. 16:25; Gal. 1:12; 2:2; Eph. 1:17; 3:3.

20. In both the Hebrew and Greek, "hear" has the meaning of listening with the intention of obeying.

21. Adam Clarke, *Clarke's Commentary, Matthew–Revelation* (Abingdon Press), p. 533.

CHAPTER 13

The Resurrection

To the apostle Paul the resurrection of Messiah Yeshua is an integral part of the gospel. But was a resurrection by itself the proof that gave Paul and the other apostles and disciples such confidence? Did a resurrection miracle alone assure them that what they were proclaiming was from God? No, it was much more than that. Their proclamation of the Good News was based on Yeshua's resurrection as the confirmation and fulfillment of God's prophetic Word given throughout the *Tanach*. Their Good News was "according to the Scriptures..."

> Moreover, brethren, I declare unto you the gospel which I preached unto you, which also ye have received, and wherein ye stand; By which also ye are saved, if ye keep in memory what I preached unto you, unless ye have believed in vain. For I delivered [committed] unto you first of all that which I also received, how that Messiah died for our sins *according to the scriptures*; And that he was buried, and that he rose again the third day *according to the scriptures...*   (1 Cor. 15:1–4)

The importance of the *Tanach* to our faith bears repeating. The New Testament calls the *Tanach* "the Holy Scriptures."[1] In the days of Yeshua, the *Tanach* was the Holy Scripture. Yeshua preached from the Word of God, but He never read a word out of New Testament texts. New Testament teaching was in the process of being written down by the Spirit of God through the early Body of Messiah. The only way these first believers knew their teaching was from God was to compare its agreement with that Word of God which they already possessed, the *Tanach*. They would have been especially mindful of *Tanach* teachings concerning resurrection.

In the *Tanach* are a number of foreshadows, types, and teachings about the resurrection of the dead. The New Testament confirms the concept of resurrection and adds that, as believers, we will have glorified bodies like our resurrected Messiah. Even this amazing truth was hinted at previously.

There are many scriptures in the *Tanach* which had to be fulfilled by the Messiah. Some await fulfillment at His return and reign, but all the *Tanach* prophecies about Messiah being resurrected have been fulfilled by Yeshua.

New Testament and *Tanach* Resurrection

Many of the New Testament writers found evidence for a resurrection in the *Tanach*. The writer to the Hebrews knew by the Holy Spirit that Abraham believed God could raise Isaac from the dead if Isaac had been sacrificed:

> By faith Abraham, when he was tried [tested], offered up [lit: presented] Isaac: and he that had received the promises offered up his only begotten son ... Accounting [reckoning, considering] that God was able to raise him up, even from the dead; from whence also he received him in a figure [likeness]. (Heb. 11:17, 19)

Some rabbis believe Isaac died of terror when Abraham lifted the knife and that God then raised Isaac from the dead.[2] Although not scriptural, and we do not agree with it, this interpretation implies a strong belief in the resurrection of the dead.

To us, it seems a result of God's spiritual blinding of them (Rom. 11:25) that the rabbis could conceive of Isaac, but not the Messiah, raised from the dead. Isaac is a distinct type of Messiah Yeshua – the promised son whom his father loved; the son who carried his own wood on which he was to be offered; he whom his father was willing to sacrifice – and one whom some rabbis see as being resurrected![3]

Yeshua teaches about the resurrection of the dead when He speaks of Moses at the burning bush,

> Now *that the dead are raised, even Moses shewed* [intimated] at the bush, when he [God] calleth [Himself] the Lord the God of Abraham, and the God of Isaac, and the God of Jacob. For he is not a God of the dead, but of the living: for all live unto him.
> (Luke 20:37–38)

By using that *Tanach* verse, Exodus 3:6, Yeshua was stating that the forefathers were alive. Of course, their bodies were in the grave until Yeshua's resurrection, the event after which, according to Paul, Yeshua "took captivity captive" (Eph. 4:8; cf. Matt. 27:52–53).

The writer of Ecclesiastes agrees. He says that when a person dies,

> Then shall the dust return to the earth as it was: and the spirit shall return unto God who gave it.   (Eccl. 12:7)

And Paul in that great chapter on the resurrection, 1 Corinthians 15, also declares a similar belief.[4]

James Orr writes, "The point to be observed is that Jesus quotes this passage, not simply in proof of the continued subsistence of the patriarchs in some state of being, but in proof of the resurrection of the dead. And how does it prove that? Only on the ground, which Jesus assumes, that the relation of the believer to God carries with it a whole immortality, and this ... implies life in the body. If God is the God of Abraham and Isaac and Jacob, this covenant relation pledges to these patriarchs not only continuance of existence, but redemption from the power of death, i.e., resurrection."[5]

Tanach Examples of the Resurrection

In the *Tanach*, there are types but also examples of life after death, or, as in the case of Enoch and Elijah, heavenly life after earthly life. The translation from earth to heaven that these two men of God had before they died[6] can be viewed as *Tanach* examples of the first resurrection, or "rapture," referred to by Paul in 1 Corinthians 15:51–53 and 1 Thessalonians 4:13–17.

Elijah, by prayer, saw a widow's dead son restored to life.

> And he stretched himself upon the child three times, and cried unto the LORD, and said, O LORD my God, I pray thee [please], let this child's soul come into him again. And the LORD heard the voice of Elijah; and the soul of the child came into him again, and he revived.
>
> (1 Kgs. 17:21–22)

Elisha, whose many miracles often foreshadow the miracles of Yeshua (feeding the multitudes; causing an axe-head to "walk on water"; healing lepers), also raised a dead boy to life and returned him to his mother (2 Kgs. 4:32–35). Compare that to the following miracle in the ministry of our Messiah:

> And he came and touched the bier: and they that bare him stood still. And he said, Young man, I say unto thee, Arise. And he that was dead sat up, and began to speak. And he delivered him to his mother.

And there came a fear on all: and they glorified God, saying, That a
great prophet is risen up among us; and, That God hath visited his
people.   (Luke 7:14–16)

In 2 Kings 13:20–21, when a dead man was placed in the same
cave and touched the bones of Elisha, that man came back to life.
Even after death, God used this prophet to bring life. The picture is
clear – all who "touch" Yeshua, the Prophet sent from God,[7] after His
death also receive life.

Of course, Elisha's body remained in the grave at least until after
Messiah's resurrection when many of the saints who had died were
raised bodily[8] (maybe Elisha was one of them) to ultimately ascend,
following Messiah to heaven.

Wherefore he saith, When he ascended up on high, he led captivity
captive, and gave gifts unto men.   (Eph. 4:8)

Tanach Teaching on the Resurrection

The book of Job contains a number of references to life after death.
Believing that Job lived at the time of Abraham, many scholars think
the book to be one of the oldest in the Scriptures.

If any saint needed assurance of a better life to come it was Job. He
makes some of the strongest *Tanach* statements about resurrection,
even applying it to himself,

For I know that my redeemer [kinsman-redeemer] liveth, and that he
shall stand [rise] at the latter day [or "the last days"] upon the earth:
And though after my skin [mortality][9] worms destroy this body, yet in
my flesh shall I see God: Whom I shall see for myself, and mine eyes
shall behold, and not another; though my reins [mind] be consumed
within me.   (Job 19:25–27)

Job is speaking about a bodily resurrection from the dead. Although
the Hebrew of this passage is difficult, there is no doubt that he is
stating a belief in life after death and that he has a Redeemer who will
vindicate and save him.

Earlier, Job had already referred to his being changed in the
resurrection,

If a man die, shall he live again? all the days of my appointed time [lit:
warfare; army service!] will I wait [hope, expect], till my change
[renewal] come.   (Job 14:14)

Paul agrees in 1 Corinthians 15:35–44, saying that our resurrected bodies will not be the same as our current bodies. Not only does the Bible give us these two voices, but here is a third witness to this truth – King David:

> As for me, I will behold thy face in righteousness: I shall be satisfied, when I awake, with thy likeness.　　　　　　　　　　(Ps. 17:15)

This affirms a resurrection with glorified bodies like Yeshua's.

On *Shavuot* the Spirit of God was poured out on the disciples who were waiting in obedience to the Lord's last command. Then Peter proclaimed the gospel with power to the Jewish multitudes by using many *Tanach* verses. Referring to the resurrection, he quoted Psalm 16:9–11 (Acts 2:29–32),

> Therefore my heart [inner man] is glad, and my glory rejoiceth: my flesh [body] also shall rest [abide, dwell] in hope [lit: safety, security]. For thou wilt not leave my soul [*nephesh* – life, that which breathes] in hell [*sheol* = grave, pit; metaphor for death]; neither wilt thou suffer [permit] thine Holy One to see corruption [pit, animal trap; metaphor for destruction]. Thou wilt shew me the path of life: in thy presence is fulness of joy; at thy right hand there are pleasures for evermore.

After three days a dead body has begun to stink with decay, of which Martha tries to remind Yeshua in John 11:39. But Yeshua Himself was raised at or before dawn of the third day. In truth God did not allow His "Holy One to see corruption."

Other places in the Psalms also refer to resurrection. David wrote,

> O LORD, thou hast brought up my soul [*nephesh* = life, being] from the grave [*Sheol* = fig. death]: thou hast kept me alive, that I should not go down to the pit.　　　　　　　　　　(Ps. 30:3)

Though David was speaking figuratively about death, since the context is his healing, his mind was dwelling on resurrection.

Here are several other verses:

> But God will redeem [ransom, rescue, deliver] my soul [life, being] from the power of the grave: for he shall receive [take] me. Selah.
> 　　　　　　　　　　　　　　　　　　　　(Ps. 49:15)

> Thou, which hast shewed me great and sore troubles, shalt quicken me again [return me to life], and shalt bring me up again from the depths of the earth.　　　　　　　　　　(Ps. 71:20)

Thou shalt guide me with thy counsel, and afterward receive [take] me
to glory. (Ps. 73:24)

The prophets make some strong declarations about the resurrection. For example, Isaiah says,

Thy dead men shall live, together with my dead body shall they
arise. Awake and sing [shout for joy], ye that dwell in dust: for thy
dew is as the dew of herbs, and the earth shall cast out the dead.
(Isa. 26:19)

Kimchi, a noted Jewish commentator, states that these words concern
the days of the Messiah.[10]

Revelation 20:5–6 indicates that there will be two resurrections,

But the rest of the dead lived not again until the thousand years were
finished. This is the first resurrection. Blessed and holy is he that hath
part in the first resurrection: on such the second death hath no power,
but they shall be priests of God and of Messiah, and shall reign with
him a thousand years.

But does the idea of two resurrections have support in the *Tanach*?
Daniel also refers to the concept of a double resurrection,

And many of them that sleep in the dust of the earth shall awake, some
to everlasting life, and some to shame and everlasting contempt.
(Dan. 12:2)

The New Testament confirms this. Yeshua speaking about the
"sheep" and "goats" before His throne of judgment says,

And these shall go away into everlasting punishment: but the righteous
into life eternal. (Matt. 25:46)

Proclamations and Prophecies of Resurrection[11]

Maimonides' thirteen principles of faith are the closest thing Judaism
has to a creed. The final one is, "I believe with perfect faith that there
will be a revival of the dead at the time when it shall please the
Creator..."[12]

We have already mentioned that some rabbis believe Isaac died and
was resurrected when Abraham was willing to sacrifice him. They
also hint at Jonah being resurrected.[13] Jonah cried out to God from
his "grave," at least figuratively in the as-good-as-dead sense.

> Then Jonah prayed unto the LORD his God out of the fish's belly, And
> said, I cried by reason of mine affliction unto the LORD, and he heard
> me; out of the belly of hell [Sheol = grave, death] cried I, and thou
> heardest my voice . . . I went down to the bottoms of the mountains; the
> earth with her bars was about me for ever: yet hast thou brought up my
> life from corruption [the pit, grave, fig. destruction], O LORD my God.
> (Jon. 2:1–2, 6)

Why did Yeshua say Jonah's three days in the "fish" would be the
only confirming sign given to His generation? Because it pointed to
His resurrection.

> But he answered and said unto them, An evil and adulterous genera-
> tion seeketh after [desires] a sign [token, miracle – here and following];
> and there shall no sign be given to it, but the sign of the prophet
> [Jonah]: For as [Jonah] was three days and three nights in the whale's
> belly; so shall the Son of man be three days and three nights in the heart
> of the earth.   (Matt. 12:39–40; see Jon. 1:17)

Was the rabbinical belief in Jonah's resurrection current in Yeshua's
day? We don't know for sure, but if it was, then His use of Jonah was
directly to the point.

Ezekiel's vision of the valley of dry bones (Ezek. 37:7–10) points
to a resurrection of the whole house of Israel. Whether that passage
is meant to be taken literally, figuratively, or both ways, it proclaims
an understanding of God's ability by His Spirit to raise the dead to
life.

The same chapter of Ezekiel contains the Passover week *Shabbat
Haftorah* portion, a selection from the Prophets which is read with
the weekly *Torah* portion in synagogues. These Haftorah selections
were first developed before Yeshua's day, during the time of the
Maccabees, when Jews were not allowed to read the "Law." These
same readings were probably in use during Yeshua's day.[14] Where
was Yeshua after His crucifixion during the *Shabbat* of the Passover
week? In the grave. So on the yearly *Shabbat* of the Hebrew calendar
when the Messiah was in the grave, Jewish people are reading Ezekiel
37 and thinking about resurrection!

Yeshua's resurrection fulfilled a Jewish holy day, a day that the
Lord proclaimed as His *moed*,[15] a feast of the Lord. This specific feast
is called the "Firstfruits" of the barley harvest (see Lev. 23:9–14).
Paul refers to this in 1 Corinthians 15, where he calls Messiah "the
firstfruits" twice,

But now is Messiah risen from the dead, and become the firstfruits of them that slept. For since by man came death, by man came also the resurrection of the dead. For as in Adam all die, even so in Messiah shall all be made alive. But every man in his own order: Messiah the firstfruits; afterward they that are Messiah's at his coming.

(1 Cor. 15:20–23)

Finally, we see two powerful verses on resurrection in the book of the prophet Hosea. Chapter 6 has a reference to being raised from the dead on the third day:

Come, and let us return unto the LORD: for he hath torn, and he will heal us; he hath smitten, and he will bind us up. After two days will he revive us: in the third day he will raise us up, and we shall live in his sight [lit. to His face; fig. in His presence]. (Hos. 6:1–2)

In Hosea 13:14a we have one of God's most far-reaching promises concerning His ultimate victory over the last enemy – death,[16]

I will ransom [lit. sever; fig. rescue, deliver] them from the power of the grave; I will redeem them [as a kinsman-redeemer] from death: O death, I will be thy plagues; O grave, I will be thy destruction...

Why should it be thought a thing incredible with you,
that God should raise the dead?
(Acts 26:8)

Notes

1. See the following verses to confirm this fact: Matt. 21:42; 22:29; Luke 24:27, 44–46; John 5:39; 19:36–37; Acts 8:32–35; 17:10–11; Rom. 1:1–2; 16:25–26; Gal. 3:8; 2 Tim. 3:15–17. (See Chapter 1 on the *Tanach*'s relation to the New Testament.)
2. Louis Ginzberg, *Legends of the Bible*, Abridged Edn (Jewish Publication Society of America, 1909), p. 133.
3. See Chapter 13 section "The Binding of Isaac."
4. See 1 Cor. 15:20–24, 35–38, 42–44, 51–54.
5. *Classical Evangelical Essays in OT Interpretation*, "Immortality in the Old Testament" by James Orr, ed. by Walter C. Kaiser Jr (Baker Book House Co., 1972), pp. 258–259.
6. See Gen. 5:22–24 and 2 Kgs. 2:11.
7. See Chapter 8, "A Prophet Like Moses."
8. Matt. 27:52–53: "And the graves were opened; and many bodies of the saints which slept arose, And came out of the graves after his resurrection, and went into the holy city, and appeared unto many."

9. Skin in Scripture is often used as a symbol for mortality. God "covered" Adam and Eve with mortality, represented by the skins of dead animals (Gen. 3:21). The animal skins were to signify Adam's and Eve's own sure death as well as to remind them of the efficacy of blood sacrifice. God killed the animals, shedding blood, then used their skins as a covering (the literal meaning of atonement). Thus our first parents lived for many more years before death took its toll.

10. Clarke's Commentary, Vol. IV (Nashville: Abingdon Press), p. 118.

11. In Chapters 10 and 11, we examined the resurrection of Israel's Messiah as prophesied in Isaiah 53 and Psalm 22.

12. Dr Joseph H. Hertz, *The Authorised Daily Prayer Book* (NY: Bloch Pub. Co., 1948), p. 255.

13. Rev. Dr A. Cohen (ed.), *The Twelve Prophets* (Soncino Press, 1948), pp. 144–145.

14. Some scholars think that Luke 4 could be an example of this.

15. *Moed* is the Hebrew word translated in Leviticus 23 as "feast." It is more than a holiday. It is a time divinely appointed by God during which He meets with His people.

16. See 1 Cor. 15:26.

CHAPTER 14

The Deity of Messiah

It is difficult to comprehend the New Testament claim that God came in the flesh as Yeshua our Messiah. This chapter, while not an attempt to explain the incarnation scientifically, will show that the *Tanach* points to a divine, as well as human, Messiah.

I and the Father Are One

Yeshua is not the Father, but as the promised Messiah He must be Deity – God in the flesh. He authoritatively declares in John 14:9b, "he that hath seen[1] me hath seen the Father . . . " He had previously stated in John 10:30, "I and my Father are one," and repeats that claim in His prayer in John 17:11, 21–22. There can be no doubt that Yeshua knew Himself to be one with the Father. Since most of the formal education of Yeshua and his audience centered on the *Tanach*, we must understand the concept of "one" within that framework.

Two biblical Hebrew words can be translated as "one" in English. *Yachid* means "one" in the sense of singular, indivisible, the only one (Gen. 22:2 and Judg. 11:34: "only"), and is not used often in Scripture. The other word translated as "one," *echad*, "stresses unity while recognizing diversity within that oneness,"[2] and is an important word/concept throughout the *Tanach*.

Here are several examples in which the word translated "one," *echad*, indicates the concept of diversity in unity.

One "day" includes both day and night.

> And God called the light Day, and the darkness he called Night. And the evening and the morning were the *first* [one] day.   (Gen. 1:5)

Marriage joins two people in a relationship so close that God says they are one flesh.

> Therefore shall a man leave his father and his mother, and shall cleave
> unto [join closely with] his wife: and they shall be one flesh.
>
> (Gen. 2:24)

When the numerous people of Israel were united, they spoke with
"one voice."

> And Moses came and told the people all the words of the LORD, and all
> the judgments: and all the people answered with *one* voice, and said,
> All the words which the LORD hath said will we do.   (Exod. 24:3)[3]

Considering that definition of *echad*, look at the most important
commandment in both Judaism and Christianity, the *Sh'ma*
("Hear!"),

> Hear, O Israel: The LORD our God is *one* LORD [lit: LORD is one/
> *echad*]: And thou shalt love the LORD thy God with all thine heart, and
> with all thy soul, and with all thy might.
>
> (Deut. 6:4–5; cf. Mark 12:28–30)

Moses, inspired by God's Spirit, used *echad* to describe God's nature
in the *Sh'ma* as a diversity in unity.

Yeshua, speaking according to *Tanach* Hebraic thought, said, "I
and my Father are *one*" (John 10:30). Yeshua is not the Father, but is
one with the Father in a unique way. If the Father is God, can Yeshua,
who claims unity with Him, be less than divine? The Jews rightly
understood His statement as a claim to Deity.

> Then the Jews took up stones again to stone him. Yeshua answered
> them, Many good works have I shewed you from my Father; for which
> of those works do ye stone me? The Jews answered him, saying, For a
> good work we stone thee not; but for blasphemy; and because that
> *thou, being a man, makest thyself God.*   (John 10:31–33)

And if Yeshua is not God in the flesh, then according to God's law, He
should have been stoned to death.

The Angel of the LORD

John 1:18 states,

> No man hath seen God at any time; *the only begotten Son*, which is in
> the bosom of the Father, he *hath declared him.*

It is clear from this verse and others, for example, Exodus 33:20b, in which God says to Moses, "Thou canst not see my face: for there shall no man see me, and live," that *no man has ever seen God* with his physical eyes. But we have many recorded appearances of God in the *Tanach*. Who did those Old Testament saints see? According to John's statements in 1:1 and 1:18, it must have been the pre-incarnate Son/Word of God declaring or revealing Him.

Yeshua seemed to appear as a different person to some of His followers after assuming His glorified state.[4] This was nothing new, since He had appeared in different manifestations before the incarnation. One of the most frequent was as "The Angel [lit: Messenger] of the LORD." In the Bible, in both the Hebrew and the Greek, the word translated "angel" is also translated "messenger." Scriptures show that this Angel explicitly identifies Himself with, and was called by, God's personal name (see below – The Name of God). He was also recognized by people as divine and received worship. This particular Angel carried the authority of God into the world of men, yet was inseparable from God in Heaven. The following scriptures, among others, identify this Angel as God.

Genesis 32:4 relates that Jacob wrestled with a "Man" whom he identified as God in 32:30,

> And Jacob called the name of the place Peniel: for I have seen God face to face, and my life is preserved.

Later, the prophet Hosea identifies this Man/God as the Angel:

> He took his brother by the heel in the womb, and by his strength he [Jacob] had power [prevailed] with God: Yea, he had power over *the angel*, and prevailed: he wept, and made supplication unto him: he found him in Bethel, and there he spake with us... (Hos. 12:3–4)

Hosea goes on to proclaim in 12:5 that this God/Angel is "Even the LORD God of hosts; the LORD [personal name of God] is his memorial."

In Genesis 48:15–16, Jacob on his deathbed makes a comparison between God and the Angel, stating that they are one. Although he starts with God, he ends asking that "The Angel"[5] would bless his grandsons in a way that only God would be able to do,

> And he [Jacob] blessed Joseph, and said, God, before whom my fathers Abraham and Isaac did walk, the God which fed [shepherded] me all my life long unto this day, *The Angel* which redeemed me from all evil, bless the lads; and let my name be named on them, and the name of my

fathers Abraham and Isaac; and let them grow into a multitude in the midst of the earth.

In describing his encounter with God, Moses wrote in Exodus 3:2a, "And *the angel* of the LORD appeared unto him in a flame of fire out of the midst of a bush..." Then in verse 4b, he said, "God called unto him out of the midst of the bush." He who was originally called "the angel of the LORD" goes on to identify Himself in verse 6b declaring, "I am the God of thy father, the God of Abraham, the God of Isaac, and the God of Jacob..."

When reading Exodus 23:20–23, it is important to understand that in biblical Hebraic thought "the name was considered to be a description of the essential nature of the person or thing..."[6] God says that He is sending an angel before Israel to guard them as they travel and bring them to the land He has promised to give them. But in verse 21, God declares,

> Beware of [Give heed to] him [the Angel], and obey his voice, provoke him not; for he will not pardon your transgressions [rebellions]: for *my name is in him.*

One could say that the essential nature of this Angel was the Name of the Lord. This Angel had God's Name, His "essential nature," in Him.

In a beautiful portion of Isaiah, the prophet portrays this Angel as Israel's Savior, Redeemer, and Shepherd, the One who carried them through life:

> For he said, Surely they are my people, children that will not lie [deal falsely]: so he was their Saviour. In all their affliction [trouble] he was afflicted, and *the angel* [messenger] *of his presence* saved them: in his love and in his pity [mercy] he redeemed them; and he bare them, and carried them all the days of old.   (Isa. 63:8–9)

One final example is found in Malachi 3:1:

> Behold, I will send my *messenger* [or angel], and he shall prepare the way before me: and the Lord, whom ye seek, shall suddenly come to his temple, even *the messenger* [or the Angel] of the covenant, whom ye delight in: behold, he shall come, saith the LORD of hosts.[7]

Notice that the temple is "his," the Lord's/Angel's, temple.

The Angel of the Lord revealed God to many *Tanach* saints. They saw, touched and talked with Him. According to John 1:18, this

Angel must have been the pre-incarnate Son/Word of God who finally entered the world as Yeshua.

The Name of God

We want to emphasize again what "name" in biblical Hebraic thinking means. "The concept of personal names in the OT often included existence, character and reputation (1 Sam. 25:25)."[8] "Declaring one's name was a chief means of revealing or manifesting oneself."[9]

Here are two of many examples. Through Moses, God states to Pharaoh,

> And in very deed for this cause have I raised thee up, for to shew in thee my power; and that *my name* may be declared throughout all the earth.
>
> (Exod. 9:16)

In fear the Hivites lied to Joshua about their home territory. As God said in the verse quoted above, fear of Him had fallen on them because they heard what He had done in Egypt.

> And they said unto him, From a very far country thy servants are come because of the *name* of the LORD thy God: for we have heard the *fame* of him, and all that he did in Egypt.   (Josh. 9:9)

Their declaration concerning God's name is true, and note the conceptual parallel[10] between "name" and "fame."

The meaning of "name" in Hebrew is another strong proof of the divinity of the promised Messiah. In Isaiah 9:6b Messiah is prophesied to be more than a man because His name – that which He will be – shall be proclaimed as, "Wonderful, Counsellor, The mighty God, The everlasting Father, The Prince of Peace." Also Isaiah 7:14b informs us that the name of the virgin's Son would be called "Immanuel," which means His essential nature would be "God with us" as Matthew 1:23 confirms.

YHWH – God's Personal Name

Some believers do not know that God constantly uses His personal name in the *Tanach*. "One of the most fundamental and essential features of the biblical revelation is the fact that God ... has a personal name..."[11] His name of four letters, the tetragrammaton, is composed of the four Hebrew letters – *yod, hay, vav* and *hay*. In some translations and commentaries it is written Yahweh or YHWH. However, in most Bible versions God's Name in Hebrew is translated "LORD" (infrequently "Jehovah" or "Yah" or "GOD").

Most of the following verses use "the LORD." We have eliminated the added "the" because it is not found in the original scriptures. Doing so gives a much better sense of God revealing His personal name. So you will see just "LORD" instead of "the LORD" in these verses.

Genesis 12:7–8 is one of the foundational scriptures concerning the promise of the Land of Israel to Abraham's descendants:

> And LORD appeared unto Abram, and said, Unto thy seed [offspring] will I give this land: and there builded he an altar unto LORD, who appeared unto him. And he removed [moved on] from thence unto a mountain on the east of Bethel ... and there he builded an altar unto LORD, and called upon the name of LORD.

In Exodus 33:18, Moses begged God to show him His glory. God said Moses would have to be satisfied with having Him proclaim His name (33:19) because no one could see His glory and live (33:20–22). Exodus 34:5–6 describes what happened:

> And LORD descended in the cloud, and stood with him there, and proclaimed the name of LORD. And LORD passed by before him, and proclaimed, LORD, LORD God, merciful and gracious, longsuffering, and abundant in goodness [*chesed*] and truth.

Note how God proclaims His name as His nature.

Throughout Leviticus 18:1–22, God's reason for expecting Israel to obey His commands is based on who He is. In that short section, He states thirty-two times that "I am LORD."

The Aaronic benediction found in Numbers 6:22–27 is one of the more traditional blessings heard in both church and synagogue. Reread it here with the concept of God's name in mind:

> And LORD spake unto Moses, saying, Speak unto Aaron and unto his sons, saying, On this wise ye shall bless the children of Israel, saying unto them, LORD bless thee, and keep [guard] thee: LORD make his face shine upon thee, and be gracious unto thee: LORD lift up his countenance [face] upon thee, and give thee peace. [12] And they shall put *my name* upon the children of Israel; and I will bless them.

Look at the *Sh'ma* again and focus on the use of "LORD":

Hear, O Israel: LORD our God is one LORD: And thou shalt love LORD
thy God with all thine heart, and with all thy soul, and with all thy
might.   (Deut. 6:4–5)

One of the best examples of the use of God's proper name is
Elijah's challenge to the people of Israel and their response once the
fire of LORD fell:

And Elijah came unto all the people, and said, How long halt [hop;
skip] ye between two opinions? if LORD be God, follow him: but if
Baal, then follow him. And the people answered him not a word ...
Then the fire of LORD fell, and consumed the burnt sacrifice, and the
wood, and the stones, and the dust, and licked up the water that was in
the trench. And when all the people saw it, they fell on their faces: and
they said, LORD, he is the God; LORD, he is the God.

(1 Kgs. 18:21, 38–39)

Is it not appropriate that Elijah's name means "My God is YHWH?"
The Psalms contain many excellent examples of the use of God's
personal name. See this endnote for some of the more pertinent
verses.[13]
Through His *Tanach* prophets God uses His personal name
consistently to make sure that everyone understands that He is the
only true and living God.

I am LORD, *that is my name*; and my glory will I not give to another ...
(Isa. 42:8a)

Therefore, behold, I will this once cause them to know, I will cause
them to know mine hand and my might; and *they shall know that my
name is* LORD.   (Jer. 16:21)

Thus saith LORD the maker thereof, LORD that formed it, to establish
it; LORD *is his name* ...   (Jer. 33:2)

So will I make *my holy name* known in the midst of my people Israel;
and I will not let them pollute [profane; defile] *my holy name* any
more: and the heathen [gentiles] shall know that *I am* LORD, the Holy
One in Israel.   (Ezek. 39:7)

And I will bring the third part through the fire, and will refine them as
silver is refined, and will try [test; prove] them as gold is tried: they
shall call on *my name*, and I will hear them: I will say, It is my people:
and *they shall say,* LORD *is my God.*   (Zech. 13:9)

Elohim is another Hebrew word for "God." It literally means "mighty ones," and is usually translated as "God," "gods" or "judges," but the Hebrew word YHWH, or "LORD," is never used for anyone other than God. How many times does the *Tanach* use God's personal name, "YHWH?" According to the Logos Bible Software Program, a total of 6,668 times!

YHWH – The Name of God's Son

The use of "LORD" in the following verses applies to God the Father but can also be linked to God the Son, in essence declaring that the nature of the pre-incarnate Son is the same as the nature of His Father. Genesis 18:1a says, "And LORD appeared unto [Abraham] ... "; verse 22b, "Abraham stood yet before LORD." Again, according to John 1:18 which states that no one can see God and live, the only "LORD" with whom Abraham could have had a face-to-face encounter is the Son, the pre-incarnate Word of God.

The Good Shepherd

The Jewish apostle Peter[14] writes to believers that Yeshua is "the Shepherd and Bishop [Overseer] of your souls" (1 Pet. 2:25b). In John 10:11 and 14 Yeshua Himself proclaims that He is the Good Shepherd:

> *I am the good shepherd*: the good shepherd giveth his life for the sheep ... *I am the good shepherd*, and know my sheep, and am known of mine.

What does the *Tanach* say about this Shepherd?

Psalm 23:1 is the best-known verse for the *Tanach* identification of Israel's Shepherd as "LORD":

> LORD *is my shepherd*; I shall not want.

Isaiah 40:10–11 comes within the context of a prophecy of Messiah Yeshua's first coming. Verses 1 and 2 command "comfort" to Jerusalem because her iniquity is forgiven; verse 3 prophesies of John the Baptist as the voice in the wilderness; verses 6 to 8 proclaim that only God's Word endures forever; verse 9 says to Judah, "Behold your God!" And then verses 10–11 identify this One as Israel's Shepherd:

Behold, the Lord GOD [YHWH] will come with strong hand, and his arm shall rule for him: behold, his reward is with him, and his work before him. He shall feed his flock like a *shepherd*: he shall gather the lambs with his arm, and carry them in his bosom, and shall gently lead those that are with young.

Note that Israel's Shepherd is identified here as Lord GOD [YHWH].[15]

Asaph, the author of Psalm 80, calls on the "Shepherd of Israel" in verse 1,

Give ear, O *Shepherd* of Israel, thou that leadest Joseph like a flock; thou that dwellest between the cherubims, shine forth.

He identifies this One as YHWH God in verse 4,

O LORD God of hosts, how long wilt thou be angry against the prayer of thy people?

Asaph presents this image in Psalm 78:52 as well.

Seeing the unity between Israel's Shepherd and Israel's God helps us as we read John 10:24–33. Now we can grasp the instant reaction of the religious leaders to Yeshua's declaration that, because He is that Shepherd, He and the Father are one:

Then came the Jews . . . and said unto him, How long dost thou make us to doubt? If thou be the Messiah, tell us plainly. Yeshua answered them, I told you, and ye believed not: the works that I do in my Father's *name*, they bear witness of me. But ye believe not, because ye are not of *my sheep* . . . My *sheep* hear my voice, and I know them, and they follow me: And I give unto them eternal life; and they shall never perish, neither shall any man pluck [seize by force] them out of my hand. My Father, which gave them me, is greater than all; and no man is able to pluck them out of my Father's hand. *I and my Father are one.*

Then the Jews took up stones again to stone him.

Yeshua answered them, Many good works have I shewed you from my Father; for which of those works do ye stone me?

The Jews answered him, saying, For a good work we stone thee not; but for blasphemy . . . because that *thou, being a man, makest thyself God.*

The King

The New Testament declares that Yeshua is King of the Jews and of the world.

Where is he that is born *King of the Jews?* ...   (Matt. 2:2a)

Then shall the *King* say unto them on his right hand, Come, ye blessed
of my Father ...   (Matt. 25:34a)

Nathanael answered and saith unto him, Rabbi, thou art the Son of
God; *thou art the King of Israel.*   (John 1:49)

On the next day much people that were come to the feast [Passover],
when they heard that Yeshua was coming to Jerusalem, Took branches
of palm trees, and went forth to meet him, and cried, Hosanna [lit:
Save now!]: Blessed is *the King of Israel* that cometh *in the name of the
Lord* [from Ps. 118:25–26]. And Yeshua, when he had found a young
ass, sat thereon; as it is written, Fear not, daughter of Sion: behold,
thy King cometh, sitting on an ass's colt [from Zech. 9:9].

                                                                (John 12:12–15)

These shall make war with the Lamb, and the Lamb shall overcome
them: for he is Lord of lords, and *King of kings*: and they that are with
him are called, and chosen, and faithful.   (Rev. 17:14)

But who is the King of Israel in the *Tanach?*
   In Isaiah 44:6 God describes Himself as the *King of Israel*:

Thus saith LORD the *King of Israel*, and his redeemer LORD of hosts
[armies]; I am the first, and I am the last; and beside me there is no
God.

We will explore this verse in depth in the next two sections. It is a key
scripture for understanding Yeshua's divinity.

First and Last

In our key verse from the *Tanach*, Isaiah 44:6, quoted above, God
also calls Himself "the first" and "the last." He uses the same phrases
in Isaiah 48:12,

Hearken unto me, O Jacob and Israel, my called; I am he; *I am the first,
I also am the last.*

   In the New Testament book of Revelation Yeshua calls Himself by
the title of "the first and the last" at least four times:

I am Alpha and Omega, *the first and the last* ...   (Rev. 1:11a)

And when I saw him, I fell at his feet as dead. And he laid his right hand upon me, saying unto me, Fear not; *I am the first and the last* . . .

(Rev. 1:17)

And unto the angel of the church in Smyrna write; These things saith *the first and the last,* which was dead, and is alive . . . (Rev. 2:8)

I am Alpha and Omega, the beginning and the end, *the first and the last.* (Rev. 22:13)

If He is the first and the last, He must also be eternal. By using the same title found in that key scripture from Isaiah, "Thus saith LORD the King of Israel, and his redeemer LORD of hosts; I am the first, and I am the last . . . ," Yeshua is proclaiming His deity through *remez/* hinting, for the verse ends with, "and beside me there is no God."

LORD of Hosts

Our key verse from Isaiah includes the title "LORD of hosts." Zechariah 2:8–12 contains some verses that might cause one to believe that there are two LORDs of Hosts! In verse 2:8, LORD of Hosts says to Israel that Someone else has sent Him to the gentiles,

For *thus saith* LORD *of hosts*; After the glory *hath he sent me* unto the nations [or gentiles] which spoiled you: for he that toucheth [strikes] you toucheth the apple [pupil] of his eye.

The same LORD of Hosts goes on to say,

For, behold, I will shake mine hand upon them, and they shall be a spoil to their servants: and ye shall know that LORD *of hosts hath sent me.* Sing [Shout] and rejoice, O daughter of Zion: for, lo, I come, and I will dwell in the midst of thee, saith LORD. And *many nations* [gentiles] *shall be joined* [united] to LORD in that day, and shall be my people: and I will dwell in the midst of thee, and thou shalt know that LORD *of hosts hath sent me* unto thee. And LORD shall inherit Judah his portion in the holy land, and shall choose Jerusalem again. (Zech. 2:9–12)

How many "LORD of Hosts" are there? Yeshua is LORD of Hosts who is speaking because he repeatedly states in the gospels that God has sent Him[16] and He is also the One who has enabled many gentiles to become part of God's family, Israel's Olive Tree (Rom. 11:17–18).[17] Yeshua is God and LORD of Hosts, but He is not identical to His Father, who sent Him, who is also God and LORD of Hosts.[18] This is why Yeshua could say, "for my Father is greater than I," and still not deny His own deity (John 14:28b).

Zechariah 14:16 ends with a vision of God's kingdom on earth:

> And it shall come to pass, that every one that is left of all *the nations* which came against Jerusalem shall even go up from year to year to *worship the King, LORD of hosts,* and to keep the feast of tabernacles.

The book of Revelation identifies this King as "King of saints" and "Lord God Almighty":

> And they sing the song of Moses the servant of God, and the song of the Lamb, saying, Great and marvellous are thy works, *Lord God Almighty*; just and true are thy ways, thou *King of saints* [lit: *ethnos*, gentiles/nations]. Who shall not fear thee, O Lord, and glorify thy name? for thou only art holy: *for all nations* [*ethnos*] *shall come and worship before thee*; for thy judgments are made manifest [revealed].
> (Rev. 15:3–4)

A few chapters later, in Revelation 17:14 and 19:16, the "King of Kings and Lord of Lords" is identified as Yeshua, our Messiah.

From our key verse, Isaiah 44:6 quoted in the previous two sections, Yeshua must be "LORD of Hosts." To grasp this, first read what the apostle Peter says about Yeshua,

> Unto you therefore which believe he is precious: but unto them which be disobedient [lit: unbelieving], the stone which the builders disallowed, the same is made the head of the corner, And *a stone of stumbling, and a rock of offence*, even to them which stumble at the word, being disobedient: whereunto also they were appointed.
> (1 Pet. 2:7–8, cf. Rom. 9:32–33; 1 Cor. 1:23)

When Peter and Paul speak of Messiah Yeshua as "a stone of stumbling, and a rock of offence," they are referring to Isaiah 8:14. Now read the context of the original quote in Isaiah:

> Sanctify *LORD of hosts himself*; and let him be your fear, and let him be your dread. And he *shall be* for a sanctuary; but *for a stone of stumbling and for a rock of offence* to both the houses of Israel, for a gin [trap] and for a snare to the inhabitants of Jerusalem.
> (Isa. 8:13–14)

So Peter and Paul are equating Messiah Yeshua with "LORD of Hosts."

These and many *Tanach* scriptures call the pre-incarnate Son/ Word of God by the name "LORD" (YHWH), God's personal name.

The Savior

In looking at God as "the Savior" in the *Tanach*, we will find another "root" supporting the New Testament proclamation that Messiah Yeshua is "God ... manifest [revealed] in the flesh..." (1 Tim. 3:16b).

"Savior ... used frequently of God [in the *Tanach*] ... emphasizes a quality and initiative in Yahweh as fundamental as creatorhood, sovereignty, and [is] unique in ancient religion."[19] "In the OT [savior or deliverer] is used of men ... (Judg. 2:16; 3:9; 12:3; 2 Kgs. 13:5; Neh. 9:27) in the sense that these men were instruments of God for salvation. Otherwise, the OT is emphatic that God is the only Savior ... and salvation by man is vain (Ps. 60:11 – 'Give us help from trouble: for vain is the help [salvation; deliverance] of man.')."[20] Here are some of the many references in the *Tanach* which declare that the God of Israel is the only Savior.

God says that He created Israel (Isa. 43:1, 7, 21), redeemed her from Egypt and her other enemies, and will continue to redeem her (43:3–4), to be His witness – the same reason He created and redeemed gentile believers:

> For I am LORD thy God, the Holy One of Israel, *thy Saviour* ... I, even I, am LORD; and *beside me there is no savi*our. I have declared, and have saved, and I have shewed, when there was no strange god among you: therefore ye are my witnesses, saith LORD, that I am God. Yea, before the day was I am he; and there is none that can deliver out of my hand: I will work, and who shall let [undo] it?   (Isa. 43:3a, 11–13)

In the following verses from Isaiah, God challenges the futile worship of idols, pleading with idol worshipers to come to Him to be saved. Many such *Tanach* verses appeal to both Jews and gentiles to recognize the true and living God and to claim Him as their Savior:

> Tell ye, and bring them near; yea, let them take counsel together: who hath declared this from ancient time? who hath told it from that time? have not I LORD? and there is no God else beside me; a just [or righteous] God and a *Saviour*; there is *none beside me*. Look [Turn] unto me, and be ye saved, *all the ends of the earth*: for I am God, and there is none else.   (Isa. 45:21–22)

God pleads with Israel in Hosea 13:4 to avert His judgment by returning to Him,

> Yet I am LORD thy God from the land of Egypt, and thou shalt know no god but me: *for there is no saviour beside me.*

The *Tanach* is emphatic on this point – the God of Israel is the only Savior. The following verses differ from the previous verses only in that they do not explicitly state that He is the only Savior, although this is assumed in all of Scripture.

In David's great psalm of praise to God for delivering him from his enemies, he declares,

> The God of my rock; in him will I trust [seek refuge]: he is my shield, and the horn of my salvation, my high tower, and my refuge, *my saviour; thou savest me from violence.*   (2 Sam. 22:3)

In Psalm 27:1a, he states, "LORD *is* my light and *my salvation;* whom shall I fear ?..." Again we are faced with the straightforward declaration that "LORD," Yahweh, is our salvation.

The Psalmist states that Israel made and worshiped the golden calf because,

> They forgat [or ignored] God their *saviour,* which had done great things in Egypt...   (Ps. 106:21; see 19–20 for the context)

Isaiah cries out to his God,

> Verily thou art a God that hidest thyself, O God of Israel, *the Saviour.*
> (Isa. 45:15)

Nevertheless, the New Testament proclaims without compromising that Yeshua is the world's Savior. First look at these verses.

The angels announced this good news to the shepherds in the fields around Bethlehem,

> And the angel said unto them, Fear not: for, behold, I bring you good tidings of great joy, which shall be to all people. For unto you is born this day in the city of David a *Saviour, which is Messiah the Lord.*
> (Luke 2:10–11)

Yeshua's encounter with the Samaritan woman at the well led her to return to her city to tell her neighbors about Him. After spending some time with Yeshua, they say,

Now we believe, not because of thy saying: for we have heard him ourselves, and know that this is indeed *the Messiah, the Saviour of the world.*   (John 4:42b)

In Acts 5:29b Peter and the other apostles have disobeyed the ruling Jewish council in Jerusalem by continuing to proclaim Yeshua as Messiah and Lord, saying, "We ought to obey God rather than men." Then they boldly declare to these same rulers,

Him [Yeshua] hath God exalted with his right hand to be a Prince and a *Saviour,* for to give repentance to Israel, and forgiveness of sins.
(Acts 5:31)

Paul declared in a synagogue in Antioch,

Of this man's [David's] seed hath God according to his promise raised unto Israel a *Saviour, Yeshua...*   (Acts 13:23)

Then writing to the Philippians, Paul stated,

For our conversation [community; citizenship] is in heaven; from whence also we look for [with expectation] the *Saviour, the Lord Yeshua the Messiah...*   (Phil. 3:20)

Paul also encourages Timothy to trust "God our Saviour ... God our Saviour ... we trust [hope] in the living God, who is the Saviour of all men, specially of those that believe" (1 Tim. 1:1b, 2:3b, 4:10b).

Finally, the beloved apostle John writes a word of assurance to his family in the faith,

And we have seen and do testify that the Father sent *the Son to be the Saviour of the world.*   (1 John 4:14)[21]

We must ask ourselves whether these New Testament statements contradict the *Tanach* which, as already seen, asserts that only God is the Savior of the world. Are they talking about the same Savior? Is there any proof in the *Tanach* that the coming Messiah would also be the Savior and therefore God?

First consider that Yeshua's name itself means salvation. "It is the oldest name containing the divine name Yahweh, and means 'Yahweh is help' or 'Yahweh is salvation'."[22] Its Hebrew root means wide, spacious, free from constraint. Other Hebrew words derived from the same root mean deliverance, salvation, help, victory, and preservation.

Concerning this name, Matthew recounts what the angel said to Joseph,

> And she shall bring forth a son, and *thou shalt call his name* [nature; character] *Yeshua: for he shall save* his people from their sins.
>
> (Matt. 1:21)[23]

Matthew proceeds to root that revelation in the *Tanach*,

> Now all this was done, that it might be fulfilled which was spoken of the Lord by the prophet, saying, Behold, *a virgin*[24] shall be with child, *and shall bring forth a son*, and they shall call his name [character] Emmanuel, which being interpreted is, *God with us*.
>
> (Matt. 1:22–23; see Isa. 7:14)

So this child, this savior, is none other than God in the flesh, "Emmanuel ... God with us."

Does the *Tanach* prophesy elsewhere that the coming Messiah will be the instrument, better the embodiment, of God's salvation? Yes. The *Tanach* declares three times in the next passage that the Messiah comes as a human servant! In Isaiah 49:5–6 the pre-incarnate Son of God talks about what His Father said to Him:

> And now, saith LORD [the Father] that formed me [the Messiah] *from the womb* to be his *servant*, to bring Jacob again to him, Though Israel be not gathered, yet shall I [Messiah] be glorious in the eyes of LORD [the Father], and my God [the Father] shall be my strength. And he [the Father] said, It is a light thing that thou [Messiah] shouldest be *my servant to raise up the tribes of Jacob, and to restore the preserved of Israel*: I [the Father] will also give thee [Messiah] for a light to the Gentiles, that thou mayest be *my salvation* [*yeshuah* – the feminine of the word Yeshua] unto the end [farthest part] of the earth.

Obviously *the servant* addressed here is not Jacob or Israel because they are the ones needing to be raised up and restored.

In Zechariah 9:9, the prophet points to salvation residing in the King Messiah who is to come,

> Rejoice greatly, O daughter of Zion; shout, O daughter of Jerusalem: behold, thy King cometh unto thee: he is just [or righteous], and having *salvation*; lowly [humble like a servant], and riding upon an ass, and upon a colt the foal of an ass.[25]

Once again the *Tanach* portrays the King Messiah as a servant, yet having salvation.

What does Yeshua say about Himself? In His High Priestly prayer from John 17:6a Yeshua says to the Father, "*I have manifested thy name* unto the men which thou gavest me out of the world . . . " Here the Word witnesses that *Yeshua carries the personal name* [character] *of God.*[26]

The apostle Paul absolutely believed that although Yeshua is not the Father, He is our Savior and God manifest in the flesh. Notice how he goes back and forth in his letter to Titus, proclaiming both God and Yeshua as our Savior:

- the commandment of *God our Saviour* (Titus 1:3b)
- God the Father and the *Lord Yeshua the Messiah our Saviour* (Titus 1:4b)
- the doctrine [instruction; teaching] of *God our Saviour* (Titus 2:10b)
- Looking for that blessed hope, and the glorious appearing of the great God and *Saviour Yeshua the Messiah* (Titus 2:13)
- the kindness and love of *God our Saviour* toward man appeared (Titus 3:4b)
- through *Yeshua the Messiah our Saviour* (Titus 3:6b).

Paul based all of his theology on God's Word, the *Tanach*, as it was revealed to him by the Holy Spirit of truth, and he was always bold to declare that Yeshua is God, our Savior!

> For the LORD is our judge, the LORD is our lawgiver, the LORD is our king; *he will save us.* (Isa. 33:22)

The Redeemer

The primary Hebrew root *goel* means to perform the role of a kinsman who redeems his kin from difficulty and danger or avenges their blood. "The essential meaning of *goel* is 'kinsman-redeemer'. [His] functions . . . include all kinds of actions whereby persons or properties were brought back or restored from alienation to their proper position and relationship."[27] The word is translated into English as "redeem" or "redeemer" and underlies other biblical Hebrew words translated as "redemption" and "ransom." "Though closely allied to salvation, redemption is more specific, for it denotes the means by which salvation is achieved . . . by the payment of a ransom."[28]

The sacrificial system in the *Tanach* provided a type and picture of redemption. By "picture," we do not mean to imply that actual redemption was not accomplished by it. In offering the sacrifices ordained by God, one was able to obtain forgiveness from sin and iniquity through the death of a substitute life. Although the animal sacrifices could not deal with our basic sin nature, there was still forgiveness for sins through them.

Even the New Testament recognizes this fact. Hebrews 9:13 says,

> the blood of bulls and of goats, and the ashes of an heifer sprinkling the unclean [defiled; profane], sanctifieth [purified; made holy] to the purifying of the flesh . . .

The *Tanach* sacrifices were a type of the ultimate fulfillment in Messiah's death which the writer of Hebrews points out in the next verse,

> How much more shall the blood of Messiah, who through the eternal Spirit offered himself without spot [faultless] to God, purge [cleanse] your conscience from dead works to serve the living God?

God states that He is our Redeemer, and He has established rules about who may redeem another person. These are found in Leviticus 25:47–54. Look at how they define and limit the relationship of a legitimate *goel*, a kinsman-redeemer, for a poverty-stricken Jew who sold himself to a gentile:

> After that he is sold he may be redeemed again; *one of his brethren* may redeem him: Either his uncle, or his uncle's son, may redeem him, or *any that is nigh of kin unto him of his family may redeem him*; or if he be able, he may redeem himself.   (Lev. 25:48–49)

Accordingly, the *goel* is also known as the kinsman-redeemer.

Because of these limitations, God could accomplish His redemptive role as our kinsman-redeemer only by coming in the flesh as part of the human family. Recognizing this, the author of Hebrews stated,

> Forasmuch then as the children are partakers of flesh and blood, he [Yeshua] also himself likewise took part of the same; that through death he might destroy [render useless] him that had the power of death, that is, the devil; And deliver [release] them who through fear of death were all their lifetime subject to bondage [slavery]. For verily he took not on him the nature of angels; but he took on him the seed of Abraham. Wherefore in all things it behoved him [He was under obligation] to be made like unto his brethren, that he might be a

merciful and faithful high priest in things pertaining to God, to make reconciliation [atone] for the sins of the people.   (Heb. 2:14–17)

Yeshua is our redemption price as well as our Redeemer, as He declared,

> For even the Son of man came not to be ministered unto, but to minister, and to *give his life a ransom* [redemption price] for many...
> (Mark 10:45)

John states it in this way, "For God so loved the world, that he gave his only begotten Son..." (John 3:16a). Of course, we should expect this pattern for it says in the *Tanach*,

> For thus saith Lord, Ye have sold yourselves for nought; and ye shall be *redeemed without money*.   (Isa. 52:3)

In Egypt the blood of the Passover lamb physically saved the children of Israel, while the sudden death of Egypt's cherished heirs, their population of firstborns, became Israel's ransom. God states in Isaiah 43:3,

> For I am Lord thy God, the Holy One of Israel, thy Saviour: I gave Egypt for *thy ransom*, Ethiopia and Seba for thee.

God paid the price; He takes no pleasure in the death of unbelievers.

The biblical declaration that God is our Redeemer gives much weight to the argument that Yeshua, in order to be our Redeemer, had to be God in the flesh. With this in mind, let's look at the following verses from the *Tanach*.

In Exodus 6:6–7, God commands Moses,

> Wherefore say unto the children of Israel, I am Lord, and I will *bring you out* from under the burdens of the Egyptians, and I will *rid* [deliver; rescue] *you out of their bondage*, and I will *redeem you* with a stretched out arm, and with great judgments: And I will *take* [also acquire, marry] *you to me for a people*, and I will be to you a God: and ye shall know that I am Lord your God, which bringeth you out from under the burdens of the Egyptians.

Phrases from those two important verses give a particular structure to the Passover feast. The rabbis use those verses to explain why we drink wine four times at the Passover *seder* [order]. First is the cup of sanctification, from verse 6 "bring you out"; second is the cup of praise, from verse 6 "rid you out of their bondage"; third is the cup of *redemption,* from verse 6 "redeem you"; fourth is the cup of acceptance, from verse 7 "I will take you to me for a people."

At His last Passover supper Yeshua took what today is called the Third Cup, the Cup of Redemption, the cup after the meal (1 Cor. 11:25), and said that it represents His blood which would be shed to make the New Covenant.

Yeshua was saying this cup would now also symbolize His saving blood, the blood of the Lamb of God. At the same time, being the Cup of Redemption, it would recall the means which redeemed Israel. Is there a symbolic connection between Egypt's firstborn and the fact that Yeshua was God's firstborn and lived for some time in Egypt? In Exodus 4:22 and Hosea 11:1 God describes the people of Israel as His firstborn son who was in Egypt, but this verse is also quoted in Matthew 2:15 as a prophecy of Yeshua. Ransomed by the blood of the firstborn in Egypt might not seem fair to today's humanistic, peace-and-unity establishment, but the Lord knew it was for His glory and best for mankind.

The song of newly redeemed Israel on the shores of the Red Sea included these verses,

> Thou in thy mercy [*chesed*] hast led forth the people which thou hast *redeemed* ... till thy people pass over, O Lord, till the people pass over, which thou hast *purchased.*   (Exod. 15:13a, 16b)

Compare this with what Paul states in Acts 20:28b, "the *church of God,* which he hath *purchased with* [by means of] *his own blood.*" Paul is declaring that with His own blood God bought us from sin's slavery (Rom. 6:18, 22) as our kinsman-redeemer. That is a strong New Testament statement that Yeshua must be God. John 4:24a says, "God [the Father, in context; see v. 23] is a Spirit," and a spirit by definition has no blood. But Paul says that God's own blood (it is definite in the Greek) was our redemption price, a powerful reason why God had to come in the flesh to redeem us.

Asaph writes in Psalm 77:15,

> Thou hast with thine arm *redeemed* thy people, the sons of Jacob and Joseph. Selah.

If you trace all verses about "the arm of" or "the right hand of the Lord/God" in the *Tanach,* it soon becomes apparent that this phrase is a metaphor for the pre-incarnate Son of God.

In Psalm 130, one of the Psalms of Ascent,[29] Psalmist encourages his nation with these words,

Let Israel hope in Lord: for with Lord there is mercy [*chesed*], and with him is plenteous *redemption*. And *he shall redeem Israel* from all his iniquities.   (Ps. 130:7–8)

The only One who is able to redeem Israel is "Lord" – YHWH, in whose name (character) is mercy and redemption. Psalm 20:7 has,

Some trust in chariots, and some in horses: but we will remember the *name of* Lord our God.

God promises by Isaiah that He will fight for Israel and defeat her enemies, with the result that "all flesh shall know that I Lord am *thy Saviour* and *thy Redeemer*, the mighty One of Jacob" (Isa. 49:26b). God also states through the prophet that the oppressors and despisers of Israel (historically "Christendom") will finally serve and help her, so that Israel "shalt know that I Lord am *thy Saviour* and *thy Redeemer*, the mighty One of Jacob" (Isa. 60:16b). In these quotes from Isaiah we see Lord God of Israel claiming as His own two of the various roles we have studied to show the Deity of Messiah Yeshua, the roles of Savior and Redeemer.

Finally, in the little book of Ruth, we find in Boaz the perfect *Tanach* example of a kinsman-redeemer, and a beautiful type of the Messiah Yeshua. Boaz's name means "strength"; he is a man of wealth/property (2:3); he comes from Bethlehem, the "house of bread" (2:4); he is the lord of the harvest (2:4–9); he is a man obedient to God's Law (3:12–13; 4:1–10); he is an advocate for his non-Jewish bride (4:5); as kinsman-redeemer he redeems a wife (4:9–10). As a result, Ruth, a gentile, lived with and blessed God's people, and God used her faithfulness to contribute to the Messianic lineage destined to bring salvation to the world (4:17; Matt. 1:5–6). For every aspect of that description of Boaz we find its perfect anti-type in Yeshua.

The New Testament proclaims Yeshua as our Redeemer because through Him God ransoms fallen man.

Being justified freely [undeservedly] by his grace through the *redemption* that is in Messiah Yeshua...   (Rom. 3:24)

But of him are ye in Messiah Yeshua, who of God is made [become] unto us wisdom, and righteousness, and sanctification, and *redemption*...   (1 Cor. 1:30)

In whom we have *redemption* through his blood, the forgiveness [pardon] of sins, according to the riches of his grace...
(Eph. 1:7; cf. Col. 1:14)

Who gave himself for us, that he might *redeem* [liberate by payment of a ransom] us from all iniquity, and purify unto himself a peculiar people, zealous of good works...   (Titus 2:14)

Neither by the blood of goats and calves, but by his own blood he entered in once into the holy place, having obtained *eternal redemption* for us...   (Heb. 9:12)

And they sung a new song, saying, Thou [the Lamb] art worthy to take the book, and to open the seals thereof: for thou wast slain, and *hast redeemed us* to God by thy blood out of every kindred, and tongue, and people, and nation...   (Rev. 5:9)

Hallelujah!

God's Son

Yeshua is often called God's Son in the New Testament and Yeshua declares that truth:

The hour is coming, and now is, when the dead shall hear the voice of the *Son of God*: and they that hear shall live...   (John 5:25b)

This sickness is not unto death, but for the glory of God, that the *Son of God* might be glorified [honored] thereby.   (John 11:4b)

These things saith the *Son of God*...   (Rev. 2:18b)

Many others in the New Testament also bear witness that Yeshua is the Son of God.

Angels say,

He shall be great, and shall be called the *Son of the Highest*... And the angel answered ... her, The Holy Ghost shall come upon thee, and the power of the Highest shall overshadow thee: therefore also that holy [lit. set apart] thing which shall be born of thee shall be called the *Son of God*.   (Luke 1:32a, 35)

Demons say,

What have we to do with thee, Yeshua, thou *Son of God*? art thou come hither [here] to torment us before the time?   (Matt. 8:29b)

John the Baptist says,

And I saw [perceived; knew], and bare record [witnessed] that this is the *Son of God*.   (John 1:34)

His disciples "came and worshipped [prostrated themselves before] him, saying, Of a truth [Most certainly] thou art the Son of God" (Matt. 14:33); "And Simon Peter answered and said, Thou art *the Messiah, the Son of the living God*" (Matt. 16:16) and "Unto you [the Jewish nation] first God, having raised up his Son Yeshua, sent him to bless you, in turning away every one of you from his iniquities" (Acts 3:26).

Martha says, "Yea, Lord: I believe that thou art the *Messiah, the Son of God*, which should come into the world" (John 11:27b).

Paul says,

> that he is the *Son of God*...   (Acts 9:20b)

> Concerning *his Son Messiah* Yeshua our Lord, which was made of the seed of David according to the flesh; And declared to be *the Son of God* with power, according to the spirit of holiness, by the resurrection from the dead...   (Rom. 1:3–4)

> God is faithful, by whom ye were called unto the fellowship of *his Son* Yeshua the Messiah our Lord.   (1 Cor. 1:9)

The writer of Hebrews says,

> Seeing then that we have a great high priest, that is passed into the heavens, Yeshua the Son of God, let us hold fast [seize or retain] our profession [confession]...   (Heb. 4:14)

Other New Testament writers say,

> The beginning of the gospel of Yeshua *the Messiah, the Son of God*...
>   (Mark 1:1)

> No man hath seen God at any time; *the only begotten Son*, which is in the bosom of the Father, he hath declared him.   (John 1:18)

> But these are written, that ye might believe that Yeshua is *the Messiah, the Son of God*; and that believing ye might have life through his name.
>   (John 20:31)

Notice the significant link between Yeshua proclaimed as Messiah and also as the Son of God. For Yeshua to be Israel's Messiah He must be the only begotten Son of God, and conversely, if we deny His Deity as Son – then He cannot be the promised Messiah nor the Savior of the world.

The Messiah was (and still is) expected to be the "Son of David," but Yeshua challenged the limitations of that, showing that the *Tanach* declared the Messiah to be more than David's Son:

> While the Pharisees were gathered together, Yeshua asked them, Saying, What think ye [your opinion] of Messiah? whose son is he? They say unto him, The Son [descendant] of David. He saith unto them, How then doth David in spirit call him Lord, saying, LORD said unto my Lord, Sit thou on my right hand, till I make thine enemies thy footstool? If David then call him Lord, how is he his son?
>
> (Matt. 22:41–45; cf. Ps. 110:1)

Without denying that Messiah is the Son of David, He used the authority of Scripture to make an even greater claim for the Messiah as David's Lord.

Nonetheless, on many occasions He was receptive to the title "Son of David". For example:

> And the multitudes that went before, and that followed, cried, saying, Hosanna [lit: Please save us!] to the *Son of David*: Blessed is he that cometh in the name of the Lord [Ps. 118:25–26]; Hosanna in the highest...
>
> (Matt. 21:9)

> And he [a blind man] cried, saying, Yeshua, thou *Son of David*, have mercy on me. And they which went before rebuked him, that he should hold his peace [be silent]: but he cried [shouted] so much the more, Thou *Son of David*, have mercy on me.
>
> (Luke 18:38–39)

The title comes from the *Tanach*. In 2 Samuel 7:12–16, God makes an everlasting covenant with David and his son Solomon,

> He shall build an house [also means "family"] for my name, and I will stablish [establish] the throne of his kingdom for ever ... And thine house and thy kingdom shall be established for ever before thee: thy throne shall be established for ever.   (2 Sam. 7:13, 16)[30]

Although Solomon is the natural fulfillment of the covenant (as Solomon states in 1 Kings 8:13–20), God makes promises in the covenant that point to another "Son" [Heb.: can mean "descendant"] who is to reign forever, indicating this Son's divine nature.

Up to a point, Solomon is a beautiful type of the Messiah – the son of Israel's greatest king; a man of peace (his name in Hebrew; 1 Chr. 22:9); a man beloved by the Lord, as his God-given name, Jedidiah, indicates (2 Sam. 12:24–25); a builder of God's temple (1 Chr.

22:10–11); and the wisest man ever (1 Kgs. 3:11–12; 4:29–34).
As with all Bible types, one should not expect everything to correlate
with the anti-type – and so with Solomon.

That the meaning of "the Son of God" goes far beyond that of "the
Son of David" is apparent. In fact, several *Tanach* verses indicate that
the God of Israel has a unique Son. For instance, God's ultimate
answer to the global rebellion against His rightful rule is to remind the
world of His Ruler,

> Yet have I set [anointed] *my king* [the king of My choosing] upon
> my holy hill of Zion. I will declare the decree: LORD hath said unto
> me, *Thou art my Son*; this day have I begotten thee ... Kiss the Son, lest
> he be angry, and ye perish from the way, when his wrath is kindled
> but a little. Blessed are all they that put their trust in him.
>
> (Ps. 2:6–7, 12)

God is stating that this King is His Son. All people are encouraged to
put their trust in the King/Son. Since the *Tanach* often warns about
trusting in man,[31] the One in whom God exhorts us to trust, has to be
more than a man.

In Proverbs 30:4 there is a question which is part of the "utter-
ance," or "oracle" (the literal translation of the KJV's "prophecy" in
v. 1), of Agur,

> Who hath ascended up into heaven, or descended? who hath gathered
> the wind in his fists? who hath bound the waters in a garment? who
> hath established all the ends of the earth? what is his name, and what is
> his son's name, if thou canst tell?

In reply, the Creator, LORD God of Israel, has given (revealed) His
name to His people. And He has also given the name of His Son.

A familiar prophecy found in Isaiah also indicates that God has a
unique Son,

> For unto us a child is born, unto us *a son is given*: and the government
> [rule; dominion] shall be upon his shoulder: and his name shall be
> called Wonderful, Counsellor, The mighty God, The everlasting
> Father, The Prince [Ruler; Captain] of Peace. Of the increase of his
> government and peace there shall be no end, *upon the throne of
> David*, and upon his kingdom, to order it, and to establish it with
> judgment and with justice [or justice and righteousness] from
> henceforth *even for ever*. The zeal of LORD of hosts will perform this.
>
> (Isa. 9:6–7)

That prophecy reveals much about the coming Messiah, who will sit on the throne of David forever, fulfilling the criteria of being David's Son. A "child is born" is a normal way of talking about a birth, but why add "a son is given"? John 3:16a shows why, "For God so loved the world, that he gave his only begotten son..." Looking back, the unusual combination of terms Isaiah uses gives a fairly strong hint of the human and divine natures of the Messiah and of His sacrifice.

We repeat, a name in Hebraic thinking is more than just a label; it often indicates the essential nature of the thing named. What is the essential nature of this Son? Look again at the verse, "and His name [His essential nature] shall be called ... The mighty God, The everlasting Father..." Can there be any doubt that this points to One who is more than a mortal man?

Further evidence of Yeshua's divine nature comes from a Jew who, without ever having read the New Testament, believed Yeshua to be the Son of God. Why did Paul, an observant Jew before and after meeting Yeshua, say that he, Paul, was a blasphemer before he was saved?

> And I thank Messiah Yeshua our Lord, who hath enabled me, for that he counted me faithful, putting me into the ministry; Who was before a blasphemer, and a persecutor, and injurious: but I obtained mercy, because I did it ignorantly in unbelief.   (1 Tim. 1:12–13)

Blasphemy is slander against God. Paul had blasphemed Yeshua.

Why did Paul confess that he compelled other believers to blaspheme?

> I verily thought with myself, that I ought to do many things contrary to the name of Yeshua of Nazareth. Which thing I also did in Jerusalem: and many of the saints did I shut up in prison, having received authority from the chief priests; and when they were put to death, I gave my voice [voted] against them. And I punished them oft in every synagogue, and compelled them to *blaspheme*...   (Acts 26:9–11b)

We know that Paul would never have blasphemed, or have forced others to blaspheme, the God of Israel. In fact, that is why he was so zealous to persecute this new way, because he believed its adherents were blaspheming God. But as Paul later came to the realization that Yeshua is the Son of God, then without hesitation he could confess that, before he met his Lord, he had blasphemed and caused others to blaspheme.

The Eternal God

More evidence for the Deity of the prophesied Messiah is seen in verses stating that the One to come is eternal. God proclaims in Micah 5:2 that His Messiah, who will come from Bethlehem (Hebrew for "house of bread"), will be the "ruler in Israel; whose goings forth [origin] have been from of old, from everlasting." The word used for "everlasting," *olam*, is the same word used to describe God as everlasting,[32] and means eternal.

The Spirit of God is referring to Messiah Yeshua when He declares in Psalm 45:6,

> *Thy throne, O God*, is for ever and ever: the sceptre of thy kingdom is a right [just] sceptre.

Why do we say that verse refers to Yeshua and not God the Father? Read verse 7. The Psalmist says this God has been anointed by God. Remember, "Messiah" means "Anointed One." (Both verses are quoted in Heb. 1:8–9.) So the *Tanach*, besides identifying this Anointed One as "God," also attributes eternal duration to His throne, His kingdom rule.

The Creator

John begins his Gospel,

> In the beginning was the Word, and the Word was with God, and the Word was God. The same was in the beginning with God. All things were made by him; and without him was not any thing made that was made.   (John 1:1–3)

John's prologue calls Yeshua not only the Word of God but also describes Him as the Creator. There are other places where different New Testament writers call Yeshua the Creator.

In Ephesians, Paul writes that he received grace so that he could preach to the gentiles the "unsearchable riches" (3:8) of Israel's Messiah, in order to "make all men see what is the fellowship of the mystery, which from the beginning of the world hath been hid in *God, who created all things by Yeshua the Messiah . . .*" (Eph. 3:9).

In Colossians 1:16–17 Paul repeats the truth that God created all things through His Son,

> *For by him* [Messiah Yeshua] *were all things created*, that are in heaven, and that are in earth, visible and invisible, whether they be

thrones, or dominions, or principalities, or powers: all things were
created by him, and for him: And he is before all things, and by him all
things consist.

Paul includes all things in what Yeshua has created, both in heaven
and on earth, both visible and invisible things. There is nothing left
out except God.

The writer to the Hebrews begins his letter with this truth, saying
that God,

> Hath in these last days spoken unto us by *his Son*, whom he hath
> appointed heir of all things, *by whom also he made the worlds* . . .
>
> (Heb. 1:2)

While the New Testament abundantly proclaims Messiah Yeshua
as the Creator, the *Tanach* plainly states that God, LORD, is the
Creator.

Isaiah 40:28b links the creative and eternal aspects of God that we
have discussed, "the *everlasting God*, LORD, *the Creator* of the ends
of the earth [all the earth defined by its "boundaries"] . . . " Initially
Genesis 1:1, the most important of verses because it is the foundation
upon which all rests, states, "In the beginning *God created* the heaven
and the earth."[33]

Can we reconcile the seeming dilemma of two Creators? We know
that God created by His Word, as stated in Psalm 33:6,

> By the *word of* LORD were the heavens made; and all the host of them
> by the breath [Heb.: *ruach*, which can also be translated as "spirit"] of
> his mouth.

God the Father created everything through His Word, later manifested in the flesh as Messiah Yeshua (John 1:14), who also possessed
the fullness of the Spirit (John 3:34).

The Word of God

The apostle John uses "the Word" as a title for Messiah Yeshua in all
his writings. In the prologue of his gospel John says, "In the beginning
was *the Word*, and *the Word* was with God, and *the Word was God*"
(1:1) and a few verses later, he says that this same "*Word was made
flesh*, and dwelt among us . . . " (1:14a).

John affirms even more strongly that he and the other original
disciples were personal witnesses of,

That which was from the beginning, which we have heard, which we have seen with our eyes, which we have looked upon [contemplated], and our hands have handled, of the Word of life ... "   (1 John 1:1)

At the end of his life, while caught up in a God-given vision, John "sees" the return of Yeshua. He describes Yeshua this way,

And he was clothed with a vesture [garment or cloak] dipped [lit: "baptized," immersed] in blood: and *his name is called The Word of God...*   (Rev. 19:13)[34]

The roots of that title are found in the *Tanach*.

He sent *his word*, and healed them, and delivered them from their destructions.   (Ps. 107:20)

So shall *my word* be that goeth forth out of my mouth: it shall not return unto me void [in vain], but it shall accomplish that which I please, and it shall prosper in the thing whereto I *sent* it.   (Isa. 55:11)

John not only stated, "And the Word was made flesh, and dwelt among us ... " (John 1:14a), but he also emphasized forty times in his gospel that Yeshua was *sent* by the Father, just as God declares in Isaiah 55:11 quoted above.

We mentioned at the end of the last section that the *Tanach* says creation was accomplished by the Word of LORD (Ps. 33:6). Psalm 119:89 states,

For ever, O LORD, *thy word* is settled in heaven.

These verses are saying that the Word was the creating agent and has existed for eternity, both descriptions of God.

Psalm 119 is a beautiful psalm speaking of the great riches and glory of God's Word, or Law (*Torah* in Hebrew, which is usually translated "Law" in English, but means "teaching" and "instruction"). We do not want to lessen the importance of the literal meaning of the text, but if we temporarily substitute the word "Yeshua" as the antitype for "word," "law," "commandments," etc., it is easy for believers to see that He is the ultimate fulfillment of many of these verses.

For example, the following verses proclaim benefits of God's "Law," "Word," etc., and can also point to what we have obtained in Messiah Yeshua: verses 41, 123, 174 (salvation); 50, 93, 116 (life); 74, 116, 147 (hope); 105, 130 (light); 133 (leading); 137–138 (righteousness); 140 (purity); 140, 165, 174 (love of God's Word);

142, 160 (truth); 162 (great treasure); 165 (great peace); 170 (deliverance).[35]

Other Titles

Psalm 146:5–10 extols the praises of "LORD." It proclaims Him to be the Creator (v. 6), the Deliverer (v. 7), the Healer (v. 8), and the One who reigns forever (v. 10). The New Testament also uses all these descriptions for Messiah Yeshua,[36] implying that the nature of the Messiah is the same as the nature of His Father and that Messiah Yeshua is God in the flesh, revealing the Father.

Finally, Jeremiah 23:5–6 declares that the Messiah is LORD our righteousness,

> Behold, the days come, saith LORD, that I will raise unto David a *righteous* Branch, and a *King* shall reign and prosper, and shall execute judgment and justice in the earth. In his days [as King] Judah shall be saved, and Israel shall dwell safely: and this is *his name* whereby he shall be called, LORD OUR RIGHTEOUSNESS.

Rabbinic scholars and Christian theologians alike say this refers to the Messiah, the Righteous Branch of David. Note that His name, His essential nature, is LORD [YHWH] OUR RIGHTEOUSNESS. That is the name of God's Messiah, Yeshua!

Paul, probably thinking of this verse, wrote in 2 Corinthians 5:21,

> For he hath made him to be sin for us, who knew no sin; that we might be made the *righteousness of God in him.*[37]

This agrees with a powerful verse in the *Tanach,*

> No weapon that is formed against thee shall prosper; and every tongue that shall rise against thee in judgment thou shalt condemn. This is the heritage of the servants of LORD, and *their righteousness is of me, saith* LORD. (Isa. 54:17)

Concluding Thoughts

God declares in Isaiah 45:22–23,

> Look [lit: Turn] unto me, and be ye saved, all the ends of the earth: for I am God, and there is none else. I have sworn by myself, the word is gone out of my mouth in righteousness, and shall not return, That unto me every knee shall bow, every tongue shall swear.

Under the inspiration of the Holy Spirit, Paul sees that declaration fulfilled in Yeshua, its final goal being the Father's glory,

> Wherefore God also hath highly exalted him, and given him a name which is above every name: That at the name of Yeshua every knee should bow, of things in heaven, and things in earth, and things under the earth; And that every tongue should confess that Yeshua the Messiah is Lord, to the glory of God the Father.   (Phil. 2:9–11)

Those two verses together reveal that Yeshua must be "God ... manifest in the flesh" (1 Tim. 3:16b). The only way to avoid that conclusion is to say God changed His Plan, or found a mere man with whom He could trust all His glory. Since neither of these scenarios is possible, we must rest on the transcendent but revealed reality that Yeshua is God.

We need to make firm our commitment to "keep the Word of God," to guard its use and protect it from abuse, to depend finally not on our limited logic and world-view, but on the divinely inspired Scriptures. Usually there is no mystery, but at other times, such as with the Deity of the Messiah Yeshua, we must recognize that "without controversy great is the mystery of godliness: God was manifest [revealed] in the flesh..." (1 Tim. 3:16a).

Lon Roberts, Bible teacher, author, and friend, explained Yeshua's deity like this, "The less divine you make Him, the more you have two gods."[38] If we believers see Yeshua as God, as one with the Father, then we are monotheists, worshiping one God. If we call ourselves believers in Yeshua but do not see Yeshua as God and one with the Father, then we are polytheists, worshiping two gods.

It need not discourage us if we find it difficult to grasp Yeshua's Man/God nature. On the contrary, we should rejoice, for of all the miracles of God, the incarnation is the greatest wonder of all.

> The word which God sent unto the children of Israel, preaching peace by Yeshua the Messiah: (he is Lord of all:)...   (Acts 10:36)

I am Alpha and Omega,
the beginning and the ending, saith the Lord,
which is, and which was,
and which is to come, the Almighty.
(Rev. 1:8)

Notes

1. The Greek word for "seen" includes the figurative meanings of perceived, known, heeded, been acquainted with by experience.

2. Harris, Archer, Waltke, *Theological Wordbook of the Old Testament* (Chicago: Moody Press), Vol. 1, p. 30.

3. Other examples: Gen. 11:6 ("the people is one ... one language"); 34:16 ("one people"); Exod. 26:6 ("one tabernacle"); Judg. 20:1, 8, 11 ("one man").

4. Mark 16:12; Luke 24:16, 31; John 20:14, 15.

5. The definite article is in the original text. Jacob is referring to a specific angel, "the" Angel.

6. Pfeiffer, Vos, Rea (eds.), *Wycliffe Bible Encyclopedia* (Moody Press), Vol. 2, p. 1174.

7. For other examples, see the stories of Hagar (Gen. 16:10–11, 13), Gideon (Judg. 6:11–23) and the parents of Samson (Judg. 13:2–23).

8. Harris, Archer, Waltke, *Theological Wordbook of the Old Testament*, Vol. 2, p. 934.

9. *Wycliffe Bible Encyclopedia*, Vol. 2, p. 1174.

10. In Hebrew, parallel thoughts confirm and explain one another, as here where "name" is parallel to "fame."

11. Colin Brown (ed.), *Dictionary of New Testament Theology*, Vol. 2, p. 649.

12. *Shalom* includes physical, emotional, mental and spiritual wholeness.

13. For example, Pss. 7:17; 20:1, 7, 9; 54:6; 99:6; 113:1–5; 118:26; 135:13.

14. All the original apostles, including Paul, are Jewish.

15. See also Ezek. 34:11–13, which identifies Israel's Shepherd as YHWH in a prophecy we see coming to pass now.

16. Matt. 10:40; 15:24; 21:37; Mark 9:37; 12:6; Luke 4:18, 43; 10:16; John 3:17, 34; 4:34; 5:23–24, 30, 36–38; 6:29, 38–40, 57; 7:16, 28–29; 8:16–18, 26, 29, 42; 10:36; 11:42, 17:3, 21, etc.

17. Matt. 12:18–21; Luke 2:30–32; Acts 11:17–18; 13:36–48; 26:22–23; Rom. 15:8–12, 16; Gal. 3:14; Eph. 3:6–8; Col. 1:27; 1 Tim. 3:16.

18. Here is another verse that seems to talk about more than one LORD, "Then LORD rained upon Sodom and upon Gomorrah brimstone and fire from LORD out of heaven..." (Gen. 19:24).

19. Elwell (ed.), *Evangelical Dictionary of Theology*, p. 975.

20. *Wycliffe Bible Encyclopedia*, p. 1531.

21. There are more New Testament verses which declare the same thing about Messiah Yeshua, i.e. Eph. 5:23; 2 Tim. 1:10; 2 Pet. 1:1, 11; 2:20; 3:18.

22. *Dictionary of New Testament Theology*, Vol. 2, p. 331.

23. Note that the angel says "his people," – Israel in this context.

24. Many Jewish commentators say that the word in this *Tanach* verse is not translated "virgin," but just "young woman." However, if that dubious assertion were true, it would turn the "sign" which the previous verse in Isaiah speaks of, into an everyday occurrence.

25. The New Testament uses this verse, or references to it, in each of the four gospels to establish the link between Yeshua and the humble King who brings salvation: Matt. 21:4–5; Mark 11:7–10; Luke 19:29–38; John 12:12–16.

26. Remember, we believe that Yeshua is Lord and God, but He is not the Father, although one with Him. See the first section of this chapter (14).

27. *Wycliffe Bible Encyclopedia*, Vol. 2, p. 1447.

28. *Evangelical Dictionary of Theology*, p. 918.

29. Apparently, Israelis sang the "Psalms of Ascent" (Ps. 120–134), also known as "Songs of Degrees," as they ascended to Jerusalem to celebrate each of the three pilgrim feasts – *Pesach* (Passover), *Shavuot* (Weeks or Pentecost) and *Succot* (Booths or Tabernacles).

30. Yeshua's human descent is traced through his mother back to Solomon's brother Nathan, another son of David, in Luke 3:31. But Yeshua's legal claim to the throne of David came through his stepfather Joseph traced back to Solomon as listed in Matt. 1:6, 7.

31. Here are three verses warning us against trusting in man: "Some trust in chariots, and some in horses: but we will remember the name of the LORD our God" (Ps. 20:7); "Woe to the rebellious children, saith the LORD, that take counsel, but not of me; and that cover with a covering [or anoint with an anointing], but not of my spirit, that they may add sin to sin: That walk to go down into Egypt, and have not asked at my mouth; to strengthen themselves in the strength of Pharaoh, and to trust in the shadow of Egypt!" (Isa. 30:1–2); "Thus saith the LORD; Cursed be the man that trusteth in man, and maketh flesh his arm, and whose heart departeth from the LORD" (Jer. 17:5).

32. For example, see Gen. 21:33; Isa. 40:28; Jer. 10:10.

33. In Isa. 45:17, God states, "But Israel shall be saved in the LORD with an everlasting salvation: ye shall not be ashamed nor confounded world without end [ever again]." Since this seemed so impossible in Israel's then current situation, God immediately reminds His readers who He is, "For thus saith the LORD *that created* the heavens; *God himself that formed* the earth and made it; he hath *established* it, he *created* it not in vain, he *formed* it to be inhabited: I am the LORD; and there is none else." If God had a calling card the main title would be, "I am the LORD, your Creator." In the *Tanach* He usually presents His calling card just before or after He states that He will do something we would find difficult to believe. By this He reminds us who He is, as if to say, "If I created all this universe, I can, and will, do whatever I say."

34. The writings of John may be the most "Hebraic" in the New Testament. For example, the book of Revelation is incomprehensible without understanding the various images it draws from the *Tanach*. The picture presented in the first half of the verse just quoted (Rev. 19:13) is taken from Isa. 63:1–6.

35. Of course, David was describing the benefits of studying the written Word of God – at least the parts then extant, the first five books of Moses and maybe a few of the other earlier books. If this is how he and the Spirit of God (who inspired him to write this psalm), described parts of the *Tanach*, shouldn't we Bible-believers let the Old Testament have its God-ordained place in our lives as a source of correction and instruction in righteousness (2 Tim. 3:16–17)? Moses urges the children of Israel to recognize that "the word is very nigh unto thee, in thy mouth, and in thy heart . . .," so that they can perform what God desires (Deut. 30:14b). Even so, our Messiah Yeshua is near by His Spirit, dwelling in our hearts by faith and bringing to our remembrance all that He commanded us.

36. Yeshua as Healer is quite obvious from the gospels. Here are references to Him as the Creator – John 1:1–3, 10; Eph. 3:9; Col. 1:16. The Deliverer – Luke 4:18; Rom. 11:26; Gal. 1:4; Heb. 2:14–15. Reigning forever – 2 Sam. 7:13, 16; Ps. 45:6–7; Isa. 9:6–7; Luke 1:31–33; Rev. 1:56; 5:13; 11:15.
37. See also Rom. 4:5.
38. Lon Roberts, *A Stone in Zion*, p. 4.

CHAPTER 15

The Holy Spirit in the *Tanach* – Part 1

Have you noticed that when Yeshua talked about the Holy Spirit, no one in the gospels ever asked, "What is this new doctrine He declares?" It is because the work of the Holy Spirit was part of the revelation given in the *Tanach*. Although the full revelation of the personal relationship between the Holy Spirit and the believer is stated most clearly in the New Testament, there are many examples and promises of it in the *Tanach*. The New Testament doctrine surrounding God's Spirit was not completely new.[1]

God's Spirit Reveals God

Yeshua's declarative statement about the relationship between God and His worshipers is found in John 4:24,

> God is a Spirit:[2] and they that worship him must *worship him in spirit and in truth.*

This fact has crucial implications for how we relate to and understand our God. Paul states that we understand the things of God only by the Holy Spirit,

> For what man knoweth the things of a man, save [except] the spirit of man which is in him? even so the things of God knoweth [are understood, perceived by] no man, but [by] the Spirit of God ... But the natural [sensual][3] man receiveth not the things of the Spirit of God: for they are foolishness unto him: neither can he know them, because they are spiritually discerned [examined, judged].
> (1 Cor. 2:11, 14, see context vv. 9–14)

The New Testament explicitly teaches that to understand who Yeshua is requires revelation by the Holy Spirit,

> But when the Comforter[4] is come, whom I will send unto you from the Father, even the Spirit of truth, which proceedeth from the Father, *he shall testify* [witness] *of me*...
> (John 15:26)

> Wherefore I give you to understand, that no man speaking by the Spirit of God calleth Yeshua accursed [Gk: anathema]: and that no man can [has the power or ability to] say [truthfully] that Yeshua is the Lord, *but by* [through] *the Holy Ghost* [Spirit].
>
> (1 Cor. 12:3)

The Holy Spirit and Creation

> In the beginning God created the heaven and the earth. And the earth was without form, and void; and darkness was upon the face of the deep. And the *Spirit of God* moved upon [brooded or hovered over] the face of the waters. (Gen. 1:1–2)

The Holy Spirit was active in creation. God's Spirit can be seen as that "part" of the Godhead (Father, Son, and Holy Spirit) carrying out the plan of God. Such is not an inferior position, as we would understand it in talking about the things of man. Scriptures show interrelationship in the workings of the Godhead, but there is no rigid separation. At times, what the Father does is also attributed to His Son or His Spirit. Often we realize that what we see Yeshua do is done through the agency of the Holy Spirit.

Although we are studying the teaching on God's Spirit, it is important not to separate the various aspects of God that are revealed to us. The more we separate them, the less we have only One God! We must always remember that *Elohim*,[5] the Godhead, is a mystery we cannot hope to understand with our finite minds, except in those areas God has chosen to reveal in His Word.

> And without controversy great is the mystery of godliness: God was manifest in the flesh, justified in the Spirit, seen of angels, preached unto the Gentiles, believed on in the world, received up into glory.
>
> (1 Tim. 3:16)

Concerning God's activity in creation, we read in Psalm 33:6,

> By the word of the LORD were the heavens made; and all the host of them by the breath [lit: *ruach*, or Spirit] of his mouth.

This *Tanach* verse shows God's Son, "the word of the LORD" (see John 1:1–3), and God's Spirit, "the breath [or spirit] of his mouth," acting together from "the beginning."

Yeshua Creates

Many New Testament verses confirm that God created everything by
Messiah Yeshua:

> And to make all men see what is the fellowship of the mystery, which
> from the beginning of the world [eternity] hath been hid in God, who
> *created all things by Messiah Yeshua* ...   (Eph. 3:9)

> *All things were made by him*; and without him was not any thing made
> that was made ... He was in the world, and the world was made by
> him, and the world knew him not.   (John 1:3, 10 John)

> But to us there is but one God, the Father, of whom are all things, and
> we in him; and one *Lord Yeshua the Messiah, by whom are all things*,
> and we by him ...   (1 Cor. 8:6)

> For by him were all things created, that are in heaven, and that are in
> earth, visible and invisible, whether they be thrones, or dominions, or
> principalities, or powers [authorities]: *all things were created by him,
> and for him*: And he is before all things, and by him all things consist.
>   (Col. 1:16–17)

> [God] Hath in these last days spoken unto us by his Son, whom he hath
> appointed heir of all things, *by whom also he made the worlds* ... But
> unto the Son he saith ... Thou, Lord [YHWH],[6] in the beginning hast
> laid the foundation of the earth; and the heavens are the works of thine
> hands ...   (Heb. 1:2, 8a, 10 – quoting Ps. 102:25)

The Holy Spirit Creates

The Holy Spirit is revealed as one through whom God creates. For
example, look at these *Tanach* verses:

> The *Spirit* of God hath made me, and the *breath* [*neshamah* – breath,
> spirit] of the Almighty hath given me life.   (Job 33:4)

> Thou hidest thy face, they are troubled: thou takest away their *breath*
> [lit: *ruach* – spirit], they die, and return to their dust. Thou sendest
> forth thy *spirit* [*ruach*], they are created [Heb.: *bara*]: and thou
> renewest the face of the earth.   (Ps. 104:29–30)

The Hebrew word *bara* means "to create from nothing." It is only
used in the *Tanach* when God is the active agent, as in Genesis 1:1.

King David uses the same word, *bara*, in Psalm 51:

> Create [*bara*] in me a clean [pure] heart, O God; and renew [make new, renew, repair] a right [firm, stable, steadfast] spirit within me. Cast me not away from thy presence; and take not *thy holy spirit* from me. Restore unto me the joy of thy salvation; and uphold me with thy free [generous] spirit. (Ps. 51:10–12)

Nathan the prophet had just confronted David with his sins in the Bathsheba affair. Instead of getting angry or making excuses, David, the man after God's heart, deeply repents. He comes to an understanding that in his flesh dwells no good thing and asks God to have mercy on him and restore him. That is a *Tanach* example of a convicted backslider recognizing that he needs to be remade a new creation. Although not stated in those words in the psalm, the theological concept is the same.

Many years later, during the Babylonian exile, the Lord revealed through the prophet Ezekiel that a new creation is what He has planned,

> A new heart [inner man] also will I give you, and a new *spirit* will I put within you: and I will take away the stony heart out of your flesh, and I will give you an heart of flesh. (Ezek. 36:26)

The Promise of the Spirit

Yeshua said that one of the reasons for His return to the Father was so He could pour out the promise of His Father, the baptism, the immersion into, the Holy Spirit,

> And, behold, I send the *promise of my Father* upon you: but tarry ye in the city of Jerusalem, until ye be endued [clothed] with power [also ability] from on high. (Luke 24:49, cf. Acts 1:4)

The fulfillment was confirmed by Peter,

> Therefore [Yeshua] being by the right hand of God exalted, and having received of the Father *the promise*[7] of the Holy Ghost, he hath shed forth this, which ye now see and hear. (Acts 2:33)

This promise fulfilled in the New Testament had been given by God in the *Tanach*. The main reference is Joel 2:28–29,

> And it shall come to pass afterward, that I will pour out my spirit upon all flesh; and your sons and your daughters shall prophesy, your old

men shall dream dreams, your young men shall see visions: And also upon the servants and upon the handmaids in those days will I pour out my spirit.

Peter certainly tied the outpouring of the Spirit on *Shavuot*/Pentecost (Acts 2:16–18) to that *Tanach* promise.

Here are several other verses that can be seen as part of this promise of the Father.

In Numbers 11:29 Moses expresses a prophetic desire that begins its New Testament fulfillment when Yeshua pours out Holy Spirit on His Body,

And Moses said unto him, Enviest thou for my sake? would God that all the LORD's people were prophets, and that the LORD would put *his spirit* upon them!

Isaiah 32:15–17 prophesies what will happen when God's people in the nation of Israel receive His Spirit,

Until *the spirit* be poured upon us from on high, and the wilderness be a fruitful field, and the fruitful field be counted for a forest [wild place]. Then judgment [or justice] shall dwell in the wilderness, and righteousness remain [dwell] in the fruitful field. And the work of righteousness shall be peace; and the effect of righteousness quietness and assurance [safety] for ever.   (cf. Isa. 44:3–5)

This outpouring also now applies to the redeemed from all nations.

What Scripture calls "fruit" or "fruitful" accompanying the outpouring of the Spirit is not defined by signs and miracles, although signs and miracles often do accompany an outpouring of God's Spirit. But the "fruit" which God promises is righteousness, peace, joy, and confidence (or faith), which are "fruits" of the Holy Spirit. Paul could easily have been thinking about that verse in Isaiah when he said,

For the kingdom [rulership] of God is not meat and drink; but righteousness, and peace, and joy in the Holy Ghost.
    (Rom. 14:17; see also Gal. 5:22–23 – the fruit of the Spirit)

Here is something else to consider when reading Isaiah 32:15. In the *Tanach*, "forest" represents a type of wilderness, a fruitless place. In ancient Israel a forest was not a pleasant picnic spot; it was a frightening abode of dangerous animals. So in verse 15 Isaiah is using different words to say, "Every valley shall be exalted, and every mountain and hill shall be made low . . . " (Isa. 40:4a). God's Spirit

will turn everything upside down – making things right, beginning to
return the world and mankind to God's order.

In Ezekiel 39:29 the Lord says,

> Neither will I hide my face any more from them: for I have [will have]
> poured out *my spirit* upon the house of Israel, saith the Lord GOD.

This *Tanach* verse is a root of Paul's Spirit-directed declaration in
Romans 11:26a, "And so all Israel shall be saved . . . "

Born Again by the Spirit

Sin separates us from God as Isaiah 59:1–2 plainly says,

> Behold, the LORD's hand is not shortened, that it cannot save; neither
> his ear heavy, that it cannot hear: But your iniquities [perversity,
> depravity, guilt] have separated between you and your God, and your
> sins [offences] have hid his face from you, that he will not hear.

Some of the events that usually comprise the born-again experience
are: the Father draws us to Yeshua; we receive the revelation – the
"seed" of faith – that Yeshua is the "way, the truth and the life";
the Holy Spirit revives our dead spirits and begins to convict us of sin;
God gives us a spirit of repentance, and freely forgives us.[8] Yeshua is
then always with us by His Spirit, enabling us to walk in obedience to
His Word. All this is accomplished by His grace, and in His order and
timing, which is different for everyone.[9]

In Ezekiel 36:25–27 we find one of the best descriptions of what it
means to be "born again" in all of Scripture,

> Then will I sprinkle clean [pure] water upon you, and ye shall be clean
> [pure]: from all your filthiness, and from all your idols, will I cleanse
> [purify] you. A new heart also will I give you, and *a new spirit will I put
> within you*: and I will take away the stony heart out of your flesh, and I
> will give you an heart of flesh. And *I will put my spirit within you*, and
> cause you to walk in my statutes, and ye shall keep my judgments,
> and do them.

Yeshua's imparting His Holy Spirit is integral to this experience.

Israel Redeemed

God's order in the redemption of His people means a regathering
of the Jewish people, most in unbelief. Although many Jews are

being redeemed in exile, when all Israel is saved, it will occur in the physical land of Israel. First God says that He will bring them back from all the nations to which He scattered them (Jer. 31:10), settling them in the land of Israel (see Ezek. 36 in context). Hallelujah! We see this happening today! Then, through a spirit of grace (favor), He gives them faith to believe so that they cry out for Him and He cleanses them. To some extent this also is happening today.

How will the Lord accomplish this? Zechariah 12:10 describes this event. Notice how it involves an outpouring of God's Spirit,

> And I will pour upon the house of David, and upon the inhabitants of Jerusalem, the spirit of grace [10] and of supplications: [11] and they shall look upon me whom they have pierced, [12] and they shall mourn for him, as one mourneth for his only son, and shall be in bitterness for him, as one that is in bitterness for his firstborn.

With that verse in mind, we believe Yeshua is probably talking about the tribes of Israel in the following verse when He speaks of His coming again,

> And then shall appear the sign of the Son of man in heaven: and then shall all the tribes of the earth [or land] mourn, and they shall see the Son of man coming in the clouds of heaven with power and great glory.
> (Matt. 24:30)

We think it a possibility because in Hebrew the word for either "land" or "earth" is the same word – *eretz*. The choice in translation then depends on the context, and often in Scripture it refers specifically to the land of Israel.

Here is another verse which may refer specifically to the people of Israel in regards to the Second Coming,

> Behold, he cometh with clouds; and every eye shall see him, and they also which pierced him: and all kindreds [tribes] [13] of the earth [or land] shall wail because of him. Even so, Amen.   (Rev. 1:7)

God is Faithful!

The New Testament recognizes that the Holy Spirit is given to gentile believers because, as seen above, God is faithful to His *Tanach* promises to the Jewish people!

That the blessing of Abraham might come on the Gentiles through Yeshua the Messiah; that we might receive the promise of the Spirit through faith.   (Gal. 3:14)

In whom ye also trusted, after that ye heard the word of truth, the gospel of your salvation: in whom also after that ye believed, ye were sealed with that holy Spirit of promise.   (Eph. 1:13)

Teach me to do thy will; for thou art my God:
thy spirit is good; lead me into the land of uprightness.
(Ps. 143:10)

Notes

1. The Hebrew word for "spirit" is *ruach*. It is also the word for "wind" or "breath."
2. In Greek this is literally "Spirit, the God," or "God is spirit." Just like in Hebrew, the Greek word for "spirit" (*pneuma*) can also mean "wind" or "breath."
3. This does not mean sexual; it means judging only by the carnal senses and mind, making man the center of all things. This is humanism. Secular humanism manifests as materialism and atheism. Religious humanism seeks spiritual experiences, thinking only how to benefit from them, easily falling prey to demonic influence.
4. Greek: *parakletos* – one called alongside for help; one who pleads the case of another before a judge, an advocate; also an intercessor.
5. This common Hebrew word for God is always in a plural form.
6. In Chapter 14 we learned that Yeshua is called, or identified as YHWH manifested to man (e.g. Isa. 40:3 and Matt. 3:3).
7. The "promise" in these two verses refers to the time of fulfillment of the promise.
8. The first instruction Yeshua gave His disciples after imparting the Holy Spirit to them was concerning forgiveness of sins: "And when he had said this, he breathed on them, and saith unto them, Receive ye the Holy Ghost: Whose soever sins ye remit [forgive], they are remitted unto [forgiven] them; and whose soever sins ye retain, they are retained" (John 20:22–23). They were then responsible to forgive and to seek forgiveness whenever necessary.
9. Sanctification is progress in faith and works. The Holy Spirit gives us a desire to know the Word of God and to please Him.
10. Heb. 10:29 states that everyone gets saved by "the Spirit of grace."
11. Compare this with Rom. 8:26: "Likewise the Spirit also helpeth our infirmities [weaknesses]: for we know not what we should pray for as we ought: but the Spirit itself maketh intercession for us with groanings which cannot be uttered."
12. John 19:34–37: "But one of the soldiers with a spear pierced his side, and forthwith [immediately] came there out blood and water. And he that saw it

bare record, and his record is true: and he knoweth that he saith true, that ye might believe. For these things were done, that the scripture should be fulfilled, A bone of him shall not be broken. And again another scripture saith, They shall look on him whom they pierced."

13. This same word is translated "tribes' in the verse quoted in the previous paragraph, Matt. 24:30. It can also be translated as nations, or peoples.

CHAPTER 16

The Holy Spirit in the *Tanach* – Part 2

Spirit-anointed Believers in the *Tanach*

Next let's consider examples from the *Tanach* of the Holy Spirit working with and through God's people. Although the Holy Spirit's permanent dwelling in believers occurs after the Lord Yeshua's death and resurrection, the *Tanach* contains examples of many temporarily Spirit-filled children of God.

The Call of Israel

Joseph and Daniel were recognized even by gentile rulers to have an anointing, which we know was God's Spirit fulfilling the reason God chose Israel – to bring the knowledge of Himself to the nations/gentiles.[1]

> And Pharaoh said unto his servants, Can we find such a one as this is, [Joseph] a man in whom the Spirit of God is? (Gen. 41:38)

> I have even heard of thee [Daniel], that the spirit of the gods is in thee, and that light and understanding and excellent wisdom is found in thee. (Dan. 5:14; see also 4:8–9, 18; 5:11)

How were gentiles to gain knowledge of God? It happened when gentiles saw that God was with His people! As Moses expressed it,

> For wherein shall it be known here that I and thy people have found grace in thy sight? is it not in that thou goest with us? so shall we be separated [distinct, marked out], I and thy people, from all the people that are upon the face of the earth.
>
> (Exod. 33:16. See the context: vv. 12–17)

The Ability to Obey

God's Spirit equips His children to do what He commands, as the Lord points out in Zechariah 4:6b,

> Not by might, nor by power, but *by my spirit, saith the* LORD *of hosts.*

An example of this happened when God anointed men among the children of Israel to construct the Tabernacle in the wilderness. The Lord said to Moses,

> And *I have filled him [Bezalel] with the spirit of God*, in wisdom, and in understanding, and in knowledge, and in all manner of workmanship.
> (Exod. 31:3; see also 28:3; 35:31)

The New Testament indicates that Yeshua was able to do what His Father wanted because He had the fullness of God's Spirit:

> For he whom God hath sent speaketh the words of God: *for God giveth not the Spirit by measure* [not just partially] *unto him.*   (John 3:34)

> How *God anointed Yeshua of Nazareth with the Holy Ghost* and with power: who went about doing good, and healing all that were oppressed of the devil; for God was with him.   (Acts 10:38)

Though not the hoped-for political deliverance, Yeshua's anointed works did fulfill what the *Tanach* prophesied about the coming Messiah.[2]

The Biblical Response

When the Holy Spirit comes on a person, the typical response is a verbal one, whether tongues, prophesying, confession of sins, or praising God. When God raised up seventy elders in Israel to aid Moses, He placed His Spirit on them. This resulted in the elders breaking forth in prophecy,

> And the LORD came down in a cloud, and spake unto him, and took of the *spirit* that was upon him [Moses], and gave it unto the seventy elders: and it came to pass, that, *when the spirit rested upon them*, they prophesied, and did not cease.   (Num. 11:25)

And in the New Testament,

> While Peter yet spake these words, *the Holy Ghost fell* on all them which heard the word. And they of the circumcision which believed

were astonished, as many as came with Peter, because that on the Gentiles also was poured out *the gift of the Holy Ghost.* For they heard them *speak with tongues,* and *magnify God.* Then answered Peter, Can any man forbid water, that these should not be baptized, which have *received the Holy Ghost* as well as we? (Acts 10:44–47)

God's Deliverers/Judges

The men and women whom God used as His representatives to deliver and judge His people were empowered to accomplish the task because the Spirit of God was on them. The Holy Spirit came on the following judges of Israel:

And when the children of Israel cried unto the LORD, the LORD raised up a deliverer [*moshiah* – savior] to the children of Israel, who delivered [saved] them, even Othniel ... Caleb's younger brother. And the *Spirit of the LORD came upon him,* and he judged Israel, and went out to war: and the LORD delivered ... [the] king of Mesopotamia into his hand ... (Judg. 3:9–10a)

But *the Spirit of the LORD came upon* [clothed Himself with!] Gideon, and he blew a trumpet ... (Judg. 6:34)

Then *the Spirit of the LORD came* [was] *upon Jephthah,* and he passed over Gilead ... (Judg. 11:29a)

And the woman bare a son, and called his name *Samson:* and the child grew, and the LORD blessed him. *And the Spirit of the LORD began to move* [push, impel] *him* at times in the camp of Dan.... (Judg. 13:24–25)

And *the Spirit of the LORD came mightily upon* [rushed on, pushed] *him,* and he rent [the lion] as he would have rent a kid, and he had nothing in his hand ... (Judg. 14:6a)

And the *Spirit of the LORD came upon* [see 14:6a] *him,* and he went down to Ashkelon, and slew thirty men ... (Judg. 14:19a)

the Philistines shouted against him: and *the Spirit of the LORD came mightily upon him* [see 14:6a], and the cords that were upon his arms became as flax that was burnt with fire, and his bands loosed from off his hands. (Judg. 15:14)

And *the Spirit of God came upon* [see 14:6a] *Saul* when he heard those tidings, and his anger was kindled greatly. (1 Sam. 11:6)

In all these instances God's Spirit filled His chosen deliverer/savior, leading and empowering each one to perform God's works (cf. 1 Sam. 11:6; Acts 10:38).

Spirit's Work in Salvation

The prophet Samuel declared to King Saul,

> And *the Spirit of the* LORD *will come upon* [rush on, push] *thee, and thou shalt prophesy with them, and shalt be turned* [changed, transformed] *into another man.* And let it be, when these signs are come unto thee, that thou do as occasion serve thee; for God is with thee ... behold, a company of prophets met him; and the Spirit of God came upon [rushed on, pushed] him, and he prophesied among them.
>
> (1 Sam. 10:6–7, 10b)

Although not salvation, and only temporary, this episode can be seen as a foreshadow of salvation, or being "born again," because it connects the Spirit of God coming on someone with that particular someone changing into a new person.[3]

> Therefore if any man be in Messiah, he is a new creature [creation]: old things are passed away; behold, all things are become new.
>
> (2 Cor. 5:17)

> Yeshua answered, Verily, verily [Truly], I say unto thee, Except a man be born of water *and of the Spirit*, he cannot [does not have the power or ability to] enter into the kingdom [rulership] of God. That which is born of the flesh is flesh; and *that which is born of the Spirit is spirit.* Marvel not that I said unto thee, Ye must be born again [or from above]. The wind [*ruach*, spirit] bloweth [or breathes] where it listeth [wants, desires], and thou hearest the sound [or voice] thereof, but canst not tell whence it cometh, and whither it goeth: so is every one that is *born of the Spirit.* (John 3:5–8)

As mature believers, we know we don't have the power to change ourselves. *Tanach* saints were also aware of their need and cried out for God to save them. For example:

> Turn us again [Help us to repent], O God, and cause thy face to shine; and we shall be saved. (Ps. 80:3; see vv. 7, 19)

> Turn thou us unto thee [same as above], O LORD, and we shall be turned; renew our days as of old. (Lam. 5:21)[4]

Here is a wonderful verse showing how the Spirit of God is needed to accept and submit to God's Anointed One:

> Then *the spirit* came upon [clothed Himself with] Amasai, who was chief of the captains, and he said, Thine are we, David, and on thy side, thou son of Jesse...   (1 Chr. 12:18a)

The analogy is simple. If it took the Spirit of God coming on Amasai for him to join with David, God's anointed king, how much more does it take the Holy Spirit to enable us to confess that "Yeshua is Lord"? As it says in 1 Corinthians 12:3,

> Wherefore I give you to understand [I want you to know], that no man speaking by the Spirit of God calleth [affirms or teaches] Yeshua accursed: and *that no man can* [has the power or ability to] *say that Yeshua is the Lord, but by the Holy Ghost.*

Godly Conviction

It takes the Spirit's power to convict us of sin so we can lovingly and fruitfully, from a humbled heart, show others their sins. We are commanded to do this.[5] Too easily we speak of other people's faults as though we were immune. The necessary thing is to speak in love and humility in the power of the Holy Spirit. All godly and effective correction will be motivated by love, a fruit of the Spirit.

Yeshua said the Holy Spirit is the convictor of sin,

> Nevertheless I tell you the truth; It is expedient [profitable] for you that I go away: for if I go not away, the Comforter [Advocate, Helper, Intercessor] will not come unto you; but if I depart, I will send him unto you. And when he is come, *he will reprove* [convict] the world of [concerning] sin, and of righteousness, and of judgment...
>   (John 16:7–8; cf. Acts 4:8–14)

The *Tanach* prophets could say in truth,

> But truly I am full of power by the spirit of the LORD, and of judgment, and of might, *to declare unto Jacob his transgression* [lit: rebellion], and to Israel his sin.   (Mic. 3:8)

One of Messiah Yeshua's divine characteristics was His ability, by the Spirit, to know a person's real intent. The rich young ruler, Mary Magdalene, Peter and the other disciples are examples of how Yeshua judged impartially and not by appearances. This was prophesied of the coming Messiah in a riddle,

> Who is blind, but my servant? or deaf, as my messenger that I sent? who is blind as he that is perfect [complete, mature], and blind as the LORD's servant? Seeing [perceiving, considering] many things, but thou observest not; opening the ears, but he heareth not. The LORD is well pleased for his righteousness' sake; he will magnify [honor] the law, and make it honourable.   (Isa. 42:19–21; cf. 11:3)

The interpretation cannot, as some say, be a condemnation of Israel, because God commends this servant in these verses. Only Yeshua's likeness fits here. Only He is truly righteous[6] and only He truly honors God's Law.[7]

The Anointed One

There are many *Tanach* types of the coming Messiah. The root word for Messiah means "to be smeared (anointed) with oil." "Messiah" literally means "Anointed One." King David, in particular, is a wonderful type of Yeshua as the anointed King of Israel.

> Then Samuel took the horn of oil, and anointed him in the midst of his brethren: and the Spirit of the LORD came [rushed] upon David from that day forward...   (1 Sam. 16:13)

This verse links the Spirit of God with being anointed by oil. For this reason oil is sometimes used as a symbol of God's Spirit.[8]

David understood the deep connection between the Spirit of God and His Word,

> Now these be the last words of David. David the son of Jesse said, and the man who was raised up on high, *the anointed* [Heb.: *mashiach* – messiah] of the God of Jacob, and the sweet psalmist of Israel, said, *The Spirit of the LORD spake by* [or "in"] *me, and his word was in my tongue...*   (2 Sam. 23:1–2)[9]

The prime example of this connection occurs in King David's greater Son, Messiah Yeshua, who declared the Word of God in the fullness of the Spirit,

> *The Spirit of the Lord is upon me, because he hath anointed me to preach the gospel to the poor; he hath sent me to heal the broken-hearted, to preach* [proclaim] *deliverance to the captives, and recovering of sight to the blind, to set at liberty them that are bruised,*

> *To preach* [proclaim] the acceptable year of the Lord ... This day is
> this scripture fulfilled in your ears.   (Luke 4:18–19, 21b)

In that one verse, half the things Yeshua did concerned healing and
the other half involved proclaiming God's Word – all by the Holy
Spirit.

Just as God gave directions for the pattern of the Tabernacle to
Moses (see Heb. 8:5), so God's expanded sanctuary built by Solomon
also followed a pattern revealed to David by the Spirit:

> Then David gave to Solomon ... the pattern of all that he had *by the*
> *spirit*, of the courts of the house of the LORD ...   (1 Chr. 28:11–12a)

Just so, declaring God's Word, as Moses and David did under the
anointing, builds God's House. The Body of Messiah, a geographic-
ally unconfined spiritual Temple built by the Holy Spirit's directions
given to the apostles and prophets, allows whosoever will to worship
God in spirit and in truth at any time and in any place.

> Now therefore ye are no more strangers and foreigners, but fellow-
> citizens with the saints, and of the household [family] of God; And are
> built upon the foundation of the apostles and prophets, Yeshua the
> Messiah himself being the chief corner stone; In whom all the building
> fitly framed together groweth unto *an holy temple in the Lord*: In
> whom ye also are builded together for *an habitation* [dwelling-place]
> *of God through* [by] *the Spirit*.   (Eph. 2:19–22)

Yeshua haMashiach, Jesus the Messiah

The New Testament witnessed of Yeshua that He had the fullness of
the Holy Spirit.[10]

> And John bare record, saying, I saw *the Spirit* descending from heaven
> like a dove, and *it abode upon him*. And I knew him not: but he that
> sent me to baptize with water, the same said unto me, *Upon whom*
> *thou shalt see the Spirit descending, and remaining on him*, the same is
> he which baptizeth with the Holy Ghost. And I saw, and bare record
> that *this is the Son of God*.   (John 1:32–34, cf. 3:34; 20:21)

The *Tanach* had prophesied that the coming Messiah would have
the Holy Spirit in fullness,

> And there shall come forth a rod out of the stem of Jesse, and a Branch
> shall grow [lit: bear fruit] out of his roots: *And the spirit of the* LORD

shall rest [settle down, remain] *upon him*, the spirit of wisdom and understanding, the spirit of counsel and might, the spirit of knowledge and of the fear of the LORD; And shall make him of quick understanding [sensitive, discerning] in the fear of the LORD: and he shall not judge after the sight of his eyes [not just by appearances][11] neither reprove after the hearing of his ears: But with righteousness shall he judge the poor [weak, lowly], and reprove with equity for the meek [humble] of the earth: and he shall smite the earth with the rod of his mouth, and with the breath [lit: spirit/*ruach*] of his lips shall he slay the wicked.   (Isa. 11:1–4)

Please note the following points about that portion of Scripture:

This prophecy, which was given after David's son Solomon died, must refer to David's promised son, the Messiah.

These verses explain Revelation 1:4, 3:1, 4:5 and 5:6 which mention "the seven Spirits of God." Isaiah describes the Holy Spirit using seven terms: the Spirit of the LORD, of wisdom, understanding, counsel, might, knowledge and fear of the LORD. The number seven in Scripture is often symbolic of completion or perfection. Just as we can be filled with the Spirit of the Lord without diminishing that Spirit, so the Holy Spirit can operate in these seven aspects of His power as He did in Yeshua and remain as "one Spirit."[12]

Yeshua amazed people by striking at the heart of every issue and judging with righteousness and equity. Toward the end of the portion under consideration, Isaiah (ch. 11) talks about the Second Coming, when God's Anointed One, Messiah Yeshua, comes as the Judge of the earth.[13]

The next verse was used in Matthew 12:17–21, to prove that Yeshua is Messiah and Savior of not just the Jewish people, but of the gentiles as well.

Behold my servant, whom I uphold; mine elect [chosen], in whom my soul delighteth [is completely satisfied]; I have put *my spirit upon him*: he shall bring forth judgment [also justice] to the Gentiles. (Isa. 42:1)

To announce His commission, Yeshua read part of the following passage in the synagogue in His home town of Nazareth,

The *Spirit of the Lord GOD is upon me*; because *the LORD hath anointed me* to preach good tidings unto the meek [poor, humble, afflicted]; he hath sent me to bind up the brokenhearted, to proclaim liberty to the captives, and the opening of the prison to them that are bound; To proclaim the acceptable year of the LORD, and the day of vengeance of our God;[14] to comfort all that mourn; To appoint unto them that mourn in Zion, to give unto them beauty for [instead of] ashes, the oil of joy for mourning, the garment of praise for the spirit of heaviness; that they might be called trees of righteousness, the planting of the LORD, that he might be glorified.

(Isa. 61:1–3; quoted in Luke 4:18–21)

Many understand that Yeshua stopped quoting halfway through verse 2, just before "the day of vengeance," because the rest of the text describes the "day of the Lord," when Yeshua will come the second time to set up His rulership on earth. Although the Second Coming will involve great judgment, it will also bring great joy to those who believe in Him.

Conclusion

Simeon was what we would call a *Tanach* saint because he was led by the Holy Spirit decades before Yeshua started His ministry. Simeon's Holy Spirit-led declaration becomes a bridge between the promise of the expected Messiah and the promise fulfilled:

> And, behold, there was a man in Jerusalem, whose name was Simeon; and the same man was just [righteous] and devout, waiting for the consolation [or comfort, advocate] of Israel: and *the Holy Ghost was upon him*. And it *was revealed unto him by the Holy Ghost*, that he should not see death, before he had seen the Lord's Messiah. And *he came by the Spirit into the temple*: and when the parents brought in the child Yeshua, to do for him after the custom of the law, Then took he him up in his arms, and blessed [or praised] God, and said, Lord, now lettest thou thy servant depart in peace, according to thy word: For mine eyes have seen thy salvation, Which thou hast prepared before the face of all people; A light to lighten [enlighten] the Gentiles, and the glory [honor, praise] of thy people Israel.
> (Luke 2:25–32)

Notes
_____

1. See Deut. 4:6–8; Exod. 19:4–6a; cf. 1 Pet. 2:9.
2. Isa. 61:1, 2.
3. For Saul it was only temporary and probably a warning from God.
4. See also Pss. 31:16; 85:4; 109:26; Isa. 25:9; Jer. 31:7.

5. See Gal. 6:1.
6. Rom. 3:25; 2 Cor. 5:21; 1 John 2:1.
7. Matt. 5:17–19; 23:23; Luke 24:44; Rom. 7:12–14; 8:4.
8. See Ps. 45:7; Zech. 4:11ff.
9. See Matt. 22:43 and Acts 4:24–25 for the New Testament witness that the Holy Spirit spoke through David.
10. "For he whom God hath sent [Yeshua] speaketh the words of God: for God giveth not the Spirit by measure unto him" (John 3:34).
11. Cf. John 7:24; 8:15–16.
12. See Eph. 4:4; 1 Cor. 12:13.
13. See Acts 10:40–43; 17:31; Rom. 2:16; 2 Tim. 4:1; Rev. 19:11–16.
14. Note that the time in which God's grace is available is stated as a year while, in comparison, the time of His judgment is described only as a day! See Isa. 63:4 as well.

CHAPTER 17

The Holy Spirit in the *Tanach* – Part 3

Let's look at some other aspects of the Spirit of God which were taught by the *Tanach* before the first coming of Messiah Yeshua.

Salvation and God's Spirit

In John 3, Yeshua declared to Nicodemus, "Except a man be born again, he cannot see the kingdom of God" (v. 3).[1] Nicodemus was not able to follow His thinking, asking "How can these things be?" (v. 9). Yeshua responded, "Art thou a [the] master [teacher] of Israel, and knowest not these things?" (v. 10).

As we explored in Chapter 7, Messiah Yeshua is implying that the concept of being born from above was already revealed in the *Tanach*. Ezekiel 36:25–27 is one of the most comprehensive descriptions in all of Scripture for this doctrine and connects salvation with the indwelling of the Holy Spirit.

God is gathering the scattered Jewish people to the land of Israel (36:24). He states to them,

> Then will I sprinkle clean [pure] water upon you, and ye shall be clean [purified]: from all your filthiness [impurity], and from all your idols, will I cleanse you. A new heart [mind, inner man] also will I give you, and *a new spirit* will I put within you: and I will take away the stony heart out of your flesh, and I will give you an heart of flesh. And *I will put my spirit within you*, and cause you to walk in my statutes, and ye shall keep [observe] my judgments, and do them.
>
> (Ezek. 36:25–27; see also 11:19–20)

Please note that God's Spirit enables obedience.

Although its literal, final fulfillment awaits Israel's salvation, this prophecy's continuing fulfillment establishes the true Church. The Holy Spirit placed inside us when we become believers enables us to obey God's Word. Look at how the New Testament declares it:

But ye are not in the flesh, but in the Spirit, if so be that the *Spirit of God dwell in you*. Now if any man have not *the Spirit of Messiah*, he is none of his.   (Rom. 8:9)[2]

We have God's Holy Spirit dwelling inside of us.

The Holy Spirit justifies and sanctifies us in the name (nature) of Yeshua.

And such were some of you: but ye are washed, but ye are sanctified [made holy – separated from the world to God], but ye are justified [declared righteous] in the name of the Lord Yeshua, and *by the Spirit of our God*.   (1 Cor. 6:11)[3]

We are made new creations in Messiah.

Therefore if any man be in Messiah, he is a new creature: old things are passed away; behold, all things are become new.   (2 Cor. 5:17)[4]

We have received God's Spirit who causes us to know God's will and enables us to obey His Word.

For the law of *the Spirit* of life in Messiah Yeshua hath made me free [liberated] from the law of sin and death. For what the law could not do, in that it was weak through the flesh,[5] God sending his own Son in the likeness of sinful flesh, and for sin, condemned sin in the flesh: That the righteousness of the law might be fulfilled [accomplished; realized] in us, who walk [i.e., live] not after [according to] the flesh, but after the Spirit.   (Rom. 8:2–4)[6]

God's Spirit is God's Presence

Often in the *Tanach*, God's Spirit and His presence are paralleled, which means that they indicate the same thing.

Whither shall I go from *thy spirit*? or whither shall I flee from thy presence [lit: face]?   (Ps. 139:7)

Neither will I hide *my face* any more from them: for I have poured out *my spirit* upon the house of Israel, saith the Lord God.
                                                                              (Ezek. 39:29)

"Face" is to be taken figuratively and signifies His presence by His Spirit. No man can literally "see God," that is, experience the fullness of God through his physical senses, and live. As the New Testament makes abundantly clear, if we have His Spirit, we have His presence.

And I will pray [request of] the Father, and he shall give you another
Comforter [intercessor, advocate, helper], that he may abide with you
for ever; Even the *Spirit of truth*; whom *the world cannot* [does not
have the power or ability to] *receive, because it seeth him not, neither
knoweth him: but ye know him*; for he dwelleth with you, and shall
be in you. I will not leave you comfortless [lit: orphaned]: I will come
to you.   (John 14:16–18)

Know [Perceive] ye not that ye are the temple of God, and that *the
Spirit of God dwelleth in you?*   (1 Cor. 3:16)

The Blood and the Spirit

We have already mentioned that at times in Scripture oil can
be symbolic of God's Spirit. The following passage is taken
from the procedure for the leper's cleansing, which was necessary
so that he could re-enter the community of Israel and worship his
God:

And the priest shall take some of the *blood* of the trespass offering, and
the priest shall put it *upon* the tip of the right *ear* of him that is to be
cleansed [purified], and upon the thumb of his right *hand*, and upon
the great toe of his right *foot*: And the priest shall take some of the log
[a measure] of *oil* and ... put *upon* the tip of the right *ear* of him that is
to be cleansed, and upon the thumb of his right *hand*, and upon the
great toe of his right *foot, upon the blood* of the trespass offering...
(Lev. 14:14–15a, 17)

Notice how the oil was placed on top of the blood and not
on uncovered flesh. This teaches that God's Spirit will not rest on
unconsecrated flesh but only on the one whose life is hid in the
Messiah (Col. 3:3). Hidden in Yeshua, "The LORD our righteousness"
(Jer. 33:16),[7] we can expect the Spirit to quicken our "ear," that is our
mind's perception of the things of God (1 Cor. 2:9–16),[8] to empower
our "hands" to obey God's will,[9] and to guide our feet, representing our lifestyle choices, on His Way.[10]

The Spirit as Teacher

The following verses confirm what was pointed out in the previous
section, that we need God's Spirit to understand the things of
God:

Thou gavest *also thy good spirit to instruct them*, and withheldest not thy manna from their mouth, and gavest them water for their thirst.

(Neh. 9:20)

Teach me to do thy will [that which delights You]; for thou art my God: *thy spirit is good; lead me* into the land of uprightness.

(Ps. 143:10)

Messiah Yeshua declares the same thing about God's Spirit:

But the Comforter [Advocate, Intercessor, Helper], which is *the Holy Ghost*, whom the Father will send in my name, he *shall teach you* all things, and bring all things to your remembrance, whatsoever I have said unto you.   (John 14:26)

Howbeit when *he, the Spirit of truth, is come, he will guide* [or teach] *you into all truth*: for *he shall not speak of himself*; but whatsoever he shall hear, that shall he speak: and he will shew [announce, make known to] you things to come. He shall glorify me: for he shall receive of mine, and shall shew it unto you.   (John 16:13–14)

Yeshua always speaks the truth, so we must understand that the job of the Holy Spirit is not to bring attention to Himself as Spirit. He comes to glorify Yeshua, to focus us on the Son of God, and to teach and remind us what Yeshua said.

If we find ourselves concentrating on the Holy Spirit, we are not being led by the Holy Spirit! Any Spirit-led meeting, or prayer, or church, or believer, will exalt the Lord Yeshua by name. Search the Scriptures – you will not find, except in Ezekiel 37 when the prophet is specifically commanded by the Lord to do so, one example of a saint speaking or praying directly to the Holy Spirit.

Here are a couple of further points on the Holy Spirit as God's teacher for His children. The will to repent and to seek righteousness is produced by a heart submitted to the Lord's discipline, and is a heart ready to receive God's teaching. The book of Proverbs says,

Turn [repent] you at my reproof [rebuke, correction, chastisement]: behold, I will pour out *my spirit* unto you, I will *make known my words* unto you.   (Prov. 1:23)

This verse makes a repentant heart the condition for receiving God's teaching by His Spirit.

Peter also links together repentance and receiving God's Spirit,

> Then Peter said unto them, *Repent*, and be baptized every one of you in
> the name of Yeshua the Messiah for the remission [forgiveness,
> pardon, release from the bondage] of sins, and ye shall *receive the gift
> of the Holy Ghost.*   (Acts 2:38)

A final note to always have in mind, especially during prayer, is
that we are never to command God's Spirit or angels.

> Who hath directed *the Spirit of the* LORD, or being his counselor hath
> taught him?   (Isa. 40:13)

The biblical approach to prayer is to let the Lord work out the
answers to our requests in His way and timing.

The Spirit and God's Punishment or Judgment

God is patient even if we spurn His discipline, but eventually a lack of
repentance will result in our punishment. Nehemiah proclaims that
by the Spirit of God God's prophets warned disobedient Israel of
danger,

> Yet many years didst thou forbear them, and *testifiedst against them by
> thy spirit* in thy prophets: yet would they not give ear: therefore gavest
> thou them into the hand of the people of the lands.   (Neh. 9:30)

Here is an example. Through the prophet Isaiah God warns His
stubborn children not to partake of an anointing that is of a different
spirit from the Holy Spirit,

> Woe to the rebellious [and/or stubborn] children, saith the LORD, that
> take counsel [make plans], but not of me; and that cover with a
> covering [lit.: anoint with an anointing], but *not of my spirit*, that they
> may add sin to sin...   (Isa. 30:1)

The result of this rebellion is that dependence on Egypt brings Israel's
downfall (see vv. 2–3).

In that familiar passage of John 16:8, Yeshua assures us that the
Holy Spirit will convict the world concerning sin, righteousness, and
justice,

> And when he is come, *he will reprove* [convict] the world of
> [concerning] sin, and of [concerning] righteousness, and of [concern-
> ing] judgment [justice]...

Finally, Stephen links Israel's rebellion, especially that of her leadership, to resisting the influence of God's Spirit.

> Ye stiffnecked [stubborn] and uncircumcised in heart and ears, ye do always *resist the Holy Ghost*: as your fathers did, so do ye.
>
> (Acts 7:51)

Of course this verse implies what we have been stating, that the Spirit of God was at work in the lives of God's people even before Yeshua came.

God's Redeemer and the Holy Spirit

In the Old Testament avenging the shedding of innocent blood is part of the job description of a redeemer. Isaiah 59:19b–21 ties together the coming of God's Redeemer with the Spirit of God fighting against the enemy,

> When the enemy shall come in like a flood, *the Spirit of the* LORD shall lift up a standard against [to attack, put to flight] him.[11] And the *Redeemer* [or Avenger] shall come to Zion, and unto them that turn [repent] from transgression [rebellion] in Jacob, saith the LORD.[12] As for me, this is my covenant with them,[13] saith the LORD; *My spirit* that is upon thee, *and my words* which I have put in thy mouth, shall not depart out of thy mouth, nor out of the mouth of thy seed, nor out of the mouth of thy seed's seed, saith the LORD, from henceforth and for ever.[14]

According to that prophecy, after the Redeemer comes, God's Spirit is promised to be on or in the remnant of Israel forever. Also note that the Spirit's coming on someone anoints their "mouth," the spoken word, so that by His Spirit we can proclaim the Good News. As Yeshua said to His disciples,

> But ye shall receive power [or ability], *after that the Holy Ghost is come upon* [overtakes] *you: and ye shall be witnesses unto me* both in Jerusalem, and in all Judaea, and in Samaria, and unto the uttermost part of the earth. (Acts 1:8)

Isaiah 63:9–14 – God's Spirit in Redemption

This meaty portion of Isaiah has a number of points we want to explore and confirm from elsewhere in the Scriptures. First, here is the entire passage of Isaiah 63:9–14 with verse numbering and some Hebrew word meanings:

> **9.** In all their affliction [trouble] he was afflicted, and the angel of his presence [lit. face] saved[15] them: in his love and in his pity [or mercy] he redeemed [ransomed] them; and he bare them, and carried them all the days of old. **10.** But they rebelled, and vexed [hurt, grieved] *his holy Spirit*: therefore he was turned to be [transformed into] their enemy, and he fought against them. **11.** Then he remembered the days of old, Moses, and his people, saying, Where is he that brought them up out of the sea with the shepherd of his flock? where is he that put his holy Spirit within [or, in the midst of] him? **12.** That led them by the right hand of Moses with his glorious arm, dividing the water before them, to make himself an everlasting name? **13.** That led them through the deep, as an horse in the wilderness, that they should not stumble? **14.** As a beast goeth down into the valley, the *Spirit of the* LORD caused him to rest [settle]: so didst thou lead thy people, to make thyself a glorious name.

Let's study parts of this passage more closely.

Isaiah 63:9

God is afflicted when His people suffer, whether Israel or the Church. Here is another *Tanach* verse that agrees with this:

> And the children of Israel said unto the LORD, We have sinned: do thou unto us whatsoever seemeth good unto thee; deliver [rescue] us only, we pray thee, this day. And they put away the strange [foreign] gods from among them, and served the LORD: and *his* [God's] *soul was grieved for the misery of Israel.*   (Judg. 10:15–16)

The New Testament also contains a confirming passage:

> And as he [Saul] journeyed, he came near Damascus: and suddenly there shined round about him a light from heaven: And he fell to the earth, and heard a voice saying unto him, Saul, Saul, why persecutest thou me? And he said, Who art thou, Lord? And the Lord said, *I am Yeshua whom thou persecutest*: it is hard for thee to kick against the pricks.[16]   (Acts 9:3–5)

When the Lord's people were persecuted, He was persecuted.

Isaiah 63:9, 13

After redemption, God still needs to "carry" us to the "Promised

Land." It is still His work of grace – working with our faith in that grace – to see us all the way home.

> Ye have seen what I did unto the Egyptians, and how *I bare you* on eagles' wings, and brought you unto myself.   (Exod. 19:4)

Though God carries us as He did Israel, we still must walk.

> Come unto me, all ye that labour and are heavy laden, and *I will give you rest.* Take my yoke upon you, and learn of me; for I am meek and lowly [humble] in heart: and ye shall find [obtain] rest unto your souls. For my yoke is easy, and my burden is light.   (Matt. 11:28–30)

Though we rest in Him, we still must serve.

> Wherefore, my beloved ... work out your own salvation with fear and trembling. For it is *God which worketh* [is active] *in you* both to will and to do [for the sake] of his good pleasure.   (Phil. 2:12–13)

Though God works in us, we still must choose.

Isaiah 63:10
After redemption we (just like Israel) can grieve His Spirit, turning God into an adversary who resists what we want to do, or who even afflicts us!

> And *grieve* [offend] *not* the holy Spirit of God, whereby ye are sealed unto the day of redemption [i.e., full deliverance].
>   (Eph. 4:30; cf. Heb. 3:7–15; 12:22–29)

> Ye adulterers and adulteresses [fig: apostates], know ye not that the friendship of the world is *enmity* [conflict] *with God?* whosoever therefore will [deliberately desire to] be a friend of the world is [declares or shows himself] the enemy [adversary] of God.
>   (Jas. 4:4)

Isaiah 63:11
Even in the *Tanach,* God's Holy Spirit was in the midst of His people.

> Yet now be strong [and/or courageous], O Zerubbabel, saith the LORD; and be strong, O Joshua ... the high priest; and be strong, all ye people of the land, saith the LORD, and work: for I am with you, saith the LORD of hosts: According to the word that I covenanted with you when ye came out of Egypt, so *my spirit remaineth among you:* fear ye not.
>   (Hag. 2:4–5)

Isaiah 63:14

The Holy Spirit causes us to enter into God's rest, the *Shabbat* rest of redemption, which has been promised to God's people. Through ongoing repentance and obedience we enter God's rest. But, we are only able to enter Yeshua's rest with the Holy Spirit's help in convicting us of sin, leading us to repent, and enabling us to declare truthfully that "Yeshua is Lord" (1 Cor. 12:3):

> And in that day there shall be a root of Jesse [David's Son – Yeshua], which shall stand for an ensign of the people; to it shall the Gentiles seek: and *his rest* shall be glorious.   (Isa. 11:10)

Yeshua declares the fulfillment,

> Come unto me, all ye that labour and are heavy laden, and *I will give you rest*. Take my yoke upon you, and learn of me; for I am meek and lowly in heart: and *ye shall find rest* unto your souls.
>
> (Matt. 11:28–29)[17]

Another spirit will not lead us into rest in Yeshua.

> Arise ye, and depart; for *this is not your rest*: because *it is polluted*, it shall destroy you, even with a sore destruction. If a man walking in the spirit and falsehood [NKJV– in a false spirit] do lie, saying, I will prophesy unto thee of wine and of strong drink; he shall even be the prophet of this people.   (Mic. 2:10–11)

Isaiah 63:12, 14

God's purpose in all of salvation history is to glorify His name, in His Son through His Spirit, so that the world will know the real Creator and Father, the God of Israel. When God says that He will sanctify His name through Israel, He specifies that it will happen when Israel is regathered and then redeemed:

> And I will sanctify my great name [character, reputation, glory], which was profaned [defiled, polluted] among the heathen [nations, gentiles] ... and the heathen shall know that I am the LORD, saith the LORD God, when *I shall be sanctified* in you [Israel] before their eyes. For I will ... gather you out of all countries, and will bring you into your own land. *Then* will I sprinkle clean [pure] water upon you, and ye shall be clean [purified]: from all your filthiness, and from all your idols, will I cleanse you. A new heart [inner man] also will I give you, and a new spirit will I put within you ... And *I will put my spirit within*

you, and cause you to walk in my statutes, and ye shall keep [guard, observe] my judgments, and do them.   (Ezek. 36:23–27)

Yeshua tells us that sanctifying God's name should be our number one priority when we pray,

> After this manner therefore pray ye: Our Father which art in heaven, *Hallowed* [holy, sanctified] *be thy name*. Thy kingdom come. Thy will be done in earth, as it is in heaven.   (Matt. 6:9–10)

Sanctifying His name will be the final result of God's making history – His story.

> Who shall not fear thee, O Lord, and *glorify* [magnify, praise, celebrate] *thy name*? for thou only art holy: for all nations shall come and worship before thee; for thy judgments are made manifest.
>   (Rev. 15:4)[18]

God Speaks by His Spirit

The Holy Spirit is the One enabling Ezekiel to speak the word of the Lord.

> Therefore prophesy against them, prophesy, O son of man. And *the Spirit of the* LORD fell upon me, and said unto me, Speak; Thus saith the LORD; Thus have ye said, O house of Israel: for I know the things that come into your mind [*ruach* – spirit], every one of them.
>   (Ezek. 11:4–5)

God also spoke by His Spirit in the New Testament,[19] and He is still speaking by His Spirit to and through the Church today. But we are cautioned not to be deceived. The Spirit of God will only speak that which agrees with the Word of God. Because He is called "the Spirit of truth" (John 14:17; 16:13), we must expect Him to bear witness to God's truth, which is in the Scripture.

> Sanctify them through thy truth: thy word is truth.   (John 17:17)

Yeshua is praying that God will sanctify us – keep us separated from the world and for Himself, for His purposes – inasmuch as His Word finds a home in us.

We all need the Holy Spirit's power to fulfill the Great Commission. That is why Satan counterfeits that power by causing excitement or a deceptive appearance of godliness. Yeshua spoke strongly on this subject in the context of the end times,

For there shall arise false Messiahs [false anointed ones], and false prophets, and shall shew *great signs and wonders*; insomuch that, if possible, they shall deceive the very elect. Behold, I have told you before.   (Matt. 24:24–25)

Ezekiel 37:1–14 – The Spirit of Life Is Restoring Now!

The following prophecy is being fulfilled today in the modern nation of Israel through the power of God's Spirit. The words in italic are the same Hebrew word, *ruach*. Depending on context it is translated either "spirit," "breath" or "wind":

> The hand of the LORD was upon me, and carried me out in the *spirit* of the LORD, and set me down in the midst of the valley which was full of bones . . . and, lo, they were very dry. And he said unto me, Son of man, can these bones live? And I answered, O Lord GOD, thou knowest. Again he said unto me, Prophesy . . . unto them, O ye dry bones, hear the word of the LORD. Thus saith the Lord GOD . . . Behold, I will cause *breath* to enter into you, and ye shall live: And I will lay sinews upon you, and will bring up flesh upon you, and cover you with skin, and put *breath* in you, and ye shall live; and ye shall know [by experience conforming to God's Word] that I am the LORD. So I prophesied as I was commanded: and as I prophesied, there was a noise [or voice], and behold a shaking, and the bones came together . . . the sinews and the flesh came up upon them, and the skin covered them above: but there was no *breath* in them. Then said he unto me, Prophesy unto the wind . . . and say to the *wind*, Thus saith the Lord GOD; Come from the four *winds*, O *breath*, and breathe upon these slain, that they may live. So I prophesied as he commanded me, and the *breath* came into them, and they lived, and stood up upon their feet, an exceeding great army. Then he said unto me, Son of man, these bones are the whole house of Israel: behold, they say, Our bones are dried, and our hope is lost: we are cut off for our parts [divided from each other]. Therefore prophesy and say unto them, Thus saith the Lord GOD; Behold, O my people, I will open your graves, and cause you to come up[20] out of your graves, and bring you into the land of Israel. And ye shall know that I am the LORD, when I have opened your graves, O my people, and brought you up[21] out of your graves, And shall put my *spirit* in you, and ye shall live, and I shall place you [settle you permanently] in your own land: then shall ye know that I the LORD have spoken it, and performed it, saith the LORD.   (Ezek. 37:1–14)

In this portion the *ruach*, or spirit, is associated with life. A number of times here it is prophesied that the dead will be resurrected when touched by the *ruach*, the Spirit of the Lord. Although by analogy this section can apply to being born from above, the plain meaning, especially from the context (Ezek. 34–39), points to the current resurrection of the nation of Israel out of the grave of the Holocaust. Very many "dry bones," having "our hope ... lost," and being "cut off" one from another describe the Holocaust, while "an exceeding great army" and settling us in our "own land" describe current events in Israel.

A Closing Thought

God's word to Zerubbabel is relevant to all of God's people. When it comes to doing His work, we must always remember that it is "Not by might, nor by power, but by *my spirit*, saith the LORD of hosts" (Zech. 4:6).

*Notes*_____

1. Here is an alternative rendering of the Greek: "Unless a man is born from above, he cannot know the rulership of God."
2. See also Rom. 8:11, 14–16; Eph. 1:13–14; 1 John 3:24.
3. See also 2 Cor. 5:21; 1 Pet. 1:22; Rev. 19:8.
4. See also Matt. 9:16–17; 1 Cor. 5:7.
5. Paul often uses "flesh" to mean man's earthly nature (mind and body apart from divine influence) which is predisposed to sin and opposed to God.
6. See also Acts 2:16–17; Rom. 8:13–14; Heb. 8:10; 1 John 3:24.
7. Cf. Ps. 24:5; 31:1; Isa. 45:24; 54:17; 1 Cor. 1:30; 2 Cor. 5:21.
8. "But as it is written, Eye hath not seen, nor ear heard, neither have entered into the heart [soul, mind] of man, the things which God hath prepared for them that love him. *But God hath revealed them unto us by his Spirit*: for the Spirit searcheth [investigates] all things, yea, the deep things of God. For what man knoweth [understands] the things of a man, save the spirit of man which is in him? even so *the things of God knoweth no man, but the Spirit of God. Now we have received*, not the spirit of the world, *but the spirit which is of* [from] *God; that we might know the things that are freely given to us of God.* Which things also we speak, not in the words which man's wisdom teacheth, but which *the Holy Ghost teacheth*; comparing [or interpreting] spiritual things with spiritual. But the natural man receiveth not the things of the Spirit of God: for they are foolishness [absurd] unto him: neither can he know [able to perceive, understand] them, because they are spiritually discerned [examined, judged]. But he that is spiritual judgeth all things, yet he himself is judged of no man. For who hath known the mind [thoughts, purposes, counsel] of the Lord, that he may instruct him? But *we have the mind of Messiah*" (1 Cor. 2:9–16).

9. See Deut. 14:28–29; Ps. 90:17; Matt. 7:21, 24; 1 Cor. 4:12; Eph. 6:8; 1 John 3:7.

10. See Deut. 10:12; Ps. 86:11; Prov. 3:5–6; Rom. 6:4; 8:4; 2 Cor. 5:7; Eph. 5:8.

11. Cf. 2 Thess. 2:8, "And then shall that Wicked [lit: lawless] be revealed, whom the Lord shall consume [abolish, destroy] with the spirit of his mouth, and shall destroy with the brightness [appearance] of his coming . . . "

12. "And so all Israel shall be saved: as it is written, There shall come out of Sion the Deliverer, and shall turn away [remove] ungodliness from Jacob . . . " (Rom. 11:26; cf. Acts 3:19, 26).

13. See Jer. 31:31–34; Ezek. 36:26–27; Heb. 8:6–13.

14. See John 7:37–39; Rom. 8:9.

15. Hoshea comes from the same root word as Yeshua.

16. According to Thayer's definition (PC Study Bible, Biblesoft Co.) "*to kick against the pricks*" is an idiomatic saying that means "to offer vain and perilous or ruinous resistance."

17. In Heb. 3:11–4:11 the word "rest" occurs eleven times.

18. See also John 12:28; 17:6, 26; Rom. 9:17.

19. See Acts 1:2, 16; 8:29; 10:19; 21:11; 28:25.

20. This is from the same Hebrew root word as *aliyah*, the word used today for Jews immigrating to Israel. It literally means "to go up," since Jerusalem, with the location of God's Temple on top of a ridge, was always the ultimate goal for returning Jews. From whatever the direction of approach, it was necessary to go up.

21. See previous note.

PART THREE

Taught Ones

Israel's Olive Tree has a healthy *Tanach* rootstock, but many of the natural branches are weak or broken. The Gardener prunes the weak branches to strengthen them. He also grafts in many branches taken from wild olive trees. The two kinds of branches joined in one tree, bear spiritual fruit for the glory of God.

CHAPTER 18

The Bride in the *Tanach*

The Mystery of Messiah

Have you ever read Ephesians 3:3–6 and considered what Paul, as a Jewish believer, must have been thinking?

> How that by revelation he made known unto me the *mystery*; (as I wrote afore in few words, Whereby, when ye read, ye may understand my knowledge in the *mystery* of Messiah) Which in other ages was not made known unto the sons of men, as it is now revealed unto his holy apostles and prophets by the Spirit; That the Gentiles should be *fellowheirs* [with whom? with the Jews!], and *of the same body* [again, with the Jews], and *partakers* [once more, with the Jews] *of his promise in Christ* [the Jewish Messiah] *by the gospel.*

Paul was declaring that the mystery which God revealed to him and the other apostles was the extraordinary inclusion of gentiles, uncircumcised in flesh, with Jews[1] in God's plan of salvation!

Let's explore the *Tanach* roots of gentile salvation, as well as the concept of a global body of believers, the Bride. First we need to understand that the New Testament word "mystery" means "a divine truth, formerly hidden, but now supernaturally revealed to men, which can be fully understood only by the saved individual though the illumination of the Holy Spirit."[2]

The most surprising act of God in the life of the early "Church"[3] was not Jewish salvation, but that He had "also to the Gentiles granted repentance unto life" through Yeshua, the Jewish Messiah (Acts 11:18b). Can you hear Rabbi Saul's (Paul's) delight and joy, even amazement, when he proclaims in Colossians 1:25–27,

> Whereof I am made a minister [servant], according to the dispensation [stewardship] of God which is given to me for you, to fulfil the word of God; Even *the mystery* which hath been hid from ages and from

generations, but now is made manifest [revealed] to his saints: To whom God would make known what is the riches of the glory *of this mystery among the Gentiles; which is Christ* [the Jewish Messiah] *in you, the hope of glory* ...

Through the Messiah promised to Israel, Jews and gentiles now have equal access to God. And, although like male and female they are not identical, they are one in Messiah Yeshua.

Now, where was this mystery "formerly hidden?" It was hidden in the *Tanach*.

Prophecies of Gentile Salvation

The New Testament declares that the universal gospel was proclaimed before the birth of the Messiah.

> And the scripture [the *Tanach*], foreseeing that God would justify the *heathen*[4] through faith, preached [announced] before [beforehand] the gospel unto Abraham, saying, In thee shall *all nations* be blessed.
>
> (Gal. 3:8)

That part where Paul quotes from the *Tanach*, "In thee shall all nations be blessed," is found in Genesis 12:3, and confirmed to Abraham twice, in Genesis 18:18 and 22:17–18. The Lord proclaimed that same "gospel" to Isaac in Genesis 26:3–4 and to Jacob in Genesis 28:13–14. God thereby prophesied that all nations/gentiles would be blessed through the seed, or line, of Abraham, Isaac and ultimately Jacob (the children of Israel – the Jewish people).[5]

Looking back through the filter of the New Testament, we see the ultimate Seed to be Yeshua, the perfect representative of Israel. He was the One who accomplished Israel's task completely, bringing gentiles to a saving knowledge of the God of Israel. In fact one of His prophesied names is "Israel":

> Listen, O isles, unto me; and hearken, ye people, from far; The LORD hath called me from the womb; from the bowels of my mother hath he made mention of my name ... And said unto me, *Thou art my servant, O Israel* [lit: Prince with God], *in whom I will be glorified.*
>
> (Isa. 49:1, 3)[6]

As you read these other verses concerning gentile salvation in the *Tanach*, remember that the Hebrew word *goyim* can be translated "nations," "heathen," or "gentiles."

In the midst of apparent end-time upheavals, God says to Israel through the psalmist,

> Be still, and know that I am God; I will be exalted among the *heathen*, I will be exalted in the earth [or land].　　　　　　　　(Ps. 46:10)

God declares He will be exalted in defending His people against the world's persecution. A theme that occurs often in the *Tanach* is God's reputation and glory increasing among the gentiles because of what He does in and through Israel in the last days.[7]

These next two quotes relate to the gentiles under God's coming Messianic kingdom. In Psalm 72 the author, although writing specifically about King Solomon, prophesies about the ultimate King,

> Yea, all kings shall fall down [bow down in worship] before him: *all nations* shall serve him.　　　　　　　(Ps. 72:11, cf. Rev. 11:15)

Isaiah, whose prophecies often touch on Messiah's kingdom, states in 2:2,

> And it shall come to pass in the last days, that the mountain of the LORD's house shall be established in the top of the mountains, and shall be exalted above the hills; and *all nations* shall flow unto it.

Based on "even" gentiles being saved through Yeshua's sacrifice for their sins, we can apply to the present day the following Scripture promises. [Following each quotation and its *Tanach* reference are superscript numbers referring to endnotes which give some New Testament verses showing the fulfillment of these *Tanach* promises.]

> And in that day there shall be a root of Jesse, which shall stand for an ensign [banner, sign] of the people; to it shall the *Gentiles* seek: and his rest shall be glorious.　　　　　　　(Isa. 11:10)[8]

> Behold my servant, whom I uphold; mine elect [chosen One], in whom my soul delighteth; I have put my spirit upon him: he shall bring forth judgment [and/or justice] to the Gentiles ... I the LORD have called thee in righteousness, and will hold [strengthen] thine hand, and will keep [sustain; guard over] thee, and give thee for a covenant of the people, for a light of the *Gentiles* ... (Isa. 42:1, 6; see the context, vv. 1–12)[9]

> Also *the sons of the stranger*, that join themselves to the LORD, to serve [or obey] him, and to love the name [nature; character] of the LORD, to be his servants, every one that keepeth the sabbath from polluting [profaning; desecrating] it, and taketh hold of my covenant; Even them

will I bring to my holy mountain, and make them joyful in my house of prayer: their burnt offerings and their sacrifices shall be accepted upon mine altar; *for mine house shall be called an house of prayer for all people.* The Lord GOD which gathereth the outcasts of Israel saith, Yet will I gather *others* to him, beside those that are gathered unto him.

(Isa. 56:6–8; see the context, vv. 3–8)[10]

Here are several verses that apply to the end of this current period, the end of the time of the gentiles.[11] The following verse from Jeremiah occurs in the context of God sending fishers and hunters to gather His people back to their land (16:16). One of the results of this final regathering of Israel is a revelation among the gentiles that God is still the God of Israel. Or as Jeremiah says,

O LORD, my strength, and my fortress, and my refuge in the day of affliction [distress], the Gentiles shall come unto thee from the ends of the earth, and shall say, Surely our fathers have inherited lies [also deceptions], vanity [emptiness], and things wherein there is no profit.

(Jer. 16:19)[12]

At some time during that same period,[13] God defends Israel from the invasion of Gog and Magog, not because Israel is sinless, but to fulfill His Word for His glory.

Thus will I magnify myself, and sanctify myself; and I will be known in the eyes of *many nations*, and they shall know that I am the LORD.

(Ezek. 38:23; cf. Rev. 15:3–4)

Finally a verse that applies to that timeframe as well as to the millennium reign of Messiah Yeshua,

For from the rising of the sun even unto the going down of the same my name [reputation; fame] shall be great among the *Gentiles*; and in every place incense shall be offered unto my name, and a pure offering: for my name shall be great among the *heathen*, saith the LORD of hosts.

(Mal. 1:11)[14]

Many other verses point to believing gentiles having a part in the Messiah of Israel. We list more of these in endnote 15.[15]

Tanach Examples of Gentile Salvation

Once we know what to look for, we discover many examples of gentile salvation throughout the *Tanach*. Some might object to using the word "salvation" for what occurs in the Old Testament because it took place before the cross. However, chapter 11 of the New Testament book of Hebrews states that there will be many Old Testament saints in heaven. Yeshua also refers to Tanach saints in His kingdom,

> And I say unto you, That many shall come from the east and west, and shall sit down with Abraham, and Isaac, and Jacob, in the kingdom of heaven.   (Matt. 8:11; also see Luke 13:28)

Their salvation rested on the same foundation as ours – faith/trust in the Word of God, made possible by God's grace in their lives.[16]

All the early faith heroes, Abel, Enoch, Noah, etc., were gentiles. Technically speaking, there were no Jews before Abraham had a great-grandson named Judah. Even Abraham and Sarah were gentiles. According to the Word, Abraham was the son of an idol worshiper:

> And Joshua said unto all the people, Thus saith the LORD God of Israel, Your fathers dwelt on the other side of the flood [lit: river, i.e., the Euphrates] in old time, even Terah, the father of Abraham, and the father of Nachor: and they served other gods.   (Josh. 24:2)

Genesis 14:18b calls Melchizedek, who was a gentile, "priest of the most high God." As King-Priest of Salem (later, Jerusalem) he blessed Abraham and accepted a tithe from him (14:19–20). That shows that God always had His people who declared His Name before men.

In the story of Moses, a Midianite priest named Jethro becomes Moses' father-in-law (Exod. 3:1) as well as his counselor (Exod. 18:19). Jethro was blessed when he blessed Israel in caring for the fugitive Moses (Exod. 2:20–21). Jethro recognized the God of Israel as the only "capital-G" God. Not only did Jethro sacrifice to Him, but he also ate a covenant meal with Moses, Aaron, and the elders of Israel, indicating that he was now an integral part of the common-wealth of the house of Israel.

> And Jethro said, Blessed be the LORD, who hath delivered you out of the hand of the Egyptians, and out of the hand of Pharaoh, who hath delivered the people from under the hand of the Egyptians. Now I know that the LORD is greater than all gods [lit.: mighty ones]: for in the thing wherein they dealt proudly he was above them. And *Jethro*, Moses' father in law, took a burnt offering and sacrifices for God: and Aaron came, and all the elders of Israel, to eat bread with Moses' father in law before [in the presence of] God.   (Exod. 18:10–12)[17]

Two gentile women, Rahab and Ruth, joined the household of Israel (Josh. 6:25; Ruth 1:16–17; 2:12), and became ancestors of the promised Messiah (Matt. 1:5).

God calls Job, a gentile of the land of Uz and probably contemporary with Abraham and Melchizedek, "my servant Job, that there is none like him in the earth, a perfect [morally complete] and an upright man, one that feareth God, and escheweth [turns from] evil ... " (Job 2:3b, see 1:1).

Balaam,[18] Naaman the Syrian general, and Nebuchadnezzar[19] are a few well-known *Tanach* figures from among the nations who once had, or came to, a knowledge of the true and living God. These examples clarify that gentile salvation (in many cases without circumcision), did occur in the *Tanach*. Yet the fullness of gentile salvation comes only after our Lord Yeshua's death and resurrection.

God Speaks to Gentile Believers in the *Tanach*

The Lord speaks directly to the "nations," the gentiles, in the *Tanach*. Who are these gentiles to whom He gives vital marching orders? Consider which gentiles are the only ones reading and believing His Word today. They are those who have been grafted into Israel's Olive Tree; they are part of Messiah's Bride; they are servant believers in Messiah Yeshua. In His House, the "Commonwealth of Israel" (Eph. 2:12), they have been given spiritual "permanent residency."[20]

The following verses indicate that when God speaks in the *Tanach* directly to His Body/Bride it is in reference to their response and responsibility to the restoration of the nation of Israel. In Isaiah 40:1–2a, the most familiar verse in this regard, God is speaking to those of His people who are not of Israel,

> Comfort ye, *comfort ye my people* [Israel],[21] *saith your God*. Speak ye comfortably to [lit: "Speak to the heart of"] Jerusalem ...

God speaks to a people and calls Himself "your God." Besides Israel there has never been, nor will there ever be, any people God would declare His own other than gentile believers.

Isaiah 52:7 says,

> How beautiful [feeling at home; comfortable] upon the mountains are the feet of *him that bringeth good tidings*, that publisheth [proclaims] peace; that bringeth good tidings [good news, gospel] of good, that publisheth salvation; that *saith unto Zion*, Thy God reigneth!

Who else could that be speaking of, other than the Body of Messiah, who are commissioned to bring good news and proclaim peace and salvation to the whole world, to the Jew first (Rom. 1:16)?

The Lord is saying that His Church should proclaim to Israel, "*Your* God reigns!" [NKJV].[22] Our Lord, the God of all born-again believers, is still the God of Israel. Paul says that in Romans 11:24–29. We are not proclaiming to the Jewish people some strange god, but their God, and their promised Messiah. If the gospel were presented to Jewish people in this way, the response might be different from the common, "Jesus may be for the gentiles, but I'm Jewish." Gentile believers, we urge you to proclaim to Jewish people the good news that their God reigns!

God speaks to the Body of Messiah in parts of Isaiah 62 also. In verses 6b–7, God wants the watchmen He has placed on Jerusalem's walls to be zealous in intercession for Israel, or as these verses state, keep not silent, and give him [God] no rest til he establish, and til he make Jerusalem a praise in the earth." Then in verses 10–11a, the Body is commanded:

> Go through, go through the gates; prepare ye the way of the people [Israel]; cast up, cast up [build up] the highway; gather out the stones; lift up a standard [banner] for the people. Behold, the LORD hath proclaimed unto *the end* [farthest part] *of the world, Say* ye *to* the daughter of Zion, *Behold, thy salvation cometh . . .*

Those stones on the highway causing Israel to stumble – what can they represent? Here are some strong possibilities:

- the Church's past and present anti-Semitism and persecution of the Jews
- replacement theology appropriating Israel's blessings for the Church while leaving God's curses for Israel
- anti-Judaism insisting that a Jew who accepts Yeshua must become a gentile in lifestyle and commitments
- resisting God's work of restoring Israel to her land
- believers thinking that they must take an anti-Zionist stance in order to evangelize Moslems
- interpreting the Bible by a humanistic world-view instead of by a Hebraic/*Tanach* perspective.

Each one of these "stones" in the "highway" is a method used by the Adversary to weaken, deceive, and destroy God's people, both Jew and gentile, for gentiles who do these things come under God's curse (Gen. 12:3).

Another area with which God commands the believer to be involved is *aliyah* (literally "going up"). In modern Hebrew *aliyah* means Jewish immigration to Israel – Jews returning to the land God has sworn to give them forever. A major goal of God's redemptive plan is to inspire, guide, and support *aliyah*.

> For, lo, the days come, saith the LORD, that I will bring again the captivity of my people Israel and Judah, saith the LORD: and *I will cause them to return* to the land that I gave to their fathers, and they shall possess it.   (Jer. 30:3)

> Yea, *I will* rejoice over them to *do them good*, and *I will plant* [establish] *them* in this land assuredly *with my whole heart and with my whole soul*.   (Jer. 32:41)

The Church is prophesied to facilitate this move of God. While reading the following scripture remember that God is speaking to Israel about the gentiles:

> Thus saith the Lord GOD, Behold, I will lift up mine hand to the Gentiles, and set up my standard [signal; banner] to the people: and they shall bring thy sons in their arms, and thy daughters shall be carried upon their shoulders.   (Isa. 49:22)[23]

Is the Bride of Messiah carrying Zion's sons in her arms, Zion's daughters on her shoulders? Is she heeding the warning in Isaiah 60:12,

> For the nation [gentile] and kingdom that will not serve thee [Israel] shall perish; yea, those nations shall be utterly wasted.

We bless the Lord that He is revealing this to many believers throughout His kingdom. There are many individual Christians, as well as many Christian organizations, who are standing in the gap now, helping to carry home Israel's children – for God's glory.[24]

There is an amazing prophecy in the *Tanach* that mentions Christians by name! In Jeremiah 30:24b God says, "in the latter days ye shall consider it" concerning what He has just declared in that chapter. The Hebrew for "latter days" is, literally, "last days" and the very next verse (a new chapter) immediately continues with, "At the same time..." So during these last days, in 31:6, there shall be a day, that the *watchmen* upon the mount Ephraim shall cry, Arise ye, and let us go up to Zion unto the LORD our God.

The biblical Hebrew word for "watchmen" is *notzrim,* which is the modern Hebrew word for "Christians"!

Obviously *notzrim* did not mean "Christians" in Jeremiah's day, but God, who knows the end from the beginning, used that specific word in this verse to leave no doubt that He is speaking to last days' believers. (There are other Hebrew words for "watchmen" that He could have used.) And what does God then say to these believers?

For thus saith the LORD; Sing with gladness for Jacob [the Jewish people], and shout among the chief of the nations: *publish* [proclaim] *ye, praise ye, and say, O* LORD, *save thy people, the remnant of Israel.*
(Jer. 31:7)

God is speaking to a people who are not Israel, but who will be able to hear His voice in the last days. He gives a command to "Sing . . . shout . . . publish . . . praise . . . and say," which seems to mean sing/praise, educate, and intercede for the salvation of Israel.

In response to His Bride's obedience, especially in intercession, the Lord has brought and will continue to bring His people back to the land of Israel (31:8–9). Why is that? Because He has declared that the majority of Jewish people who will be saved, will be saved in the land of Israel. They will be brought back as unbelievers. Ezekiel 36:24–27 is one of the foremost examples of this sequence:

For I will take you from among the heathen, and gather you out of all countries, and will bring you into your own land. Then will I sprinkle clean [pure] water upon you, and ye shall be clean [pure]: from all your filthiness, and from all your idols, will I cleanse [purify] you. A new heart also will I give you, and a new spirit will I put within you: and I will take away the stony heart out of your flesh, and I will give you an heart of flesh. And I will put my spirit within you, and cause you to walk in my statutes, and ye shall keep my judgments, and do them.[25]

The Lord continues in Jeremiah 31:10,

Hear the word of the LORD, O *ye nations,* [gentiles who are listening for His voice] *and declare* it in the isles afar off, and say, He that scattered Israel *will gather* him, *and keep* [guard] him, as a shepherd doth his flock.

God desires His Bride to proclaim this to the world. In the midst of the news, views and confusion of the current situation in Israel, this is what our Father is doing. He wants the Church and the world to wake up to His mighty acts as He fulfills His Word before our eyes (Jer. 1:12). Israel's national deliverance from both her enemies and her sins, has global consequences, and God desires the Church to take an active role in bringing it about. Paul sums up what is at stake in these verses:

> Now if the fall of them be the riches of the world,
> and the diminishing of them the riches of the Gentiles;
> how much more their fulness [completeness]? . . .
> For if the casting away [rejection; repudiation] of them
> be the reconciling [restoration] of the world,
> what shall the receiving of them be,
> but life from the dead?
> (Rom. 11:12, 15)

Notes

1. Paul is saying, *with* the Jews, not instead of the Jews. Replacement "theology" says instead of the Jews.
2. *Wycliffe Bible Encyclopedia* (Moody Press), Vol. 2, p. 1164.
3. "Church" is in quotes because many people think of it as a gentile institution, even a physical building, as opposed to what it really denotes – the living community of believers, both Jew and gentile, in Messiah Yeshua.
4. The Hebrew word *goyim* and the Greek word *ethnos* can both be translated as "nations," or "peoples."
5. Ishmael (Gen. 17:18–21; 21:12) and Esau (Gen. 25:23; 28:3–4, 12–15) were not recipients of this specific covenant.
6. For proof that this verse refers to Messiah Yeshua and not the people Israel, see verses 5 and 6 of this passage in Isa. 49.
7. For example, see Jer. 33:7–9; Ezek. 36:23; Rom. 11:12, 15.
8. Cf. Matt. 2:1–2; 11:28–29; 12:17–21; Rom. 15:9–12; Heb. 4:9–11.
9. Cf. Luke 2:32; John 8:12; Acts 26:22–23.
10. Cf. John 10:16; Eph. 2:11–22; 1 Thess. 1:9–10.
11. God's economy seems to contain periods of overlap. Yeshua died but the sacrifices still went on in the Temple for forty years. In June 1967, Jerusalem was no longer under gentile rule, and although Jews are receiving Messiah Yeshua in greater numbers than at any time since the first century, we are still in that overlap as the time of the gentiles comes to a close and before all Israel is saved.
12. Cf. 1 Thess. 1:9–10; 1 Pet. 1:18–19; Rev. 7:9–10.
13. Some scholars see two fulfillments of this event, one here and one at the end of the Millennial reign of Messiah (see Rev. 20:7–8).

14. Cf. Matt. 28:19–20; Acts 15:16–17; Rev. 11:15.
15. Deut. 32:21; 1 Chr. 16:31; Pss. 65:2, 5; 66:4; 68:32; 86:9; Isa. 45:22–24; 49:1–7; 52:15; 55:4–5; Jer. 3:17; Dan. 7:13–14; Zech. 8:20–23; 14:8–9, 16.
16. See 2 Tim. 3:14–15; Heb. 11:39–40.
17. Covenant meals (also see Gen. 26:26–30; 31:44–47) are the *Tanach* foundation for our covenant meal, Communion or the Lord's Supper. Read the following scripture about Aaron's and his sons' consecration to the priesthood and recognize that believers are now a kingdom of priests: "And they shall eat those things wherewith the atonement was made, to consecrate and to sanctify them: but a stranger shall not eat thereof, because they are holy" (Exod. 29:33). Notice the parallels with the Bible's commands to us as found in 1 Cor. 11:23–29.
18. Although there is no doubt that Balaam knew the true God, as he used God's covenant name Yahweh in addressing Him (Num. 22:8–9, 18, 34–35; 23:3–5, 8, etc.) we are not saying that Balaam was a *Tanach* saint (Num. 24:1). The fruit of this particular prophet in facilitating Israel's apostasy (Rev. 2:14), reminds us of Yeshua's warning against false prophets found in Matthew 7:15–23.
19. Naaman – 2 Kgs. 5:17; Nebuchadnezzar – Dan. 4:34–37.
20. In the present-day nation of Israel a non-Jew who has shown himself invaluable to the nation is often given what is termed "permanent residency," which includes almost all the rights of a citizen except voting in national elections.
21. In the *Tanach*, the expression "My people" of necessity refers to the descendants of Jacob.
22. It is regrettable that this scripture was altered when a song using it was written. To Jewish ears it sounds like replacement theory when gentile believers sing, "Our God reigns." Although technically correct, scripturally and especially in context, it borders on changing the Word of God.
23. See also Isa. 60:1–16; 61:5; 66:18–23.
24. For practical ways to participate in fulfilling these prophecies, contact: Christian Friends of Israel (see contact information at the back of this book); Bridges For Peace (www.bridgesforpeace.com or write BFP, Box 1093, Jerusalem, Israel, or call 972-2-624-5004); International Christian Embassy, Jerusalem (email <icej@icej.org.il> or write ICEJ, Box 1192, Jerusalem 91010, Israel or call 972-2-566-9823); Ebenezer Emergency Fund (www.ebenezer-ef.org or write EEF, Ebenezer House, 5a Poole Road, Bournemouth BH2 5QJ, UK, or call 01202 294455 in UK, or in USA call 252-491-9201). All these Christian organizations plus many more are actively involved in helping with the restoration of Israel.
25. Other examples include Jer. 31:7–9; 32:37ff.; Joel 2:18ff. (in context this can only be Israel's salvation); Zech. 12:10; Matt. 23:37–39.

CHAPTER 19

Israel and Our Salvation

The last days restoration of the state of Israel is essential for believers' assurance of their eternal salvation. As extreme as this statement appears, it is a biblical fact.

Replacement Theory

A fundamental concept of our biblical faith has been eaten away by centuries of anti-Semitism and replacement theology (better yet, "replacement theory" since there is no biblical basis for the idea). Replacement theory teaches that the Church has replaced Israel as the people of God and that Israel as a people and nation now have no special significance in the purposes and plan of God. The part of the Church which endorses replacement thinking claims all the *Tanach* promises of blessing while saying the Jewish people, because they rejected their Messiah, receive all the *Tanach* curses. But concerning this issue Paul, the apostle to the gentiles, cries by the Holy Spirit in Romans 11, "God forbid!"

Unfortunately, replacement thinking is still entrenched in the Church. Many Christians especially in the West give little credence to the 1948 rebirth of the nation of Israel as a miracle. Other believers see it only as a fulfillment of prophecy. Yet without the fulfillment of the promised miracle of Israel's resurrection in the last days, we would have little physical evidence, aside from archaeological interpretations, that the Bible is the word of the living, faithful, promise-keeping God. If we have doubts about God keeping His promises to Israel, how can we trust in what God says about the "foolishness"[1] of Yeshua's death on the cross for our salvation? Let's follow this reasoning step by step.

Whose World?

The Scriptures state that God is the Lord of the earth. Therefore, any teaching that Satan gained dominion over this world at the Fall, is not based on the Word. Yes, he is the god of this world's man-made system, but only because man is a slave to sin. In spite of this, some teach that when Adam fell, he forfeited dominion of the world to Satan who then became the god of the earth. Such teachers imply that God had to figure out a legal way to come back into the world, so He decided to do this through a virgin's womb.

The Word tells us a different story. When Adam and Eve fell, God did not ask Satan's or anyone else's permission for what He was about to do. He cursed the serpent, then proclaimed the curses which the sin of Adam and Eve would bring, finally cursing the very ground. Both before and after the Fall, God is Lord of the world. Here are some post-Fall verses to verify this key doctrine:

> And I will sever in that day the land of Goshen, in which my people dwell, that no swarms of flies shall be there; to the end thou mayest know that *I am the* LORD *in the midst of the earth.* (Exod. 8:22)

> And Moses said unto him [Pharaoh], As soon as I am gone out of the city, I will spread abroad my hands unto the LORD; and the thunder shall cease, neither shall there be any more hail; that thou mayest know how that *the earth is the* LORD*'s.* (Exod. 9:29; see 9:14–16)

> *The earth is the* LORD*'s,* and the fulness thereof; the world, and they that dwell therein. (Ps. 24:1)

> Ye are my witnesses, saith the LORD, and my servant whom I have chosen: that ye may know and believe me, and understand that I am he: *before me there was no God formed, neither shall there be after me.* (Isa. 43:10)

Even Messiah Yeshua proclaims that His Father is God of the world, "At that time Yeshua answered and said, I thank thee, O Father, Lord of heaven and earth..." (Matt. 11:25a).

God is still God, the only Lord of the earth, even after the Fall. Satan is not a god of anything except deception, embodied in the world system. The above scriptures indicating this are only a small sample of what the Bible says about God's sovereignty over His planet.

Whose Land?

Not only does God own the whole planet, but He has chosen a plot of ground in the Middle East which He calls His land and His inheritance, the land of Israel.

> The land shall not be sold for ever: *for the land is mine*; for ye are
> strangers and sojourners with me.   (Lev. 25:23)

God could not be more precise about to whom the land of Israel
belongs. Some confirming verses follow:

> LORD, thou hast been favourable unto *thy land*: thou hast brought
> back the captivity of Jacob.   (Ps. 85:1)

The idiomatic term, "the captivity of Jacob," refers to God's people,
the Jews, living outside the Promised Land, in exile.[2]

> And first I will recompense their iniquity and their sin double; because
> they have defiled *my land*, they have filled *mine inheritance* with the
> carcases of their detestable and abominable things.   (Jer. 16:18)

In that verse, the Lord calls the land of Israel His inheritance (see
Exod. 15:17).
    He also calls the people of Israel His inheritance![3]

> In that day shall Israel be the third with Egypt and with Assyria, even a
> blessing in the midst of the land [earth]: Whom the LORD of hosts shall
> bless, saying, Blessed be Egypt my people, and Assyria the work of my
> hands, and Israel mine inheritance.   (Isa. 19:24–25)

Clearly land and people are inseparably linked in God's mind. Both
are His inheritance and He uses them together to demonstrate to the
world His sovereignty and faithfulness.

> Therefore thus saith the Lord GOD; Surely in the fire of my jealousy
> have I spoken against the residue of the heathen, and against all
> Idumea [Edom, Esau], which have appointed *my land* into their
> possession with the joy of all their heart, with despiteful minds, to
> cast it out for a prey.   (Ezek. 36:5)

All of Ezekiel 36 describes what the Lord has done and prophesies
what He will do with the land and people of Israel. It is a chapter
pinpointing God's acts in and through Israel today!

> For, behold, in those days, and in that time, when I shall bring again
> [return] the captivity of Judah and Jerusalem [after 1967], I will also
> gather all nations, and will bring them down into the valley of
> Jehoshaphat [meaning "the LORD is judge"], and will plead with
> [judge] them there for my people and for my heritage Israel, whom
> they have scattered among the nations, and *parted* [partitioned,
> divided] *my land*.   (Joel 3:1–2)

God declares that He will judge nations involved in carving up Israel, including in any "land for peace" process. The more nations try to push Israel to give away what ultimately is not hers to give, the more those nations will suffer judgments, either what insurance companies label "acts of God" (natural disasters of all kinds), or terror attacks, vicious crimes, lawlessness, immorality, and even war.[4] These will intensify if nations ignore these as warnings from God.

The Gospel To and Through the Jews

When God first called Abraham He promised him a land and blessings:

> Now the LORD had said unto Abram, Get thee out of thy country, and from thy kindred, and from thy father's house, unto a land that I will shew thee: And I will make of thee a great nation, and I will *bless* thee, and make thy name great; and thou shalt be a *blessing*: And I will *bless* them that *bless* thee, and curse him that curseth thee: *and in thee shall all families of the earth be blessed.*   (Gen. 12:1–3)

Part of God's initial promise declared that through Abraham's seed all the "families," meaning nations or gentiles[5] of the earth, would be blessed. Paul states that this was the gospel preached to Abraham:

> And the scripture, foreseeing that God would justify the heathen through faith, preached before *the gospel* unto Abraham, saying, In thee shall all nations be blessed.   (Gal. 3:8)

The promise of the gospel was confirmed to Abraham after he obeyed God in his willingness to sacrifice Isaac, the son of the promise:

> By myself have I sworn, saith the LORD, for because thou hast done this thing, and hast not withheld thy son, thine only son: That in blessing I will bless thee, and in multiplying I will multiply thy seed as the stars of the heaven, and as the sand which is upon the sea shore; and thy seed shall possess the gate of his enemies; And in thy seed shall all the nations of the earth be blessed; because thou hast obeyed my voice.
> (Gen. 22:16–18)

Then the promise was passed on through Isaac:

> And I will make thy seed to multiply as the stars of heaven, and will give unto thy seed all these countries; *and in thy seed shall all the nations of the earth be blessed . . .*   (Gen. 26:4)

After Isaac the promise of the good news was confirmed to Jacob as he was fleeing from the wrath of Esau:

> And, behold, the LORD stood above it [the ladder], and said, I am the LORD God of Abraham thy father, and the God of Isaac: the land whereon thou liest, to thee will I give it, and to thy seed; And thy seed shall be as the dust of the earth, and thou shalt spread abroad to the west, and to the east, and to the north, and to the south: *and in thee and in thy seed shall all the families of the earth be blessed.*
>
> (Gen. 28:13–14)

We need to understand that what Messiah Yeshua said to the Samaritan woman applies to all unbelieving gentiles,

> Ye worship ye know not what: we know what we worship: for *salvation is of the Jews.* (John 4:22)

Remember why God says He created the Jewish people:

> for I have created him for my glory, I have formed him; yea, I have made him ... This people have I formed for myself; they shall shew forth my praise. (Isa. 43:7b, 21)

And it was through the Jewish people[6] that Yeshua came as Abraham's greatest Seed, to make possible global salvation and the reality of God's indwelling Spirit in new hearts, thereby fulfilling the "blessing" part of God's promise.

> Now to Abraham and his seed were the promises made. He saith not, And to seeds, as of many; but as of one, And to *thy seed, which is Messiah.* (Gal. 3:16)

God's Land for God's People

Besides promising blessings for Abraham and his seed, as well as the gospel blessing to the world, God also gave His land to Abraham, and to his seed through Jacob/Israel, as an inheritance. The following verses bring out the dual aspect of the children of Israel as God's inheritance, with the land of Israel as the inheritance of the children of Israel:

> But the LORD hath taken you, and brought you forth out of the iron furnace, even out of Egypt, *to be unto him a people of inheritance,* as ye are this day. Furthermore the LORD was angry with me for your sakes, and sware that I should not go over Jordan, and that I should not

go in unto *that good land, which the* LORD *thy God giveth thee for an inheritance . . .* (Deut. 4:20–21)

This verse from Jeremiah is being fulfilled today:

In those days the house of Judah shall walk with the house of Israel, and they shall come together out of the land of the north to *the land that I have given for an inheritance unto your fathers.* (Jer. 3:18)

As already mentioned previously in "Whose Land?," Ezekiel 36 is a currently relevant chapter describing prophecies – past, present and future – in the Middle East. In verse 12, God speaks to the land of Israel itself,

Yea, I will cause men to walk upon you, even my people Israel; and they shall possess thee, and *thou shalt be their inheritance,* and thou shalt no more henceforth bereave them of men. (Ezek. 36:12)[7]

How serious is God about giving the Land to the Jewish people? The Spirit of God speaks through King David,

He hath remembered his covenant for ever, the word which he commanded to a thousand generations. Which covenant he made with Abraham, and his oath unto Isaac; And confirmed the same unto Jacob for a law, and to Israel for an everlasting covenant: Saying, Unto thee will I give the land of Canaan, the lot of your inheritance . . . (Ps. 105:8–11)

God is stating something so important that He uses five different terms to describe it, *"his covenant for ever,* the *word* ... he commanded to a thousand generations ... his *oath* ... *law* ... *everlasting covenant . . ."* And that whole section appears in the Word twice (see 1 Chr. 16:15–18)![8] What is God stating in such strong terms?

Unto thee *will I give the land of Canaan,* the lot of *your inheritance.*

Why does God stress this so strongly? He knows that virtually no unbelievers, not even many believers, will want to believe that His relationship with the Jewish people and the unconditional promise of the land really do endure forever (Jer. 31:35–37).

If understanding that passage in Psalms has not convinced you that God is serious about bringing the Jewish people back to the land of Israel, then read this:

Yea, I will rejoice over them to do them good, and *I will plant them in this land assuredly with my whole heart and with my whole soul.*
(Jer. 32:41)

Nowhere else in all of God's Word does He declare that He is going to do something with His whole heart and soul! Who will be able to resist His desire? Who in their right mind would want to resist what the Lord God Almighty is determined to do with all of His heart and soul? And yet a self-centered part of the Church ignores this God-centered part of His Word as if it has no importance. Can you imagine the spiritual condition of one who ignores God's heart and soul?

The Sanctification of God's Name

Therefore say unto the house of Israel, Thus saith the Lord GOD; I do not this for your sakes, O house of Israel, but *for mine holy name's sake,* which ye have profaned among the heathen, whither ye went. And *I will sanctify my great name,* which was profaned among the heathen, which ye have profaned in the midst of them; and *the heathen shall know that I am the* LORD, *saith the Lord* GOD, *when I shall be sanctified in you before their eyes.*

For I will take you from among the heathen, and gather you out of all countries, and will bring you into *your own land.* Then will I sprinkle clean water upon you, and ye shall be clean: from all your filthiness, and from all your idols, will I cleanse you. A new heart also will I give you, and a new spirit will I put within you: and I will take away the stony heart out of your flesh, and I will give you an heart of flesh. And I will put my spirit within you, and cause you to walk in my statutes, and ye shall keep my judgments, and do them. *And ye shall dwell in the land that I gave to your fathers; and ye shall be my people, and I will be your God.* (Ezek. 36:22–28)

That crucial section reveals the reason God is determined to plant His people in His land. It is because He has chosen this way to sanctify His name. And sanctifying God's name is the first thing Yeshua told us to pray,

After this manner therefore pray ye: Our Father which art in heaven, Hallowed [sanctified] be thy name. (Matt. 6:9)

What does "sanctifying" God's name mean? In Hebraic thinking, which is the mindset of the Scriptures, a person's name describes his essential character. God's Name represents who He is. Our God is holy, faithful, merciful, just, good, true, gracious, and long-suffering (Exod. 34:5–7), etc. That is Who He is and there is nothing we can do either to add to or subtract from His nature.

We "sanctify His name" when we proclaim to the world and to the heavens that our God is indeed the Holy One, faithful in all His acts, merciful yet just, good and true, etc. And as we have just read in Ezekiel 36:23–24, we can use the restoration of Israel as the best last days example of the sanctification of God's name. God said that Israel's rebirth (as a nation and also spiritually when all Israel is saved) would sanctify His name among the nations. And God builds the fulfillment of His Word on the sure foundation of who He is!

> I will worship toward thy holy temple, and praise thy name for thy lovingkindness and for thy truth: for *thou hast magnified thy word above* [not "over," but *"upon"*] *all thy name.*   (Ps. 138:2)

Physical Land and Eternal Salvation

What then is the connection between Israel's end-time physical restoration and our eternal salvation? It is simply that the promise of the land of Israel given as an everlasting covenant, sworn to by God, and the promise of eternal life given to those who trust in Yeshua, are both guaranteed by God's faithfulness and ability to keep His Word.

If God is fickle as opposed to faithful, or if He is a God who proclaims but cannot perform, then what assurance do we have of salvation? And if God, who made such remarkable promises to the Jewish people about their homecoming and inheritance, cannot or will not fulfill these promises, then what assurance do we have that He will fulfill His promises to us?

After a meeting someone asked if Yeshua's resurrection wasn't all the proof we needed for our assurance of salvation? Chuck responded, "How did Yeshua's resurrection prove He was the One whom God had sent? There were many Jews crucified during Yeshua's time, and there were others, like Lazarus, who were also raised from the dead. But the promised Messiah was prophesied to be crucified and raised from the dead on the third day. His death and resurrection are proof of Yeshua's Messiahship for only one reason – they fulfill God's prophetic Word about Messiah."

Hiding His glorified body, Yeshua refused to focus on the miracle of His resurrection as proof of His Messiahship. Instead, He quoted prooftexts to two depressed disciples and reminded them that those *Tanach* prophecies of Messiah's life, death, and resurrection must be fulfilled:

> Then he said unto them, O fools, and slow of heart to believe all that the prophets have spoken: Ought not the Messiah to have suffered these things, and to enter into his glory? And beginning at Moses and all the prophets, he expounded unto them in all the scriptures [the Old Testament] the things concerning himself.
>
> (Luke 24:25–27)

Even later, after revealing His identity to them, He repeated the point to make it unmistakable:

> And he said unto them, These are the words which I spake unto you, while I was yet with you, that all things must be fulfilled, which were written in the law of Moses, and in the prophets, and in the psalms, concerning me. Then opened he their understanding, that they might understand the scriptures [the Old Testament], And said unto them, Thus it is written, and thus it behoved the Messiah to suffer, and to rise from the dead the third day ...
>
> (Luke 24:44–46)

If He so magnified the Scriptures, the *Tanach*, in the presence of the awesome miracle of His resurrection, can we do any less concerning the prophesied resurrection of Israel in the last days? May He open every disciple's understanding of the prophecies promising Israel's miraculous restoration today – for the sanctification of His Name!

Be encouraged! Trust God! God is fulfilling His Word right before our eyes! Israel has been resurrected from the dead; the Jewish people are returning to their ancient homeland; ancient cities are being rebuilt; Hebrew is being spoken and sung and prayed again; and all the world is so deceived that they are preparing to war against Jerusalem just as the prophet has spoken,

> Behold, I will make Jerusalem a cup of trembling unto all the people round about, when they shall be in the siege both against Judah and against Jerusalem. And in that day will I make Jerusalem a burdensome stone for all people: all that burden themselves with it shall be cut in pieces, though all the people of the earth be gathered together against it.
>
> (Zech. 12:2–3)

Conclusion

Where is all this in the New Testament? Romans 15:8 says,

> Now I say that Yeshua the Messiah was a minister [servant] of the circumcision [the Jews] for the truth of God, to *confirm the promises* made unto the fathers...

As we have seen, those promises include the inheritance of the land of Israel. Yeshua's life, death, and resurrection confirm those promises.

The Word talks about having at least two witnesses testify to truth.[9] The Church testifies to Yeshua's resurrection, confirming the promises made to Israel, and Israel testifies by her resurrection, confirming the promises made to the Church.

> The grass withereth, the flower fadeth: but the word of our God shall stand for ever. (Isa. 40:8)

> Oh that the salvation of Israel were come out of Zion!
> when the LORD bringeth back the captivity of his people,
> Jacob shall rejoice, and Israel shall be glad.
> (Ps. 14:7)

Notes

1. See 1 Cor. 1:18, 23, 25; 2:14.
2. Other examples of this usage are found in Ezra 6:21; 8:35; Jer. 30:3, 10; 33:7; 46:27; Ezek. 39:25; Amos 7:17 and 9:14–15:3.
3. 2 Kgs. 21:14; Isa. 47:6.
4. Abortion, homosexuality, drugs, the occult, divorce, abuse – these things do not bring God's judgment; they *are* God's judgment!
5. In Hebrew, the word is *goyim*, which can be translated "nations," "gentiles," or "heathen" depending on the context and the theological bent of the translator.
6. Rom. 1:3; 9:5.
7. See also Num. 34:2; Deut. 19:14; Josh. 1:6; 1 Kgs. 8:36; Jer. 12:14.
8. Matt. 18:16; 2 Cor. 13:1.
9. Deut. 17:16; 19:15; 2 Cor. 13:1; 1 Tim. 5:19.

CHAPTER 20

Your People Will Be My People – Part 1

We have already demonstrated that Israel and the Church have the same biblical roots – the *Tanach*. But there is something more, something that most of the Church has missed through the centuries, something usually missed also by those trying to restore "Jewish" roots to the modern Church – the intimate connection between the Jewish people and true Christians.

Shavuot

Shavuot, or literally in Hebrew "Weeks," known in the Church as "Pentecost" or "Whitsunday," is one of the three pilgrim feasts when all Israeli males were to appear before God in Jerusalem (Exod. 23:14–17; Deut. 16:16). In the Church it is no longer observed according to the Hebrew lunar calendar and so usually no longer falls on the Hebrew calendar Feast of *Shavuot*. As early as the second century, gentile church leaders made efforts to avoid celebrations on Jewish holy days and eventually created different holy days.

Many see Pentecost as the birthday of the Church. In Acts 2, on *Shavuot*, the risen and glorified Messiah poured out on the waiting disciples that Promise which was promised by His Father – the Holy Spirit (Luke 24:49; Acts 1:4–5; 2:32–33). At that moment the first "Messianic Jews" began to be empowered by one Spirit in one Body (1 Cor. 12:13–14).

We can see that process in the symbolism of *Shavuot* and *Bikkurim*, first fruits of the barley harvest, which was the biblical feast on which Messiah rose from the dead (Lev. 23:9–14). *Bikkurim* always occurs on the day after the *Shabbat* of Passover week (Lev. 23:11). There are different opinions as to which *Shabbat* is meant – the weekly feast, or Passover itself, also called a *Shabbat*. If the weekly, then *Bikkurim* would always occur on the first day of the week, the day when Yeshua rose from the dead as the *Bikkurim*, the first fruits of the resurrection (1 Cor. 15:20).

During *Bikkurim*, sheaves of individual grain stalks were offered in a wave-offering before God in the Temple. But the *Shavuot* offering, after forty-nine (7 × 7) days or seven "Weeks," on the fiftieth day (Greek: *pentecoste*), is a wave-offering of two loaves of bread.

Think of the ancient process of making bread. After cutting, the stalks are immediately assembled into bundles. Taken to a threshing floor, they are beaten to separate the grain, which is gathered into shallow baskets and repeatedly tossed into the air on a windy day – "winnowed," to blow out worthless bits. The cleaned grain is then thoroughly smashed to powder between stones to make flour. The flour is combined with oil and water, repeatedly pressed and squeezed – "kneaded," put in a hot oven and finally – bread, the staff of life.[1]

Isn't this what Yeshua does with us after we are harvested? We are saved as individuals, but immediately become part of a community, His Body. We also are transformed through the powerful processes of conviction and repentance resulting in sanctification, all of which is overseen by the Holy Spirit, so that we, like Yeshua, can be broken bread and poured out wine for others (thanks to Oswald Chambers for that analogy).

Yeshua's death and resurrection made possible the harvest of individual grains but it takes the infilling of the Holy Spirit's power to enable us to function according to His spiritual gifts as part of His Body. For that reason *Shavuot* is the birthday of the Church.

Rabbis say that after Israel left Egypt, Moses received the Ten Commandments on *Shavuot*.[2] Although Israel was given freedom on Passover, freedom without law leads to anarchy. So God gave the tablets of the Law and Israel became a nation. Because of that, Judaism recognizes *Shavuot* as the birthday of the people of Israel!

Although historically Israel and the Church have despised each other and felt they have little in common, is it coincidence that both have claimed *Shavuot* as their birthday?

Ruth and the Church

Jewish sages have assigned certain *Tanach* books to be read on the holy days. On *Shavuot*, Ruth is read, mainly because it occurs in the spring, like *Shavuot*, during barley harvest time (Ruth 1:22). Note that the book of Ruth is named for a gentile (1:4) who was willing to leave her country and family to stay with and minister to Naomi, her Jewish mother-in-law.

Naomi and her family had left Bethlehem because of a famine. She is about to return after losing her husband and both sons in Moab. Her two Moabite daughters-in-law want to go with her. One is convinced by Naomi to stay in Moab, but not Ruth. In one of the most touching declarations of faith and loyalty in the Bible, Ruth says,

> Intreat me not to leave thee, or to return from following after thee: for whither thou goest, I will go; and where thou lodgest, I will lodge: *thy people shall be my people, and thy God my God*: Where thou diest, will I die, and there will I be buried: the LORD do so to me, and more also, if ought but death part thee and me.   (Ruth 1:16–17)

In Israel Ruth finds a husband, Boaz, a wonderful foreshadow of Messiah Yeshua in the following points: he is a kinsman-redeemer (2:1), a mighty man of wealth (2:1), a man of the law (3:12–13), the lord of the harvest (2:4, 15–16), an advocate (4:1–6) and a bride-groom (4:13) with a gentile bride who becomes part of the household of Israel (4:11). Boaz not only mirrors Yeshua in all these things, but he and Ruth are blessed to become ancestors of the Davidic line (4:17) and of Yeshua Himself (Matt. 1:5). Ruth's faithfulness to her Jewish mother-in-law birthed a desire to become grafted into Israel's Olive Tree, resulting in incredible blessing not just for her, but also for the world.

This poor gentile widow, who followed love and truth at whatever cost, becomes a matriarch in God's plan to bring salvation to the world. Ruth went the extra mile, not only leaving her country, but also seeking shelter under the wings of Naomi's God – the God of Israel, becoming part of Naomi's people – the people of Israel.

The Church has claimed the "thy God shall be my God" part of Ruth's confession. But down through the centuries the "thy people shall be my people" part has been ignored, rejected, and "replaced." As Psalm 102:13 says, the set time has come – the time to have mercy on Zion. The gentile Church is coming into a new revelation of them-selves as the "other" part of the greater commonwealth of spiritual Israel, past, present, and future. Now is the time for the Church to proclaim its debt to the Jewish people (Rom. 15:27) and stand with the Jews of today, the brethren of Yeshua and the Apostles.

The Church and Israel – Romans 11

Many believers today are excited about the truth they see in Romans 9–11. This convicting part of God's Word has historically been ignored or misinterpreted by the Church. The context is clear – Paul is proclaiming God's faithfulness to Israel despite the blindness of most of Israel to Yeshua as the promised Messiah.

But Romans 10:18–21 states that none of this took God by surprise. He knew Israel's response beforehand (see Acts 4:27–28).

> But to Israel he saith, All day long I have stretched forth my hands unto a disobedient [willfully, perversely disbelieving] and gainsaying [speaking against, contradicting, disobeying, refusing to relate] people. I say then, Hath God cast away his people? *God forbid.* For I also am an Israelite, of the seed of Abraham, of the tribe of Benjamin. God hath not cast away his people which he foreknew.   (Rom. 10:21–11:2a)

What is your answer to Paul's question, "Has God cast away His disbelieving and stubborn people?" The Church historically has answered, "Of course, and we have replaced Israel." The Holy Spirit's answer through Paul is, "God forbid!" Why? Because God will not contradict His Word, break His promises, or annul His everlasting covenant.

In Romans 11:7–10, Paul points to dire accusations and curses in the *Tanach* against disbelieving Israel. But even against such a background, he asks again,

> I say then, Have they stumbled [erred, sinned] that they should fall [perish under judgment/condemnation]? *God forbid*: but rather through their fall [sin, offense] salvation is come unto the Gentiles, for to provoke them to jealousy.   (Rom. 11:11)

Why make the Jews jealous? To torment them? No! To cause them to recognize their Messiah!

Twice in that chapter God's Word gives a powerful "God forbid" to answer whether God has rejected or will reject Israel forever as His chosen nation. Yet the Church in many places continues to teach otherwise. What will you believe, the Word of God or traditional teachings that oppose His Word?

Paul twice points out the worldwide blessings that will result from Israel's national salvation (11:12, 15), and finally he shares about the relationship between gentiles and Israel in God's plan.

The Olive Tree Connection

In the context of Romans 9–11, Paul talks about Israel as an ancient olive tree, some of whose natural branches have undergone heavy

pruning because of the "disease" of unbelief. This cultivated olive tree
(11:16–24) is the commonwealth citizenship or community – of Israel
(Eph. 2:12). The healthy branches are living Jewish believers along
with, as we shall see shortly, living gentile believers. The healthy roots
are all the past *Tanach* saints, Messianic Jews, and gentile believers
whose lives of faith in God and His promises have channeled
nourishment for the growth of the tree.[3]

Yeshua, the greatest fulfillment and fulfiller of God's promises,
came as the model for our faith, the DNA if you will, for this Tree
of Life – from taproot to branch. He is the first, the greatest, the
strongest, the prophesied Root of Jesse and David, and He is God's
Servant called the Branch.[4] The olive tree under discussion is Rabbi
Shaul's picture of the Commonwealth of the House of Israel.

What happens when gentiles trust in Yeshua? They are cut out of
wild olive trees (Rom. 11:17) representing paganism and heathenism
and grafted into Israel's cultivated tree nourished by faith in the God
of Abraham, Isaac, and Jacob. Or as Paul states elsewhere, believers
turn "from idols to serve the living and true God" (1 Thess. 1:9b).
However, even though gentile believers are grafted into Israel's Olive
Tree, much of the Church has acted, and still acts, as though it has
been grafted into a Christmas tree – flashing its attractive lights and
decorations, but unconcerned about its loss of roots and wondering
why it is spiritually drying up and dying.

Saved gentiles are to share in "the root and fatness of the olive tree"
(11:17). They do not take the Jews' place, but are "among them, and
with them." Hear God's Spirit speaking through Paul to gentile
believers,

> Boast not [exult not] against the branches [natural branches that were
> cut off]. But if thou boast, thou bearest [support] not the root, but the
> root thee.   (11:18)

After Paul warns Christians about pride against the Jews (Rom.
11:20, 24), and says a day will come when all Israel will be saved
(11:26), he states,

> As concerning the gospel, they are enemies [enemies of the gospel –
> very strong in the original] for your sakes: but as touching the election,
> they are beloved for the fathers' sakes. For the gifts and calling of God
> are without repentance.   (11:28–29)

Jews – many still enemies of the gospel, haters of Yeshua, despising
and opposing Christians – are yet beloved by God. But that's not all.

Turn it around and look at the other side of that coin – enemies of the Jews and haters of Israel are cursed by God (Gen. 12:3; Num. 24:9; Isa. 49:25–26; Zech. 12:9; Matt. 25:40, 45).

Saved gentiles have been supernaturally grafted against nature into a tree not their own, but saved Jews are natural branches. Yet when a Jew gets saved, gentile believers are often amazed. This shows how far the Church has strayed from a biblical perspective. Remember, the unbelievable miracle in Acts was that gentiles were being saved! But in regards to the Jewish people, Paul says that God is able to graft those natural branches in again, if they believe (11:23). They are more easily grafted back in because they belong there. Those branches need to hear this Good News.

Bride of Messiah, honor your spiritual forefathers through their physical descendants, just as you love your physical brothers and sisters even if they are unsaved. How? Paul completes this chapter using the word "mercy" four times (Rom. 11:30–32). We can't imagine how different a situation we would be facing today if only the Church had obeyed God's Word and had mercy on Israel, provoking them to jealousy instead of forcing them to convert or die.

Not only do the Jewish people need the Good News, they need support and prayer covering as protection from the Adversary's attempts to destroy them. Church, wake up to the biblical truth that the existence of Israel is imperative to our very lives as believers! Israel's faith in the *Tanach* promises are the roots of Israel's Olive Tree. Remember, you do not bear the root but the root bears you (Rom. 11:18b). If Israel is ever destroyed, the Word of God and His promises to Israel, His everlasting covenant, are proved to be lies and the Church's spiritual foundation crumbles.

The Enemy is prowling the corridors of churches, including Israel-loving churches, looking for a meal. Don't cut yourself off from your roots of faith! Stay in the Word of God and prayer; seek holiness; refuse the ways of the world; test every spirit.

No Longer Strangers

Another New Testament section that talks about the Jew/gentile relationship is Ephesians 2:11–3:12. Paul says that before salvation, gentiles were "without Messiah, being aliens [shut out from fellowship and intimacy] from the commonwealth [community, citizenship] of Israel, and strangers from [without knowledge of or a share in] the covenants of promise, having no hope, and without God in the world..." (Eph. 2:12).

But Paul has good news for gentiles,

> now in Messiah Yeshua ye who sometimes were far off are made nigh by the blood of Messiah. For he is our peace, who hath made both one... (Eph. 2:13–14a; cf. 2:17 and Isa. 57:19)

Yeshua foresaw our being one when He said,

> And other sheep I have, which are not of this fold: them also I must bring [lead], and they shall hear my voice; and there shall be one fold, and one shepherd. (John 10:16)

Paul says that gentiles in Messiah "are no more strangers and foreigners [noncitizens], but fellowcitizens with the saints [who are Messianic Jews], and of the household [family] of God..." (Eph. 2:19). Redeemed gentiles, even uncircumcised, could be saints along with redeemed Jews! This was news!

Finally, Paul shares concerning gentile believers and the "mystery of Messiah" which God has now revealed (Eph. 3:1–5). The mystery is,

> That the Gentiles should be fellowheirs [joint heirs], and of the same body, and partakers of his promise in Messiah by the gospel...
> (Eph. 3:6)

To grasp this, remember Paul was a rabbi immersed in Hebraic culture.

Here is what we guess such a Pharisee might have thought when he first realized that gentiles could be saved without converting to Judaism:

> The mystery of Messiah is that those gentiles, whom I used to look on as unclean dogs, should be joint heirs with God's people, my people – Israel, even a part of the same flock and able to partake of God's promises in the Jewish Messiah by this Good News!

Or, as Paul says in another letter,

> Even the mystery which hath been hid from ages [eternity] and from generations, but now is made manifest to his saints: To whom God would make known what is the riches of the glory of this mystery among the Gentiles; which is Messiah in you, the hope of glory...
> (Col. 1:26–27)

Hear that! The Jewish Messiah in you gentiles is your hope of glory!

Church, could you be brought any closer to Israel and the Jewish people? You are saved because the God of Israel has placed the promised, prophesied Messiah of the Jews in you by His Spirit!

Welcome to the family!!

> Behold, how good and how pleasant it is
> for brethren to dwell together in unity!
> It is like the precious ointment [anointing oil] upon the head,
> that ran down upon the beard, even Aaron's beard:
> that went down to the skirts of his garments;
> As the dew of Hermon, and as the dew
> that descended upon the mountains of Zion:
> for there the LORD commanded the blessing,
> even life for evermore.
> (Ps. 133)

Notes

1. If one wants bread to seem more than it really is, be softer and easier to chew and swallow, and appear light and pure, the grain must have the life-germinating factor removed along with the protective seed cover. A rapidly reproducing fungus in an oil/liquid mixture is added which causes the dough to expand with gas and puff up to even twice normal size. The oven heat causes the outer layer to become rigid so that the bread remains fixedly puffed up. Once the outer layer is breached, the many air holes caused by the gas facilitate a rapid loss of moisture resulting in a dry unpalatability. The Bible compares false doctrine and hypocrisy to this rapidly reproducing fungus (Matt. 16:12; Luke 12:1). The Bible also compares the grain seed to the Word of God (Matt. 13:19–23; Luke 8:11–15).

2. Whether this was the actual day or not, is irrelevant to the point under consideration.

3. Rom. 4:1–3, 9–22; Gal. 3:6–9; Heb. 11:8–21.

4. See Isa. 11:1, 10; Jer. 23:5–6; Zech. 3:8; Rom. 15:12; Rev. 5:5; 22:16.

CHAPTER 21

Your People Will Be My People – Part 2

Gentiles Who Became Part of Israel in the *Tanach*

We have just discovered that the Church's relationship to the Jewish people should be in agreement with Ruth's commitment to Naomi, "your people, my people, and your God, my God" (lit. translation, Ruth 1:16), and we have looked at some New Testament teachings which illustrate that relationship.[1] The *Tanach* also contains teachings on this subject. We barely touched on this relationship in a previous chapter,[2] so the emphasis here will explore beyond prophesied gentile salvation, and penetrate to that relationship between the Jewish people and redeemed gentiles as described in the *Tanach*.

The *Tanach* mentions by name two non-Jewish women, Rahab and Ruth, who by choice became part of the greater community of Israel.

> And Joshua saved Rahab the harlot alive, and her father's household, and all that she had; and she dwelleth [settled, remained] in Israel even unto this day... (Josh. 6:25a)

Rahab, like Ruth, is listed in Yeshua's genealogy (see Matt. 1:5), and the New Testament cites her also as an example of faith proven by her works:

> By faith the harlot Rahab perished not with them that believed not, when she had received the spies with peace. (Heb. 11:31)

> Likewise also was not Rahab the harlot justified by works, when she had received the messengers, and had sent them out another way? For as the body without the spirit is dead, so faith without [separated from] works is dead also. (Jas. 2:25–26)

In Ruth's case, her faith in Israel's God made her eligible to marry Boaz. When Ruth questioned his kindness to her, a stranger, Boaz replied,

It hath fully been shewed me, all that thou hast done unto thy mother in law . . . and how thou hast left [to desert, leave behind] . . . the land of thy nativity, and art come unto a people which thou knewest not heretofore. The LORD recompense thy work, and a full reward be given thee of *the* LORD *God of Israel, under whose wings thou art come to trust* [seek refuge, have hope in].   (Ruth 2:11–12)

In using the phrase, "LORD God of Israel" ("LORD," the tetragrammaton, God's personal name), Boaz indicates that Ruth knew Israel's God was different from her ancestors' gods. Ruth left her family and nation and joined herself to the Jewish people, putting her trust in their God, the only true God – the God of Israel.

The Law of Foreigners and Strangers

The *Torah*, God's teaching, instructs Israel to differentiate between gentiles who serve other gods, and gentiles who join themselves to Israel by trusting Israel's God. It seems this is not known or taught in today's Church, so there is much misunderstanding among believers concerning the relationship of the nation of Israel with the gentiles in her midst.

Many Christians say that Israel needs to accept and love the Moslems and that Moslems have an equal right to the Promised Land. We do believe Israel needs to treat all her citizens righteously, including her Moslem citizens. But, biblically, there is a huge difference between Moslems, or any other people group who belong to another god, and Jews and Christians who belong to the God of Israel. This is misunderstood for two main reasons. The first reason is simply a lack of awareness that the Moslem god, Allah (the spirit principality behind Islam), has nothing in common with the Judeo-Christian God of Israel.[3] The second reason is more complex because most translations do not make a consistent difference between several Hebrew words.

The *Ger*

The Hebrew noun *ger* (*Strong's* #1616) comes from a root which means "to live among a people who are not blood relatives." The *ger*,[4] without the protection of his homeborn "civil rights," was dependent on his host's hospitality, an important custom in the Middle East then and now. *Gerim* (plural) in Israel were for that reason considered a protected people.

The patriarchs and David, looking to God as their Protector, called themselves *gerim* in the Promised Land,

> By faith Abraham, when he was called to go out into a place which he should after receive for an inheritance, obeyed; and he went out, not knowing whither he went. By faith he sojourned [resided as a foreigner] in the land of promise, as in a strange [foreign] country, dwelling in tabernacles with Isaac and Jacob, the heirs with him of the same promise: For he looked for a [lit: the] city which hath foundations, whose builder and maker is God ... These all died in faith, not having received the promises, but having seen [known, perceived] them afar off, and were persuaded of them, and embraced them, and *confessed that they were strangers and pilgrims on the earth.*
>
> (Heb. 11:8–10, 13 referring to Gen. 23:4)

King David is humbled that God would allow his and the people's offerings for the building of the Temple. He prays to the Lord,

> But who am I, and what is my people, that we should be able to offer so willingly after this sort? for all things come of thee, and of thine own [lit: hand] have we given thee.　　　　　(1 Chr. 29:14)

On what does he base his point of view? On the reality that all of God's people are strangers and sojourners.

> *For we are strangers* [*gerim* – people in need of grace and hospitality] before thee, *and sojourners* [*toshavim* – see below], *as were all our fathers*: our days on the earth are as a shadow, and there is none abiding [remaining alive].　　　　　(1 Chr. 29:15)

In Psalm 39:12, David pleads with God to hear his prayer based on the same theme,

> Hear my prayer, O LORD, and give ear unto my cry; hold not thy peace at my tears: *for I am a stranger* [*ger*] *with thee, and a sojourner* [*toshav* – see below], *as all my fathers were.*

Concerning the land of Israel itself, God tells His people that they may not sell it because He is the owner and they are His protected guests:

> The land shall not be sold for ever: for the land is mine; *for ye are strangers* [*gerim*] *and sojourners* [*toshavim*] *with me.*
>
> (Lev. 25:23)

Likewise, the New Testament bears witness with the *Tanach*'s point of view when it states that as believers we need to see ourselves as in the world but not of it:

> If ye were of the world, the world would love his own: but because *ye are not of the world*, but I have chosen you out of the world, therefore the world hateth you.   (John 15:19; see 17:14–16)

John goes on to warn the Church:

> *Love not the world*, neither the things that are in the world. If any man love the world, the love of the Father is not in him.
>   (1 John 2:15)

James, also writing to believers, declares in no uncertain terms:

> Ye adulterers and adulteresses [fig: apostates] know ye not that the friendship of the world is enmity with God? *whosoever therefore will be a friend of the world is the enemy of God.*   (Jas. 4:4)

The *Ger* in Israel

God told Israel to see *gerim* as proselytes, part of the community with most of the same rights as the native-born Israeli, yet not as children of Israel according to the flesh. In the following verses, the Hebrew for "stranger" is *ger*.

Shabbat laws applied to them.

> But the seventh day is the sabbath of the LORD thy God: in it thou shalt not do any work, thou, nor thy son, nor thy daughter, thy manservant, nor thy maidservant, nor thy cattle, nor *thy stranger* [*ger*] *that is within thy gates* . . .   (Exod. 20:10; also 23:12)

If they were circumcised, *gerim* could celebrate Passover.[5]

> And when *a stranger shall sojourn with thee*, and will keep the passover to the LORD, let all his males be circumcised, and then let him come near and keep it; and he shall be as one that is born [a native] in the land: for no uncircumcised person shall eat thereof. *One law shall be to him that is homeborn, and unto the stranger* [*ger*] *that sojourneth among you.*
>   (Exod. 12:48–49; also Num. 9:14)

Along with the congregation of Israel the *gerim* were obligated to observe other Feasts of the LORD as well.

Unleavened Bread [*Hag haMatzot*]:

> Seven days shall there be no leaven found in your houses: for who-
> soever eateth that which is leavened, even that soul shall be cut off
> from the congregation of Israel, whether he be a *stranger*, or born in
> the land.   (Exod. 12:19)

The Day of Atonement [*Yom Kippur*]:

> And this shall be a statute for ever unto you: that in the seventh month,
> on the tenth day of the month, ye shall afflict [or humble] your souls,
> and do no work at all, whether it be one of your own country, *or a*
> *stranger that sojourneth among you*: For on that day shall the priest
> make an atonement for you, to cleanse [purify] you, that ye may be
> clean from all your sins before the LORD.   (Lev. 16:29–30)

So we see that the blood atonement which purchased forgiveness for
sins for all of the congregation of Israel included the believing
strangers (*gerim*) who lived in the midst of her.

Tabernacles [*Succot*]:

> Thou shalt observe the feast of tabernacles seven days, after that thou
> hast gathered in thy corn and thy wine: And thou shalt rejoice in thy
> feast, thou, and thy son, and thy daughter, and thy manservant, and
> thy maidservant, and the Levite, *the stranger*, and the fatherless,
> and the widow, that are within thy gates.   (Deut. 16:13–14)

The *ger* was to be present in the assembly when the Law was read
and was also held accountable to its demands.

> When all Israel is come to appear before the LORD thy God in the place
> which he shall choose, thou shalt read this law before all Israel in their
> hearing. Gather the people together, men, and women, and children,
> *and* thy stranger that is within thy gates, that they may *hear*, and that
> they may *learn*, and *fear* the LORD your God, and *observe to do* all the
> words of this law...   (Deut. 31:11–12; see Lev. 18:26)

Just like the children of Israel, the *ger* was condemned to death if he
sacrificed to other gods.

> Whosoever he be of the children of Israel, *or of the strangers that*
> *sojourn in Israel*, that giveth [sacrifice] any of his seed [children] unto
> Molech; he shall surely be put to death: the people of the land shall
> stone him with stones. And I will set my face against that man, and will
> cut him off from among his people; because he hath given of his seed

unto Molech, to defile my sanctuary, and to profane [defile, desecrate, pollute] my holy name [reputation].　　(Lev. 20:2b–3; see 17:8–9)

In this verse, the Lord affirmed that the *ger's* behavior, just as much as the native Israelite's behavior, had an impact on Israel's witness to Himself.

The *ger* was also forbidden to eat blood, though unlike the Israelite, he could eat what had died by itself or was torn.

> And whatsoever man there be of the house of Israel, *or of the strangers that sojourn among you*, that eateth any manner of blood; I will even set my face against that soul that eateth blood, and will cut him off from among his people.　　(Lev. 17:10; but see Deut. 14:21a)

Like the Israelite, he also underwent special cleansing, qualifying to be cleansed by the ritual of the red heifer.

> And he that gathereth the ashes of the heifer shall wash his clothes, and be unclean until the even: and it shall be unto the children of Israel, and *unto the stranger that sojourneth among them*, for a statute for ever.　　(Num. 19:10)

The *ger* enjoyed most of the same rights as the Israelite, and was not to be oppressed.

> Thou shalt *neither vex* [maltreat] *a stranger, nor oppress him*: for ye were *strangers* in the land of Egypt.　　(Exod. 22:21, see Jer. 7:6)

He was to be treated righteously in judgment.

> And I charged your judges at that time, saying, Hear the causes between your brethren, and judge righteously between every man and his brother, and *the stranger that is with him*.
>　　　　　　(Deut. 1:16, see also 24:17; 27:19; Jer. 22:3)

Even the cities of refuge were available to him.

> These six cities shall be a refuge, both for the children of Israel, *and for the stranger, and for the sojourner among them*: that every one that killeth any person unawares [mistakenly] may flee thither.
>　　　　　　　　　　(Num. 35:15)

Ultimately, he was expected to show the same honor and commitment to the LORD God as every Israelite. Moses sums up in Leviticus 24:22 by saying,

> Ye shall have one manner of law, as well *for the stranger* [*ger*], as for one of your own country: for I am the LORD your God.

Finally, God specifically states that He loves the *gerim*, and then commands Israel to love them as well:

> For the LORD your God is God of gods, and Lord of lords, a great God, a mighty, and a terrible, which regardeth not persons, nor taketh reward: He doth execute the judgment of the fatherless and widow, and loveth the stranger, in giving him food and raiment. Love ye therefore the stranger: for ye were strangers in the land of Egypt.
>
> (Deut. 10:17–19; also Lev. 19:34)

The *Ger* – a Type of the Christian

The *ger* is a wonderful foreshadow of the gentile believer grafted into Israel's Olive Tree. He became an actual part of the Commonwealth of Israel with most of the same obligations toward God as the Israelite. Because he had made a deep commitment to the God of Israel *and* the people of Israel, there can be no comparing the *ger* with the native Canaanites, demonized idol worshipers practicing human sacrifice, whom God commanded Israel to destroy.[6]

There are instructions concerning the lifestyle of the *ger* that Christians should consider. Have you ever celebrated Passover? Have you ever fasted on *Yom Kippur*? As we have already noted,[7] the Feasts of the Lord are specific times of the year when God wants to meet with His people – and the true Christian has certainly become an integral part of His people. Other instructions to *gerim* are also mentioned, but the point is that the *ger* was to accept the descendants of Jacob as his community, and the God of Jacob as his God. He stood with Israel. And we believe that the God of Israel desires the same attitude from His Church.

The *Toshav*

There are other Hebrew words which are also translated "strangers," "sojourners" or "aliens" [foreigners]. *Toshav* (*Strong's* #8453) is often paralleled with *ger*. In the following verses, *ger* is translated "stranger," while *toshav* is translated "sojourner."

When buying the burial plot in Hebron for Sarah, Abraham uses both terms to describe himself: "I am a *stranger* and a *sojourner*

with you: give me a possession of a buryingplace with you…"
(Gen. 23:4a). God uses both terms in describing Israel's relationship
to the Land:

> The land shall not be sold for ever: for the land is mine; for ye are
> *strangers* and *sojourners* with me.   (Lev. 25:23)

Israel was commanded to have compassion on the *ger* and the
toshav when they were in distress.

> And if thy brother be waxen poor, and fallen in decay with thee; then
> thou shalt relieve [strengthen] him: yea, though he be a *stranger*, or a
> *sojourner*; that he may live with thee.   (Lev. 25:35)

The *ger* and *toshav* were to be dealt with just as the Israelis would deal
with their flesh and blood brothers.
Both could flee to the cities of refuge for protection.

> These six cities shall be a refuge, both for the children of Israel, and for
> the *stranger*, and for the *sojourner* among them: that every one that
> killeth any person unawares may flee thither.   (Num. 35:15)

King David describes his people's position before God with these
same terms:

> For we are *strangers* before thee, and *sojourners*, as were all our
> fathers: our days on the earth are as a shadow, and there is none
> abiding.   (1 Chr. 29:15)

> Hear my prayer, O LORD, and give ear unto my cry; hold not thy peace
> at my tears: for I am a *stranger* with thee, and a *sojourner*, as all my
> fathers were.   (Ps. 39:12)

But there are differences from the *ger*. The *toshav* could not
participate in Passover. "A *foreigner* [toshav] and an hired servant
shall not eat thereof" (Exod. 12:45). He could also be bought as a
slave.

> Moreover of the children of the *strangers* [toshavim] that do sojourn
> among you, of them shall ye buy, and of their families that are with
> you, which they begat in your land: and they shall be your possession.
> And ye shall take them as an inheritance for your children after you, to
> inherit them for a possession; they shall be your bondmen for ever…
>   (Lev. 25:45–46a)

The *Nekar*

Another word sometimes translated "stranger" is *nekar* (*Strong's* #5236). The words translated from *nekar* are highlighted in the following verses.

The *nekar* was to be circumcised after he was bought and then became part of an Israeli's household.

> And he that is eight days old shall be circumcised among you, every man child in your generations, he that is born in the house, or bought with money of any *stranger*, which is not of thy seed.   (Gen. 17:12)

But whether circumcised or not, he could not celebrate Passover.

> And the LORD said unto Moses and Aaron, This is the ordinance of the passover: There shall no *stranger* eat thereof...   (Exod. 12:43)

Israel was forbidden to lend among themselves based on usury, or interest, but they could do so with the *nekar*.

> Unto a *stranger* thou mayest lend upon usury; but unto thy brother thou shalt not lend upon usury: that the LORD thy God may bless thee in all that thou settest thine hand to in the land whither thou goest to possess it.   (Deut. 23:20)

Also, the *nekar* could never be king over Israel.

> Thou shalt in any wise set him king over thee, whom the LORD thy God shall choose: one from among thy brethren shalt thou set king over thee: thou mayest not [do not have the authority or right to] set a *stranger* over thee, which is not thy brother.   (Deut. 17:15)

One of God's accusations against rebellious Israel was that they brought "into my sanctuary *strangers* [lit. sons of *nekarim*], uncircumcised in heart, and uncircumcised in flesh ... to pollute [defile, desecrate] it..." (Ezek. 44:7a). Obviously, those *nekarim should* have been circumcised in flesh according to Genesis 17:12 quoted before. This was Israel's neglected responsibility. Not only that, the Levites had allowed unbelievers among these uncircumcised *nekarim* into God's sanctuary to do the work they should have done themselves, as recorded in the same passage,

> And ye have not kept the charge of mine holy things: but ye have set keepers of my charge in my sanctuary for yourselves. Thus saith the Lord GOD; No *stranger*, uncircumcised in heart, nor uncircumcised in

flesh, shall enter into my sanctuary, of any *stranger* that is among the children of Israel.   (Ezek. 44:8–9)

Here God implies that the *nekarim* who become circumcised in both heart and flesh would have access to His house. Unlike the caste system of India, God's regulations provide for "upward mobility." *Nekarim* could rise above their spiritual lot in life by submitting themselves to the God of Israel. This foreshadows the "stranger" of today who, having been circumcised in heart, becomes a living stone in God's Holy Spirit temple.

All of the following verses can also be seen as foreshadows of the Christian. For example, look at what Isaiah 56:3a, 6–8 states,

> Neither let the son of the *stranger* [*nekar*], that hath joined himself to the LORD, speak, saying, The LORD hath utterly separated me from his people ... Also the sons of the *stranger* [*nekar*], that join themselves to the LORD, to serve him, and to love the name of the LORD, to be his servants [includes worshipers], every one that keepeth the sabbath from polluting it, and taketh hold of [with determination, courage and strength] my covenant; Even them will I bring to my holy mountain, and make them joyful in my house of prayer: their burnt offerings and their sacrifices shall be accepted [approved] upon mine altar; for mine house shall be called an house of prayer for all people. The Lord GOD which gathereth the outcasts of Israel saith, Yet will I gather others to him, beside those that are gathered unto him.

Here again we see the joining, or "grafting in," of the stranger/gentile to the commonwealth of the house of Israel because of the stranger's commitment to Israel's God.

Solomon prayed for the *nekarim* who would come to pray in Jerusalem to find favor with God because of His great name,

> Moreover concerning a *stranger*, that is not of thy people Israel, but cometh out of a far country for thy name's sake; (For they shall hear of thy great name, and of thy strong hand, and of thy stretched out arm;) when he shall come and pray [or intercede] toward this house; Hear thou in heaven thy dwelling place, and do according to all that the *stranger* calleth to thee for: that all people of the earth may know thy name, to fear thee, as do thy people Israel; and that they may know that this house, which I have builded, is called by thy name.
>
> (1 Kgs. 8:41–43)

So come!

Finally, Isaiah prophesies that *nekarim* will minister to Israel, helping in her end-time restoration,

> And the sons of strangers [*nekarim*] shall build up thy walls ... And strangers [*zarim* – see below] shall stand and feed your flocks, and the sons of the *alien* [*nekar*] shall be your plowmen and your vinedressers.
>
> (Isa. 60:10a; 61:5)

The *Zar*

One final word translated as "stranger" is *zar* (*Strong's* #2114), which means neither an acquaintance nor one related to the community in any way. The following verses show the distinction between the *zar* and the *ger, toshav* and even the *nekar*.

A *zar* was not to eat any of the holy sacrifices. In a foreshadow of Communion,[8]

> And Aaron and his sons shall eat the flesh of the ram, and the bread that is in the basket, by the door of the tabernacle of the congregation. And they shall eat those things wherewith the atonement was made, to consecrate and to sanctify them: but a *stranger* [*zar*] shall not eat thereof, because they are holy.   (Exod. 29:32–33)

In Leviticus, the same thought is continued but with added parameters,

> There shall no *stranger* [*zar*] eat of the holy thing: a sojourner of the priest, or an hired servant, shall not eat of the holy thing. But if the priest buy any soul with his money, he shall eat of it, and he that is born in his house: they shall eat of his meat. If the priest's daughter also be married unto a *stranger* [*zar*], she may not eat of an offering of the holy things.   (Lev. 22:10–12)

There is a rich parallel here between a priest buying a soul who is then able to eat of the holy things and God purchasing us with His own blood (Acts 20:28), called redemption, and our freedom to then take communion.

The *zar* was forbidden to be anointed with the holy oil (see Exod. 30:33). They were not allowed to help with the Tabernacle or priesthood. Their presence defiled God's House.

> And when the tabernacle setteth forward, the Levites shall take it down: and when the tabernacle is to be pitched, the Levites shall set it up: and the *stranger* that cometh nigh shall be put to death.
>
> (Num. 1:51)

And thou shalt appoint Aaron and his sons, and they shall wait on [protect or attend to] their priest's office: and the *stranger* that cometh nigh shall be put to death. (Num. 3:10; see also 16:40)

David says that the *zar* does not believe in the God of Israel,

For *strangers* are risen up against me, and oppressors seek after my soul: they have not set God before them. Selah. (Ps. 54:3)

God is angry with Israel for being corrupted by *zarim*.

Only acknowledge thine iniquity, that thou hast transgressed [rebelled] against the LORD thy God, and hast scattered thy ways to the *strangers* under every green tree, and ye have not obeyed my voice, saith the LORD. (Jer. 3:13)

Accordingly He uses them as an instrument of judgment on His people.

Like as ye have forsaken me, and served strange gods in your land, so shall ye serve *strangers* in a land that is not yours. (Jer. 5:19b)

And I will ... deliver you into the hands of *strangers*, and will execute judgments among you. (Ezek. 11:9; also 7:21; 28:10)

When Jerusalem was finally destroyed, Israel experienced the fulfillment of God's threatened judgments.

Our inheritance is turned [turned over] to *strangers* [*zarim*], our houses to aliens [*nekarim*]. (Lam. 5:2)

However, when God saves Israel, she will no more be in bondage to *zarim*.

For it shall come to pass in that day, saith the LORD of hosts, that I will break his yoke from off thy neck, and will burst thy bonds, and *strangers* shall no more serve themselves of him [Israel]: But they [Israel] shall serve the LORD their God, and David their king [metaphor for Messiah], whom I will raise up unto them. (Jer. 30:8–9)

Isaiah praises God because of His judgment on the *zarim* (25:2, 5), but he also foresees a time when God will use even the *zarim* to help with Israel's final restoration. Today we see many gentile non-believers helping to restore the nation.

And *strangers* [*zarim*] shall stand and feed your flocks, and the sons of the alien shall be your plowmen and your vinedressers. (Isa. 61:5)

Could this also foresee Israel's population of Moslem Arabs, descendants of thousands who flooded in from surrounding nations in
the twentieth century to find work? It must include the unbelievers
among the imported Eastern European and Far East laborers in Israel
today.

After our Lord's return, His city of Jerusalem, will allow no
unbelievers, no *zarim*.

> So shall ye know that I am the LORD your God dwelling in Zion, my
> holy mountain: then shall Jerusalem be holy, and there shall no
> *strangers* pass through her any more.   (Joel 3:17)

Was Paul thinking of this when he said to gentile believers,

> Now therefore *ye are no more* [no longer] *strangers and foreigners, but
> fellowcitizens* with the saints [in context: believing Jews], and of the
> household of God...   (Eph. 2:19)

The Stranger in the Land

So who has a biblical right to live in Israel peacefully with the children
of Israel? Anyone law-abiding, including the heathen, the *zarim* (Isa.
61:5). Who has a right to the land itself? The sojourners, the *gerim*,
who trust in the God of the land of Israel and obey His laws, settling
down as part of the people of Israel.

> And it shall come to pass, that ye shall divide it by lot for an inheritance
> unto you, and to the *strangers* [*gerim*] *that sojourn among you*, which
> shall beget children among you: and they shall be unto you as born in
> the country among the children of Israel; they shall have inheritance
> with you among the tribes of Israel. And it shall come to pass, that
> in what tribe the *stranger sojourneth*, there shall ye give him his
> inheritance, saith the Lord GOD.   (Ezek. 47:22–23)

Biblically, a believer who recognizes Israel's covenant stewardship
in this land and considers himself part of the people of Israel could
have an inheritance here. But biblically, a Moslem or any other kind
of heathen does not have an inheritance here. How God deals with
this today politically is up to Him, but that is the scriptural principle.
God is not happy with people who bring strange gods into His land or
with Israel's accepting them (see Jer. 3:13 above; also see Jer. 12:14–
17). In many nations politics and religion are kept separate. In Israel

they cannot be separated. The God of Creation has chosen this land for His physical home, and He is coming soon to take up residency once more.

Conclusion

Queen Esther can be seen as a portrait of the last days' Church. She is chosen to become the bride of the world's most powerful king, yet she hides her Hebrew roots! At a time when the existence of her people is threatened, Esther reveals her true family connection and intercedes for her people.

Bride of Messiah, Israel is being threatened with extinction through satanic attacks in every area right now – spiritual, socio-cultural, and political – and you have access to the King's throne. Plead for grace and mercy for Israel. As Mordecai says to Esther,

> Think not with thyself [lit: in your soul] that thou shalt escape in the king's house, more than all the Jews. For if thou altogether holdest thy peace at this time, then shall there enlargement [relief] and deliverance arise to the Jews from another place; but thou and thy father's house shall be destroyed...   (Esth. 4:13–14a)

The Hebrew word translated "destroyed" means just that: to perish, vanish, or go astray. Yes, precious Bride of Christ, your spiritual life is at stake. Israel's roots support you, not the other way around (Rom. 11:18). If you think Israel's existence does not matter to you – you are walking in deception!

God will save Israel because of His covenant promises, and because He is the faithful God who has acted, and will act, not for Israel's sake, but for His holy name's sake (Ezek. 36:22–23). But He wants His Bride's help.[9]

The encouragement Mordecai speaks to Esther applies to the Church today, "and who knoweth whether thou art come to the kingdom for such a time as this?"

May He give us all grace for the courage to do what He calls us to do. "Your kingdom come – Your will be done on earth as it is in heaven," in the name of our Messiah and Lord, Yeshua. Amen!

Notes

1. Rom. 11 and Eph. 2:11–3:10.
2. Chapter 18, "The Bride in the Tanach."
3. See the following for more information on this subject: *Inside Islam* by Reza F. Safa (Creation House, 1996); *Who is this Allah?* by G.J.O. Moshay (Dorchester House Pub., 1995); *The Islamic Invasion* by Robert A. Morey (Harvest House Pub., 1992).
4. See *The Theological Wordbook of the Old Testament*, edited by Harris, Archer and Waltke (Chicago: Moody Press), Vol. I, pp. 155–156.
5. Believers in Yeshua have their hearts circumcised. Foreskin circumcision, according to Paul, "avails nothing" for them, although Jewish believers are still to circumcise their sons as a sign of God's eternal covenant with Israel (Gen. 17:9–14). But gentile believers can get so caught up in their "Jewish" roots that they forget that it is a spiritual and social connection, not a fleshly one. We personally know of one young man who circumcised himself with dire results! (Rom. 10:2).
6. Do not extrapolate this fact into a modern-day command to destroy pagans – something the Church has wrongly condoned off and on down through the ages. Yeshua's disciples are commanded to love and pray for enemies, although nations still have every right to defend themselves.

   God's command to Israel to cleanse the Promised Land from pagan influence can be seen from two perspectives. One, it was necessary to protect Israel from the corrupting effect of paganism in their new life as a nation separated to God (Num. 23:9; Deut. 7:1–6, 16). Two, Israel was God's instrument of judgment on those nations who were given adequate time to repent, but chose not to serve God (Gen. 15:16; Deut. 9:1–6).
7. See Chapter 3, note 1.
8. See Chapter 11, section "After the Resurrection," commentary on Ps. 22:26.
9. Whatever your general prayer burden for your community – whether concerning salvation, government, media, pollution, youth, crime, abortion, the elderly, whatever it is – if it applies – pray it for Israel first, and be prepared for spiritual warfare as well as blessings.

Epilogue

In Psalm 1 the person who delights in God's teaching and meditates on it day and night is likened to a tree planted by a river. Such a tree never dries up and its fruit never fails. It is nourished when the water from the river penetrates the soil of the riverbank and picks up nutrients from the soil. The tree is not immersed in the river or it would drown. The water or the soil, separately, cannot sustain life. The river represents the Spirit of God. The tree must be planted in the soil of Truth – the Word of God. The Word of God is said to be "alive" because it is saturated with the Spirit of God, just as cells are always in contact with blood vessels, and just as riverbanks never lack moisture.

If you want to grow spiritually, you cannot separate the Spirit of God from the Word of God. They are a unity, a channel of spiritual power and life. Yeshua said,

> It is the Spirit who gives life ... *The words that I speak to you are spirit* and they are life. (John 6:63 NKJV)

> If you abide in Me and *My words* abide in you, you will ask what you desire, and it shall be done for you. By this My Father is glorified, that you bear much fruit; so you will be My disciples.
> (John 15:7–8 NKJV)

Yeshua said that those who believe in Him would receive spiritual power, that "rivers of living water" would flow from them. However, there is a requirement for receiving this power (John 7:38–39). Yeshua stated this requirement when He "cried out, saying, 'If anyone thirsts, let him come to Me, and let him who believes in Me drink' " (John 7:37b NKJV). In Proverbs 1 Wisdom personified cries out,

> Turn [repent] you at my reproof: behold, I will pour out my spirit unto you, *I will make known my words* unto you. (Prov. 1:23)

Spiritual power filters through the Word of God, bringing the nourishing Truth into the roots of our faith. The roots of our faith transport that power upward through Israel's Olive Tree, into the branches which turn that power, that "living water," into spiritual fruit.

In order to bring Yeshua's life to the world, believers need to "eat, drink and breathe" the Word of God, to immerse themselves and be refreshed in God's Word and to dialogue with Yeshua while doing so. This is communion with God, helped by the Holy Spirit.

> God is faithful, by whom you were called into the fellowship of His Son.   (1 Cor. 1:9 NKJV)

There is no other "formula" for receiving daily spiritual power from God.

We desire to see Yeshua's Body rooted in truth and ripening spiritual fruit while standing strong against temptations and the storms of false teaching. Pray that the Lord raises up pastors, teachers, and other workers to edify His Body. The night is coming when no one can work. Do you desire to be fully equipped for the end of the age?

> Study to shew thyself approved unto God, a workman that needeth not to be ashamed, rightly dividing the word of truth.   (2 Tim. 2:15)

> And he showed me a pure river of water of life, clear as crystal, proceeding from the throne of God and of the Lamb. In the middle of its street and on either side of the river, was the tree of life, which bore twelve fruits, each tree yielding its fruit every month. And the leaves of the tree were for the healing of the nations. And there shall be no more curse, but the throne of God and of the Lamb shall be in it, and His servants shall serve Him.   (Rev. 22:1–3 NKJV)

About the Authors

Chuck and Karen Cohen, ex-hippies, have been ministering in the Messianic movement since 1979. In 1989, they were called to live in Jerusalem with their two sons and have gained a broad historic and cultural perspective. God has given them a burden for the restoration of the Church to its biblical foundations, the roots of our faith.

As one of the directors of Intercessors For Israel, Chuck preaches, teaches and writes about believers' God-given commission to Israel and the Jewish people, as well as other issues that speak to the heart of Messiah's end-time Bride, such as intercessory prayer, the roots of our faith, and end-time deception.

Chuck, an intense and entertaining speaker, can keep the interest of seminary students, pastors, and their congregations through three-day seminars. He is involved in several international conferences in Jerusalem, travels and speaks internationally and has bee featured on Christian television and radio programs.

Chuck and Karen, contributors to *Sword* magazine, also write a biblical perspective on the news, *Watchmen from Jerusalem*, providing a prophetic understanding about Israel's current situation – with the goal of encouraging prayer.

To subscribe to their bi-monthly newsletter, *Watchmen from Jerusalem*, please visit the website:

> www.ifij.org
> (on the bottom left go to "E-Mails – Subscribe")

To schedule Chuck for a teaching seminar or conference email:

> wfj@ifij.org

or write:

> Chuck Cohen
> c/o Intercessors For Israel
> PO Box 28368
> Jerusalem 91281
> Israel

Homecoming – Our Return to Biblical Roots (first published under the title *Roots of Our Faith*) was created from articles originally written for Christian Friends of Israel and sent out regularly in their mailings as well as in our own newsletter, *Watchmen from Jerusalem*. In 1995 the first twelve articles were published by CFI as a book, which has since sold out.

After twelve more articles of the *Roots of Our Faith* series were written, we and CFI decided that all of the articles should be combined in one book. This required expansion and extensive revision, re-formatting, plus a new cover – in other words, a new book.

Homecoming – Our Return to Biblical Roots, published by Sovereign World, is an excellent resource for personal study, as a Bible study guide, as a reference for sermon preparation, or as a class textbook.

Scripture Index

Genesis
1:1 *18, 91, 202, 211*
1:1–2 *210*
1:5 *175*
1:27 *25*
2:23–24 *25*
2:24 *176*
3:14 *160*
3:21 *174*
4:4 *72*
5:1–3 *67*
5:22–24 *173*
6:5 *65*
6:8 *38, 56*
6:9 *38, 56*
8:21 *66*
9:4 *69*
11:6 *206*
12:1 *119*
12:1–3 *19, 119, 257*
12:3 *158–159, 244, 250, 269*
12:7–8 *180*
14:18 *247*
14:19–20 *247*
15:6 *59–61*
15:16 *286*
16:10–11 *206*
16:13 *206*
17:9–14 *286*
17:12 *280*
17:15–19 *152*
17:18–21 *252*
17:19 *152*
18:1 *182*
18:18 *244*
18:22 *182*
19:24 *206*
21:12 *252*
21:33 *207*
22 *151, 155*
22:1–2 *151*

22:2 *152, 154, 175*
22:3–4 *154*
22:5–6 *154*
22:7–8 *156*
22:8 *157*
22:9–10 *156*
22:11–12 *156*
22:12 *157*
22:13 *157*
22:14 *158*
22:15–18 *158*
22:16–18 *257*
22:17–18 *244*
23:4 *274, 279*
25:23 *252*
26:3–4 *244*
26:4 *257*
26:26–30 *253*
28:3–4 *252*
28:12–15 *252*
28:13–14 *244, 258*
31:44–47 *253*
32:4 *177*
32:30 *177*
34:16 *206*
41:38 *218*
48:15–16 *177*

Exodus
1:8–10 *101*
1:22 *101*
2:3 *101*
2:5–6 *101*
2:5–10 *102*
2:9 *101*
2:9–10 *102*
2:11–14 *115*
2:15 *102*
2:16–21 *115*
2:20–21 *247*
2:23–25 *46*
3:1 *247*
3:2 *178*

3:4 *178*
3:6 *167, 178*
3:9–10 *109*
3:10–15 *106*
3:19 *47*
3:20 *113*
4:12 *111*
4:21 *102*
4:22 *41, 194*
4:23 *41*
4:28 *113*
4:29–31 *116*
5:1 *46*
6:6 *193–194*
6:6–7 *193*
6:7 *194*
7:5 *27, 53*
7:11 *110*
7:14–12:30 *47*
7:16–17 *44*
7:17 *53, 113*
7:22 *110*
8:2 *113*
8:10 *44, 53*
8:16 *113*
8:19 *44, 53*
8:21 *113*
8:22 *44, 47, 53, 255*
9:4 *53*
9:14 *53*
9:14–16 *44, 255*
9:16 *25, 47, 179*
9:20 *44*
9:26 *53*
9:29 *44, 47, 53, 255*
10:1 *89*
10:1–2 *44*
10:23 *53*
11:7 *44, 48*
12 *49–50*
12:1–2 *49*
12:2 *49*
12:3–11 *111*

12:5 *49*
12:6 *49*
12:7 *51, 110*
12:8 *50*
12:8–11 *50*
12:11 *50*
12:11–13 *110*
12:12 *47, 50*
12:13 *51*
12:19 *51, 276*
12:21 *50*
12:23 *51*
12:25–27 *111*
12:26–27 *52*
12:27 *50–51*
12:29 *51*
12:42–49 *111*
12:43 *280*
12:45 *279*
12:47–49 *52*
12:48–49 *275*
14:4 *44, 53*
14:10–11 *102*
14:13 *52*
14:18 *44, 53*
14:31 *44*
15:13 *33, 194*
15:13–14 *72*
15:16 *64, 72, 194*
15:17 *256*
15:24 *103*
15:24–25 *114*
16:2 *103*
16:15 *104*
16:35 *104*
17:5–6 *114*
17:8–13 *110*
18:10–12 *247*
18:19 *247*
18:21–22 *112*
18:23–23 *112*
19:3–6 *64*
19:4 *235*
19:4–6 *226*
19:5–6 *79*

291

Exodus (*cont.*)
19:9 105, 121
19:19 105
20:10 275
20:18–19 105
20:19 111
21:23 69
21:30 67
22:21 277
23:12 275
23:14–17 264
23:20–23 178
23:21 178
24:3 105, 176
24:7–8 107
25:1–40:38 61
25:8 80
25:21–22 78
26:6 206
28:3 219
29:32–33 282
29:33 253
30:33 282
31:3 219
32 56
32–33 39
32:11–14 108
32:26–28 110
32:31–32 108
32:34–33:3 44
33:12–17 218
33:12–19 38
33:16 218
33:17 56
33:18 33, 180
33:19 180
33:20 176
33:20–22 180
34:5–6 105, 180
34:5–7 261
34:5–9 38
34:6 36, 56
34:6–7 33
34:28 103
34:29–30 104
35:31 219
39:1–31 76

Leviticus
1:1–7:38 61
1:3–9 153, 164
4:29 61
4:31 61

4:33 61
4:35 61
10:1–5 61
11:44–45 71
14:2–7 76
14:14–15 230
14:17 230
16 20, 66, 73, 79, 86
16:2 74, 78
16:3 74
16:4 75
16:5 76
16:6 71, 76–77, 79
16:7–8 76
16:9 77
16:10 77
16:11 71, 77
16:12–13 77
16:14 78
16:15 76, 78–79, 83
16:16 80
16:17 71, 80
16:18–19 81
16:20–21 77, 81
16:20–22 77
16:21 73
16:21–22 85
16:22 76, 82
16:23 76
16:23–24 83
16:24 71
16:27 84
16:29 84
16:29–30 276
16:30 81, 85
16:31 85
16:32 86
16:33–34 71
17:8–9 277
17:10 71, 277
17:11 68, 73, 75, 77
17:11–12 68
18:1–22 180
18:5 122
18:26 276
19:16 69
19:34 278
20:2–3 277
20:10 56

22:10–12 282
23 45–46, 52, 174
23:5 52, 111
23:6–8 52
23:9–14 52, 172, 264
23:11 264
23:15–21 52
23:24–25 53
23:26–32 53, 73
23:33–43 53
24:17 56
24:22 277
25:23 256, 274, 279
25:35 279
25:45–46 279
25:47–54 192
25:48–49 192

Numbers
1:51 282
3:10 283
6:22–27 180
6:24–26 39
9:14 275
11:1–2 108
11:16 103
11:25 219
11:29 213
12 105
12:1 102, 115
12:3 104
12:7 59, 106
12:68 105
13:1–2 103
14:19 34
16:20–22 108
16:28 89
16:40 283
16:41–48 79
16:48 79
19:10 277
21 161
21:5 161
21:5–9 160
21:6 161
21:7 161
21:8 161–162
21:8–9 160
21:9 162
22:8–9 253
22:18 253

22:34–35 253
23–25 30
23:3–5 253
23:8 253
23:9 286
24:1 253
24:9 269
34:2 263
35:15 277, 279

Deuteronomy
1:16 277
4 36
4:6–8 226
4:9 95
4:20–21 259
4:25 36
4:26–27 36
4:29 95
4:30 36
4:31 36
5:5 107
5:29 44, 95
5:31 107
6:4–5 176, 181
6:4–6 95
6:13 25
6:16 25
7:1–6 286
7:7–8 29
7:9 59
7:12–13 30
7:16 286
8:2 95
8:3 25
8:5 95
9:1–6 286
9:4–5 95
9:13–20 108
10:10 108
10:12 95, 240
10:15 30
10:16 92
10:17–19 278
10:20 25
12:23 69
14:1 42
14:21 277
14:28–29 240
16:13–14 276
16:16 264
17:15 280
17:16 263

17:17 95
18 99–100
18:15 53
18:15–19 99
18:18 111
18:18–19 53
19:14 263
19:15 263
19:21 69
21:22–23 160
23:5 30
23:20 280
24:17 277
27:19 277
28:47 95
30:4 23
30:6 90, 92
30:12 122
30:12–14 21
30:14 95, 122, 207
31:11–12 276
32:6 42
32:21 123, 253
32:48–52 114
34:5 114
34:10 105

Joshua
1:6 263
6:25 248, 272
9:9 179
11:20 89
24:2 247
24:14 44

Judges
2:16 187
3:9 187
3:9–10 220
6:11–23 206
6:34 220
9:3 89
10:15–16 234
11:29 220
11:34 175
12:3 187
13:2–23 206
13:24–25 220
14:6 220
14:19 220
15:14 220
20:1 206

20:8 206
20:11 206

Ruth
1:4 265
1:16 272
1:16–17 248, 266
1:22 265
2:1 266
2:3 195
2:4 195, 266
2:4–9 195
2:11–12 273
2:12 248
2:15–16 266
3:9 44
3:12–13 195, 266
4:1–6 266
4:1–10 195
4:5 195
4:9–10 195
4:11 266
4:13 266
4:17 195, 266

1 Samuel
2:35 59
10:6–7 221
10:10 221
11:6 220–221
12:14 44
15:22 72, 164
16:13 223
25:25 179

2 Samuel
7:10 119
7:12–14 119, 152
7:12–16 198
7:13 198, 208
7:14 43
7:16 119, 198, 208
11 56
12:24–25 198
22:3 188
23:1–2 223

1 Kings
3:11–12 199
3:12 66, 89
4:29–34 66, 199
8:13–20 198

8:36 263
8:41–43 281
8:46 66
10:9 44
17:21–22 168
18:21 181
18:38–39 181

2 Kings
2:11 173
4:32–35 168
5:17 253
13:5 187
13:20–21 169
13:23 39
21:14 263

1 Chronicles
12:18 222
16:15–18 259
16:31 253
22:9 198
22:10–11 198
28:11–12 224
29:10 42
29:14 274
29:15 274, 279

2 Chronicles
2:11 44
3:1 153
9:23 89
12:14 89
20:20 61

Ezra
6:21 263
8:21 84
8:35 263

Nehemiah
9:7–8 59
9:20 231
9:27 187
9:30 232
9:31 36

Esther, 4:13
285

Job
1:1 79, 248
1:8 79

2:3 248
9:32–33 79
14:14 169
19:25–27 169
33:4 211

Psalms
1 287
1:1–3 12
2 19
2:1–9 53
2:6–7 199
2:11 44
2:12 199
4:1 40
5–10 204
6:2 39–40
7:17 206
8:2 22
9:13 40
9:16 27, 48
14:7 263
16:9–11 170
17:15 170
19:4 123
19:9 44
20:1 206
20:7 195, 206–207
20:9 206
22 44, 138–139, 141, 143, 147–149, 165, 174
22:1 138
22:1–22 44
22:6 139–140
22:7–8 140
22:9–10 140
22:12 141
22:14 141
22:15 141
22:16 142
22:17 142
22:18 143
22:20 143
22:21–22 143, 150
22:22 144
22:23 144–145
22:25 145
22:26 146, 286
22:27 146, 150

Psalms (*cont.*)
22:28 146, 150
22:29 147
22:30 147
22:31 148
23:1 182
23:4–5 51
24:1 53, 255
24:3–4 91
24:5 239
25:16 40
27:1 188
30:3 170
31:1 239
31:16 226
32 82
32:1 82
32:5 82
33:6 202–203, 210
34:4–5 162
34:8 52
34:22 72
35:13 84
39:12 274, 279
40:6–8 154
41:4 40
41:5–13 44
42 149
45:6 201
45:6–7 208
45:7 201, 227
46:10 245
49:15 170
51 56, 212
51:1 34, 37, 40, 56
51:5 67
51:10 90–91
51:10–12 212
51:16–19 72
54:3 283
54:6 206
58:3 67
60:4 162, 165
60:11 187
63 149
65:2 253
65:5 253
66:4 253
68:5 43
68:32 253

69:4 44
69:7–9 44
69:10 84
69:19–26 44
69:21 141
69:26 132, 135
71:20 170
72 245
72:11 245
73:24 171
77:15 194
77:20 113
78:52 183
80 183
80:1 183
80:3 221
80:4 183
80:7 221
80:19 221
84:11 40
85:1 256
85:4 226
85:9 44
86:5 34
86:9 253
86:11 240
89:26 43
89:28 60
90:17 240
95:11 124
96:12–13 112
97:10 35
98:3 48
99:6 206
101:2–3 44
102:13 40, 266
102:25 211
103:10–11 34
104:29–30 211
105:8–11 259
106:19–20 188
106:21 188
106:23 108
107:20 203
107:23–31 13
109:26 226
110:1 198
113:1–5 206
115:9–13 144
116:5 37
118:2–4 144
118:22–23 135, 155

118:25–26 184, 198
118:26 206
119 203
119:18 162
119:40 87
119:41 203
119:50 203
119:58 40
119:74 203
119:89 203
119:93 203
119:104 44
119:105 203
119:113 44
119:116 203
119:123 203
119:128 44
119:130 203
119:133 203
119:137–138 203
119:140 203
119:142 204
119:147 203
119:160 204
119:162 204
119:163 44
119:165 203–204
119:170 204
119:174 203
120–134 207
130 194
130:3 66
130:7–8 195
133 271
135:13 206
136 34
138:2 261
139:7 229
139:21–22 44
143 149
143:2 66
143:10 216, 231
146:6 204
146:7 204
146:8 204
146:10 204

Proverbs
1 287
1:7 44
1:23 20, 231, 287
3:5–6 240

3:11–12 20
3:34 56
3:34 40
6:16 44
8:13 44
11:9 137
15:8 78
16:23 89
20:9 66
21:27 72
25:25 125
28:13 37
30:1 199
30:4 199

Ecclesiastes
7:20 66
12:7 168
12:13 44

Song of Solomon
2:4 32

Isaiah
1:10–20 72
2:2 245
5 120
6 120
7:9 62
7:14 179, 190
8:13 44
8:13–14 186
8:14 186
8:20 65
9:6 179
9:6–7 199, 208
11 225
11:1 271
11:1–4 225
11:3 223
11:10 131, 162, 165, 236, 245, 271
11:11 162
11:12 162
13:10 23
19:24–25 256
25:2 283
25:5 283
25:9 226
26:19 171
27:12–13 23
28:16 123

29:18–19 24
30:1 232
30:1–2 207
30:2–3 232
30:18–19 40
32:15 213
32:15–17 213
33:22 191
34:4 23
35:4–6 24
40:1 182
40:1–2 248
40:2 182
40:3 182, 216
40:4 213
40:6 124
40:6–8 182
40:8 124, 263
40:9 182
40:10–11 182
40:13 232
40:17–26 53
40:28 202, 207
42:1 225, 245
42:1–12 245
42:6 245
42:8 181
42:18 163
42:19–21 223
43:1 187
43:3 187, 193
43:3–4 187
43:7 187, 258
43:10 255
43:11–13 187
43:21 187, 258
44:3–5 213
44:6 184, 186
44:20 89
45:15 188
45:17 207
45:21–22 187
45:22–23 147, 204
45:22–24 253
45:22–25 164
45:24 239
45:24–25 87
46:12–13 87
47:6 263
48:12 184
49 252
49:1 244

49:1–7 253
49:3 87, 244
49:5 252
49:5–6 190
49:6 252
49:7 60, 63, 129, 139
49:22 162, 250
49:23 123
49:25–26 269
49:26 195
51:1–2 163
52:3 193
52:7 123, 130, 248
52:7–10 130
52:10 130
52:13 127
52:13–53:12 87, 127
52:14 128, 139
52:15 87, 128–129, 253
53 20, 70, 82, 134, 137, 174
53:1 123, 129–130
53:2 131
53:3 131, 139
53:4 53, 70, 82, 131–132
53:4–6 48
53:5 53, 70, 132
53:6 53, 67, 70, 132, 155
53:7 133, 156
53:8 70, 134
53:9 134
53:10 69–70, 135, 155
53:11 136
53:12 70, 82, 108, 136
54:17 87, 204, 239
55:4–5 253
55:7 37
55:11 116, 143, 203
56:3 281
56:3–8 246
56:6–8 246, 281
57:19 270

59:1–2 27, 48, 139, 214
59:2 76
59:19–21 233
60:1–16 253
60:10 282
60:12 250
60:16 195
61:1 226
61:1–2 24
61:1–3 226
61:2 226
61:5 253, 282–284
61:8 44
62 249
62:6–7 249
62:10–11 249
63:1–6 207
63:4 227
63:7 30
63:7–64:12 30
63:8–9 178
63:9 30, 234
63:9–14 233–234
63:10 235
63:11 113, 235
63:12 236
63:13 234
63:14 236
63:16 42
64:6 61, 64, 66
64:8 42
65:1 123
65:2 123
65:17 21
66:18–23 253

Jeremiah
1:12 130, 144, 252
3:12 34
3:13 283–284
3:17 253
3:18 259
3:19 42
5:19 283
6:16 124
7:6 277
7:21–23 72, 164
10:10 207
12:14 263
12:14–17 284

16:16 246
16:18 256
16:19 246
16:21 181
17:1 92
17:5 207
17:9 66, 89, 92
17:9–10 95
22:3 277
23:5–6 87, 204, 271
30–33 57
30:3 250, 263
30:8–9 283
30:10 263
30:23–31:1 30
30:24 250
31:1–3 40
31:2 57
31:3 30
31:6 250
31:7 226, 251
31:7–9 253
31:8–9 251
31:9 42
31:10 215, 251
31:31–34 50, 90, 93, 240
31:35–37 39, 259
32:37 253
32:39–40 90–91
32:41 250, 260
33:2 181
33:7 263
33:7–9 252
33:16 230
33:20–21 60
33:25–26 60
44:4 44
46:27 263
51:5 39

Lamentations
2:20 35
3:22–23 35, 37, 60
4:10 35
5:2 283
5:21 221

Ezekiel
7:21 283
11:4–5 237

Ezekiel (*cont.*)
11:9 *283*
11:19 *93*
11:19–20 *90,*
228
11:20 *94*
16 *31*
16:1–14 *31*
16:8 *31*
16:15–34 *31*
16:35–59 *31*
16:60–63 *31*
18:4 *77*
18:20 *68, 77*
20:7 *53*
20:8 *53*
20:16 *53*
20:18 *53*
20:24 *53*
28:10 *283*
34–39 *239*
34:11–13 *206*
36 *215, 256,*
259
36:5 *256*
36:12 *259*
36:22–23 *285*
36:22–28 *260*
36:23 *145, 252*
36:23–24 *261*
36:23–27 *237*
36:24 *228*
36:24–27 *251*
36:25 *90*
36:25–27 *90–91,*
214, 228
36:26 *212*
36:26–27 *240*
36:37 *40*
37 *172, 231*
37:1–14 *238*
37:7–10 *172*
38:23 *246*
39:7 *181*
39:25 *263*
39:29 *214, 229*
44:7 *280*
44:8–9 *281*
47:22–23 *284*

Daniel
4:8–9 *218*
4:17 *53*

4:18 *218*
4:25 *53*
4:32 *53*
4:34–35 *53*
4:34–37 *253*
5:11 *218*
5:14 *218*
5:21 *53*
7:13–14 *23, 253*
9:9 *36*
9:26 *134*
12:2 *171*

Hosea
3:1 *44*
6 *173*
6:1–2 *173*
6:6 *72*
11:1 *194*
11:4 *44*
12:3–4 *177*
12:5 *177*
13:4 *188*
13:14 *173*
14:1–2 *31*
14:4 *31*

Joel
2:12 *84*
2:13 *37*
2:18 *253*
2:28–29 *212*
2:32 *123*
3:1–2 *256*
3:17 *284*

Amos
5:14–15 *44*
5:21 *44*
5:21–24 *72*
7:17 *263*
9:11 *145*
9:11–12 *145*
9:14–15:3 *263*

Jonah
1:17 *172*
2:1–2 *172*
2:6 *172*

Micah
2:10–11 *236*
3:8 *222*

5:2 *201*
6:6–8 *72*
7:18 *35*
7:19 *83*

Nahum, 1:15
123

Habakkuk
1:5 *163*
2:4 *21, 55, 62,*
125

Zephaniah,
3:17 *32*

Haggai
2:4–5 *235*
2:8 *53*

Zechariah
2:6 *23*
2:8 *185*
2:8–12 *185*
2:9–12 *185*
3:8 *271*
4:6 *219, 239*
4:6–7 *41*
4:11 *227*
7:5 *87*
8:17 *44*
8:20–23 *253*
9:9 *184, 190*
12 *41*
12:2–3 *262*
12:2–11 *41*
12:9 *269*
12:10 *41, 57,*
142, 163, 215,
253
12:10–12 *23*
13:7 *80*
13:9 *181*
14:8–9 *253*
14:8–16 *253*
14:16 *186*

Malachi
1:11 *246*
3:1 *178*
3:3 *72*
3:6 *12, 26, 58*
4:2 *44*

Matthew
1:1 *101, 118–119,*
152
1:5 *248, 266, 272*
1:5–6 *195*
1:6 *207*
1:7 *207*
1:18–25 *102*
1:21 *190*
1:22 *119*
1:22–23 *190*
1:23 *179*
2:1–2 *252*
2:2 *184*
2:13 *101–102*
2:14–15 *102*
2:15 *125, 194*
2:16 *101*
2:19–21 *102*
2:23 *125*
3:3 *216*
3:17 *164*
4:1–2 *104*
4:1–11 *110*
4:4 *25*
4:7 *25*
4:10 *25*
5:3 *146*
5:8 *89, 91*
5:16 *94–95*
5:17 *70*
5:17–18 *21*
5:17–19 *227*
6:9 *260*
6:9–10 *237*
6:21 *89*
7:12 *23*
7:15–23 *253*
7:21 *240*
7:24 *58, 94, 240*
7:24–27 *62*
7:26 *58*
7:28–29 *111*
8:2 *70*
8:11 *247*
8:16–17 *131*
8:17 *125*
8:25–26 *35*
8:28–32 *110*
8:29 *196*
9:16–17 *239*
9:36 *35*
10:1 *103*

10:5 *103*
10:28 *27*
10:40 *206*
11:5 *24*
11:25 *47, 255*
11:28–29 *236, 252*
11:28–30 *104, 235*
12:1–7 *22*
12:17 *125*
12:17–21 *225, 252*
12:18–21 *206*
12:34 *89*
12:39–40 *172*
13:19–23 *271*
13:35 *125*
14:14 *35*
14:19–21 *104*
14:29–31 *35*
14:33 *197*
15:7–8 *90*
15:24 *206*
16:12 *271*
16:16 *197*
16:16–17 *130*
17:1–2 *104*
17:3 *114*
17:14–18 *110*
18:16 *263*
18:35 *89*
19:4–5 *25*
19:16–19 *23*
20:28 *69*
21:4 *125*
21:4–5 *206*
21:9 *198*
21:12–13 *35*
21:16 *22*
21:37 *206*
21:42 *164, 173*
22:29 *125, 173*
22:29–46 *25*
22:41–45 *198*
22:41ff. *25*
22:43 *227*
23:23 *227*
23:37–39 *25, 253*
24:4–5 *25*
24:11 *25*
24:23–25 *87*
24:24 *25, 125*

24:24–25 *238*
24:29–31 *23*
24:30 *215, 217*
25:31–46 *113*
25:34 *184*
25:40 *269*
25:45 *269*
25:46 *171*
26:24 *25*
26:26–28 *107*
26:27–28 *68*
26:31 *87*
26:39 *156*
26:42 *156*
26:44 *156*
26:56 *87*
27:4 *69*
27:29 *141*
27:30–31 *131*
27:35 *143*
27:39–44 *140*
27:44 *134*
27:46 *25, 139*
27:52–53 *167, 173*
27:57–60 *134*
28:19–20 *253*

Mark
1:1 *197*
1:21–22 *111*
1:27 *111*
3:5 *35*
7:1–13 *22*
7:6 *89*
7:7–13 *22, 25*
8:31 *117*
9:9–10 *117*
9:37 *206*
10:45 *79, 108, 193*
11:7–10 *206*
12:6 *206*
12:10–11 *164*
12:23–25 *117*
12:24 *22*
12:28–30 *176*
12:33–34 *72*
12:36 *22*
13:21–23 *87*
13:22 *125*
15:3–5 *133*
15:27–28 *136*

15:29 *140*
16:12 *206*

Luke
1:17 *89*
1:26–33 *102*
1:31–33 *208*
1:32 *152, 196*
1:35 *196*
1:66 *89*
2:1 *101*
2:3–5 *101*
2:7 *101*
2:10–11 *188*
2:22–24 *63*
2:25–32 *226*
2:25–38 *118*
2:30–32 *145, 206*
2:32 *24, 252*
2:51 *89*
3:15 *89*
3:23–32 *102*
3:31 *207*
4 *174*
4:1–13 *23*
4:18 *206, 208*
4:18–21 *226*
4:18–19 *24, 109, 224*
4:20–21 *111*
4:21 *24, 224*
4:43 *206*
7:14–16 *169*
8:11–15 *271*
9:8 *117*
9:19 *117*
10:1 *103*
10:16 *206*
10:17–22 *35*
12:1 *271*
12:49–53 *25*
13:28 *247*
14:26–27 *157*
16:29 *22*
16:31 *22, 117*
18:31–34 *25*
18:38–39 *198*
19:29–38 *206*
19:41 *35*
20:17 *164*
20:37–38 *167*
22:14–20 *111*

22:19 *50*
22:20 *50*
22:22 *25*
22:37 *25, 137*
23:33–34 *109*
23:35–37 *140*
24:13 *114*
24:16 *206*
24:25–27 *25, 149, 262*
24:25-27 *120*
24:27 *173*
24:31 *206*
24:44 *125, 227*
24:44–46 *149, 173, 262*
24:44–48 *149*
24:44–49 *25*
24:45–46 *154*
24:46 *117*
24:49 *212, 264*

John
1:1 *177, 202*
1:1–3 *201, 208, 210*
1:3 *211*
1:10 *208, 211*
1:14 *43, 202–203*
1:18 *44, 176–178, 182, 197*
1:21 *100*
1:25 *100*
1:29 *52–53, 79, 156*
1:32–34 *224*
1:34 *196*
1:36 *53*
1:45 *117*
1:49 *184*
3 *228*
3:3 *88, 228*
3:5–8 *221*
3:6–7 *67*
3:7 *88*
3:9 *228*
3:10 *88, 228*
3:14 *162*
3:14–15 *159*
3:16 *152, 193, 200*
3:17 *206*

John (*cont.*)
3:34 *106, 202,*
   206, 219, 224,
   227
4:22 *258*
4:23 *194*
4:24 *67, 194, 209*
4:34 *206*
4:42 *189*
4:48 *125*
5:19–20 *107,*
   114
5:23–24 *206*
5:24–27 *112*
5:25 *196*
5:30 *206*
5:39 *18, 24–25,*
   116, 121, 173
5:45–47 *25, 121*
5:46–47 *100*
6:14 *100*
6:29 *206*
6:31–35 *161*
6:38–40 *206*
6:41 *103*
6:47–54 *71*
6:54 *117*
6:57 *206*
6:63 *287*
7:3–5 *103*
7:16 *206*
7:24 *227*
7:28–29 *206*
7:37 *287*
7:37–39 *240*
7:38–39 *287*
7:40–41 *100*
8:12 *252*
8:15–16 *112,*
   227
8:16–18 *206*
8:26 *106–107,*
   206
8:29 *206*
8:42 *206*
8:46 *50*
10:11 *113, 182*
10:14 *182*
10:14–15 *153*
10:14–16 *113*
10:16 *252, 270*
10:17–18 *153*
10:18 *77*

10:24–33 *183*
10:30 *175–176*
10:31–33 *176*
10:35 *18, 22*
10:36 *106, 206*
11:4 *196*
11:23–24 *117*
11:27 *197*
11:35 *35*
11:39 *170*
11:42 *206*
12:12–15 *184*
12:12–16 *206*
12:23 *105*
12:27–28 *105*
12:28 *240*
12:32 *128*
12:37–38 *103,*
   129
12:37–40 *120*
12:39–40 *129*
12:47 *112*
12:49–50 *106*
13:2 *89*
14:6–9 *158*
14:6–11 *35*
14:9 *175*
14:15 *58, 92*
14:16–18 *230*
14:17 *237*
14:21 *92*
14:21–24 *64*
14:23 *80, 92*
14:24 *92*
14:26 *231*
14:28 *186*
15:7–8 *287*
15:13 *153*
15:19 *275*
15:25 *125*
15:26 *209*
16:7–8 *222*
16:8 *232*
16:13 *237*
16:13–14 *231*
16:32 *87*
16:33 *48*
17:3 *206*
17:6 *191, 240*
17:9 *109*
17:11 *175*
17:12 *125*
17:14–16 *275*

17:17 *237*
17:21 *206*
17:21–22 *175*
17:26 *144, 240*
18:9 *125*
18:11 *135, 141,*
   155
19:11 *141*
19:17 *155*
19:23–24 *143*
19:24 *125*
19:28 *125, 149*
19:28–29 *142*
19:30 *79*
19:34–37 *216*
19:36–37 *125,*
   173
20:9 *117*
20:14 *206*
20:15 *206*
20:21 *224*
20:22–23 *216*
20:31 *197*
36–38 *206*

Acts
1:2 *240*
1:3 *114*
1:4 *212*
1:4–5 *264*
1:8 *233*
1:16 *240*
2 *264*
2:16 *140*
2:16–17 *239*
2:16–18 *213*
2:23 *155*
2:24 *117*
2:29–32 *170*
2:32 *117*
2:32–33 *264*
2:33 *212*
2:38 *232*
3:18 *100*
3:19 *240*
3:22–24 *100*
3:26 *197, 240*
4:8–14 *222*
4:11 *164*
4:12 *80*
4:24–25 *19, 227*
4:27–28 *135,*
   155, 267

5:1–11 *28*
5:11 *28*
5:29 *189*
5:31 *189*
6:7 *125*
7:13 *117*
7:21–22 *102*
7:23–28 *115*
7:25 *109*
7:35 *115*
7:37 *100*
7:51 *233*
8:21 *89*
8:29 *240*
8:32–35 *173*
8:32–35 *134*
8:37 *90*
9:3–5 *234*
9:20 *197*
10:19 *240*
10:36 *53, 205*
10:38 *219, 221*
10:40–42 *113*
10:40–43 *227*
10:44–47 *220*
11:17–18 *206*
11:18 *243*
11:23 *89*
13:16 *145*
13:22 *89*
13:23 *189*
13:33–34 *117*
13:36–48 *206*
13:38 *136*
15 *144*
15:8–9 *89*
15:14–17 *145*
15:16–17 *253*
15:29 *71*
17:10–11 *173*
17:31 *227*
20:28 *53, 64, 71,*
   194, 282
21:11 *240*
24:14 *121*
26:8 *173*
26:9–11 *200*
26:22–23 *206,*
   252
27:9 *87*
28:23 *21*
28:25 *240*
28:26–27 *89*

Romans
1:1-2 122, 173
1:3 159, 263
1:3-4 197
1:16 249
1:16-17 25, 62, 125, 148
1:21 89
2:15 89
2:16 227
3:23 65
3:23-25 69
3:24 195
3:24-25 77, 148
3:25 78, 83, 87, 227
3:31 122
4 60
4:1-3 271
4:3 25
4:3-6 64
4:5 208
4:9 64
4:9-22 271
4:20-22 63
4:20-25 64
4:25 83
5-6 87
5:6-8 157
5:14-21 71
6 109
6:2-8 83
6:4 82, 240
6:11-12 83
6:16-23 110
6:17-18 110
6:18 194
6:22 194
6:23 77
7:12 55, 93
7:12-14 227
7:18 91
8:2-4 229
8:4 93, 227, 240
8:9 229, 240
8:11 239
8:13-14 239
8:14-16 239
8:15 45
8:26 216
8:27 75
8:29 67
8:32 159

8:34 75, 109, 137
9-11 33, 266-267
9:4-5 101, 159
9:5 263
9:17 25, 47, 240
9:27 45
9:31-32 54
9:32-33 186
10 90, 95, 130
10:2 286
10:5-6 25
10:5-8 122
10:6 95
10:6-8 21
10:8-10 90
10:9-21 122
10:9-10 89
10:15-16 130
10:18-21 267
10:21-11:2 267
11 12, 17, 129, 254, 266, 286
11:1 123
11:2-4 126
11:5 45
11:5-6 64
11:7-10 267
11:7-12 126
11:11 267
11:11-15 137
11:12 130, 252, 267
11:15 130, 145-146, 252, 267
11:15-16 126
11:16-24 25, 268
11:17 32, 117, 268
11:17-18 185
11:18 268-269, 285
11:20 268
11:20-21 126
11:23 269
11:24 268
11:24-29 126, 249
11:25 117, 130, 167
11:25-26 116
11:25-32 137

11:26 57, 208, 214, 240, 268
11:28-29 268
11:30-32 269
11:33-36 126
14:17 213
15:8 263
15:8-12 206
15:9-12 252
15:12 271
15:16 206
15:27 266
16:17-18 25
16:25 44, 165
16:25-26 173

1 Corinthians
1:9 197, 288
1:18 263
1:23 186, 263
1:25 263
1:30 87, 148, 195, 239
2:2 127
2:9-14 209
2:9-16 230, 239
2:11 209
2:14 209, 263
3:16 230
3:16-17 87
4:12 240
5:6-8 50
5:7 49-50, 111, 239
6:11 229
6:19-20 87
8:6 211
10:1-2 63
10:9 161
10:11 33, 46
11:23-29 253
11:25 194
11:26 52, 111
12:3 210, 222, 236
12:13 227
12:13-14 264
14:21-22 124
15 168, 172
15:1-4 166
15:3-4 114, 123, 154
15:20 264

15:20-23 173
15:20-24 173
15:21-22 71
15:26 174
15:35-38 173
15:35-44 170
15:42-44 173
15:51-53 168
15:51-54 173

2 Corinthians
1:21 44
4:6 89
5:7 240
5:10 112
5:10-11 28
5:17 49, 87, 91, 117, 221, 229
5:20-21 148
5:21 40, 87, 163, 204, 227, 239
6:16 87
11:2 115
13:1 263

Galatians
1:4 208
1:12 165
2:2 165
3:3 60
3:6 60
3:6-9 271
3:6-14 64
3:8 19, 119, 159, 173, 244, 257
3:11 25, 62
3:13 160
3:13-14 30
3:14 206, 216
3:16 258
4:6 45
5:4 60
5:22-23 58, 213
6:1 227
6:7-8 56

Ephesians
1:7 53, 195
1:11 56
1:13 216
1:13-14 239
1:17 165
2:1 67

Ephesians (*cont.*)
2:5 67
2:8 92, 130
2:8–9 55, 64, 94
2:10 75
2:11–3:10 286
2:11–3:12 269
2:11–22 252
2:12 248, 268, 270
2:13–14 270
2:17 270
2:19 270, 284
2:19–22 87, 224
3:1–5 270
3:3 165
3:3–6 243
3:6 270
3:6–8 206
3:8 201
3:9 201, 208, 211
3:16–17 90
4:4 227
4:8 167, 169
4:14 17
4:30 235
5:8 240
5:14 117
5:23 206
5:30–32 75, 115
6:8 240

Philippians
1:6 44
2:5–8 136
2:9–11 147, 205
2:12–13 40, 235
2:13 44
3:9 40
3:20 189

Colossians
1:14 195
1:15 43
1:16 208
1:16–17 201, 211
1:19 43
1:22 44
1:25–27 243

1:26–27 270
1:27 206
2:17 12
3:3 230

1 Thessalonians
1:9 268
1:9–10 252
1:10 51
3:13 89
4:13–17 168
4:14 117
4:16 117
5:9 49, 51
5:24 44

2 Thessalonians
2:2–4 25
2:8 240
2:9 125
3:3–4 44

1 Timothy
1:1 189
1:12–13 200
2:3 189
2:5 80, 86
2:5–6 108
3:16 159, 187, 205–206, 210
4:10 189
5:19 263

2 Timothy
1:10 206
2:13 63
2:15 288
3:14–15 21, 253
3:15 65
3:15–17 173
3:16–17 18–20, 53, 207
4:1 113, 227
4:18 44

Titus
1:3 191
1:4 191
2:10 191
2:13 191
2:13–14 71, 94
2:14 196
3:4 191

3:6 191
3:8 58, 71, 94
3:14 71, 94

Hebrews
1:2 44, 202, 211
1:3 44
1:8 211
1:8–9 201
1:10 211
2:10–12 144
2:14–15 208
2:14–17 193
2:17 87
3:1 74, 86
3:1–6 106
3:7–15 235
3:11–4:11 240
3:12 90
4:1–3 124
4:9–11 252
4:10 57
4:14 197
4:14–15 87
4:14–16 78
4:15 49
5:10 87
6:20 87
7:25 109, 137
7:26–27 76, 79
7:26–28 87
8:1 135
8:1–2 74
8:2 75
8:5 12, 224
8:6–13 240
8:8–12 93
8:10 239
8:13 93
9:5 78
9:11 87
9:11–12 75
9:11–15 78, 111
9:12 53, 196
9:12–14 75
9:13 192
9:13–14 81
9:14 192
9:22 53, 68, 75
9:24 75
9:24–26 85
9:28 136
10:1 12

10:5–10 75, 153, 164
10:5–12 154
10:16–17 93
10:18 135
10:19–21 75
10:19–22 87
10:21 87
10:29 216
10:30–31 28
10:37–38 62
10:38 25, 55
11 62, 247
11:4 72
11:6 62, 70
11:8 64
11:8–21 271
11:8–10 274
11:10 84
11:13 274
11:17 167
11:19 167
11:29 54
11:31 272
11:39–40 253
12:1 62, 70
12:2 63
12:5–11 48
12:22–29 235
12:29 28
13:8 27
13:11–14 84
13:20 113

James
2:14 58, 95
2:17–18 95
2:18 58
2:20 58, 71
2:21–23 151
2:23 60
2:25–26 272
2:26 58
4:4 235, 275
4:6 40, 57
4:7 57

1 Peter
1:2 128
1:10–11 127
1:16 71
1:18–19 50, 252
1:19 53

1:22 *239*
1:23–25 *124*
2:5 *87, 113*
2:7–8 *186*
2:9 *226*
2:21–24 *137*
2:22 *134*
2:25 *182*
5:4 *113*
5:5 *40, 57*
5:6 *57*

2 Peter
1:1 *206*
1:11 *206*
1:17 *164*
1:20–21 *20*
2:20 *206*
3:18 *206*

1 John
1:1 *203*

1:9 *37*
2:1 *80, 227*
2:3–5 *64*
2:3–6 *92*
2:15 *275*
3:7 *240*
3:8 *51*
3:16 *71, 77, 153*
3:20–21 *89*
3:24 *239*
4:8 *26*
4:14 *189*
4:16 *26*
5:2–3 *64*

Jude
24–25 *44*

Revelation
1:4 *225*
1:7 *215*

1:8 *205*
1:11 *184*
1:17 *185*
1:56 *208*
2:6 *44*
2:8 *185*
2:14 *253*
2:15 *44*
2:18 *196*
2:23 *28*
3:1 *225*
3:14 *63*
3:16 *28*
4:5 *225*
5:5 *271*
5:6 *225*
5:6–13 *133*
5:8 *78*
5:9 *196*
5:13 *208*
7:9–10 *252*
8:3–4 *78*

11:15 *208, 245, 253*
12:11 *71*
13:8 *49*
14:12 *95*
15:3–4 *186, 246*
15:4 *237*
17:14 *184, 186*
19:8 *75, 239*
19:11 *113*
19:11–16 *227*
19:13 *203, 207*
19:16 *186*
20:5–6 *171*
20:7–8 *252*
22:1–3 *288*
22:13 *185*
22:16 *271*

Topic Index

A

Aaronic benediction 39, 180
  See also blessing
Abba 41, 45
Abraham 163
  as *ger* and *toshav* 278
  believed in resurrection 167
  blessing for the gentiles 244, 257–258
  faith of 59–60, 63–64, 151
  father of Ishmael 152
  obedience of 153
  saw God 182
  son of a pagan 247
access to God 244
  See also believers: access to God
  for Jew and gentile 244
adultery
  Israel's 31
Adversary, *see* Satan
ahavah/love 29
  See also love: of God
  Akedah, see binding of Isaac
aliyah 240, 250
  See also Israel: immigration to
All the Messianic Prophecies of the Bible 159
Allah
  god of Moslems 273
allegory
  of love 32
altar
  bronze 161
Amasai
  Spirit on 222
amen
  related to faith and truth 59, 63
Ananias and Sapphira 28
anarchy 265

angel 39
  as messenger 177, 188
Angel of the LORD, the 157, 176–179
  See also Son of God: pre-incarnate
  divine 177
  God's Name in 177
  His temple 178
  Moses meets 178
  reveals God 177
  Savior, Redeemer, Shepherd 178
  Son/Word 179
  worshiped 177
  wrestles Jacob 177
anger
  God's 31
animal sacrifice 157
  See also atonement: substitutionary
  as type of Yeshua 69
  See also type: of Messiah
Anointed One 201, 223, 225
  See also Messiah
anointing 218, 223–224
  counterfeit 232
  false 207
  for judgment 225
  oil 223
  to build Tabernacle 219
apostasy, *see* rebellion; sin; transgression
  Israel's 34, 253
apostles
  all Jewish 206
  and prophets 224
apostles' faith
  in *Tanach* 18–19
  in Yeshua's sacrifice 135
appearance
  of godliness 237
  Yeshua judges not by 223
appointed time 85

Ark of the Covenant 150
arm of God, *see* right hand: of God
ArtScroll Tanach Series
  Bereshis/Genesis (Hirsch) 61
  Psalms (Feuer) 149
Asaph 183
asking God 40
  for grace 41
  for mercy 42, 56
assurance 261
atheism 216
atonement 55, 83
  before Yeshua 174
  See also forgiveness: in *Tanach*
  Hebrew root word for 67
  relation to Moses and Yeshua 110
  substitutionary 70, 95, 132, 134, 136
  See also animal sacrifice; blood sacrifice; offering; sacrifice: substitutionary
  teaching on 52, 61, 67–70
  in NT 68
  Yom Kippur 65, 73–86
Authorised Daily Prayer Book, The (Hertz), *Yom Kippur* 174
authority
  of Moses and Yeshua 111
azazel scapegoat

B

Balaam 30, 253
banner, *see nes*/sign foreshadows cross
baptism
  Holy Spirit 212

Pentecost/*Shavuot*
    213
    promised in *Tanach*,
        see Promise of the
        Spirit
Israel's 54
"belief in"
    definition of 61
believer
    Paul as Jewish 243
believers
    access to God 75, 214
    and God's wrath 48
    as *gerim* 275
    as monotheists 205
    as polytheists 205
    assurance of 254
    before Yeshua 218–222,
        225
    Bible 18
    established 62
    faith witness 62, 187
    gentile 248, 268–269
        in *Tanach* 243–251
    God as Father of 41
    God's discipline on 48,
        232
    growth of 21
    heart circumcision of
        286
    idolatry by 53
    in olive tree 17, 248,
        278
    Jewish 268
    last days 250
        to pray for Israel 251
    maturity of 21, 221
    New Testament 17–18
        faith in *Tanach* 19,
            49, 127
    nominal Israelite 120
    priesthood of 75
    problems 127
    reason redeemed 187
    relationship with Holy
        Spirit 209, 214
    righteous in Yeshua 204
    sanctification of 265
    Spirit-led 231
    submission
        to each other 57
        to God 57
    to praise God 144
    to preach salvation 249

walk 17, 214
    examples in *Tanach*
        46
    in unbelief 34
Beshore, Kenton 117
Bethlehem 195, 201
Bible, *see* Word of God
Bikkurim, see First Fruits
binding of Isaac 151
    See also Akedah
blasphemy
    against Yeshua 200
    definition of 200
blessing
    from Israel's salvation
        267
    of Israel 39
    of prayer for Israel
        286
blood
    consuming forbidden
        71, 277
    God's 71, 194
    lamb's 46, 50–51, 54
    on mercy seat 78, 150
    power of 61, 68, 74, 81,
        174
    purifies 81, 128
        See also cleansing
    sign for God 51
    Yeshua's 50–52, 69, 75,
        81
        makes new covenant
            50, 194
blood sacrifice 51, 55, 61,
    69, 79–80
    See also animal sacrifice;
        atonement:
        substitutionary;
        offering; sacrifice
Boaz
    kinsman-redeemer 195
    type of Messiah 195,
        266
Body of Messiah 265
    See also believers: as
        Temple
body of Yeshua 50
Booths, *see* Tabernacles
born again 159, 214, 228
    See also new birth
    believers 249
    elements of experience
        214

OT description of 214,
    221, 228
born from above 67, 228
    See also new birth; born
        again
Branch, the 268
bread
    from Heaven 161
    leavened 271
    making 265, 271
    manna 161
    of affliction 50
    offering 265
    unleavened 50
Bride of Messiah 243, 248,
    250
    See also believers
    Esther type of 285
    obedience of 251
    to declare Israel's
        deliverance 251
    to help Israel 285
    to love Israel 269
Brown, Colin 55
Brown-Driver-Briggs
    Hebrew lexicon
    (PC Study Bible) 53

C
Calvary
    type in *Tanach* 20
Canaanites 278
carnal nature 216
    See also flesh; man; old
        man
caste 281
Chambers, Oswald 265
character
    in a name 33
characteristics
    of God 27, 195
    of spiritual fruit 58
chen/grace 33, 38–39, 41,
    55–56
    See also chen/grace of
        God; God's grace,
        chen/grace; God's
        grace
    and Aaronic benediction
        39
    and peace 39
    as unmerited favor 33,
        39
    definition of 38

chen/grace *(cont.)*
  on Zion 40
  to Israel 40–41
  to Moses 39
chesed/love 29, 32–34,
  59–60
  and God's Name 33
  and hope of salvation 33
  as covenant love 32, 35,
    71
  God's eternal 34
  God's pleasure in 34
  in forgiveness 37, 56
children, *see* believers:
  maturity of
children of God, *see*
  believers
choice 230, 235, 286
Christ in All the Scriptures
  (Hodgkin) 149
Christianity
  first commandment in
    176
Christians 250
  See also believers
  in *Tanach* 250
  organizations helping
    Israel 253
Church 17
  anti-Semitism in 249
  as *gerim* 278
  birthday on Pentecost
    264–265
  definition of 252
  dry 268
  early 144
    mostly Jewish 144
  election of 29
  foundation destroyed
    269
  God's Spirit establishes
    228
  lost perspective of 269
  loved by God 32
  membership 116
  mercy on Israel 269
  replacement theory in
    254, 266–267
    See also replacement
      theory
  revelation of spiritual
    Israel 266
  security of 29
  self-centeredness of 92

to confess Jewish
  Messiah to Jews
  249
unbelief in God's Law
  100, 121
will help *aliyah* 165,
  250
Church and Israel
  266–267
  despised each other 265
  relationship 267, 272
  roots in *Tanach* 264
  witness to resurrection
    263
circumcision
  of *nekar* 280–281
  physical 286
Classical Evangelical Essays
  in OT Interpretation
  (ed. Kaiser) 173
cleansing 215
  See also blood: purifies
  of lepers 230
  ritual 277
Cohen, Rev. Dr A. 43, 45,
  138–139, 141, 143,
  146
command
  most important 29, 92
  not angels 232
  to correct 222
  to do good works 94
  to eat no blood 69
  to wait 170
commandment, *see*
  command; commands
commands 180
  obeyed through Spirit
    219, 222
common meal, *see*
  Communion
commonwealth of Israel
  268–269, 278
  gentiles joined to 281
Communion 52–53, 146,
  253
  See also covenant meal;
    Passover: Yeshua's
    last
community 265
confession
  of David 56
  of sins 85, 219
congregation 145

contacts to help Israel 253
contexts in *remez* 138
convert 270
conviction of sin 81
  by Spirit of God
    222–223, 232, 265
correction, scripture for 20
covenant 79
  eternal
    with Israel 31, 60, 91,
      267, 285
  new 68
  obligation of 15
  promise of resurrection
    168
  sealed by blood 68
  with Abraham 118–119
  with David 118–119
  with Isaac 152
  with Noah 69
covenant meal 253
  See also Communion;
    Passover: Yeshua's
    last
  Jethro and Moses at 247
  relation to Moses and
    Yeshua 111
covenant-love 56
  See also chesed
covering for sin 61, 74, 80,
  174
  See also atonement
creation 210
Creator
  faith in 18
  identity of 199
  right to judge 66
cross
  and curse 30
  as burden of obedience
    155
    See also principle: of
      suffering
  as judgment on sin 27,
    48
  exaltation of 162
  exchange on 163
  in the *Tanach* 20, 61,
    151, 162
    See also Chapters 10
      and 11
  reveals God's love 152
crown of thorns 141
crucifixion 121, 141–143

in *Tanach* 138
of Yeshua 127,
134–136, 159
origin of 127
prophesied in *Tanach*
127, 132, 134
questions about the 139,
155
Cup of Redemption 50,
68, 194
See also Communion
cup of suffering 141,
155
cups of Passover, *see*
Passover: four cups of
curse
into blessing 30
of God 125, 250, 254,
269
first occurrence 160,
255
of sin 160
curses
against Israel 267
cut off 17
from roots 18

D
Daniel 218
David
as a *ger* 274
declared God's Word and
built God's House
224
promised son of 152,
225
repentant 212
type of Messiah 223
Davidic lineage 266
Day of Atonement 20, 43,
53, 65
See also Yom Kippur;
atonement
gospel in 73, 86
Day of Blowing, *see* Rosh
haShanah
day of the Lord 226
Days of Awe 31
reconciliation during 31
dead raised 168, 172
See also resurrection
death 170
and unbelief 161
as last enemy 173

deliverance from 162
faithful until 62
of a sacrifice 153
of Adam and Eve 174
of Moses and Yeshua
114
second 171
death on the cross 83, 133,
136, 143
God's will 135, 139
death penalty 56, 82, 163,
276
See also curse: of sin
deception 17, 21
See also false: doctrines;
heresies
as error 285
as sin 132
defense against 17
in world 262
of Satan 79, 255
spiritual 237
Deity of Yeshua 175–176,
186
deliverance 51, 146–147
from enemy territory 51
through Moses and
Yeshua 109
deliverers
Spirit upon 220–221
demonic influence 216
Devil, *see* Satan
*Dictionary of New
Testament Theology*
(Brown) 206
disciples 170
taught by *Tanach* 21,
120, 262
witness of 202
discipline 231
See also correction
disobedience, *see* sin
*Distinctive Ideas of the Old
Testament, The*
(Snaith) 29, 44
diversity 175–176
doctrines
and tradition 22
false, compared to
leaven 271
See also false: religions/
dualism
of New Testament,

validated by
Tanach 18–19, 26
dualism, *see* false: religions/
dualism

E
echad 175
See also yachid
Tanach examples
175–176
Egypt
and God's fame 179
dependence on 232
firstborn of 193–194
gods of 47, 53
plagues on 47–48
election 55
election-love, *see* ahavah
Elijah 168
Elisha 168
Ellison, H.L. 164
Elohim 182
See also God; God's;
Name of God
encouraging 19, 148
end time, *see* last days
deception 17, 237
See also heresies
prophecies
about Israel 40, 42
restoration of Israel 261
upheavals 245
Enemy 79
See also Satan
Enoch 168
ensign, *see* nes/sign
foreshadows cross
error
and ignorance 22, 125
as sin 132, 155
errors, *see* heresies
Esau 252
Esther
type of Church 285
*Evangelical Dictionary of
Theology* (ed.) Elwell)
95
evangelization, *see*
believers: faith witness;
believers: to preach
salvation
evangelization of Moslems
249
See also god: of Moslems

Everyman's Talmud
  (Cohen) 43, 45
evil, hating 35
exaltation
  of the cross 162
example
  of Yeshua 137
exchange, *see* atonement:
  substitutionary
exegesis 46
exile of the Jews 31, 256
  redemption in 214

F
Face of God
  metaphor for Spirit 229
  See also God's:
    presence
faith 18
  and righteousness 21,
    90
  and works 54, 58, 71,
    88
  as trust and obedience
    59–61
  for heart cleansing 89
  foundation of 18
  foundations to be
    studied 15
  in God 62, 215, 268
    as Creator 18
  in the *Tanach* 60–63,
    147
  in Yeshua's blood 70
  of Jeremiah 34
  pleases God 154
  related to truth 59
  test of 151
  to believe promises, *see*
    promises
  verified by *Tanach* 18
  within the *Tanach* 18,
    54, 58–63
faith/belief, meanings of
    58, 61
faithfulness 59
  of God 44, 59–60, 63,
    116, 215, 256
  of men 59
  of Ruth 195
Fall of Man 160, 254
false
  anointed ones 238
  doctrines 17, 26

  See also deception;
    heresies
  religions/dualism 47
  spirit 236
fasting 84–85
father
  as Lord 255
  God as 41
    and LORD of hosts
      185
    offered Son 153
  Pharaoh as symbolic 41
  revealed in Yeshua 158
  sees Son's blood 51
Father's separation from
    Yeshua 139, 149, 175
Fathers of the Covenant
    (Ellison) 164
favor, *see* *chen*/grace
fear 95
fear of the Lord 28, 40,
    44, 91, 145, 179
Feasts of LORD 45–46,
    51–52, 172, 207, 278
  See also moed
feasts, pilgrim 264
feelings, of God 35–36
fellowship
  of Jew and gentile 71
Feuer, Rabbi A.C. 141,
    145
first and last 184–185
First Fruits 52, 172, 264
first priority in prayer 260
fishers and hunters 246
flesh, *see* carnal nature;
    man; old man
  definition of 239
  Messiah came in 159,
    192
  no good thing dwells in
    212
foreshadow
  of atonement 78
  of gentile believers 85,
    278, 281
  of Messiah 41, 78, 84,
    86
  of salvation 61, 221
  of the cross 156
forest, *see* wilderness
forgiveness
  and the Spirit of God
    216

  by God 34, 36, 61, 69,
    82
  by Yeshua's blood 51
  in *Tanach* 61, 70, 81,
    85, 192
  on *Yom Kippur* 65
free will offering 153
fruit of the Spirit 17, 58,
    213
  in obedience 61
  love as 222

G
gentiles/nations 125, 252
  See also heathen
  against Jerusalem 41
  as faith heroes 247
  as part of Israel 32, 51,
    85, 185, 195, 215,
    278
  God speaks to in
    Tanach 248
    about Israel 248–249
  Good News to 145,
    158, 201, 270–271
Gethsemane 135, 139
gift 151
  of faith for salvation
    130
gifts
  spiritual 265
Ginzberg, Louis 173
glorified 177
  bodies 166
glorify
  God's name 236
glory of God
  to fulfill His Word 246
gnosticism 17, 26
  See also heresies; false:
    religions/dualism
god
  See also *Elohim*; God's;
    Name of God;
    Tetragrammaton
  as an adversary 235
  as Creator 202, 207
    foundation of 202
    through Word 202
  as destroyer 51
  as Father 41–43, 182
    See also Father: God as
    in Judaism 43
    of individuals 43

of orphans and
    widows 43
of the remnant 42
of Yeshua 43
to Israel 41–42
as Judge 257
as Lord 255
as Redeemer 191, 194
as Savior 187, 190
    See also Messiah: as
        Savior
    Tanach references for
        187–188
as Shepherd 182
    See also shepherd: the
        good
as Son 182
as Spirit 67
commanded Passover 51
covenant keeper 34, 36,
    285
defends Israel 245–246,
    285
faithful to Israel 129,
    285
feelings of 35
fulfills His Word 129,
    143
grace of, see chen/grace
    of God; God's: grace
love for, see love: for
    God
of Israel 145, 246, 248
    the only Savior
        187–188
of Moslems 273
    See also evangelization
        of Moslems
of world system 255
    See also Satan
prophesied submission
    to 205
relationship with
    Israel 39
    Moses 39
resists the proud 57
revelation of Himself 18
Scripture inspired by 20
speaks in Tanach 19
suffers with His people
    234
will defend Israel 285
God in the flesh 175–176,
    193–194, 203, 205

See also Deity: of Yeshua;
    Incarnation
God's, see God; Name of
    God; Elohim
characteristics 27, 36
faithfulness 63, 215,
    254
    to Israel 267, 285
forgiveness 34, 36–37
glory 180
grace 37–39, 54–56, 64
    See also chengrace;
        chen/grace of God
    and Israel's salvation
        57
    and mercy 56
    and Noah 56
    and rest 57
    and the Law 54
    definition of 38, 55
    examples in Tanach
        56–58
    for salvation 214–215
    in the Tanach 54–56
    to believers 40, 85
    to the humble 56
home on earth 285
inheritance
    land and people 256
judgment 27
    for Israel 48
    from love 27, 135
    in NT 27–28
    results in 263
love 26, 32
    in OT 27, 29
    leads and guides 33
mercy 35–36
name 253, 260
    See also Name of God:
        personal;
        Tetragrammaton
sanctification of
    260–261
supports His Word
    261
nature 176, 261
    same as Yeshua 204
order 61, 144, 214
patience 232
presence 229
protection 87, 161
    withdrawn 161
provision 61, 161

sacrifice 117
sovereignty 47–48
way 61, 74, 232
    in Tabernacle 80
will 135, 152
    Yeshua's submission
        to 133, 141, 153,
        155
God-fearers 28, 144
godliness, appearance of
    237
gods 182, 273, 276, 284
    See also idolatry
goel 192
    See also kinsman-
        redeemer; Redeemer
Gog and Magog 246
golden calf, see idolatry: of
    Israel
Good News 26, 83, 118
    and resurrection 166
    of salvation by grace 55
    of Yeshua 124, 145
    proclaimed through
        Spirit 233
    to gentiles 159
    to Jew first 249,
        268–269
good works 71, 94–95
    See also works
Gorelik, Robert R. 137
gospel 118, 170
    and resurrection 166
    in Tanach 21, 118–125,
        244
    rejection of prophesied
        130
    to Abraham 257
    to gentiles 119
    to the Jews 257–258
grace 235
    See also chen/grace;
        chen/grace of God;
        God's grace
Great Commission 237
Great Hallel 34
grieve the Spirit 235
growth of believers, see
    believers: maturity of
guidance 231

H
Haftorah, see Torah:
    portion

hate 157
  evil 35
hear, *see* Sh'ma
heart 89–90, 94
  circumcision 90, 92
    See also new birth
  condition of 70, 88–89,
    91
  definition of 66, 88–89
  evil 66
  Pharaoh's 47
  purification of 89–91
  ruled by God 144
  written on 93
heathen 268, 284
  See also gentiles/nations
Hebraic
  perspective 249, 260
    See also humanism
Hebraism
  for atonement 53
Hebrew
  idiom 55
  language 263
  mistranslations 273
  roots 285
  theology 55
Hebrew prayer book,
  see Siddur
heresies 17
  See also deception
  gnosticism 26
  Marcionism 26
Hertz, Dr J.H. 157, 160
High Priest 75, 78
  See also priesthood
  believers as body of 75
  garments 75
  on *Yom Kippur* 65, 73,
    150
    ministers alone 80,
      85
  warned by God 74
  Yeshua as 74, 79, 93
  Yeshua's prayer as 191
hinting, *see* remez/hinting
history
  Church 17
  in *Tanach* 46
Hivites 179
Hodgkin, A.M. 138
Holocaust 239
holy
  definition of 75

Holy Ghost, *see* Spirit of
  God
Holy of Holies 74, 76, 78,
  150
  of Scripture, *see* Song of
    Songs
Holy Scriptures, *see*
  Scripture
Holy Spirit, *see* Spirit of
  God
  empowers 59, 94
  grieving 235
  inspires 205
human sacrifice, *see*
  sacrifice: human
humanism 194, 216, 249
  religious 216
  secular 216
humble 146
humilty
  of heart 89, 222
  of Moses and Yeshua
    104
hypocrisy and leaven 271

I

Ibn Ezra 143
idolatry 53
  Elijah's challenge to 181
  from ignoring God 187
  God saves from 187
  judgment on 188
  of believers 53, 151
  of Israel 56
image, *see* likeness
immortality 168
Incarnation 175, 205
incense 78
iniquity 164
  See also sin; transgression
  and repentance 31
  definition of 82
inner man, *see* heart
Inside Islam (Safa) 286
inspiration
  Scripture given by 20,
    143, 176
intercession 164
  and God's love
    for Israel 34
  by Esther 285
  by grace 56
  by Moses and Yeshua
    108

  by Yeshua 75, 132, 136
  for Israel 30, 249, 251,
    285
    and Church 85
    by Moses 34, 56
Isaac
  as son of promise 152,
    257
  as type of Yeshua 152,
    159, 167
  blessing for the gentiles
    244
Ishmael 252
Islam, god of 273
  *See also Allah Islamic
    Invasion, The*
    (Morey)
Israel
  and baptism 54
  and God's covenant 32,
    34
  and idols 53
  apostasy of 36
    as unbelief in *Tanach*
      100
  applied the blood
    51–52, 54
  as a nation 265
  as *gerim* before God
    274
  as God's children 41
  as God's firstborn 194
  as God's wife 31
  as God's witness 187
  as *toshavim* 279
  blinded 129, 267
  chosen by God 29, 31,
    33, 44, 218
  Christian groups helping
    253
  Church to stand with
    266
  commonwealth of 247,
    266, 278
  compassion on *gerim* and
    toshavim 279
  deliverance of 252
  destruction of 269
  elect of God 29–30
  exile of 36, 39
  God sanctifies His name
    in 236, 261
  God waiting for cry of
    40–41, 215, 221

importance to Church
269
land of 215
See also Israel: to
possess the Land;
Promised Land
dividing 257
God's inheritance
255–256
Jews' inheritance 258
loved by God 29,
31–32, 34
national rebirth 254
Olive Tree of 267–268
See also Olive Tree of
Israel
people of God's
inheritance 258
See also Jews
promised healing 31
promises by God for 40,
140
Messianic 118
reason redeemed 187
rebellion of 280
redemption of 44, 46,
194
by God 54, 195, 236
reason for 187
rejection of 123, 267
relation to Moses and
Yeshua 115
repentance of 161
restoration of 30, 57,
246, 248, 254, 263
resisting 249, 260
sanctifies God's name
261
zarim in 283
salvation of 207, 215,
228, 285
blessings from 267
spiritually dry 131
stewardship of land 284
stone of stumbling to
186
threatened 285
to obey 180
to possess the Land 42,
215, 279
See also Israel: Land
of; Promised Land
to remember 51
tribes of 215

ways to help 253
witness to gentiles 218
Israel and Church
despised each other 265
roots in *Tanach* 264
witness to resurrection
263
Israel's Olive Tree, *see*
Olive Tree of Israel

J
Jacob 145
blessing for the gentiles
244
God of 278
identifies Angel as God
177
wrestles with God 177
Jedidiah 198
Jerusalem 153
Council 71, 144
forbidden to *zarim* 284
goal of *aliyah* 240
nations against 41, 262
pardoned 182
worship in 145
Jethro
Midianite priest 247
*Jewish New Testament
Commentary* (Stern)
149
Jewish New Year, *see* Rosh
haShanah
Jews, *see* Israel: people of
gospel to 17, 21, 120,
145
in exile 256
See also exile of the
Jews
inherit the promise 158,
215
loved by God 268
Messianic 243, 264,
268
saved 268
saved in Israel 251
Jews and gentiles
belong to God of Israel
273
fellowship of 71
one in Messiah 244,
270–271
Job 79, 169, 248
John the Baptizer 156

Joseph 218
Judah as first Jew 247
Judaism
anti 249
conversion to 270
fast in 73
first commandment in
176
holy days of 31, 85, 265
principles of faith 171
Judas 69
judges 182
Moses and Yeshua as
112
Spirit upon 220–221
judgment of God 27, 66,
171
See also punishment: and
God's Spirit
after the cross 28
and justice 40, 69
and redemption 48
and sin 48
at altar 161
for unbelief 161
mercy and love in 27
on idolatry 188
results in 263
terror of 28
justification 77, 83

K
Kaiser, Walter Jr 19, 25,
43
Kimchi 171
King
of gentiles/nations 183
of Israel 183–184, 223
in NT 184
in OT 184
of kings 184
of the Jews 184
king crucified 143
kingdom/rulership
as rulership 144, 146,
149, 239
eternal 198
inherit the 146
Messianic 226, 245
See also Millennium
of priests
Israel as 54
on earth 186, 225
See also Millennium

kinsman-redeemer 44,
    191, 194
  See also goel; Redeemer
  Boaz as 195, 266
Knowledge of the Holy,
    The (Tozer) 27, 44

L

lamb
  is the Passover 50
  of Passover 49
Lamb of God 50, 52, 133,
    194
  kills 28
  provided 158
  redeems by blood 196
  song of 186
  Tanach prophecy of
    157
land, *see* Promised Land
last days 17, 250, 254
  See also end time
  Israel in 36, 262
last supper 68
Law 54–55
  See also Tanach, Law:
    of Moses; *Torah*
  and salvation 37, 54,
    58, 61, 122–123
  as the standard 55, 93,
    122
  benefits of 203
  definition of 203
  for holiness and
    protection 54
  fulfilled in Yeshua
    203
  fulfilling
    conditions for 93
  given at Sinai 46, 54
  given on *Shavuot*
    265
  gospel in 73
  in NT 63
  judgment for breaking
    30, 55, 78, 81
  of foreigners and
    strangers 273–285
  of life for life 69
  of Moses 17, 30, 54
  summary in
    Deuteronomy 92
  unbelief by Israel 100
  under the 55, 122

law and prophets, *see*
    Tanach
Law of Moses, *see* Law:
    of Moses
Law of the Lord, *see* Law
leaven
  as type of sin 50
  compared with
    hypocrisy/false
    doctrine 271
Legends of the Bible
    (Ginsberg) 173
leper, offering of 70
Levites 280
  See also priesthood
Lexical Aids to the Old
    Testament, The
    Hebrew – Greek Key
    Study Bible (ed.
    Zodhiates) 95
life 17
  after death 168
  as warfare 169
  in blood 69
  of faith 62
  spiritual 285
lifestyle 278
likeness
  of Adam 67
  of God 67
  of Yeshua 67, 159
literal fulfillment of
    prophecy 140, 143
  See also Word of God:
    fulfilled
Lockyer, Herbert 159
Logos Bible Software
    Program 182
Lord 145, 147
  See also God: as Lord
LORD of hosts 185–186
love
  for enemies 286
  for God 29, 92
    See also Yeshua: love
    for
  of God 32
    Hebrew terms for 29
    rest in 32
  word first used 152
loving-kindness, *see chesed*
loyalty of Ruth 266
lying to God, judgment on
    28

M

Maccabees 172
Maimonides
  thirteen principles of
    171
man, *see* carnal nature;
    flesh; old man
  sensual 209
  slave to sin 255
manifestations 177
Marcionism 26
  See also heresies
marriage of God and Israel
    32
martyr, *see* witness: and
    martyr
Mashiach, see Messiah
materialism 216
Matthew Henry's
    Commentary (Henry)
    87
Matthew shows *Tanach*
    fulfillments 119
matzah 53
  See also Unleavened
    Bread; bread:
    unleavened
mediator 79
  See also High Priest;
    intercession
  Moses and Yeshua as
    107
Melchizedek
  King-Priest of Jerusalem
    247
Memra 160
mercy, *see rechamim/*
    mercies; *chesed*
  as an action 35
  as compassion 35, 39
  for Jews 269
  God of 35, 195
    See also God's: mercy
  on Zion 266
  rebuke part of 20
mercy seat 74, 78, 150
messenger, *see* angel
Messiah
  as Abraham's Seed 258
  as firstfruits 172
  as priest and sacrifice 79
  as Savior 187–191
  as Sevant of the LORD
    87, 133, 190

as son of David 119,
198–199, 204
as Word of God
incarnate 202
credentials in *Tanach*
18–19, 21, 23–24,
118, 120, 139, 142,
203, 262
as prophet like Moses
99–116
cut off for Israel 134
definition of 201, 223
divinity of 179, 196, 201
See also Chapter 14
eternal 201
for gentiles 129
foreshadow of 41
has God's Name 179
in you 271
more than human 128,
175, 179
name of 204
obligation of Body of
15, 147
one with believers 144
promised to Israel 249
rejected by His people
129, 131
rose on First Fruits 264
Tanach metaphor for
165
titles of 203–204
*Messiah in the New
Testament, The*
(Santala) 150
*Messiah in the Old
Testament in the Light
of Rabbinical Writings,
The* (Santala) 117,
149
*Messiah of the Targums,
Talmuds and
Rabbinical Writers,
The* (Beshore) 117
*Messiah, A Rabbinic and
Scriptural Viewpoint*
(Yellin) 137
*Messiah, Another Jewish
View* (Gorelik) 137
Messianic Jews 145, 264
See also Jews: Messianic
Millennium 186, 246, 252
See also kingdom/
rulership

miracles
by Elisha 168
by Moses and Yeshua
113
by Yeshua 168
no proof of *per se* 120,
129
moed, see Feasts of LORD
as God's appointment
45, 172
definition 174
moneylending 280
Morey, Robert A. 286
Moriah 153
site of sacrifice
of Isaac 153
of Temple 153
of Yeshua 153
mortality, *see* death
Moses
and God's grace 38, 45
as intercessor 56, 161
as Lawgiver 176
as prophet 36, 46
desires spirit
outpouring 213
as symbol of God's Law
100
as type of Yeshua 46,
101–116
declared God's Word
built God's House 224
sent by God 46
song of 186
writings of 22, 121
Moshay, G.J.O. 286
Moslems
evangelization of 249
in Israel 273, 284
mystery
definition of 243
of gentile salvation 130
of the Trinity/*Elohim*
210
mystery of Messiah
243–244
See also gentiles/nations:
salvation of: in
Tanach

N

name as nature 33, 144,
177, 179–180, 199,
204, 260

Name of God 33, 36,
38–39, 47, 179–182
defended by God 285
glorify 236
is eternal 42
LORD OUR
RIGHTEOUSNESS
204
personal 179–182, 195
translations of 180
revealed 199
in Yeshua 199
See also Yeshua:
has God's name
to be declared 179
used by Angel 178
used by Boaz 273
nations/gentiles/heathen,
see gentiles/nations
nature of God 27, 32, 54,
144, 176, 182
nekar 280–282
circumcision of 280
to minister to Israel 282
nes/sign
foreshadows cross 161
new birth 88, 90, 92
See also born again; born
from above; heart:
circumcision;
salvation
benefits of 89, 93
definition of 88, 90,
95
elements in experience
of 214
in *Tanach* 88, 90–92
results of 92–95
New Covenant 88, 93
new creations 212
See also new life
by God's Spirit 221,
229
*New International
Dictionary of New
Testament Theology*
(Brown) 55
new life 49
See also new creations
*New Scofield Reference
Bible, The* (Scofield)
87
New Testament 17–18
before the 17

New Testament (*cont.*)
  believers 18
  commands 71
  doctrines
    Hebraic background
      of 15
    validated by *Tanach*
      17, 24, 65,
      118–119, 166,
      193
  God of love 26
  points to *Tanach*
    promises 152
  uses "scripture" for OT
    18
  view of *Tanach* 19
Nicodemus 88, 159
Noah and grace 56

O
obedience 79, 170
  and God's love 29
  as burden 155
  as worship 128, 154
  in Spirit 230
  of Abraham 257
  of Yeshua 128, 136
  to God's Word 79, 92,
    95
    by Abraham 154
    by faith 81–82, 88,
      95
offering, *see* animal
  sacrifice; blood
  sacrifice; atonement:
  substitutionary;
  sacrifice:
  substitutionary
  burnt 153, 164
    killed by offerer
      153
    wood for 155
  of two animals 76,
    81–82
  sin 77
  wave 265
oil, *see* anointing: oil
old man 82
  See also carnal nature;
    flesh; man
Old Testament 17
  See also Tanach; Word
    of God
  as Scripture 18, 21

God of judgment 27
  saints, *see* believers:
    before Yeshua;
    saints: in *Tanach*
  validates the New
    Testament 18
  validity for today 17,
    19, 24
Olive Tree of Israel
  266–268, 278
  See also Israel: Olive
    Tree of
  believers in 17, 185,
    248, 278
  gentiles grafted into
    32, 185
one, Hebrew concept of,
  see echad; *yachid*
order, *see* God's: order
  God's 61, 144, 214
Orr, James 168

P
paganism, *see* false:
  religions/dualism;
  heathen
parakletos 216
  See also Spirit of God
Passover 46, 52
  first 49–52
  four cups of 193
    See also Cup of
      Redemption
  freedom on 265
  Hebrew names for,
    see Pesach; *Seder*
  is the lamb 50
  lamb 49, 51–52
  redemption 46, 193
  relation to Moses and
    Yeshua 110
    See also Yeshua: as
      Lamb
  Shabbat of 172
  songs for 207
  Yeshua's last 68, 193
    See also Communion
patriarchs 167
  as *gerim* 274
pattern, *see* plan of
  salvation; salvation:
  God's plan of
  of Tabernacle 224
  of Temple 224

Paul
  apostle to gentiles 254
  as blasphemer 200
  as Pharisee 270
  as rabbi 270
  encourages*Tanach* study
    20
  Hebrew name for, *see*
    Shaul
  teachings 17
    from *Tanach* 17,
      20–21, 65
PC Study Bible 53, 149
peace, *see shalom*
  peace process 257
Pentateuch and Haftorahs,
  The (ed. Hertz) 87
Pentecost 17, 21, 52
  See also Shavuot
  birth of Church 264
perception, spiritual
  230
permanent residency
  253
persecution 200
  of the Jews 249
Pesach, *see* Passover
Peter
  use of *Tanach* by 17, 21,
    170
Pharaoh, *see* Egypt: gods of
  as a god 46
Pharisees
  accuse 22
  and God's Word 22
  Paul one of 270
phobia 28
  See also fear of the Lord
picture 20
  See also type
pierced 142
plan of salvation 52, 61,
  266
  See also salvation: God's
    plan of; purposes of
    God
  Israel in 254
politics and religion 284
poor in spirit 146
power
  spiritual 237, 265
  to obey 29
practical ways to help
  Israel 253

praise 145, 219
  by children 22
  by *nekarim* 281
prayer
  answers to 232
  delights God 78
  Elijah's 168
  first priority in 260
  for enemies 286
  for Israel 286
  for Jews 269
  Lord's 260
  to sanctify God's name
    237
  warning 232
  Yeshua's High Priestly
    191
presence of God, *see* God's:
    presence
pride, God resists 57
priesthood
  anointed 86
    See also anointing
  in *Tanach* 61, 93, 282
  of believers 253
    consecrated 253
  of Israel 79, 83
    believers from 120
  of Levites 280
principle
  of asking 40
    See also asking God
  of grace to the humble
    57
  of reaping and sowing
    56
  of Word's fulfillment
    130
promise 30, 39
  of Messiah's coming 99,
    189, 225–226
    through Abraham
      118–119, 158
    through David 119
    through Isaac 257
    through Jacob 258
    through Sarah 152
  of resurrection 173
  refers also to fulfillment
    216
  son of 198, 257
    See also Isaac; Yeshua
  to defend Israel 195,
    285

to heal Israel 31
Promise of the Spirit
  212–213, 264
  See also Yeshua:
    promises Spirit
Promised Land 91, 256
  See also Israel: land of;
    Israel: to possess the
    Land
  to Israel in NT 119
  to Israel in OT 180,
    250, 256, 258
  unconditional 259
promises 151
  See also faith
  faith in the 63
  guaranteed by God's
    name 261, 267
  of gentile salvation 245
    See also gentiles/
      nations: salvation
      of; prophecies: of
      gentile salvation
  to Church
    confirmed by Israel
      263
  to Israel 40, 57, 91, 93,
    129, 285
    confirmed by Church
      263
    include Promised
      Land 263
    Yeshua confirms 263
proof of Messiahship 261
proof texts 18, 124
  Yeshua quotes 262
prophecies
  of gentile salvation
    244–246
  require fulfillment 262
prophecy, *see* literal
    fulfillment of prophecy;
    promise; promises;
    Word of God: fulfilled
  by believers 219
  of Israel's restoration
    238, 256
  fulfillment of 254,
    262
    with Church help 250
  of John the Baptist 182
  of Lamb of God 156
  of Messiah 182, 190,
    194

as God's Son 199
  as judge 223
  as King of kings 245
  as our righteousness
    204
  to have Spirit 224
  of Middle East 259
  of new birth 93
Prophet, the
  in NT 99–100, 169
prophets 127
  declare God's name
    181
  false 253
  warn by Spirit 232
  writings of 21–22
propitiation 77–78, 150
  See also atonement
proselytes 144
  as *gerim* 275
protection 87, 161
  withdrawn 161
provision of God 61, 161
provoke to jealousy 269
Psalms 35
  of Ascent 194, 207
punishment, *see* judgment
    of God
  and God's Spirit
    232–233
purpose of God 236

Q

quotes from *Tanach*
  by Paul 17
  by Yeshua 17, 139
  frequency in NT 17–18
  longest in NT 93

R

Rabbi Akiva 32
Rabbi Saul 121
Rabbi Simeon ben Yochai
  132
rabbinic teaching
  method, *see remez/*
    hinting
  on faith 61
  on Messiah 101, 116,
    128, 131–132, 146,
    204
  on resurrection 167,
    171
  on *Shavuot* 265

rabbinic teaching (*cont.*)
  on Suffering Servant
    139
  on *Yom Kippur* 85
rachamim/mercies 35–37,
    40
  See also mercy
  in plural 35
  on Israel 40
Rahab 272
  ancestor of Messiah 248
  faith of 272
ransom 67
  See also redemption:
    price
rapture 168
Rashi 146
rebellion 199
  See also apostasy; sin
  of Israel 34, 232, 253
rebuke
  in love 222
  part of God's mercy 20
  Scripture used to 20
Redeemer 147, 169,
    191–195
  See also goel; kinsman-
    redeemer
  and Spirit 233
redemption
  and *aliyah* 250
  and judgment 27, 46, 48
  by blood 282
  definition of 191
  from death 168
  in Passover 46, 49
  of Israel 46, 71, 194,
    214
  of mankind 195
  price 191, 193–194
  See also ransom
  reason for 187
reedemer 191
regathering of Israel, *see*
  restoration: of Israel
regeneration, *see* new birth
rejection of Israel 267
relationship
  of Church and Israel
    267
  with God 70
  of Moses and Yeshua
    105
religion and politics 284

remez/hinting 138–139,
    144, 149, 162, 185
remnant
  and grace 45
  confess God as Father
    42
  doctrine of the 33
  of gentiles 145
  of Israel 131, 233
repentance, *see* turn
  and God's Spirit 231
  and submission 231
  believers' 34, 265
  Israel's 33–34, 161, 221
  lack of 231
  on *Yom Kippur* 85
  reward of 37, 82
replacement theology, *see*
  replacement theory
replacement theory 17,
    249, 252–254
  See also Church:
    replacement
    theory in
responsibility
  for the crucifixion
    155–156
  of Levites 280
rest 52
  and salvation 57, 86
  in God's love 32
  in repentance and
    obedience 236
  of redemption 236
restoration 214
  involves correction 20
  of Israel 91, 246, 248,
    253–254
  See also aliyah
  resisting 249
  sanctifies God's name
    260
  zarim in 284
  See also zarim
resurrection 121, 166–173
  See also dead raised
  as confirmation 166,
    173
  definition of 168
  first 168, 171
  in glory 170
  of forefathers 167
  of Israel 172, 239, 254,
    262

of the body 169
of Yeshua 83, 135, 139,
    144–146, 166–170
  fulfilled a *moed* 172
  on third day 154, 170
  prophesied in *Tanach*
    166, 171, 174
  Tanach examples of 168
  type of 163
  types in *Tanach* 167
revelation 17
  by God 18, 21, 26, 130,
    158
  of Israel 250
  progressive 26
  written 18
  See also Scripture;
    Word of God;
    Tanach
Revelation, book of
  images from *Tanach*
    207
right hand 165
  of God 194
righteousness
  by faith 21, 90, 151
  NT uses OT to prove
    21, 60, 122–123
  in Messiah 40, 163
  of Messiah 148, 163,
    204
  our own 92
  Scripture teaches 21
rituals, God-ordained 74,
    77–78, 81, 83, 88, 277
Romans 11 266–267
Root of Jesse 131, 268
roots 17
  cut off from 18
  Israel's 285
  spiritual and social 286
Rosh haShanah 31, 53
ruach 216, 238–239
  See also Spirit of God;
    spirit
Ruth 195, 265–266, 272
  ancestor of Messiah 248
  faith of 272–273
  loyalty of 266

S

Sabbath, *see Shabbat*
Sabbath of Repentance,
  see Shabbat Shuvah

sacrifice
  God's 152, 200
  human 157, 278
  in obedient faith
    153–154, 257
  living 83
  substitutionary 157,
    174, 192
  See also animal
      sacrifice;
      atonement:
      substitutionary;
      blood sacrifice;
      offering
sacrificial system 61, 81,
    154, 157, 161, 191
  See also animal sacrifice;
      atonement; blood;
      blood sacrifice;
      priesthood;
      Tabernacle
  fulfilled 135
  ineffectual 85, 93, 192
Safa, Reza F. 286
saints, *see* believers
  in *Tanach* 178,
    218–221, 226, 247,
    268
  Jew and gentile 270
salvation, *see* new birth
  and the Law 37, 54, 58
  as rest 57
  assurance of 254, 261
  by grace through faith
    37, 46, 52, 54–55,
    92, 94, 122–123,
    247
  connection with Israel
    261
  for gentiles 130,
    144–145
  for gentiles and Jews 55,
    144
  God's plan of, *see* plan of
      salvation; pattern;
      purpose of God
  overview of 46
  symbol of 61
  in Passover 49
  in the *Tanach* 20, 61,
    246
  Jewish 269
  of Israel 42, 55, 91, 130,
    145, 215

blessings from 267
hindering 64
outside Yeshua 55
Spirit's work in
    221–222
working out 40
sanctification
  definition of 216
  of believers 265
  of God's name 236,
    260–262
  definition of
      260–261
Santala, Risto 117
Sarah 163
Satan, *see* Enemy
  counterfeits power of
      God 237
  defeated by Yeshua 17
  god of world system
      255
  wants to destroy God's
      people 249, 269,
      285
Savior, *see* Yeshua: as
      Savior
  Messiah as 187–191,
      195
scapegoat 77, 81, 83
  carried sins 83
  Hebrew name for, *see*
      azazel
Scofield, C.I. 78
Scripture 17
  See also Word of God;
      Tanach
  in NT means *Tanach*
      125–126, 166
  inspired 18, 20
  maturity in 17
  profitable 18, 20
  for correction 20
  for rebuke 20
  for salvation 20
  for teaching
      righteousness 21
  trusting 205
Second Coming 23, 215,
    225
  type of 117
Seder 50, 52
  See also Passover
  for believers 52
Septuagint 142, 150

Sermon on the Mount 94
serpent 161–163
  as a curse 160
  as symbol 160
  bronze 160–163
Servant of LORD, *see*
      Messiah: as Servant
      of LORD
  as Messiah 132
  called Israel 87
seven
  aspects of Spirit 225
  symbolic of perfection
      225
seventy elders 219
Sh'ma 180
Shabbat
  breaking 22
  of Passover 172
  rest of redemption 236
  Shuvah 31
shalom, definition of 39,
    206
Shaul 65
  See also Paul
Shavuot 17, 264–265
  See also Pentecost
  and Spirit baptism 170
  birthday of the people of
      Israel 265
  songs for 207
shepherd
  Moses and Yeshua as
      113
  the good 182–183
Siddur
  confession of sins in
      43
sign, *see* *nes*/sign:
      foreshadows cross
  of blood 51
  of circumcision 286
  seeking a 121
signs
  accompany spiritual
      outpouring 213
  and wonders 238
  are not fruit 213
Simeon 145, 226
sin, *see* apostasy; error;
      iniquity; rebellion;
      transgression
  and God 33, 35, 80
  and *Yom Kippur* 66

sin (*cont.*)
  confession of 37
    by remnant 42
    in the Siddur 43
  curse of 160
  defeat of 91
  definition of 82, 132
  destroys God's likeness
    128
  forgiveness for 51–52
  from Adam 67
  in *Tanach* 65–67
  no one without 66–67,
    69, 92
  of unbelief, *see* unbelief
  penalty for 69, 128
  separates from God
    139, 214
    See also Father:
      separation from
      Yeshua
  Tanach terms for 67
Sinai 46
sinless 49
sinners
  as Law-breakers 55
    See also carnal nature;
      flesh; man; old
      man
  need mediator 83, 86
sins
  covering/payment for
    68, 80
  forgiven under Law 81
  judged by God 27
  on the cross 27, 48,
    137
  put on Yeshua 139
slavery
  Israel's 46
  spiritual 53
Smith, James E. 147
Snaith, Norman 29, 32, 44
Solomon 66
  as son of David 198
  temple of 153
  type of Messiah 119,
    198
Son of David, *see* Messiah:
  as son of David;
  Yeshua: son of
  Abraham and David
Son of God 196–200
  as Son of David 200

as son of Israel 159
in *Tanach* 199
nature of 200
NT says Yeshua is
  196–197
pre-incarnate 51, 157,
  182, 190, 194
  as LORD 187
  reveals the Father 44
  See also Yeshua:
    reveals the Father
*Soncino Books of the Bible,
  The Psalms* (Cohen)
  149–150
Song of Songs 32
sovereignty of God 47–48,
  255–256
Spirit of God 17, 209–215
  See also ruach
  agrees with Word of
    God 237
  and forgiveness 216
  and salvation 228–229
  as Creator 202,
    210–211
  as one 225
  as teacher 230–231
  convicts of sin 222,
    236
  declares Yeshua Lord
    236
  enables obedience 219,
    228–230
  fruit of, *see* fruit of the
    Spirit
  fullness of in Yeshua
    219
  given after repentance
    20
  glorifies Yeshua 231
  grieving 235
  has no blood 194
  illumines mysteries 243
  imparted 214
  in redemption 233–236
  inspired OT 237
  inspired Word 20–21,
    201, 223, 237
  leading 231
    to repentance 236
  linked to repentance and
    baptism 232
  lives in believers 80–81,
    93, 218, 228

makes new creations
  221
makes Yeshua Lord 210
never exalts Himself
  231
not separate from Word
  of God 210, 223
  builds God's House
    224
outpouring 212–215
  on disciples 170
  response to 219, 233
  prepares for Redeemer
    233
promised 212–213, 215
  to Israel 212–214
resisting 233
revealed in *Tanach* 209
reveals God 209–210
same as Presence 229
sanctifies 144, 216, 229
symbol for 230
through David
  promises land of
    Israel 259
with Israel 236
Spirit of life 17, 238–239
spirit, another 231, 236
spiritual
  experiences 216
  perception 230
  warfare, *see* W (most
    entries listed under)
    by Moses and Yeshua
      110
    over prayer for Israel
      286
sprinkle 150
  See also blood: purifies
stone of stumbling
  for today 249–250
  in NT 186
  in OT 186
strange gods, *see* idolatry;
  god; gods
strangers, *see* gerim;
  nekarim; toshavim;
  zarim
  as proselytes 85
*Strong's Exhaustive
  Concordance of the
  Bible* (Strong) 44, 59
submission to God
  fulfilled in Yeshua 205

Succot, see Tabernacles
suffering 147
supplication, *see* asking
symbol
  in Abraham 156
  in blood 69, 230
  in bronze 161
  in common meal 146
  in cup of redemption
    194
  in grain seeds 271
  in High Priest garments
    75
  in laying on hands 81
  in leaven 271
  in linen 75
  in manna 161
  in *matzah* 53
  in oil 223, 230
  in olive tree 185
  in serpent 160, 162–163
  in *Shavuot* and
    Bikkurim 264
  in skin 174
  in sword 143
  in Tabernacle 61
  in two goats 83
  in wine 71, 93
  Israel not just 46
synagogue 172

T
Tabernacle
  built through Spirit 219
  songs for 207
  symbolism of 61
Tabernacles 53
Tanach 17
  See also Old Testament;
    Scripture; Word of
    God
  Aramaic translations, *see*
    Targums
  as Word of God 18–19,
    21, 24
    See also Scripture:
      inspired
  Paul's use of 17–18
  describes Messiah's
    works 219
  equips for works 21,
    207
  foundation of gospel
    166–167

in Greek, *see* Septuagint
  promises new covenant
    93
  promises Spirit 215
  resurrection in 166
  roots of Israel and
    Church 264
  saints 37, 221
  source of correction 207
  source of true doctrine
    20–22, 49
  use by John 120, 125
  use by Matthew
    119–120
  use by Paul 17, 65,
    123–124, 126, 191
  use by Yeshua 21–22,
    120–121, 143–144,
    159, 163, 167, 172,
    198
  used for rebuke 20
Targum Jonathan 128,
  131, 136
Targum Pseudo-Jonathan
  160
Targums 128
teaching
  by Spirit 230–231
  next generation 52
Temple
  in the heart 90
  See also Spirit: of God:
    Temple of
  spiritual 224
  Third 64
tempting God 161
Ten Commandments 55
tetragrammaton 179, 273
thanksgiving sacrifice 146
*Theological Wordbook of
  the Old Testament,
  The* (eds. Harris,
  Archer, Waltke) 68,
  286
theology 17
  replacement 17, 249,
    252–254
thirst 141
  for God 149
three
  days 154, 170, 172
  times 17
time of the gentiles
  end of 246, 252

tongues 124, 219
Torah 93
  See also Law
  portion 172
  teaching on gentiles
    273–285
toshavim 278–279
  different from *gerim*
    279
*Toward An Old Testament
  Theology* (Kaiser) 43
Tozer, A.W. 27, 36, 44
tradition
  and doctrine 22
  without faith 70
transgression
  definition of 82
Tree of Life 268
tribes of Israel 215
triumph 143
trust 146
  See also faith
  in God's atonement 58,
    70, 254
  in God's Word 58, 62,
    70, 151
  in man 199, 207
  in the *Tanach* 18
truth
  related to faith 59
  Spirit of God speaks
    237
turn 20, 163
  See also repentance
Twelve Prophets, The
  (Cohen) 174
type
  of Church 285
  of Communion 282
  of fruitlessness 213
  of God's love 152
  of hypocrisy/false
    doctrine 271
  of Messiah 41, 49, 69,
    119, 152, 156, 159,
    161, 167, 195, 203,
    223
    See also foreshadow
      of Messiah
  of prayer 78
  of redemption 191
  of resurrection 163
  of salvation 61, 83
  of Second Coming 117

type (*cont.*)
  of the cross 151, 159,
    191–192
  reveals truth 21

U

unbelief 87, 90, 161, 267
  See also sin
  Jews regathered in 214
  prophesied 129
unbelievers
  blinded 129
  God's wrath on 48
  help Israel 283
  in God's sanctuary
    280
  stumble 186
  to know salvation from
    the Jews 258
understand
  salvation in *Tanach* 20
understanding
  Word of God
    given after repentance
      20
unity 175–176
Unleavened Bread
  Feast of 52
unrighteousness
  cleansing of 37
uprightness
  after correction 20
*Uses of the Old Testament
  in the New, The*
  (Kaiser) 19

V

vengeance 226
verse numbers 126
victory, *see* triumph
  over death 173
vinegar 142
violence 143
virgin birth 141, 206
virgin's Son
  as God with us 179

W

walk of believers 17, 66
  in Holy Spirit 82, 93
  in obedience 91, 214
war against Jerusalem
  262
  See also spiritual: warfare

warnings 17, 19, 90
  about another spirit
    in *Tanach* 231, 236
  by Paul 161, 268
  by Spirit through
    prophets 232
  by Yeshua
    about false prophets
      253
    in the *Tanach* 21
    to believers 28, 121
  from God 257
  plagues as 27
  to serve Israel 250
watchmen 249, 251
way
  of God 61, 124, 230
  See also God's: way
Weeks, Feast of, *see*
  Shavuot
*What the Bible Teaches
  About the Promised
  Messiah* (Smith) 150
Who is this Allah?
  (Moshay) 286
wilderness 17
Wisdom of Solomon 160
witness
  and martyr 72
  for God 187
  of disciples 202
  of *gerim* 277
  of Israel 87
witnesses
  two 263
womb and mercy 35
Word of God 18, 87, 160,
  202–203
  See also Tanach
  as Creator 202–203
  as grain seed 271
  built on Name of God
    261
  fulfilled 129, 142
    See also literal
      fulfillment of
      prophecy;
      prophecy;
      promise; promises
  glorifies God 246
  incarnate 202
  misunderstanding of
    17
  misuse of 17, 253

not separate from Spirit
  210
  proved a lie 269
  rejecting 22
  Spirit of God attracts to
    216, 223
  Tanach foundation of
    20–21, 123–124
works
  and salvation 37, 54,
    70
    See also Law: and
      salvation
  faith and 58, 62, 151
  of the flesh 54, 61
  of the Law 88, 90
  of Yeshua 219
  Tanach equips for 21
world
  believers not to love
    275
  deceived 262
  friendship with 275
worship
  in spirit and truth 209,
    224
  in vain 22
  is to obey 128
  is to serve 95, 147
worshiper
  as servant 128
wrath of God 48, 51
*Wycliffe Bible
  Encyclopedia* (Moody
  Press) 206

Y

yachid 175
  See also echad
Yellin, Burt 137
Yeshua 17
  See also Messiah; Son of
    God; Son of Man
  afflicted by God 132
  ancestors of 272
  and His Bride 32
  as Abraham's Seed 258
  as antitype of Law 203
  as Creator 201, 208,
    211
  as Deity 175–176, 179,
    184–205
  as God incarnate 205
  as High Priest 74, 86

Yeshua (*cont.*)
  as Judge 225
  as King and Lord 186,
    223
  as Lamb 117, 133
    See also Passover:
      lamb: relation to
      Moses and Yeshua
  as LORD of hosts
    185–186
  as LORD OUR
    RIGHTEOUSNESS
    204
  as Redeemer 195
  as redemption price 193
  as Savior 187–191
  as sin offering 75, 77,
    79, 135
  as Son of God 200
  as Word of God
    201–203
  confirms promises to
    Israel 263
  dead bow to 147
  death of
    for our sins 48,
      69–70, 132
    fulfilled Law 69–70,
      136, 138
    prophesied 139, 143
  declares Word by Spirit
    224
  deity of 184–185, 191,
    195, 205
  discernment of 222
  faith in 63
  faith in *Tanach* 18,
    21–22, 120–121,
    149, 268
  fulfills Scripture 268
  gives rest 236
  glorifies the Father 130

  has God's name
    182–205
    See also Name of God:
      revealed: in
      Yeshua
  has God's Spirit 202,
    219, 224
  hates 44
  healing by 131–132,
    224
  honors Law 223
  humanity of 131
  intercession of 75, 80
  lifted and exalted 154
  lineage of 207
  love for 92, 157
    See also love: for God
  means salvation 189
  Messiah of gentile and
    Jew 225
  more than human 128,
    176, 205
  on the cross 138, 148
  one with Father
    175–176
  our Passover 49
  praises Father
    through believers 144
  prays for believers 237
  promises Spirit 231
  representative of Israel
    244
  resurrection fulfilled
    prophecy 167, 268
  resurrection of 166–167
    on First Fruits 264
  reveals the Father 35,
    144, 158, 204
    See also Son of God:
      reveals the Father
  righteousness of 163,
    204, 223

  sent by God 185, 189
    as Word of God 203
  son of Abraham and
    David 118–119,
    152
  struggle to obey 135,
    139
  sufferings of 144
  Tanach education of
    175
  type of 41, 46
    Moses as 101–116
  victory over Satan 17
  warning by 121
  was made sin 163
  without sin 69, 76, 79,
    134, 137, 204
Yom Kippur 20, 31, 43,
  53, 65, 150
  See also Day of
    Atonement
  date of 73
  fasting on 85
  in Israel 73
Yom Teruah, see Rosh
  haShanah

Z
zarim 282–284
  as unbelievers 283
  as unredeemed 282
  defiled the holy 282
  judgment on 283
  used for judgment 283
Zerubbabel 239
  as type of Messiah 41
Zion
  mercy on 266
  sons and daughters of
    250
Zionism
  anti 249

We hope you enjoyed reading this Sovereign World book.
For more details of other Sovereign books and
new releases see our website:

www.sovereignworld.com

If you would like to help us send a copy of this book
and many other titles to needy pastors in developing countries,
please write for further information
or send your gift to:

Sovereign World Trust
PO Box 777
Tonbridge, Kent TN11 0ZS
United Kingdom

You can also visit **www.sovereignworldtrust.com.**
The Trust is a registered charity.